WRITINGS ON LO
METAPHYSI

Writings on Logic and Metaphysics

F. H. BRADLEY

Edited by

JAMES W. ALLARD

and

GUY STOCK

CLARENDON PRESS · OXFORD

Oxford University Press, Walton Street, Oxford OX2 6DP

Oxford New York
Athens Auckland Bangkok Bombay
Calcutta Cape Town Dar es Salaam Delhi
Florence Hong Kong Istanbul Karachi
Kuala Lumpur Madras Madrid Melbourne
Mexico City Nairobi Paris Singapore
Taipei Tokyo Toronto
and associated companies in
Berlin Ibadan

Oxford is a trade mark of Oxford University Press

Published in the United States by
Oxford University Press Inc., New York

First published in hardback and paperback 1994
Reprinted in paperback 1995

British Library Cataloguing in Publication Data
Data available

Library of Congress Cataloging in Publication Data
Bradley, F. H. (Francis Herbert), 1846–1924.
Writings on logic and metaphysics / F. H. Bradley;
edited by James Allard and Guy Stock.
1. Logic. 2. Metaphysics. I. Allard, James W. II. Stock, Guy.
III. Title.
B1618.B73W75 1994 192—dc20 94-10327
ISBN 0-19-824445-2
ISBN 0-19-824438-X (pbk.)

Printed in Great Britain
on acid-free paper by
Bookcraft (Bath) Ltd
Midsomer Norton, Avon

CONTENTS

ABBREVIATIONS AND CONVENTIONS

AR   *Appearance and Reality*, repr. from 9th imp. of 1930 (Oxford: Clarendon Press).

CE   *Collected Essays*, 2 vols. (Oxford: Clarendon Press, 1935).

ETR   *Essays on Truth and Reality*, repr. from the 1962 edn. (Oxford: Clarendon Press).

PL   *The Principles of Logic*, repr. from the 1928 corr. imp. of the 1922 2nd edn. (Oxford: Oxford University Press).

The numbers in square brackets in the outside margins of the text indicate the page numbers in the editions from which the selections were taken.

For the sake of convenience we have renumbered Bradley's notes to begin with 1 and run consecutively by chapter. In Part I footnote numbers which stand alone refer to footnotes from the first edition of *The Principles of Logic*. These notes were not numbered but given asterisks or daggers as designations. Footnote numbers followed by a second number in curly brackets refer to endnotes added in the second edition of *The Principles of Logic*, 38–40, 107–13, and 125–7. The number in curly brackets is Bradley's original number. We have printed both numbers in Bradley's cross-references. In Part II Bradley's notes were originally numbered by page. These original numbers are not given here. Notes cued with lower-case letters are editorial footnotes.

In addition we have changed the form of some of Bradley's numerous references and omitted many of the rest. Where Bradley refers to abbreviated titles of his own works we have printed the full title or substituted our own abbreviation. Because of the frequency of our omissions we have not marked our deletions from the texts of the notes. We have usually omitted references to passages in Bradley's work that we have not reprinted and we have also omitted a large number of references to Bosanquet's work as well as entire notes.

INTRODUCTION

In 1898, after five years of reading Bradley avidly and admiring him more than any other living philosopher, Bertrand Russell joined G. E. Moore in revolting against idealism. 'Hegelians', Russell said, 'had all kinds of arguments to prove this or that not "real" . . . Nothing was real, we were assured, except the Absolute, which could think only of itself since there was nothing else for it to think of.'[1] Russell rejected these arguments and with sudden enthusiasm became an extreme realist. 'I felt it', he says,

as a great liberation, as if I had escaped from a hot-house on to a wind-swept headland. I hated the stuffiness involved in supposing space and time were only in my mind. I liked the starry heavens even better than the moral law, and could not bear Kant's view that the one I liked best was only a subjective figment. In the first exuberance of liberation, I became a naive realist and rejoiced in the thought that grass is really green. . . . I have not been able to retain this pleasing faith in its pristine vigour, but I have never again shut myself up in a subjective prison.[2]

Readers who know something about the history of philosophy correctly conclude from passages like these that Russell is describing his emancipation from his early flirtation with Bradley's idealism. Bradley was, after all, regarded by many as the leading British Hegelian, and his august presence broods over many of Russell's youthful and polemical pages. Since most contemporary readers are acquainted with Russell rather than with Bradley, they naturally conclude that for Bradley, as for Hegel, reality is identical with some cosmic principle of thought called The Absolute. They are likely to see the origin of contemporary philosophy in Russell's and Moore's rejection of just this sort of idealism. Since Hegel's view of the relation between thought and reality is much more complex than Russell suggests, they again conclude that Bradley is a crude Hegelian who may have discovered a few interesting puzzles, but whose views on logic, epistemology, and metaphysics need not be taken seriously.

[1] Bertrand Russell, *My Philosophical Development* (London: Allen & Unwin, 1959), 62.
[2] Ibid. 61–2.

In fact, however, Bradley rejects the identification of thought and reality just as forcefully as Russell. In one of his more vivid passages he says,

Unless thought stands for something that falls beyond mere intelligence, if 'thinking' is not used with some strange implication that never was part of the meaning of the word, a lingering scruple still forbids us to believe that reality can ever be purely rational. It may come from a failure in my metaphysics, or from a weakness of the flesh which continues to blind me, but the notion that existence could be the same as understanding strikes as cold and ghost-like as the dreariest materialism. That the glory of this world in the end is appearance leaves the world more glorious, if we feel it is a show of some fuller splendour; but the sensuous curtain is a deception and a cheat, if it hides some colourless movement of atoms, some spectral woof of impalpable abstractions, or unearthly ballet of bloodless categories. Though dragged to such conclusions, we can not embrace them. Our principles may be true, but they are not reality. They no more *make* that Whole which commands our devotion, than some shredded dissection of human tatters *is* that warm and breathing beauty of flesh which our hearts found delightful. (*PL* 590–1)

These are not the words of a man who thinks that reality is some kind of cosmic thought and who wishes to confine reality to a 'subjective prison'. Although obviously indebted to Hegel, Bradley did not consider himself a Hegelian and, as the above passage illustrates, rejected what he, like Russell, took to be Hegel's central contention.

Bradley does borrow a number of things from Hegel but in his own distinctive and even sceptical way. As Richard Wollheim has said,

In contrast to so many metaphysicians who have the air of bold, perhaps reckless, travellers setting out with determination from familiar surroundings for a distant though just barely discernible destination lying on the horizon of thought, Bradley is more like a man forced backwards, step by step, down a strange labyrinth, in self-defence, until at last finding himself in the comparative safety of some murky cave he rests among the shadows.[3]

The argument for which Bradley is best known, sometimes called Bradley's regress, illustrates this. It is an infinite regress argument

[3] Richard Wollheim, *F. H. Bradley*, 2nd edn. (Baltimore: Penguin Books, 1969), 18.

which purports to prove that relations are contradictory and hence unreal. This argument, like much of Bradley's philosophy, is destructive rather than constructive, sceptical rather than dogmatic, British rather than German.

But his philosophy contains more than a few sceptical paradoxes. His destructive dialectic generates positive views for which he offers quite original arguments. Many of these arguments rest on considerations that would now be recognized as belonging to the philosophy of language. Bradley discusses demonstrative pronouns, conditional judgements, proper names, non-denoting singular terms, negative existential judgements, and a variety of problems about individuation. These are not hidden features of Bradley's philosophy and his concern with them pervades his writing. His emphasis on the philosophy of language marks a new departure in British philosophy which made Bradley a force to be reckoned with. This is why Bradley was the worthy recipient of both Russell's respect and his criticism. Unfortunately, this is not generally appreciated today. Contemporary philosophers are only familiar with a few generally received caricatures, usually inspired by Russell, of his metaphysics.[4] In order to understand his philosophy and his place in the history of philosophy, a reassessment of Bradley's writings is necessary. Our main aim in this volume is to present materials from which such a reassessment may begin. In the rest of this Introduction we will briefly sketch Bradley's life and then explain the rationale guiding our choice of selections.

Francis Herbert Bradley (1846–1924) was born in Clapham, London, one of twenty children fathered by the Revd Charles Bradley. A younger brother, A. C. Bradley, well known for his work on Shakespearian tragedy, was Professor of English Literature at Glasgow University, and of Poetry at Oxford.

Bradley was educated at Cheltenham, Marlborough, and Oxford, where he was awarded a Fellowship at Merton College in 1870. The fellowship, which was terminable only on marriage, demanded no formal teaching duties and, apparently, none were offered. This may have been a result of the fact that in 1871 Bradley was afflicted with an often severe but never diagnosed kidney ailment from which he never recovered and which made

---

[4] For a description of the received caricature see Stewart Candlish, 'The Truth about F. H. Bradley', *Mind* 98 (1989), 331–4.

his manner of living extremely reclusive. There is good evidence that Bradley was a man of amorous experience, but he never married and so he retained residence at Merton until his death. He was not a public figure although, towards the end of his life, he received the Order of Merit.

Knowledge of his private life is fascinatingly sketchy. By temperament he seems to have been at once irascible and charming. Both characteristics come out in his writing. The latter is present in many irresistible touches of humour. Bradley no doubt was a great respecter of German philosophy, but he remained irrevocably English in the manner of his philosophizing. His respect for sense-experience, together with his unsystematic method and proneness to self-doubt and scepticism, place him firmly within the British tradition.

His influence outside the context of British philosophy was not great, but within it, in the later nineteenth and early twentieth centuries, he was a quite dominating figure. He was the author of five large books which secured his position: *Ethical Studies* (1876; 2nd edn. revised 1927), *The Principles of Logic* (1883; 2nd edn., considerably enlarged, 1922), *Appearance and Reality* (1893; 2nd edn. 1897), *Essays on Truth and Reality* (1914), and the posthumously published *Collected Essays* (1935). A very limited edition of Bradley's aphorisms appeared in 1930.[5] His power of intellect was admired even by those who, like Russell and William James, criticized him heavily in their published writings. In a letter written on receiving the second edition of Bradley's *Principles of Logic*, Russell says,

I am very glad there is a new edition, & very proud of having it as a gift from you. Your *Logic* was very nearly the first philosophical book that I read carefully, nearly twenty years ago; & the admiration which I felt for it has never diminished. I see that there is a good deal of new matter, which I shall read at my first spare moment.[6]

And in an admiring letter, which acknowledges his debt to Bradley, James perceptively brings out Bradley's paradoxically irascible yet charming character:

[5] The *Aphorisms* is now available reprinted in a single volume together with Bradley's first publication *The Presuppositions of Critical History*; see F. H. Bradley, *The Presuppositions of Critical History and Aphorisms*, intro. Guy Stock (Bristol: Thoemmes Press, 1993).

[6] Russell to Bradley, 20 Nov. 1922, original in Merton College Library.

I . . . have never written to you although I am one of your more consistent readers, and to a great extent pupils, although I find much that isn't
clear and easily digestible, and überhaupt am grieved at the 'surly sullen
bell' that more and more keeps tolling through your *manner*, as if your
reader were bound to be impervious to argument, and you don't know
why you take the trouble to write at all 'in such an atmosphere and in
such company.' Your letter shows you in a different light, and you are
described to me as full of humanity and easy to be entreated, when
opposed to one in the flesh![7]

   Bradley's writings are not easily accessible today. This is not,
as it is with Kant and Hegel, because of his use of a technical
vocabulary. Bradley is, as T. S. Eliot recognized, master of a
plain English style almost perfectly suited to its purpose.[8] In fact,
if anything, it is the other way round. At least part of the inac-
cessibility is because contemporary philosophical issues are formulated within a framework of quasi-technical concepts. These
concepts derive from symbolic logic, the natural sciences, and
mathematics, and are employed in a discussion in which it is presupposed that, in one way or another, those disciplines have a
special significance for epistemology and metaphysics. Bradley,
on the other hand, for reasons which nevertheless fall within the
sphere of philosophical logic and an epistemology not natural-
ized, maintains that neither formal logic, nor any 'special' science, is to be seen as having a privileged epistemological or
metaphysical significance.
   The fundamental philosophical issues that concern Bradley,
therefore, are to be seen as logically prior to those that arise
when thinking within the framework of the quasi-technical concepts in question. For this reason it is often impossible to relate
Bradley's discussions to the issues that in recent years have domi-
nated debate within analytical philosophy. However, since
Bradley is critical of assumptions which tend to be unquestion-
ingly accepted in adopting the framework within which contemporary problems are formulated, the relevance of his writings
should be obvious. They are especially so for anybody who might
feel that there is something profoundly wrong in scientific

---

   [7] J. C. J. Kenna, 'Ten Unpublished Letters from William James, 1842–1910, to
Francis Herbert Bradley, 1846–1924', *Mind*, 75 (1966), 311–12.
   [8] T. S. Eliot, *Selected Essays*, 2nd edn. (New York: Harcourt, Brace, 1950),
445.

realism, physicalist metaphysics, utilitarianism, and so on, and something philosophically sterile (even if scientifically important) in the current debates of cognitive scientists, information technologists, symbolic logicians, and so on.

What is of contemporary relevance in Bradley is thus not his comments on topics which are deemed important but the overall thrust of his argument. For this reason we have reprinted those texts that present most forcefully and clearly Bradley's philosophical position. With some regret we have included no selections from *Ethical Studies*. This volume is readily available and it gives a comprehensive statement of Bradley's views on the nature of morality. We have also ignored Bradley's psychological essays which comprise a large part of his *Collected Essays*, another volume that is still in print. Our concern is with the rest of Bradley's philosophy, a philosophy found in three large out-of-print books, *The Principles of Logic, Appearance and Reality* and *Essays on Truth and Reality*.

Since Bradley is primarily regarded as a metaphysician, the book of his most often cited as defining his position is his metaphysical treatise, *Appearance and Reality*. This book, however, is a sequel to *The Principles of Logic* and a prerequisite for *Essays on Truth and Reality*, a volume of essays in which Bradley tries to clarify some of his more obscure metaphysical claims. The central concern of *Appearance and Reality* is to achieve an understanding of the nature of the universe as a whole. But Bradley sees the achievement of this aim (as also did, at least in their early careers, Moore, Russell, and Wittgenstein) as something that cannot proceed independently of a proper understanding of the nature of human thinking, true and false, and its relation to that of which we think: the universe. In fact it is this theme, the relation between thought and reality, that forms the central focus on Bradley's work and of the selections reprinted below. We have divided the selections into two parts, each with a separate introduction. Those in the first part deal with Bradley's view of judgements; they are taken exclusively from *The Principles of Logic*. Those in the second part, which deal with Bradley's metaphysics, are taken from both *Appearance and Reality* and *Essays on Truth and Reality*. We have further divided this part into two sections, one corresponding to each volume. The selections from *Appearance and Reality* set forth Bradley's position systematically. Those from *Essays on Truth and Reality* restate and explain the implications of particular aspects of that position. Because of the difficulty of Bradley's writing and the length of some of the selections, we have prefaced many of them with short introductions.

PART I

Logic

Introduction *to* The Principles of Logic

In *Our Knowledge of the External World* Russell complains that 'Hegel and his followers' have fallaciously identified logic with metaphysics. In the course of this complaint he criticizes Bradley (whom he takes to be one of Hegel's followers) by saying:

Mr. Bradley has worked out a theory according to which, in all judgment, we are ascribing a predicate to Reality as a whole; and this theory is derived from Hegel. Now traditional logic holds that every proposition ascribes a predicate to a subject, and from this it easily follows that there can only be one subject, the Absolute. . . . Thus Hegel's doctrine, that philosophical propositions must be of the form 'the Absolute is such-and-such,' depends upon the traditional belief in the universality of the subject-predicate form.[1]

Russell then suggests that this belief, 'being traditional, is scarcely self-conscious', that as a result it is accepted uncritically by 'Hegel and his followers', and that 'modern logic' (by which Russell means mathematical logic) has shown it to be false.

This passage contains two of Russell's common criticisms of Bradley that have been accepted by most twentieth-century philosophers. The first is that Bradley was a follower of Hegel and not an original philosopher in his own right. The second is that Hegel's logic and metaphysics both depend on the traditional but false belief that all propositions, or judgements to use Bradley's term, have the same logical form: they are all subject-predicate judgements. Taken together, these complaints license drawing the conclusion that since there are judgements which do not have subject-predicate form, Bradley's logic and metaphysics are an edifice resting on sand. Most twentieth-century philosophers have accepted this conclusion on Russell's authority.

However, Russell's first criticism is at best debatable and in any case misleading. In the preface to *The Principles of Logic* Bradley had already replied to the charge that he was 'a Hegelian'. He says:

[A]ssuredly I think him a great philosopher; but I never could have called myself a Hegelian, partly because I can not say that I have mastered his system, and partly because I could not accept what seems his main principle, or at least part of that principle. I have no wish to conceal how much I owe to his writings; but I will leave it to those who can judge better than myself, to fix the limits within which I have followed him. As for the 'Hegelian School' which exists in our reviews, I know no one who has met with it anywhere else. (PL, p. x)

---

[1] Bertrand Russell, *Our Knowledge of the External World* (London: Allen and Unwin, 1926), 48.

Bradley never says what he thinks Hegel's main principle is, but he certainly rejects what others have identified as Hegel's main conclusion: that there is an Absolute Spirit whose knowing is identical with what it knows. As Bradley admits, however, he stands in Hegel's debt. The nature of this debt is most easily seen by comparing Bradley with other British philosophers. Unlike most of them, Bradley's aim is not critical, but synthetic. His goal is not to 'remove the rubbish that lies in the way to knowledge',[2] but to show how seemingly divergent aspects of our experience are part of a larger whole. Since Bradley relies on Hegel in a number of ways in his attempt to achieve this goal, he may be in some large sense a Hegelian.

But *The Principles of Logic* is not a Hegelian work. The influence of Hegel is most apparent in Bradley's ethics, less apparent in his metaphysics, and least apparent in his logic. Even a quick comparison of Bradley's *Principles of Logic* and Hegel's *Science of Logic* shows that there is a vast difference between the two books. Unlike Hegel, Bradley is not at all concerned to determine the a priori categories of thought. *The Principles of Logic* has a very different aim: to construct what Bradley sometimes calls a 'theory' of judgement and inference. This aim and his implementation of it have very little to do with anything Bradley derived from Hegel. To interpret him as another British Hegelian is to miss most of what he has to say.

Russell's second criticism is not even debatable. It is clearly wrong. Russell is, of course, correct that many nineteenth-century philosophers held the traditional belief that 'every proposition ascribes a predicate to a subject'. Russell's godfather, John Stuart Mill, held this belief.[3] Russell is also correct that Bradley believed that 'the Absolute' is the logical subject of all judgements. But the word 'subject' in these two beliefs is ambiguous. Bradley's acceptance of the Absolute as the subject of all judgements does not prevent him from being a sharp critic of the traditional view, a fact Russell acknowledges in some of his earlier works.[4] Not only did Bradley deny that every judgement ascribes a predicate to a subject, he argued that *no* judgement ascribes a predicate to a subject. He claimed that all judgements were hypothetical or conditional; they assert that *if* something is the case, *then* something else is the case. From

[2] John Locke, *An Essay Concerning Human Understanding*, ed. P. H. Nidditch (Oxford: Clarendon Press, 1975), 10.

[3] See John Stuart Mill, *A System of Logic* (Toronto: University of Toronto Press, 1973–4), 78, where Mill says, 'A proposition . . . is a portion of discourse in which a predicate is affirmed of a subject.'

[4] In both 'On Denoting' and 'Mathematical Logic as Based on the Theory of Types' Russell explicitly credits Bradley with showing that so-called universal categorical judgements are conditionals. See Bertrand Russell, *Logic and Knowledge*, ed. Robert C. Marsh (New York: Capricorn Books, 1956), 43; 70.

the point of view of his metaphysics this is the most important thing Bradley tries to establish in *The Principles of Logic*. It is the basis of his anti-realism and the ground on which he constructs his idealism in *Appearance and Reality*.

The selections we have reprinted contain Bradley's most important arguments for this claim and for his view of judgement as a whole. They are taken from the first three chapters of *The Principles of Logic*. The first selection, 'The General Nature of Judgement', explains in a preliminary way what Bradley takes a judgement to be. The second and longest selection, 'The Categorical and Hypothetical Forms of Judgement', explains in detail why Bradley takes all judgements to be conditionals and why this is consistent with taking them all to say something about reality as a whole. The third selection, 'The Negative Judgement', explains a particular type of judgement, the negative judgement, against the background of Bradley's general view. It is important primarily because of the role negative judgements play in Bradley's metaphysics. Taken together these selections explain the main features of judgements on which Bradley builds his metaphysics in *Appearance and Reality*.

'The General Nature of Judgement', contains Bradley's initial statement and defence of his view of judgements. He says that a judgement is 'the act which refers an ideal content . . . to a reality beyond the act' (PL 10). This definition says three essential things about judgements. First, they are particular kinds of acts, mental acts. Second, they have a special sort of content which Bradley calls 'ideal content'. He uses 'ideal' as the adjectival form of 'idea' so his claim is that judgements are composed of an idea or of ideas. Third, judgements have objective reference. This is what Bradley means by saying that they refer their ideal content 'to a reality . . . beyond the act'. It is in virtue of this reference that judgements are true or false. We might paraphrase his definition by saying that a judgement is a mental act in which we characterize an object by predicating ideas of it.

The first element in Bradley's definition indicates that judgements are mental phenomena. In *The Principles of Logic* Bradley is not concerned with mental acts of judgement in their entirety, but only in so far as they are true or false. As he is aware, it is not the entire act that is true or false, but only an aspect of it, its content. This content, that something is the case, is abstracted from a datable event which is a judging by a particular person. When the content has been abstracted from the mental act in which it is embedded, it forms the subject matter of Bradley's theory of judgement. The theory *considers* this content apart from the mental act in which it is a component, but it denies that the content *exists* apart from the mental act.

The second element in Bradley's definition, the ideal content, is what is abstracted from a concrete mental event when its content is considered by itself. Like 'idea', 'ideal content' is ambiguous. It may either refer to a concrete mental event (which Bradley somewhat misleadingly calls a mental image) or to a meaning. The distinction Bradley is making is analogous to that between a particular word printed in ink and its meaning. The printed word is a particular object with a distinct location in space and time. The meaning of the word is not. It is something that is conveyed by any instance of the word, whether printed or spoken. A concrete mental event for Bradley is like a printed word. It is a particular event in the consciousness of a particular individual at a particular time. Mental events, Bradley says, 'are facts unique with definite qualities . . . the same in all points with none other in the world' (PL 4). They are unrepeatable items in the stream of consciousness and, as such, they are not elements of judgements. A meaning, by contrast, is like what is communicated using a particular word. It is the symbolic content of a unique mental event. Distinct mental events can have the same symbolic content in the same way that distinct printed words can. This is why Bradley says that a meaning 'can not as such exist . . . can not be an event, with a place in the series of time or space . . . can be a fact no more inside our heads than outside them' (PL 7). Only as meanings do ideas form the ideal content of judgements.

The third element in Bradley's definition of judgement, the reference of the ideal content to reality, is what enables a judgement to be true or false. Bradley initially explains its function in a very simple way. He says that some reference to reality is necessary for objectivity. Judgements are true or false. Truth and falsity are relational properties which hold of a judgement in virtue of its relations to something outside of itself. It is hard to see how this outside thing which determines whether a judgement is true or false can be anything but reality. So, Bradley says, a judgement must refer to reality.

Although seemingly innocuous, this definition has an important consequence, namely, that judgements are not combinations of independently existing ideas. This is because the ideal content of a judgement is constructed by abstracting it from a mental act in which all of its elements are already present, not by combining separately existing ideas. Bradley puts the point in an extreme form by saying, 'It is not true that every judgement has two ideas. We may say on the contrary that all have but one' (PL 11). Despite such statements Bradley is quite willing to admit that we can distinguish different features within the content of any judgement. We may even call these distinguishable features ideas, if we wish. What he denies is that the content of a judgement is constructed by uniting different ideas by means of relations. As he puts it, 'The relations between ideas are themselves ideal. They are not psychical relations of mental facts. They do not exist between symbols, but in the symbolized' (PL 11). Because of his view of relations (discussed in 'Substantive and Adjective' and 'Relation and Quality', reprinted below), Bradley thinks that any attempt to explain how a judgement can be constructed by relating independently existing ideas, as, for example, in Russell's multiple relation theory of judgement, will fail.[5]

In the long and difficult second selection, 'The Categorical and Hypothetical Forms of Judgement', Bradley extends his view by advancing two seemingly contradictory claims. The first is that the logical subject of all judgements is reality as a whole. The second is that all judgements are conditionals, not subject-predicate judgements. Bradley's arguments for both of these claims are quite complex and we can only sketch their general outlines here.

The first claim depends on the fact that Bradley takes the ideal content of a judgement always to be a general term and never a singular term. Consider, for example, the judgement, 'I have a toothache.' This judgement appears to contain a pronoun which functions as a singular term, a name for a specific individual. On Bradley's view this appearance is misleading. The content of this judgement is not a combination of separate terms; its entire content is one composite term. Since this term can be used by any individual to describe any number of actual or possible cases in which he or she has a toothache, Bradley concludes that it does not uniquely describe any particular case. Consequently, it functions as a general rather than as a singular term. It describes a type of case rather than an individual case. Another example of this is found in judgements containing proper names, like 'Bertrand Russell was the brother of an earl.' This seems to uniquely describe a particular state of affairs. However, Bradley argues that proper names are disguised descriptions (PL 59–61). Consequently, like other judgements containing descriptions, they describe more than one actual or possible case. If, for example, 'Bertrand Russell' abbreviates the description 'The junior co-author of *Principia Mathematica*', then the judgement asserts that the junior co-author of *Principia Mathematica* is the brother of an earl. This describes only one actual case but it could be used to describe many possible cases. A novel, for example, might contain a character who was the junior co-author of *Principia Mathematica*. In this respect the description functions as a general term. Since there is nothing distinctive about these judgements, this sort of argument can be employed in the case of any judgement. It shows, Bradley thinks, that the ideal content of a judgement is always a general term. The ideal content of a

---

[5] For a simple exposition of Russell's theory see Bertrand Russell, *The Problems of Philosophy*, ch. 12.

judgement must denote something real, but it fails to denote any *particular* real thing.

The conclusion Bradley draws from this is that the ideal content of every judgement is a general term that denotes the only real thing that is not a particular piece of reality, namely, reality as a whole. This is why Bradley says that the logical form of all judgements is 'Reality is such that S is P'. (PL 623). We are able to attribute the ideal content of a judgement of reality because we do not need to describe it to refer to it. We have a cognitive connection with it in immediate experience or presentation.

Bradley occasionally paraphrases this by saying that reality is the logical subject of all judgements or that the ideal content of a judgement is predicated of reality. These statements are all intended to make the same point: that the only thing a judgement is about is the whole of reality.[6] This is the sense in which Bradley accepts the belief that all judgements have a subject and a predicate. Contrary to Russell, this is different from the traditional belief that all judgements have subject-predicate form in that Bradley is not saying that every judgement contains a subject *term*. What Bradley takes to be the subject of all judgements is not part of the ideal content of the judgement at all; it is what the ideal content describes.[7]

Bradley's second claim is that all judgements are conditionals. This is a denial of the traditional belief that all judgements contain a subject and a predicate where the judgement is true if the object named by the subject has the attribute named by the predicate. On this analysis judgements purport to describe without qualification what their subject terms name. They say how it is. For this reason they are called categorical judgements. By denying the traditional belief that all judgements have a subject and a predicate, Bradley is also denying that there are *any* categorical judgements in this sense.

Bradley's argument depends on his analysis of conditionals. He approaches this analysis by means of a problem. According to his view, all judgements predicate their ideal content of reality as a whole. But a conditional judgement, for example, 'If this man has taken that dose, he will be dead in twenty minutes' (PL 89), does not seem to do this. It

---

[6] Bradley does sometimes speak of the '[t]wofold nature of reality as the subject of judgement' or the 'special subject' of judgement (PL 39 n. 11). As we will discuss below, Bradley argues that all judgements are conditionals. The subject of a conditional for Bradley is the whole of reality, while its special subject is the select portion of reality denoted by the grammatical subject of its consequent. Since Bradley thinks that all judgements are conditionals, reality will be the subject of all judgements in this twofold way.

[7] Russell specifically attributes this view: see Bertrand Russell, *Principles of Mathematics*, 2nd edn. (New York: W. W. Norton, n.d.), 47.

does not assert either that the man has taken the dose or that he will be dead within twenty minutes. It seems to be about what is possible rather than about reality. To solve this problem Bradley needs to explain what conditionals assert about reality.

He faces the problem by considering a particular kind of conditional, the counterfactual conditional. Typically, this is a judgement in which the antecedent is false, as, for example, the judgement, 'If you had not destroyed our barometer, it would not forewarn us' (PL 87). Judgements like this seem to be about the actual world and on Bradley's definition they must be. But the antecedent and the consequent both seem to say something about unactualized possibilities. Bradley's problem is to explain how what seems to be a judgement about unactualized possibilities can assert something about reality.

The key to Bradley's solution is found in the following quotation:

In this judgement [If you had not destroyed our barometer, it would now forewarn us] we assert the existence of such circumstances, and such a general law of nature, as would *if we suppose* some conditions present, produce a certain result. But assuredly those conditions and their result are not predicated, nor do we even hint that they are real. (PL 87)

Here he says that counterfactual conditionals assert two things: the existence of a law of nature and the existence of the circumstances under which the law obtains. Neither of these are explicitly mentioned in Bradley's example and he admits that neither could be exactly specified. The judgement must assert that barometers respond to changes in air pressure. This is the assertion of the scientific law. Furthermore, the judgement must assert that the conditions under which the law holds obtain. These two assertions, neither of which is explicit, form the basis of the counterfactual.

In addition, the judgement includes what Bradley calls the supposal that certain other conditions not actually present are present. Bradley describes the supposal in the following terms:

A supposal is, in short, an ideal experiment. It is an application of a content to the real, with a view to see what the consequence is, and with a tacit reservation that no actual judgement has taken place. The supposed is treated as if it were real, in order to see how the real behaves when qualified in a certain manner. (PL 86)

This passage specifies the nature of a supposal. 'Ideal' is again an adjectival form of 'idea', so an ideal experiment is an experiment with ideas or a thought experiment. Bradley thinks it constitutes the essence of inference (PL 431). It involves the application of a content to the real. This content is the antecedent. By applying it to the real we assume that it is true. We then perform the experiment—we use the circumstances and the law of nature implicitly asserted to deduce what would happen on the assumption that the antecedent is true.

Bradley's claim, in other words, is that a conditional is to be seen as an abbreviated argument or inference, the premisses of which are the antecedent of the conditional, a judgement about the relevant conditions under which the antecedent is asserted, and a judgement affirming the relevant scientific laws. If we agree to count the antecedent of a conditional as true, Bradley's view can be put by saying that a conditional is true if the argument it abbreviates is sound. Since the premisses of the argument, with the exception of the supposal, are judgements about reality, Bradley's treatment of conditionals explains how they predicate an ideal content of reality.

On the basis of this analysis Bradley argues that all judgements are conditionals. He backs this claim by showing why it is true of the class of judgements least likely to be taken as conditionals, the class of judgements traditionally regarded as affirmative singular categorical judgements.[8] In this argument Bradley confines his attention to the class of singular judgement that seems most likely to resist this treatment: judgements made about objects of which the person making that judgement is directly aware. Judgements like these seem to be the most obvious cases of subject-predicate or categorical judgements; if they can be shown to be conditionals, then, for similar reasons, all other singular categoricals and hence all categorical judgements can be also.

Bradley somewhat misleadingly calls the class of judgements he is concerned with analytic judgements of sense.[9] This is misleading because 'analytic' is not being used in its familiar Kantian sense and because these judgements are not, as the word 'sense' suggests, about sense-data. They are about objects. For instance, one of the analytic judgements of sense Bradley mentions is 'This bird is yellow' (PL 58), judged by someone who is directly aware of a yellow bird. Judgements like this seem to be straightforward examples of categorical judgements. They seem to assert without qualification that a fact obtains. In the case of the above judgement, the fact asserted seems to be that the particular object denoted by the subject, 'this bird', has the attribute named by the predicate, 'yellow'. It is a subject-predicate judgement which, if true, describes the properties of a particular thing and so corresponds with a fact. In virtue of doing so, it is said to be a categorical judgement.

[8] Bradley's argument that affirmation universal categorical judgements are in fact conditionals is now virtually a dogma of contemporary philosophy. For Russell's acceptance of Bradley's argument for this see n. 4 above.

[9] Bradley took this terminology from the now forgotten philosopher Christoph Sigwart. See Sigwart, *Logic*, 2nd edn. (London: Swan Sonnenschein, 1896), 102-12.

Bradley's argument at this point is extremely dense and we will only describe its general course. His basic claim is that if analytic judgements of sense are treated as categorical judgements, then they are all false. He explains this by saying:

There are more ways than one of saying the thing that is not true. It is not always necessary to go beyond the facts. It is often more than enough to come short of them. And it is precisely this coming short of the fact, and stating a part as if it were the whole, which makes the falseness of the analytic judgement. (PL 93–5)

We can understand this by means of Bradley's earlier argument for the conclusion that reality as a whole is the logical subject of all judgements. When treated as categorical in form, judgements like 'This bird is yellow' purport to correspond with a particular fact. The problem, Bradley seems to be saying, is that there are no particular facts. There is only one great fact, the state of reality as a whole. An analytic judgement of sense, if treated as categorical, must assert that this fact obtains. But no analytic judgement of sense can do this. Each one is confined to that portion of reality of which the person making the judgement is immediately aware. At best an analytic judgement of sense asserts a fact about some limited aspect of reality. It thus describes a part as if it were the whole and so is false. Since not all judgements that seem to be analytic judgements of sense are false, Bradley concludes that they are not categorical judgements.

All judgements somehow assert that some facts obtain. Categorical judgements assert this without qualification. By showing that analytic judgements of sense are not categorical, Bradley has in effect shown that they assert facts subject to a qualification. But this is to say that they assert that a fact obtains subject to a condition. In other words, analytic judgements of sense are conditionals. Since Bradley thinks that the class of judgements least likely to be conditional, affirmative singular categorical judgements, are conditionals, he concludes that all judgements are conditionals.

The third selection, 'The Negative Judgement', is Bradley's discussion of the peculiarities of this type of judgement worked out against the background of his general account of judgement. It plays very little role in the development of Bradley's theory of judgement in *The Principles of Logic*, but Bradley does rely on it in his account of the nature of the absolute (see 'The General Nature of Reality', reprinted below). The most important feature of his account of negative judgements is his claim that they presuppose a positive ground (PL 117). For example, if it is true that a surface is not 10 degrees C, then it must be of some temperature that excludes the possibility. As Bradley understands it, this positive ground is a system of conditionally related ideal contents which are mutually exclusive. Negative judgements thus presuppose an extensive background of affirmative conditional judgements.

We can summarize Bradley's theory of judgement at this point by saying that we are able to make judgements only because we are able to predicate ideas of reality as we encounter it in immediate experience. We can never fully describe this experience, even in an analytic judgement of sense. In all of our judgements, even negative judgements, we predicate ideas of reality subject to conditions which are not explicitly stated. In this sense all of our judgements are conditionals which predicate their contents of reality as a whole.

This view of judgement has an important consequence for Bradley's metaphysics: that judgements lack determinate truth values. The reason Bradley holds this is that on his treatment of conditionals, no conditional is complete. A conditional is an abbreviated argument which is true if and only if the argument it abbreviates is sound. But to determine soundness one must determine the truth value of the premises and this requires evaluating the soundness of the arguments they abbreviate. The same problem recurs with them and so on indefinitely. Because of this regress the argument abbreviated by a judgement cannot be specified in full detail. The content of a judgement is in principle not fully determinate. Since judgements lack determinate content, Bradley concludes that their truth values are likewise indeterminate.[10]

This doctrine forms the core of Bradley's idealism and his opposition to realism. Philosophical realism takes many forms and it can be described in a number of ways. But however it is described, Michael Dummett seems correct when he says:

The primary tenet of realism, as applied to some given class of statements, is that each statement in the class is determined as true or not true, independently of our knowledge, by some objective reality whose existence and constitution is, again, independent of our knowledge.[11]

If this is correct, then, by denying that judgements are determinately true or false, Bradley is denying the main tenet of realism. Since for him all judgements are incomplete and hence of indeterminate truth value, they are not determined as true or false by anything. As Bradley will later argue, this can only be because judgements are not independent of their objects (see 'Thought and Reality', reprinted below).[12] Bradley's

[10] This is the basis of Bradley's doctrine of the degrees of truth and reality. See 'Degrees of Truth and Reality', reprinted below.

[11] Michael Dummett, *The Interpretation of Frege's Philosophy* (Cambridge, Mass.: Harvard University Press, 1981), 434.

[12] Bradley's subtle and complex account of the relation between thought and reality is what he describes as the 'main thesis' of *Appearance and Reality* (AR 493). In his view thought is neither identical with reality nor independent of it.

theory of judgement is thus firmly anti-realistic. It is on the basis of this staunch rejection of realism that Bradley builds his idealistic metaphysics in *Appearance and Reality*.

J.A.

Introduction to The General Nature of Judgement

Bradley's announced aim in *The Principles of Logic* is not to construct a
system of logic, but 'to provide a sceptical study of first principles', 'to
clear the ground so that English Philosophy, if it rises, may not be
choked with prejudice' (PL, p. x). Consistent with this aim Bradley provides no introductory discussion of the province of logic, of the problems of logic, or even a rationale for his selection of topics. He simply
begins with one of his main topics, the nature of judgement. After giving
a preliminary sketch of his theory of judgement, he criticizes other theories of judgement and explains how the ability to judge occupies a definite stage in the evolution of mind.

The selection reprinted below, 'The General Nature of Judgement', is
the first third of Chapter I. It contains Bradley's preliminary sketch of
his theory of judgement. He summarizes his theory in §10 by saying,
'Judgement proper is the act which refers an ideal content (recognized as
such) to a reality beyond the act.' Bradley prepares the way for this
summary by discussing the ideal content of a judgement. 'Ideal' is an
adjectival form of 'idea', so the ideal content of a judgement is its repre-
sentational element, the idea that forms its content. Bradley's main concern in §§2–9 is to show that the ideal content is a universal, not a
particular, a meaning, not a mental image. According to the analysis
given in §4, a meaning is an aspect of a datable psychical event (Bradley
somewhat misleadingly calls it a mental image) which has been separated
or 'abstracted' by he mind from that event. Since it has been abstracted,
it can be used to refer to objects independently of the occurrence of the
psychical event from which it has been taken. Only as a meaning does
an idea become an element in a judgement.

Not all meanings, however, are constituents of judgements. Bradley's
way of describing those that are not is unusual. Since a meaning is an
aspect of a particular thing (i.e. the event from which it has been
abstracted), Bradley calls it an adjective. If it is not being used to refer
to anything, it is what Bradley calls a floating adjective. It is an adjective
that has been detached from one substantive and not reattached to
another. Meanings become elements in judgements when they are reattached. This occurs when a meaning is used in characterizing something.
This is what Bradley means when he says that a judgement involves an
act that refers its ideal content (i.e. a meaning) to reality. Without such
an act ideas would not be contents of judgements. They would continue
to float. Bradley describes this act in §10.

By the time he wrote the second edition of *The Principles of Logic* Bradley had come to reject the view that ideas could float. (He explains his revised view in his essay 'On Floating Ideas and the Imaginary', the relevant parts of which are reprinted below.) According to this revised view, a mental act is still needed to abstract an aspect of an image, but this act also refers the resulting meaning to reality. This changes Bradley's view of judgement in a number of ways. Many of these corrections are mentioned in footnotes added in the second edition. The relevant notes have been included below.

In the final two sections of his preliminary sketch Bradley makes two further points about judgements. First, in §11 he asserts that judgements contain only one indefinitely complex idea. This is a rejection of any view, like Russell's, that takes a judgement to involve relations between individually representative components.[1] Second, in §12, he claims that the subject of a judgement is never an idea but always reality. Both of these points are developed in more detail in Chapter 2 of *The Principles of Logic*, most of which is reprinted below.

J. A.

---

[1] Bertrand Russell, *The Problems of Philosophy* (Oxford: Oxford University Press, 1959), 119–30.

I

The General Nature of Judgement

§ 1. It is impossible, before we have studied Logic, to know at [1] what point our study should begin. And, after we have studied it, our uncertainty may remain. In the absence of any accepted order I shall offer no apology for beginning with Judgement. If we incur the reproach of starting in the middle, we may at least hope to touch the centre of the subject. . . .

In a book of this kind our arrangement must be arbitrary. The general doctrine we are at once to lay down, really rests on the evidence of the following chapters. If it holds throughout the main phenomena of the subject, while each other view is in conflict with some of them, it seems likely to be the true view. But it can not, for this reason, be put forward at first, except provisionally.

Judgement presents problems of a serious nature to both psychology and metaphysics. Its relation to other psychical phenomena, their entangled development from the primary basis of soul-life, and the implication of the volitional with the intellectual side of our nature on the one hand, and on the other hand the difference of subject and object, and the question as to the existence of any mental activity, may be indicated as we pass. But it will be our object, so far as is possible, to avoid these problems. We do not mainly want to ask, How does judgement stand to other psychical states, and in ultimate reality what must be said of it. Our desire is to take it, so far as we can, as a given mental [2] function; to discover the general character which it bears, and further to fix the more special sense in which we are to use it.

§ 2. I shall pass to the latter task at once. Judgement, in the strict sense, does not exist where there exists no knowledge of truth and falsehood; and, since truth and falsehood depend on the relation of our ideas to reality, you can not have judgement proper without ideas. And perhaps thus much is obvious. But the

Repr. from *PL*, book I, 'Judgement', 1–13.

point I am going on to, is not so obvious. Not only are we unable to judge before we use ideas, but, strictly speaking, we can not judge till we use them *as* ideas.[1{2}] We must have become aware that they are not realities, that they are *mere* ideas, signs of an existence other than themselves. Ideas are not ideas until they are symbols, and, before we use symbols, we can not judge.

§ 3. We are used to the saying, 'This is nothing real, it is a mere idea.' And we reply that an idea, within my head, and as a state of my mind, is as stubborn a fact as any outward object. The answer is well-nigh as familiar as the saying, and my complaint is that in the end it grows much too familiar. In England at all events we have lived too long in the psychological attitude. We take it for granted and as a matter of course that, like sensations and emotions, ideas are phenomena. And, considering these phenomena as psychical facts, we have tried (with what success I will not ask) to distinguish between ideas and sensations. But, intent on this, we have as good as forgotten the way in which logic uses ideas. We have not seen that in judgement no fact ever *is* just that which it *means*, or can mean what it is; and we have not learnt that, wherever we have truth or falsehood, it is the signification we use, and not the existence. We never assert the fact in our heads, but something else which that fact stands for. And if an idea *were* treated as a psychical reality, if it were taken by itself as an actual phenomenon, then it would not represent either truth or falsehood. When we use it in judgement, it must be referred away from itself. If it is not the idea *of* some existence, then, despite its own emphatic actuality, its content remains but 'a mere idea'. It is a something which, in relation to the reality we mean, is nothing at all.

[3]   § 4. For logical purposes ideas are symbols, and they are nothing but symbols. And, at the risk of common-place, before I go on, I must try to say what a symbol is.

In all that is we can distinguish two sides, (i) existence and (ii) content. In other words we perccive both *that* it is and *what* it is. But in anything that is a symbol we have also a third side, its signification, or that which it *means*. We need not dwell on the two first aspects, for we are not concerned with the metaphysical problems which they involve. For a fact to exist, we shall agree,

---

[1{2}] 'We can not judge till we use them *as* ideas.' This requires correction. See ['On Floating Ideas and the Imaginary', repr. below], pp. [229–47].

it must be something. It is not real unless it has a character which is different or distinguishable from that of other facts. And this, which makes it what it is, we call its content. We may take as an instance any common perception. The complex of qualities and relations it contains, makes up its content, or that which it is; and, while recognizing this, we recognize also, and in addition, *that* it is. Every kind of fact must possess these two sides of existence and content, and we propose to say no more about them here.

But there is a class of facts which possess an other and additional third side. They have a meaning; and by a sign we understand any sort of fact which is used with a meaning. The meaning may be part of the original content, or it may have been discovered and even added by a further extension. Still this makes no difference. Take anything which can stand for anything else, and you have a sign. Besides its own private existence and content, it has this third aspect. Thus every flower exists and has its own qualities, but not all have a meaning. Some signify nothing, while others stand generally for the kind which they represent, while others again go on to remind us of hope or love. But the flower can never itself *be* what it *means*.

A symbol is a fact which stands for something else, and by this, we may say, it both loses and gains, is degraded and exalted. In its use as a symbol it forgoes individuality, and self-existence. It is not the main point that *this* rose or forget-me-not, and none other, has been chosen. We give it, or we take it, for the sake of its meaning; and that may prove true or false long after the flower has perished. The word dies as it is spoken, but the particular sound of the mere pulsation was nothing to our minds. Its existence was lost in the speech and the significance. [4] The paper and the ink are facts unique and with definite qualities. They are the same in all points with none other in the world. But, in reading, we apprehend not paper or ink, but what they represent; and, so long as only they stand for this, their private existence is a matter of indifference. A fact taken as a symbol ceases so far to be fact. It no longer can be said to exist for its own sake, its individuality is lost in its universal meaning. It is no more a substantive, but becomes the adjective that holds of another. But, on the other hand, the change is not all loss. By merging its own quality in a wider meaning, it can pass beyond itself and stand for others. It gains admission and influence in a world which it otherwise could not enter. The paper and ink cut the throats of men, and the sound of a breath may shake the world.

We may state the sum briefly. A sign is any fact that has a meaning, and meaning consists of a part of the content (original or acquired), cut off, fixed by the mind, and considered apart from the existence of the sign.[2] . . .

[5] § 6. We might say that, in the end, there are no signs save ideas but what I here wish to insist on, is that, for logic at least, all ideas are signs. Each we know exists as a psychical fact, and with particular qualities and relations. It has its speciality as an event in my mind. It is a hard individual, so unique that it not only differs from all others, but even from itself at subsequent moments. And this character it must bear when confined to the two aspects of existence and content. But just so long as, and because, it keeps to this character, it is for logic no idea at all. It becomes one first when it begins to exist for the sake of its meaning. And its meaning, we may repeat, is a part of the content, used without regard to the rest, or the existence. I have the 'idea' of a horse, and that is a fact in my mind, existing in relation with the congeries of sensations and emotions and feelings, which make my momentary state. It has again particular traits of its own, which may be difficult to seize, but which, we are bound to suppose, are present. It is doubtless unique, the same with no other, nor yet with itself, but alone in the world of its fleeting moment. But, for logic, and in a matter of truth and falsehood,

[6] the case is quite changed. The 'idea' has here become an universal, since everything else is subordinate to the meaning. That connection of attributes we recognize as horse, is one part of the content of the unique horse-image, and this fragmentary part of

---

[2] It would not be correct to add, 'and referred away to another real subject'; for where we think without judging, and where we deny, that description would not be applicable. Nor is it the same thing to have an idea, and to judge it possible. To think of a chimaera is to think of it as real, but not to judge it even possible. And it is not until we have found that all meaning must be adjectival, that with every idea we have even the suggestion of a real subject other than itself.[3(7)]

[3(7)] This footnote is wrong throughout, for there are no ideas not so 'referred'. See ['On Floating Ideas and the Imaginary', repr. below' Part II, Sect. 2, Ch. 1]. The words in the text, 'cut off, etc.' are also incorrect. There are no ideas before or apart from their use, and that at first is unconscious. See Note 1{2}.

the psychical event is all that in logic we know of or care for. Using this we treat the rest as husk and dross, which matters nothing to us, and makes no difference to the rest. The 'idea', if that is the psychical state, is in logic a symbol. But it is better to say, the idea *is* the meaning, for existence and unessential content are wholly discarded. The idea, in the sense of the mental image, is a sign of the idea in the sense of meaning.[4][8]

§ 7. These two senses of idea, as the symbol and the symbolized, the image and its meaning, are of course known to all of us. But the reason why I dwell on this obvious distinction, is that in much of our thinking it is systematically disregarded. 'How can any one', we are asked, 'be so foolish as to think that ideas are universal, when every single idea can be seen to be particular, or talk of an idea which remains the same, when the actual idea at each moment varies, and we have in fact not one identical but many similars?' But how can any one, we feel tempted to reply, suppose that these obvious objections are unknown to us? When I talk of an idea which is the same amid change, I do not speak of that psychical event which is in ceaseless flux, but of one portion of the content which the mind has fixed, and which is not in any sense an event in time. I am talking of the meaning, not the series of symbols, the gold, so to speak, not the fleeting series of transitory notes. The belief in universal ideas does not involve the conviction that abstractions exist, even as facts in my head. The mental event is unique and particular, but the meaning in its use is cut off from the existence, and from the rest of the fluctuating content. It loses its relation to the particular symbol; it stands as an adjective, to be referred to some subject, but indifferent in itself to every special subject.

The ambiguity of 'idea' may be exhibited thus. *Thesis*, On the one hand no possible idea can be that which it means. *Antithesis*, On the other hand no idea is anything but just what it means. In the thesis the idea is the psychical image; in the antithesis the

[4][8] Here again we must remember that we are not to say (i) that an idea is there apart from its being used, or (ii) that, in using it, we must be aware of it as a mental thing. Further (iii) I was wrong to speak, here and elsewhere, as if with every idea you have what may be called an 'image'. How far and in what sense the psychical existence is always capable of being verified in observation is a difficult point to which I have perhaps not sufficiently attended. Still every idea, I must assume, has an aspect of psychical event, and so is qualified as a particular existence.

[7] idea is the logical signification. In the first it is the whole sign,
but in the second it is nothing but the symbolized. In the sequel I
intend to use idea mainly in the sense of meaning.[5]

§ 8. For logical purposes the psychological distinction of idea
and sensation may be said to be irrelevant, while the distinction
of idea and fact is vital. The image, or psychological idea, is for
logic nothing but a sensible reality. It is on a level with the mere
sensations of the senses. For both are facts and neither is a meaning. Neither is cut from a mutilated presentation, and fixed as a
connection. Neither is indifferent to its place in the stream of psychical events, its time and relations to the presented congeries.
Neither is an adjective to be referred from its existence, to live on
strange soils, under other skies and through changing seasons.
The lives of both are so entangled with their environment, so one
with their setting of sensuous particulars, that their character is
destroyed if but one thread is broken. Fleeting and self-destructive
as is their very endurance, wholly delusive their supposed individuality, misleading and deceptive their claim to reality, yet in some
sense and somehow they *are*. They have existence; they are not
thought but given.[6] But an idea, if we use idea of the meaning, is
neither given nor presented but is taken. It can not as such exist.
It can not ever be an event, with a place in the series of time or
space. It can be a fact no more inside our heads than it can out-
[8] side them. And, if you take this mere idea by itself, it is an adjective divorced, a parasite cut loose, a spirit without a body
seeking rest in another, an abstraction from the concrete, a mere
possibility which by itself *is* nothing.

§ 9. These paradoxical shadows and ghosts of fact are the ideas
we spoke of, when we said, Without ideas no judgement; and,

---

[5] There are psychological difficulties as to universal ideas, and we feel them
more, the more abstract the ideas become. The existence and the amount, of the
particular imagery or sensuous environment, give rise to questions. But these
questions need not be considered here, for they have no logical importance whatever. I assume, after Berkeley, that the mental fact contains always an irrelevant
sensuous setting, however hard it may be to bring this always to consciousness.
But I must repeat that this is not a vital question. It is a mistake in principle to
try to defend the reality of universals by an attempt to show them as psychical
events existing in one moment. For if the universal we use in logic had actual existence as a fact in my mind, at all events I could not *use* it as the fact. You must
at any rate abstract from the existence and external relations, and how much further the abstraction is to go seems hardly an important or vital issue.

[6] This statement is subject to correction by Chapter II ['The Categorical and
Hypothetical Forms of Judgement', repr. below, Part I, Ch. 2].

before we proceed, we may try to show briefly that in predication we do not *use* the mental fact, but only the meaning. The full evidence for this truth must however be sought in the whole of what follows.

(i) In the first place it is clear that the idea, which we use as the predicate of a judgement, is not my mental state as such. 'The whale is a mammal' does not qualify real whales by my mammal-image. For that belongs to me, and is an event in my history; and, unless I am Jonah, it can not enter into an actual whale. We need not dwell on this point, for the absurdity is patent. If I am asked, Have you got the idea of a sea-serpent? I answer, Yes. And again, if I am asked, But do you believe in it, Is there a sea-serpent? I understand the difference. The enquiry is not made about my psychical fact. No one wishes to know if *that* exists outside of my head; and still less to know if it really exists inside. For the latter is assumed, and we can not doubt it. In short the contention that in judgement the idea is my own state as such, would be simply preposterous.

(ii) But is it possible, secondly, that the idea should be the image, not indeed as my private psychical event, but still as regards the whole content of the image? We have a mental fact, the idea of mammal. Admit first that, as it exists and inhabits my world, we do not predicate it. Is there another possibility? The idea perhaps might be used apart from its own existence, and in abstraction from its relations to my psychical phenomena, and yet it might keep, without any deduction, its own internal content. The 'mammal' in my head is, we know, not bare mammal, but is clothed with particulars and qualified by characters other than mammality; and these may vary with the various appearances of the image.[7] And we may ask, Is this *whole* image used in [9] judgement? Is *this* the meaning? But the answer must be negative.

We have ideas of redness, of a foul smell, of a horse, and of death; and, as we call them up more or less distinctly, there is a kind of redness, a sort of offensiveness, some image of a horse, and some appearance of mortality, which rises before us. And

---

[7] I may point out that, even in this sense, the idea is a product of abstraction. Its individuality (if it has such) is conferred on it by an act of thought. It is *given* in a congeries of related phenomena, and, as an individual image, results from a mutilation of this fact (Vid. Chapter II ['The Categorical and Hypothetical Forms of Judgement', repr. below, Part I, Ch. 2]).

should we be asked, Are roses red? Has coal gas a foul smell? Is that white beast a horse? Is it true that he is dead? we should answer, Yes, our ideas are all true, and are attributed to the reality. But the idea of redness may have been that of a lobster, of a smell that of castor-oil, the imaged horse may have been a black horse, and death perhaps a withered flower. And *these* ideas are *not* true, nor did we apply them. What we really applied was that part of their content which our minds had fixed as the general meaning.

It may be desirable (as in various senses various writers have told us) that the predicate should be determinate, but in practice this need can not always be satisfied. I may surely judge that a berry is poisonous, though in what way I know not, and though 'poisonous' implies some traits which I do not attribute to *this* poison. I surely may believe that AB is bad, though I do not know his vices, and have images which are probably quite inapplicable. I may be sure that a book is bound in leather or in cloth, though the sort of leather or cloth I must imagine I can not say exists. The details I have never known, or at any rate, have forgotten them. But of the universal meaning I am absolutely sure, and it is this which I predicate.

The extreme importance of these obvious distinctions must excuse the inordinate space I allot to them. Our whole theory of judgement will support and exemplify them; but I will add yet a few more trivial illustrations. In denying that iron is yellow, do I say that it is not yellow like gold, or topaze, or do I say that it is not any kind of yellow? When I assert, 'It is a man or a woman or a child,' am I reasonably answered by, 'There are other possibilities. It may be an Indian or a girl'? When I ask, Is he ill? do I naturally look for 'Oh no, he has cholera'? Is the effect of, 'If he has left me then I am undone,' removed by 'Be happy, it was by the coach that he deserted you'?

[10] The idea in judgement is the universal meaning; it is not ever the occasional imagery, and still less can it be the whole psychical event.

§ 10. We now know what to understand by a logical idea, and may briefly, and in anticipation of the sequel, dogmatically state what judgement does with it. We must avoid, so far as may be, the psychological and metaphysical difficulties that rise on us.

Judgement proper is the act which refers an ideal content (recognized as such) to a reality beyond the act.[8]{[10]} This sounds perhaps much harder than it is.

The ideal content is the logical idea, the meaning as just defined. It is recognized as such, when we know that, by itself, it is not a fact but a wandering adjective. In the act of assertion we transfer this adjective to, and unite it with, a real substantive. And we perceive at the same time, that the relation thus set up is neither made by the act, nor merely holds within it or by right of it, but is real both independent of and beyond it.[9]

If as an example we take once more the sea-serpent, we have an idea of this but so far no judgement. And let us begin by asking, Does it exist? Let us enquire if 'it exists' is really true, or only an idea. From this let us go on, and proceed to judge 'The sea-serpent exists.' In accomplishing this what further have we done? And the answer is, we have qualified the real world by the adjective of the sea-serpent, and have recognized in the act that, apart from our act, it is so qualified. By the truth of a judgement we mean that its suggestion is more than an idea, that it is fact or in fact. We do not mean, of course, that as an adjective of the real the idea remains an indefinite universal. The sea-serpent, if it exists, is a determinate individual; and, if we knew the whole truth, we should be able to state exactly how it exists. Again when in the dusk I say, That is a quadruped, I qualify the reality, now appearing in perception, by this universal, while the actual quadruped is, of course, much besides four legs and a head. But, while asserting the universal, I do not mean to exclude [11] its unknown speciality. Partial ignorance need not make my

---

[8]{[10]} Judgement (proper) is etc.' (i) In this definition the word 'act' raises a question, important in psychology and in metaphysics but (so far as I see) not necessary in logic. (ii) 'Recognized as such' is wrong (see Note 1{2}). What I *should* recognize on reflection I may in fact ignore. Cf. § 10. (iii) 'Beyond the act', and (below) 'independent of it', are right for logic. For metaphysics, on the other hand, the problem raised here can not be ignored. But as to recognition of the act (to return to that) the text is wrong. A perceived object changed by an idea, and the change ignored except as the development of the object—though not of the mere perceived object—here is the beginning of judgement in the proper sense. But, again, to take judgement as present wherever we have an object at all before the mind—is a view which is tenable.

[9] I may remark that I am dealing at present only with affirmation; the negative judgement presents such difficulties that it can hardly be treated by way of anticipation.

knowledge fallacious, unless by a mistake I assert that knowledge as unconditional and absolute.

'Are the angles of a triangle equal to two right angles?'[10]{13} 'I doubt if this is so,' 'I affirm that this is so.' In these examples we have got the same ideal content; the suggested idea is the relation of equality between the angles of a triangle and two right angles. And the affirmation, or judgement, consists in saying, This idea is no mere idea, but is a quality of the real. The act attaches the floating adjective to the nature of the world, and, at the same time, tells me it was there already. The sequel, I hope, may elucidate the foregoing, but there are metaphysical problems, to which it gives rise, that we must leave undiscussed.

§ 11. In this description of judgement there are two points we may at once proceed to notice. The reader will have observed that we speak of a judgement asserting *one* idea, or ideal content, and that we make no mention of the subject and copula. The doctrine most prevalent, on the other hand, lays down that we have always *two* ideas, and that one is the subject. But on both these heads I am forced to dissent. Our second chapter will deal further with the question, but there are some remarks which may find a place here.

(i) It is not true that every judgement has two ideas. We may say on the contrary that all have but one.[11]{14} We take an ideal content, a complex totality of qualities and relations, and we then introduce divisions and distinctions, and we call these products separate ideas with relations between them. And this is quite unobjectionable. But what is objectionable, is our then proceeding to deny that the whole before our mind is a single idea; and it involves a serious error in principle. The relations between the ideas are themselves ideal. They are not the psychical relations of mental facts. They do not exist between the symbols, but hold in the symbolized. They are part of the meaning and not of the existence. And the whole in which they subsist is ideal, and so one idea.

[10]{13} (i) 'Are the angles &c.?'. The false doctrine of 'floating ideas' is involved here. (ii) 'The same ideal content.' Not so.

[11]{14} This statement (cf. pp. [39], [45]) requires correction. It is true that the ideal meaning is one; but it is also true that the subject is a special subject, and that it, in its special sense, must be there within the meaning. The twofold nature of Reality as the subject of judgement was not sufficiently recognized by me.

Take a simple instance. We have the idea of a wolf and we call
that one idea. We imagine the wolf eating a lamb, and we say,
There are two ideas, or three, or perhaps even more. But is this
because the scene is not given as a whole? Most certainly not so. [12]
It is because in the whole there exist distinctions, and those
groupings of attributes we are accustomed to make. But, if we
once start on this line and deny the singleness of every idea
which embraces others, we shall find the wolf himself is anything
but one. He is the synthesis of a number of attributes, and, in the
end, we shall find that no idea will be one which admits any sort
of distinction in itself. Choose then which you will say, There are
no single ideas, save the ideas of those qualities which are too
simple to have *any* distinguishable aspects, and that means there
are no ideas at all—or, Any content whatever which the mind
takes as a whole, however large or however small, however simple or however complex, is one idea, and its manifold relations
are embraced in an unity.[12]

We shall always go wrong unless we remember that the relations within the content of any meaning, however complex, are
still not relations between mental existences. There is a wolf and
a lamb. Does the wolf eat the lamb? The wolf eats the lamb. We
have a relation here suggested or asserted between wolf and
lamb, but the relation is (if I may use the word) not a *factual*
connection between events in my head. What is meant is no psychical conjunction of images. Just as the idea of the wolf is not
the whole wolf-image, nor the idea of the lamb the imagined
lamb, so the idea of their synthesis is not the relation as it exists
in my imagination. In the particular scene, which symbolizes my
meaning, there are details that disappear in the universal idea,
and are neither thought of nor enquired after, much less asserted.

To repeat the same thing—the imagery is a sign, and the
meaning is but one part of the whole, which is divorced from the
rest and from its existence. In this ideal content there are groups
and joinings of qualities and relations, such as answer to nouns
and verbs and prepositions. But these various elements, though

---

[12] The psychological controversy as to the number of ideas we can entertain at
once, can hardly be settled till we know beforehand what is one idea. If this is to
exclude all internal complexity, what residuum will be left? But, if it admits plurality, why is it one idea? If, however, what otherwise we should call plurality, we
now call single just because we have attended to it as one, the question must
clearly alter its form.

you are right to distinguish them, have no validity outside the
[13]   whole content. That is one idea, which contains all ideas which
you are led to make in it; for, whatever is fixed by the mind as
one, however simple or complex, is but one idea. But, if this is
so, the old superstition that judgement is the coupling a pair of
ideas must be relinquished.

§ 12. I pass now (ii) to the other side of this error, the doctrine
that in judgement one idea is the subject, and that the judgement
refers another to this. In the next chapter this view will be finally
disposed of, but, by way of anticipation, we may notice here two
points. (*a*) In 'wolf eating lamb' the relation is the same, whether
I affirm, or deny, or doubt, or ask.[13{16}] It is therefore not likely
that the *differentia* of judgement will be found in what exists
apart from all judgement. The *differentia* will be found in what
differences the content, as asserted, from the content as merely
suggested. So that, if in all judgement it were true that one idea
is the subject of the assertion, the doctrine would be wide of the
essence of the matter, and perhaps quite irrelevant. But (*b*) the
doctrine (as we shall see hereafter) is erroneous. 'B follows A,' 'A
and B coexist,' 'A and B are equal,' 'A is south of B,'—in these
instances it is mere disregard of facts which can hold to the doctrine. It is unnatural to take A or B as the subject and the
residue as predicate. And, where existence is directly asserted or
denied, as in, 'The soul exists,' or, 'There is a sea-serpent,' or,
'There is nothing here,' the difficulties of the theory will be found
to culminate.

I will anticipate no further except to remark, that in every
judgement there is a subject of which the ideal content is
asserted. But this subject of course can not belong to the content
or fall within it, for, in that case, it would be the idea attributed
to itself. We shall see that the subject is, in the end, no idea but
always reality; and, with this anticipation, we must now go forward, since we have finished the first division of this chapter. . . .

13{16} 'The relation is the same.' But see Note 10{13}.

Introduction to 'The Categorical and Hypothetical Forms of Judgement'

Bradley's stated goal in Chapter 2 of *The Principles of Logic* is to support and deepen his account of the general nature of judgement contained in the previous selection. This chapter, 'The Categorical and Hypothetical Forms of Judgement', falls into three uneven, overlapping parts. In the first part, §§1–9 and 20–1, Bradley discusses an argument he derives from Johann Friedrich Herbart which purports to show that all judgements are hypothetical. Bradley thinks this is a valid argument which contains the false premiss that judgements are composed exclusively of ideas. He avoids Herbart's conclusion by denying this premiss and asserting that judgements are not composed merely of ideas. They also contain a reference to reality. Bradley claims they do so by attributing their ideal content to the whole of reality. This is made possible by the fact that we have access to the whole of reality in immediate experience. This deepens Bradley's theory of judgement by specifying the reality to which judgements refer. In §§10–14, which form an appendix to this argument, Bradley clarifies his position by distinguishing between reality and immediate experience and discussing the connection between them.

In the rest of the chapter Bradley attempts to reconcile this conclusion with a modified form of Herbart's contention. His argument for this conclusion takes up the second and third parts of the chapter. In the second and longest part, §§6–7 and 15–56, Bradley supports his theory by showing how both categorical and hypothetical judgements can be interpreted as referring to reality as it is given in presentation. In most of these sections Bradley is concerned with singular categorical judgements (§§15–41). These judgements purport to state facts unconditionally. In §7 Bradley provisionally divides them into three groups, analytic judgements of sense, synthetic judgements of sense, and a third, unnamed group. He then shows how these judgements, in their different grammatical forms, can all be interpreted as predicating their contents directly of reality as it is given in our direct, waking sense perceptions or, in Bradley's vocabulary, presentation. According to this interpretation, reality is the logical subject of judgement and the entire ideal content is the predicate. Since the content is directly attributed to reality, singular judgements are categorical. They state facts unconditionally. This is not true of universal categorical judgements. They predicate their contents indirectly of reality by asserting that *if* a condition holds, then reality is characterized by the predicate. What they attribute directly to reality is the ground of the connection between antecedent and consequent (§§49–51). They do not directly attribute their contents to reality but only indirectly, under a condition. For this reason they are hypothetical judgements. This theory of judgement allows Bradley to interpret affirmative singular categoricals as referring to reality as it is given in presentation, while allowing him to distinguish between categorical and hypothetical judgements. It also treats all affirmative judgements as asserting something about reality and hence as existential judgements. Consequently, Bradley denies that there is a separate category of existential judgements (§§43–4).

In the third and final part of the chapter, §§57–81, Bradley further deepens his theory by revising his account of singular judgements. He argues that on the interpretation he has just given all singular judgements are false (§59). Bradley defends this claim by returning to analytic judgements of sense. His position is that if these judgements are construed as predicating their contents directly of reality, then what they say is false. They come short of the facts (§61). In order to remedy this defect analytic judgements of sense and other singular categoricals must be reconstrued as hypotheticals and so as predicating their content indirectly of reality. Thus Bradley concludes that all judgements have the logical form of conditionals and attribute their contents to the whole of reality as it is given in our direct, waking sense experience.

J.A.

2

The Categorical and Hypothetical
Forms of Judgement

§ 1. In the foregoing chapter we have attempted roughly to settle [41] the main characteristics of judgement. The present chapter will both support and deepen our conclusion. It will deal with problems, in part familiar to those who have encountered the well-known discussion aroused by Herbart.[a] The length and the difficulty of this second chapter may perhaps be little warranted by success, but I must be allowed to state beforehand that both are well warranted by the importance of the subject in modern logic.

A judgement, we assume naturally, says something about some fact or reality. If we asserted or denied about anything else, our judgement would seem to be a frivolous pretence. We not only must say something, but it must also be about something actual that we say it. For consider; a judgement must be true or false, and its truth or falsehood can not lie in itself. They involve a reference to a something beyond. And this, about which or of which we judge, if it is not fact, what else can it be?

The consciousness of objectivity or necessary connection, in which the essence of judgement is sometimes taken to lie, will be found in the end to derive its meaning from a reference to the real. A truth is not necessary unless in some way it is compelled to be true. . . . And compulsion is not possible without something that compels. It will hence be the real, which exerts this force, of which the judgement is asserted. We may indeed not affirm that the suggestion S—P itself is categorically true of the fact, and *that* is not our judgement.[1] The actual judgement

Repr. from *PL*, book I, 'Judgement', 41–73, 77–83, 85–107.

[1] 'S—P.' This form I found of course in use, and I employed it in this volume where that seemed convenient. I neither did nor do attach importance to its use.

---

[a] Johann Friedrich Herbart, *Lehrbuch zur Einleitung in die Philosophie*, in *Sämmtliche Werke*, i, ed. G. Hartenstein (Leipzig: Leopold Voss, 1850), esp. 91–106.

asserts that S—P is forced on our minds by a reality *x*. And this reality, whatever it may be, is the subject of the judgement. It is the same with objectivity.[2{2}] If the connection S—P holds outside my judgement, it can hardly hold nowhere or in nothingness.

[42] It must surely be valid in relation to something, and that something must be real. No doubt, as before, S—P may not be true directly of this fact; but then that again was not what we asserted. The actual judgement affirms that S—P is in connection with *x*. And this once again is an assertion about fact.

There is a natural presumption that truth, to be true, must be true of reality. And this result, that comes as soon as we reflect, will be the goal we shall attain in this chapter. But we shall reach it with a struggle, distressed by subtleties, and perhaps in some points disillusioned and shaken.

§ 2. Less serious difficulties we may deal with at once. 'A four-cornered circle is an impossibility,' we are told, does not assert the actual existence of a four-cornered circle (Herbart,[b] I. 93). But the objection is irrelevant, unless it is maintained that in every case we affirm the reality of the *grammatical* subject. And this clearly is not always what we mean to assert. And such further examples as 'There are no ghosts,' or 'This thought is an illusion,' may be likewise disposed of. It is not the first form and haphazard conjunction of every proposition which represents reality. But, in every proposition, an analysis of the meaning will find a reality of which something else is affirmed or denied. 'The nature of space excludes the connection of square and round,' 'The world is no place where ghosts exist,' 'I have an idea, but the reality it refers to is other than its meaning,'—we may offer these translations as preliminary answers to a first form of attack. And when Herbart assails us with 'The wrath of the Homeric gods is fearful'[c] (I. 99), we need give no ground before such a weapon. In Homer it *is* so; and surely a poem, surely any imagination, surely dreams and delusions, and surely much more our words and our names are all of them facts of a certain kind. Such plain distinctions as those between existences of different

---

[2{2}] 'Objectivity.' What this means is that it is *the object itself* which is this or that. The 'subjective' = the irrelevant.

---

[b] Johann Friedrich Herbart, *Lehrbuch zur Einleitung in die Philosophie*, in *Sämmtliche Werke*, i, ed. G. Hartenstein (Leipzig: Leopold Voss, 1850),
[c] Ibid.

orders[3{3}] should never have been confused, and the paradox lies on the side of those who urge such an objection.

And if, further, the discussion take the misleading form of an [43] enquiry into the copula, we find merely the same misunderstandings unknowingly reproduced. Wherever we predicate, we predicate about something which exists beyond the judgement, and which (of whatever kind it may be) is real, either inside our heads or outside them. And in this way we must say that 'is' never can stand for anything but 'exists'.

§ 3. But Herbart, we shall find, is not so easily disposed of. He was not the man first uncritically to swallow the common-sense doctrine that judgement is of things, and then to stagger at the discovery that things are not words, or fall prostrate before a supposed linguistic revelation of the nature of the copula. In denying that judgement asserts a fact, he knew well what he stood on. It was no puzzle about the grammatical subject, but a difficulty as to the whole nature of truth and of ideas. We reflect about judgement, and, at first of course, we think we understand it. Our conviction is that it is concerned with fact; but we also see that it is concerned with ideas. And the matter seems at this stage quite simple. We have a junction or synthesis of ideas in the mind, and this junction expresses a similar junction of facts outside. Truth and fact are thus given to us together, the same thing, so to speak, in different hemispheres or diverse elements.

But a further reflection tends to dissipate our confidence. Judgements, we find, are the union of ideas, and truth is not found except in judgements. How then are ideas related to realities? They seemed the same, but they clearly are not so, and their difference threatens to become a discrepancy. A fact is individual, an idea is universal; a fact is substantial, an idea is adjectival; a [44] fact is self-existent, an idea is symbolical. Is it not then manifest that ideas are *not* joined in the way in which facts are? Nay the essence of an idea, the more it is considered, is seen more and more to diverge from reality. And we are confronted by the conclusion that, so far as anything is true, it is *not* fact, and, so far as it is fact, it can never be true. Or the same result may have a

---

[3{3}] 'Existences of different orders.' Cf. *Essays on Truth and Reality*, Chap. III ['On Floating Ideas and the Imaginary', repr. below, Part II, Sect. 2, Ch. 1]. 'Existence' and 'exist' (like 'fact') are used in the present work often in a wide sense.

different form. A categorical judgement makes a real assertion in which some fact is affirmed or denied. But, since no judgement can do this, they all in the end are hypothetical. They are true only of and upon a supposition. In asserting S—P I do not mean that S, or P, or their synthesis, is real. I say nothing about any union in fact. The truth of S—P means that, *if I suppose* S, I am bound *in that case* to assert S—P. In this way *all* judgements are hypothetical.[4]

The conclusion, thus urged upon us by Herbart, follows, I think, irresistibly from the premisses. But the premisses are not valid. Judgement, we saw in the foregoing chapter, can not consist in the synthesis of ideas. And yet it will repay us to pause awhile, and to enlarge on the consequences of this erroneous doctrine. To see clearly that, if judgement is the union of ideas, there then can be no categorical judgement, is a very great step in the understanding of Logic. And, through the next few sections, we shall endeavour to make this conclusion plain.

§ 4. The contrast and comparison of reality and truth no doubt involve very ultimate principles. To enquire what is fact, is to enter at once on a journey into metaphysics, the end of which might not soon be attained. For our present purpose we must answer the question from a level not much above that of common sense.[5{4}] And the account which represents the ordinary view, and in which perhaps we may most of us agree, is something of this sort.

The real is that which is known in presentation or intuitive knowledge. It is what we encounter in feeling or perception. Again it is that which appears in the series of events that occur in space and time. It is that once more which resists our wills; a [45] thing is real if it exercises any kind of force or compulsion, or exhibits necessity. It is briefly what acts and maintains itself in existence. And this last feature seems connected with former ones. We know of no action, unless it shows itself by altering the series of either space of time, or both together; and again perhaps there is nothing which appears unless it acts. But the simplest account, in which the others possibly are all summed up, is

---

[4] Herbart, [*Sämmtliche*] *Werke*, I. 92.

[5{4}] Unfortunately in this work, with regard to 'reality', neither the view of Common Sense (whatever that is) nor any other view has been kept to consistently. Cf. § 72.

given in the words, The real is self-existent. And we may put this otherwise by saying, The real is what is individual.

It is the business of metaphysics to subject these ideas to a systematic examination. We must content ourselves here with taking them on trust, and will pause merely to point out a common misunderstanding. It is a mistake to suppose that 'The real is individual' means either that the real is abstractly simple, or is merely particular. Internal diversity does not exclude individuality, and still less is a thing made self-existent by standing in a relation of exclusion to others. Metaphysics can prove that, in this sense, the particular is furthest removed from self-existence. The individual is so far from being merely particular that, in contrast with its own internal diversity, it is a true universal. . . . Nor is this a paradox. We are accustomed to speak of, and believe in, realities which exist in more than one moment of time or portion of space. Any such reality would be an identity which appears and remains the same under differences; and it therefore would be a real universal.

§ 5. Such, we may say, are some of the points which constitute reality. And truth has not one of them. It exists, as such, in the world of ideas. And ideas, we have seen, are merely symbols. They are general and adjectival, not substantive and individual. Their essence lies within their meaning and beyond their existence. The idea is the fact with its existence disregarded, and its content mutilated. It is but a portion of the actual content cut off from its reality, and used with a reference to something else. No [46] idea can be real.

If judgement is the synthesis of two ideas, then truth consists in the junction of unreals. When I say, Gold is yellow, then certainly some fact is present to my mind. But universal gold and universal yellowness are not realities, and, on the other hand, what *images* of yellow and gold I actually possess, though as psychical facts they have real existence, are unfortunately not the facts about which I desired to say anything. We have seen (Chap. I[d]) that I do *not* mean, This image of gold is in my mind joined psychically with this other image of yellow. I mean that, quite apart from my mental facts, gold in general has a certain kind of colour. I strip away certain parts from the mental facts, and, combining these adjectival remnants, I call the synthesis truth.

---

[d] 'The General Nature of Judgement', repr. above, Part I, Ch. 1.

But reality is not a connection of adjectives, nor can it so be represented. Its essence is to be substantial and individual. But can we reach self-existence and individual character by manipulating adjectives and putting universals together? If not, the fact is not given *directly* in any truth whatsoever. It can never be stated categorically. And yet, because adjectives depend upon substantives, the substantive is implied. Truth will then refer to fact *indirectly*. The adjectives of truth presuppose a reality, and in this sense all judgement will rest on a supposal. It is all hypothetical; itself will confess that what directly it deals with, is unreal.

§ 6. More ordinary considerations might perhaps have led us to anticipate this result. The common-sense view of facts outside us passing over into the form of truth within us, or copying themselves in a faithful mirror, is shaken and perplexed by the simplest enquiries. What fact is asserted in negative judgements? Has every negation I choose to invent a real counterpart in the world of things? Does *any* logical negation, as such, correspond to fact? Consider again hypothetical judgements. *If* something is, *then* something else follows, but should neither exist, would the statement be false? It seems just as true without facts as with them, and, if so, what fact can it possibly assert? The disjunctive judgement will again perplex us. 'A is *b* or *c*' must be true or false, but how in the world can a *fact* exist as that strange ambi-

[47] guity '*b* or *c*?' We shall hardly find the flesh and blood alternative which answers to our 'or'.

If we think these puzzles too technical or sought out, let us take more obvious ones. Have the past and the future we talk of so freely any real existence? Or let us try a mere ordinary categorical affirmative judgement, 'Animals are mortal.' This seems at first to keep close to reality; the junction of facts seems quite the same as the junction of ideas. But the experience we have gained may warn us that, if ideas are adjectives, this can not be the case. If we are unconvinced, let us go on to examine. 'Animals' seems perhaps to answer to a fact, since all the animals who exist are real. But, in 'Animals are mortal,' is it only the animals now existing that we speak of? Do we not mean to say that the animal born hereafter will certainly die? The complete collection of real things is of course the same fact as the real things themselves, but a difficulty arises as to future individuals. And, apart from that, we scarcely in general have in our minds a complete collection. We *mean*, 'Whatever is an animal will die,' but that is the same as *If* anything is an animal *then* it is mortal. The assertion really is about mere hypothesis; it is not about fact.

In universal judgements we may sometimes understand that the synthesis of adjectives, which the judgement expresses, is really found in actual existence. But the judgement does not say this. It is merely a private supposition of our own. It arises partly from the nature of the case, and partly again from our bad logical tradition. The fact that most adjectives we conjoin in judgement can be taken as the adjectives of existing things, leads us naturally to expect that this will always be the case. And, in the second place, a constant ambiguity arises from the use of 'all' in the subject. We write the universal in the form 'All animals', and then take it to mean each actual animal, or the real sum of existing animals. But this would be no more an universal judgement than 'A B and C are severally mortal.' And we *mean* nothing like this. In saying 'All animals', if we think of a collection, we never for a moment imagine it complete; we mean also 'Whatever besides may be animal must be mortal too.' In universal judgements we never mean 'all'. What we mean is 'any', and 'whatever', and [48] 'whenever'. But these involve 'if'.

We may see this most easily by a simple observation. If actual existence were really asserted, the judgement would be false if the existence failed. And this is not the case. It would be a hazardous assertion that, supposing all animal life had ceased, mortality would at once be predicated falsely, and, with the reappearance of animal existence, would again become true. But cases exist where no doubt is possible. 'All persons found trespassing on this ground will be prosecuted,' is too often a prophecy, as well as a promise. But it is not meant to foretell, and, though no one trespasses, the statement may be true. 'All triangles have their angles equal to two right angles' would hardly be false if there were no triangles. And, if this seems strange, take the case of a chiliagon. Would statements about chiliagons cease to be true, if no one at the moment were thinking of a chiliagon? We can hardly say that, and yet where would any chiliagons exist? There surely must be scientific propositions, which unite ideas not demonstrable at the moment in actual existence. But can we maintain that, if the sciences which produce these became non-existent, these judgements would have *ipso facto* become false, as well as unreal?

The universal judgement is thus always hypothetical. It says '*Given* one thing you will *then* have another,' and says no more. No truth can state fact.

§ 7. This result is however not easy to put up with. For, if the truth is such, then all truths, it would seem, are no better than false. We can not so give up the categorical judgement, for, if that is lost, then everything fails. Let us make a search and keep to this question, Is there nowhere to be found a categorical judgement? And it seems we can find one. Universal judgements were merely hypothetical, because they stated, not individual substantives, but connections of adjectives. But in singular judgements the case is otherwise. Where the subject, of which you affirm categorically, is one individual, or a set of individuals, your truth expresses fact. There is here no mere adjective and no hypothesis.

These judgements are divisible into three great classes.[6]{[7]} And [49] the distinction will hereafter be of great importance. (i) We have first those judgements which make an assertion about that which I now perceive, or feel, or about some portion of it. 'I have a toothache,' 'There is a wolf,' 'That bough is broken.' In these we simply analyze the given, and may therefore call them by the name of *Analytic judgements of sense*.[7] Then (ii) we have *Synthetic judgements of sense*, which state either some fact of time or space, or again some quality of the matter given, which I do not here and now directly perceive. 'This road leads to London,' 'Yesterday it rained,' 'Tomorrow there will be full moon.' They are synthetic because they extend the given through an ideal construction, and they all, as we shall see, involve an inference. The third class (iii), on the other hand, have to do with a reality which is never a sensible event in time. 'God is a spirit,' 'The soul is a substance.' We may think what we like of the validity of these judgements, and may or may not decline to rec-

---

[6]{[7]} 'Three great classes.' These distinctions are all in the end untenable. All judgements without exception are conditional.

[7] These analytic and synthetic judgements must not for one moment be confounded with Kant's. Every possible judgement, we shall see hereafter, is both analytic and synthetic. Most, if not all, judgements of sense are synthetic in the sense of transcending the given.

ognize them in metaphysics. But in logic they certainly must have a place.

§ 8. But, if judgement is the union of two ideas, we have not so escaped. And this is a point we should clearly recognize. Ideas are universal, and, no matter what it is that we try to say and dimly mean, what we really express and succeed in asserting, is nothing individual. For take the analytic judgement of sense. The fact given us is singular, it is quite unique; but our terms are all general, and state a truth which may apply as well to many other cases. In 'I have a toothache' both the I and the toothache are mere generalities. The *actual* toothache is not any other toothache, and the *actual* I is myself as having this very toothache. But the truth I assert has been and will be true of all other toothaches of my altering self. Nay 'I have a toothache,' is as true of another's toothache as of my own, and may be met by the assertion, 'Not so, but *I* have one.' It is in vain that we add to the original assertion 'this', 'here', and 'now', for they are all universals. They are symbols whose meaning extends to and covers innumerable instances.

Thus the judgement will be true of any case whatsoever of a [50] certain sort; but, if so, it can not be true of the reality; for that is unique, and is a fact, not a sort. 'That bough is broken,' but so are many others, and we do not say which. 'This road leads to London' may be said just as well of a hundred other roads. 'Tomorrow it will be full moon,' does not tell us what tomorrow. Hereafter it will constantly be true that, on the day after this day, there will be a full moon. And so, failing in all cases to state the actual fact, we state something else instead. What is true of all does not express this one. The assertion sticks for ever in the adjectives; it does not reach the substantive. And adjectives unsupported float in the air; their junction with reality is supposed and not asserted. So long as judgements are confined to ideas, their reference to fact is a mere implication. It is presupposed outside the assertion, which is not strictly true until we qualify it by a suppressed condition. As it stands, it both fails as a singular proposition, and is false if you take it as a strict universal (cf. § 62 foll.).

§ 9. But judgement, as we saw in the foregoing Chapter,[e] is not

---

[e] 'The General Nature of Judgement', repr. above, Part I, Ch. I.

confined to ideas, and can not by any means consist in their synthesis. The necessity for two ideas is a mere delusion, and, if before we judged we had had to wait for them, we certainly should never have judged at all. And the necessity for the copula is a sheer superstition. Judgements can exist without any copula and with but one idea.

In the simplest judgement an idea is referred to what is given in perception, and it is identified therewith as one of its adjectives. There is no need for an idea to appear as the subject, and, even when it so appears, we must distinguish the fact from grammatical show. It is present reality which is the actual subject, and the genuine substantive of the ideal content. We shall see hereafter that, when 'this' 'here' and 'now' seem to stand as subjects, the actual fact which appears in perception is the real subject, to which these phrases serve to direct our attention. But of this in the sequel; we have seen already, and have further to see, that all judgements predicate their ideal content as an attribute of the real which appears in presentation.

[51] It is from this point of view that we must resume the discussion. Standing on this basis, we must examine afresh the various judgements which have passed before us, and must ask for their meaning and further validity. Some difficulties in our search for categorical judgements may have already disappeared; but others as formidable must perhaps be awaited. And, if we come to the result that all truth in the end is true of reality, we must not expect to maintain that doctrine in its crude acceptation.

§ 10. Our first movement however must be towards a definition. A phrase we have used was designedly ambiguous. Are we to hold that the real, which is the ultimate subject, and which, as we said, appears in perception, is identical with the merely momentary appearance? We shall see that this can not be, and that such a view could not possibly account for the facts. At present we may offer a preliminary argument against this mistake.

The subject which appears in the series of time, and to which we attribute our ideas as predicates, must itself be real. And, if real, it must not be purely adjectival. On the contrary it must be self-existent and individual. But the particular phenomenon, the momentary appearance, is not individual, and is so not the subject which we use in judgement.

§ 11. We naturally think that the real, at least as we know it, must be present. Unless I come into contact with it directly, I can never be sure of it. Nothing in the end but what I feel can be real, and I can not feel anything unless it touches me. But nothing again can immediately encounter me save that which is present.[8]{[10]} If I have it not here and now, I do not have it at all.

'The present is real'; this seems indubitable. And are we to say that the momentary appearance is *therefore* real? This indeed would be mistaken. If we take the real as that which is confined to a single 'here' or a single 'now' (in this sense making it particular), we shall have questions on our hands we shall fail to dispose of. For, beside the difficulties as to the truth of all universal judgements, we are threatened with the loss of every proposition which extends beyond the single instant. *Synthetic* judgements must at once be banished if the real is only the phenomenon of a moment. Nothing either past or future in time, nor any space I do not directly perceive, can be predicated as adjectives of our [52] one 'now' and 'here'. All such judgements would be false, for they would attribute to the existent qualities which confessedly are non-existent, or would place the real as one member in a series of utter unrealities.

But perhaps we feel we may escape this consequence; or at all events feel so sure of our premiss that we can not give it up. 'The real is confined to one here or one now.' But supposing this true, are we sure we know what it is we understand by our 'now' and 'here'? For time and extension seem continuous elements; the here is one space with the other heres round it; and the now flows ceaselessly and passes for ever from the present to the past.

We may avoid this difficulty, we may isolate the time we call the present, and fix our now as the moment which *is*, and has neither past, nor future, nor transition in itself. But here we fall into a hopeless dilemma. This moment which we take either has no duration, and in that case it turns out no time at all; or, if it has duration, it is a part of time, and is found to have transition in itself.

If the now in which the real appears is purely discrete, then first we may say that, as characterized by exclusion, the

---

[8]{[10]} A view, such as that advocated, e.g., by Mr. Russell, I take (i) to deny the reality of apparent change, and (ii) to be incompatible with the fact of the appearance.

phenomenon, if apparent, is not self-subsistent, and so not real. But apart from that objection, and to return to our dilemma, the now and the here must have some extension. For no part of space or time is a final element. We find that every here is made up of heres, and every now is resolvable into nows. And thus the appearance of an atomic now could not show itself as any one part of time. But, if so, it could never show itself at all. Or, on the other hand, if we say the appearance has duration, then, like all real time, it has succession in itself, and it would not be the appearance of our single now.[9] From all which it is clear that a momentary appearance will not give us the subject of which we are in search.

[53]   § 12. It is a mistake to suppose that the present is a part of time, indivisible and stationary, and that here and now can be solid and atomic. In one sense of the word the present is no time. Itself no part of the process, it is a point we take within the flow of change. It is the line that we draw across the stream, to fix in our minds the relations of one successive event to another event. 'Now', in this sense, stands for 'simultaneous with'; it signifies not existence but bare position in the series of time. The reality is not present in the sense of given in one atomic moment.

What we mean, when we identify presence with reality, is something different. The real is that with which I come into immediate contact, and the content of any part of time, any section of the continuous flow of change, is present to me if I directly encounter it. What is given in a perception, though it change in my hands, is now and here if only I perceive it. And within that perception any aspect or part, which I specially attend to, is specially present, is now and here in another sense than the rest of that content. The present is the filling of that duration in which the reality appears to me directly; and there

---

[9] It is the business of metaphysics to prove these points at length. If time consists of discrete parts, it is hard to see how the fact of succession can possibly be explained, unless time be taken between these parts of time. And that would lead to untenable conclusions. But it is the fact of change which shows that time is continuous. The rate of change, the number of events in every part of time, may, so far as we know, be increased indefinitely; and this means that in every part of time more than one event may take place. If the parts be discrete, then not only will motion imply that a thing is in several places in one time (and this is a fact), but also (which is absurd) that throughout all these places no time elapses, that they are strictly contemporaneous. I should be glad to enter into the discussion at length, but the subject cannot properly be treated by logic.

can be no part of the succession of events so small or so great, that conceivably it might not appear as present.

In passing we may repeat and may trace the connection of those shades of meaning we have found in 'presence'. (i) Two events in time are now to one another, if both are given simultaneously in *my* series. (ii) Since the real appears in the series of time, the effort to find it both *present* and *existing* within that series, creates the fiction of the atomic now. (iii) If the real can never exist *in* time, but only appear there, then that part of the series in which it touches me is my present. (iv) And this suggests the reflection that presence is really the negation of time, and never can properly be given in the series. It is not the time that [54] can ever be present, but only the content.

§ 13. But we must leave these intricacies. We must be satisfied with knowing that the real, which (we say) appears in perception, does not appear in one single moment. And if we will pause and reflect for a little, we shall see how hardened we are in superstitions. When we ask for reality, we at once encounter it in space and time. We find opposed to us a continuous element of perpetual change. We begin to observe and to make distinctions, and this element becomes a series of events. And here we are tempted to deceive ourselves grossly. We allow ourselves to talk as if there existed an actual chain of real events, and as if this chain were somehow moved past us, or we moved along it, and as if, whenever we came to a link, the machinery stopped and we welcomed each new link with our 'here' and our 'now'. Still we do not believe that the rest of the links, which are *not* here and now, do all equally exist, and, if so, we can hardly be quite sure of our chain. And the link, if we must call it so, which is now and here, is no solid substance. If we would but observe it, we should see it itself to be a fluid sequence whose parts offer no resistance to division, and which is both now, and itself without end made up of nows.

Or we seem to think that we sit in a boat, and are carried down the stream of time, and that on the banks there is a row of houses with numbers on the doors. And we get out of the boat, and knock at the door of number 19, and, re-entering the boat, then suddenly find ourselves opposite 20, and, having there done the same, we go on to 21. And, all this while, the firm fixed row of the past and future stretches in a block behind us and before us.

If it really is necessary to have some image, perhaps the following may save us from worse. Let us fancy ourselves in total darkness hung over a stream and looking down on it. The stream has no banks, and its current is covered and filled continuously with floating things. Right under our faces is a bright illuminated spot on the water, which ceaselessly widens and narrows its area, and shows us what passes away on the current. And this spot that is light is our now, our present.

[55] We may go still further and anticipate a little. We have not only an illuminated place, and the rest of the stream in total darkness. There is a paler light which, both up and down stream, is shed on what comes before and after our now. And this paler light is the offspring of the present. Behind our heads there is something perhaps which reflects the rays from the litup now, and throws them more dimly upon past and future. Outside this reflection is utter darkness; within it is gradual increase of brightness, until we reach the illumination immediately below us.

In this image we shall mark two things, if we are wise. It is possible, in the first place, that the light of the present may come from behind us, and what reflects the light may also bestow it. We can not tell that, but what we know is, that our now is the source of the light that falls on the past and future. Through it alone do we know there exists a stream of floating things, and without its reflection past and future would vanish. And there is another point we must not lose sight of. There is a difference between the brightness of the now, and the paler revelation of past and future. But, despite this difference, we see the stream and what floats in it as one. We overcome the difference. And we do so by seeing the continuity of the element in past, present and future. It is because, through the different illuminations, there are points of connection offered by what floats, in other words, a sameness of content, that the stream and its freightage become all one thing to us, and we even forget that most of what we see is not self-subsistent but borrowed and adjectival. We shall perceive hereafter that time and space beyond here and now are not strictly existent in the sense in which the present is. They are not given directly but are inferred from the present. And they are so inferred because the now and here, on which the light falls, are the appearance of a reality which for ever transcends them, and upon which resting we go beyond them.

§ 14. But this is to anticipate. The result, which at present we have wished to make clear, is that the now and here, in which the real appears, are not confined within simply discrete and resting moments. They are any portion of that continuous content with which we come into direct relation. Examination shows that not only at their edges they dissolve themselves over into there [56] and then, but that, even within their limits as first given, they know no repose. Within the here is both here and there; and in the ceaseless process of change in time you may narrow your scrutiny to the smallest focus, but you will find no rest. The appearance is always a process of disappearing, and the duration of the process which we call our present has no fixed length.

It will be seen hereafter that in the above reflections we have not been wandering. Nor will it be long before we return to them, but we must now rediscuss from a better point of view those forms of judgement we before laid down (§ 7).

§ 15. Judgement is not the synthesis of ideas, but the reference of ideal content to reality. From this basis we must now endeavour to interpret the various kinds of judgement we have met with. And, beginning with the singular judgement of § 7, let us take the first division of these, which were called Analytic judgements of sense.

I. The essence of these is to hold only of the now, and not to transcend the given presentation. They may have neither grammatical subject nor copula, or again, on the other hand, may possess one or both.

A. In the judgements that have neither copula nor subject, an idea is referred (α) to the whole sensible reality, or (β) to some part of it.

(α) When we hear the cry of 'Wolf', or 'Fire', or 'Rain', it is impossible to say that we hear no assertion. He who raises the cry is always taken to affirm, to have uttered a sign and to have used it of the real. The practical man would laugh at your distinction that, in exclaiming 'Wolf', I can not be a liar, because I use no subject or copula, but that, if I go so far as 'This is a wolf,' I am thereby committed. Such a plea, we must allow, would be instantly dismissed. In the 'Wolf' or 'Rain' the subject is the unspecified present environment, and that is qualified by the attribution of the ideal content 'Wolf' or 'Rain'. It is the *external* present that is here the subject. But in some moment of both outward squalor and inward wretchedness, where we turn to one another with the one word 'miserable', the subject is here the whole given reality.

[57] Such single words, it may perhaps be said, are really interjections and never predicates. If they were really interjections, we must stubbornly maintain, they could not be the vehicle of truth and falsehood. And a real interjection that is nothing besides, is not so common as some persons suppose. An *habitual* interjection soon gets a meaning, and becomes the sign of a received idea, which, in reference to the content, may be an assertion of truth or falsehood.

But the fact is really beyond all question. You may utter a word which conveys to you, and which you know conveys to others also, a statement about fact. Unless then you are deceiving, you must be judging. And you certainly are judging without any other subject than the whole sensible present.

(β) But this is an extreme case; in nearly all instances but one piece of the present is the real subject. We qualify by our idea some one given aspect. But no subject or copula appears even here. A common understanding, or the pointing of a finger, is all that serves to limit the reference. Of a visible wolf I may predicate the words 'asleep' or 'running,' or in watching a sunset, it is enough for me to say the word 'down' or 'gone,' and every one knows I am judging and affirming. It might be said, no doubt, that the subject is elided, but this would be a mere linguistic prejudice. The genuine subject is not an idea, elided or expressed, but it is the immediate sensible presentation.

And again it might be said that what we call the predicate is really the subject of an unexpressed existential judgement. But this cardinal mistake will be soon disposed of, when hereafter we deal with that class of judgements (§ 42).

§ 15.[f] B. We pass next to those analytic judgements where a subject is expressed. The ideal content of the predicate is here referred to another idea, which stands as a subject. But in this case, as above, the ultimate subject is no idea, but is the real in presentation. It is this to which the content of both ideas, with their relation, is attributed. The synthesis of the ideal elements is

---

[f] This is a misprint. There are two sections numbered 15 in Bradley's text.

predicated either (α) of the whole, or (β) of a part, of that which appears.

(α) In such judgements as 'Now is the time,' 'It's all so dreary,' or 'The present is dark,' an idea takes the place of the unspoken [58] reference of the preceding section. But the subject remains in both cases the same. An idea, it is true, intervenes between the reality and the predicate, and holds the place of immediate subject. But a moment's consideration will assure us that the subject of our assertion is still the presented. The immediate subject is the sign of a reference, either simple or embodying implications, to the whole given reality.

(β) We have a further advance when the presented fact is not the whole sensible environment, but only a part of it. In 'There is a wolf,' 'This is a bird,' or 'Here is a fire,' 'there' 'this' and 'here' are certainly ideas, and stand no doubt for the subject of the judgement:[10] but, the moment we examine them, we find once more a reference to the reality, not now indefinite and embracing the whole, but still no more than a sign of distinction and indication. If these ideas are the true subject of a judgement, then so is a silent pointing with the finger.

§ 16. There is really no change when we go a step further, and take such judgements as 'This bird is yellow,' 'That stone is falling,' 'This leaf is dead.' The idea, which stands as the grammatical subject, is certainly more than an indefinite reference, more even than a sign of indication. It not only distinguishes a part from the environment, but it also characterizes and qualifies it. But if, before, the subject we *meant* was not an idea, but was presented fact, so also now does this remain the truth. It is not the bare idea, symbolized by 'this bird', of which we go on to affirm the predicate. It is the fact distinguished and qualified by 'this bird', to which the adjective 'yellow' is really attributed. The genuine subject is the thing as perceived, the content of which our analysis has divided into 'this bird' and 'yellow', and of which we predicate indirectly those ideal elements in their union.

The same account holds throughout all the variety of these analytic judgements. Let us complicate our assertion. 'The cow, which is now being milked by the milkmaid, is standing to the [59]

---

[10] It sounds, perhaps, rather shocking to call 'there' or 'here' subjects, but, if the text is understood, I need make no defence. On the nature of the ideas of 'this', 'now', and 'here', we shall find later on a good deal to say.

right of the hawthorn tree yonder.' In this judgement we have
not one thing but several, and more than one statement about
their relations. But it is still a part of the presented environment
which is actually the subject and the real substantive of which
this whole complex is indirectly asserted. If you deny this, then
show me where you draw your line, and what point it is in the
scale of judgements at which the idea takes the place of the sensible fact, and becomes the true subject. And confine the assertion
to mere ideas. Take the ideal elements of a cow and a hawthorn
tree and a milkmaid, and combine them ideally in any way you
please. Then after they are combined, stand in presence of the
fact, and ask yourself if *that* does not enter into your judgement.
If, with the fact before you, you begin to reflect, you will find
that, if you keep to mere ideas, you remove from the assertion
just the thing you mean. In § 20 we shall return to this point, but
at present we may deal with a popular error.

§ 17. There is a curious illusion, now widely spread, on the
subject of proper names. We find it laid down that a proper
name has not got *connotation*, or, to use the more common technical term, it has no *intension*. In ordinary language, it *stands* for
something but does not *mean* anything.

If this were true, it would be hard to understand what is
signified by such judgements as 'John is asleep.' There are
thinkers indeed, who fear no consequence, and who will tell us
that here the *name* John is the subject of the proposition. And
against these adversaries I confess I have no heart to enter the
lists. They may say what they please without hindrance from me.
But, if we are inclined to accept a less heroic solution, and to
suppose the *man* John to be the subject of the judgement, then I
do not quite see the purpose of the name, if we are not to mean
by it anything at all. Why not simply omit it, and, pointing to
the man, say the word 'asleep'?

'But it stands for the man,' I shall hear the reply, 'and, even
when he is present, it is a *mark* which serves to distinguish him
much more clearly than pointing.' But that is just what puzzles
me. If there *is* an idea conveyed by the name, whenever it is used,
then it surely means something, or, in the language which pleases
you, it must be 'connotative'. But if, on the other hand, it con-
[60] veys *no* idea, it would appear to be some kind of interjection. If
you say that, like 'this' and 'here', it is merely the ideal equiva-

lent of pointing, then at once it assuredly *has* a meaning, but unfortunately that meaning is a vague universal. For anything and everything is 'this' and 'here'. But if you asseverate that it is the ideal counterpart of pointing in particular to John, then you must allow me to doubt if you comprehend what you are saying.

The word 'mark' has two senses which perhaps we may confuse. It is something which *may be* made a means of distinction, or something which *has been* made such a means. I suppose, for I can do no more than suppose, that mark is not taken in the former sense, and that our man was not seen to be distinct from other men, because he was found to have the marking John. But, if it is the latter of these senses we adopt, then a name is a mark because it is a sign, and mark and sign are here identical.

Now a sign can not possibly be destitute of meaning. Originally imposed as an *arbitrary* mark, that very process, which makes it a sign and associates it firmly with the thing it signifies, must associate with it also some qualities and characters of that which it stands for. If it did not to some extent get to *mean* the thing, it never could get to *stand* for it at all. And can any one say that a proper name, if you are aware of its designation, brings *no* ideas with it, or that these ideas are mere chance conjunction? What connection, I would ask, would be left between the bare name and the thing it stands for, if every one of these ideas were removed? All would vanish together.

The matter is so plain I do not know how to explain it. The meaning of a sign need of course not be fixed. But is the thing it stands for quite invariable? If the 'connotation' is unsteady, does the 'denotation' never change? But where the latter is fixed there the former on its side (within limits) is stationary. You may have no idea what 'William' connotes, but if so you can hardly know what it stands for. The whole question arises from a simple mistake and misunderstanding.

§ 18. 'But after all the name is the sign of an individual, and meanings are generic and universal. Therefore the name can not have any content of which it is the sign.' I have purposely put an objection in that form which suggests the conclusion I wish to [61] arrive at. The name of a man is the name of an individual, which remains amid changing particulars, and therefore no judgement about such an individual is wholly analytic. It transcends the given, it becomes synthetic, and with it we pass into the second great division of singular judgements.

Proper names have a meaning which always goes beyond the presentation of the moment. It is not indeed true that such names must stand for objects, which endure through a train of altering perceptions. The unique thing they designate may appear but once, as an event shut up within one presentation. But that object would not be unique, nor proper to its own especial self, if it did not involve a reference to a series from which it was excluded. And mere analysis of sense could never suggest that limiting relation which gives it uniqueness.

And, when we take the proper names of objects which last and which reappear, then the given is transcended in a still higher sense. The meaning of such a name is universal, and its use implies a real universality, an identity which transcends particular moments. For, unless the person were recognized as distinct, he would hardly get a name of his own, and his recognition depends on his remaining the same throughout change of context. We could not recognize anything unless it possessed an attribute, or attributes, which from time to time we are able to identify. The individual remains the same amid that change of appearance which we predicate as its quality. And this implies that it has real identity. Its proper name is the sign of a universal, of an ideal content which actually *is* in the real world.

This assumption, and the practice of giving proper names, may no doubt be indefensible. What concerns us here is that the practice transcends presented reality. In 'John is asleep,' the ultimate subject can not be the real as it is now given; for 'John' implies a continuous existence, not got by mere analysis. We have reached the class of synthetic judgements.

[62] § 19. II. In this second class of singular judgements (§ 7), we make generally some assertion about that which appears in a space or time that we do not perceive, and we predicate of a presentation something not got by analysis of its content. If I say 'There is a garden on the other side of that wall,' the judgement is synthetic, for it goes beyond perception. And in 'Yesterday was Sunday,' 'William conquered England,' 'Next month is June,' I certainly do not analyze what is merely given. In synthetic judgements there is always an inference, for an ideal content is connected with the sensible qualities that are given us. In

other words we have always a construction, which depends on ideas, and which only indirectly is based on perception. . . .

And, this being so, it seems as if now we were unable to proceed. If the subject is the real that appears in perception, how can events in the past and future, or a world in space outside the presentation, and how even can qualities not given to sense be referred to the object and considered as its adjectives? We have already glanced at the solution of this problem, and what we now wish to show is the following. In synthetic judgements the ultimate subject is still the reality. That is not the same as the momentary appearance, and yet synthetic judgements are possible only by being connected with what is given at this very instant. The ideas of past and future events are projected from the base of present perception. It is only in that point that they encounter the reality of which they wish to be true.

'But past and future,' the reader may object, 'are surcly realities.' Perhaps they are, but our question is, Given a synthesis of ideas within my mind, how and where am I able to get at a reality to which to attribute them? How am I to judge unless I go to presentation? Let the past and future be as real as you please, but by what device shall I come in contact with them, and refer to them my ideas, unless I advance directly to the given, and to them indirectly? It is possible, I am aware, to assert that past realities are directly presented, and possible also (for all I know) to say the same of the future, and of all the space I am not in contact with, and of all the qualities that I do not perceive. In this way, no doubt, we dispose of the difficulty, and indeed may make a very simple matter of any kind of problem, if indeed any problems any longer will exist.

§ 20. But the persons I write for, and who are not so blessed [63] with easy intuitions, will feel this difficulty, and there may come a temptation to fall back once more on the abandoned heresy and to say, In these synthetic judgements the subject can not possibly be the reality. It must be an idea, and in the junction of ideas must lie the truth. And I think, perhaps, at the cost of repetition, we had better see where this temptation leads us.

When we say 'It rained last Tuesday,' we mean *this* last Tuesday, and not any other; but, if we keep to ideas, we do not utter our meaning. Nothing in the world that you can do to ideas, no possible torture will get out of them an assertion that is not universal. We can not escape by employing ideas of events in time, particulars as we call them. The event you describe is a single occurrence, but what you say of it will do just as well for any number of events, imaginary or real. If you keep to ideas it is useless to make a reference to the present, and say, 'The Tuesday that came before *this* day.' For we have seen before (§ 8), that in analytic judgements we are equally helpless. The real is inaccessible by way of ideas. In attempting to become concrete and special, you only succeed in becoming more abstract and wholly indefinite. 'This' 'now' and 'mine' are all universals. And your helpless iteration, 'not this but this', will not get your expression any nearer to your meaning. If judgement is only the union of ideas, no judgement is ever about the individual.

§ 21. We must get rid of the erroneous notion (if we have it) that space and time are 'principles of individuation', in the sense that a temporal or spatial exclusion will confer uniqueness upon any content. It is an illusion to suppose that, by speaking of 'events', we get down to real and solid particulars, and leave the airy region of universal adjectives. For the question arises, What space and time do we really mean, and how can we express it so as not to express what is as much something else? It is true that, in the idea of a series of time or complex of space, uniqueness is in one sense involved; for the parts exclude one another reciprocally. But they do note exclude, unless the series is taken as one continuous whole, and the relations between its members are thus [64] fixed by the unity of the series. Apart from this unity, a point on its recurrence could not be distinguished from the point as first given. And elsewhere we might ask, how far such an unity is itself the negation of mere exclusivity.

But, to pass by this question, it is clear that exclusion within a given series does not carry with it an absolute uniqueness. There is nothing whatever in the idea of a series to hint that there may not be any number of series, internally all indistinguishable from the first. How can you, so long as you are not willing to transcend ideas, determine or in any way characterize your series, so as to get its difference from every possible series within your description? It is idle to say 'this', for 'this' does not exclude except in *this* sphere, and it is idle to say 'my', for it is only in *my* element that yours and mine collide. Outside it they are indifferent, and the expression 'my' will not distinguish one world from the other. If we simply attend to the series itself, and, declining to look outside, confine ourselves to the consideration of its character, then all that it contains might be the common property of innumerable subjects, existing and enjoyed in the world of each, a general possession appropriated by none. The mere quality of appearance in space or time can not give singularity.

§ 22. The seeking for judgement in the synthesis of ideas once more has led us where there is no exit. With however little hope we must return to the doctrine, that judgement is the reference of an ideal content to the real which appears in time and space, which is to be encountered directly in presentation, but which can not be limited to a momentary instance. It is not by its quality as a temporal event or phenomenon of space, that the given is unique. It is unique, not because it has a certain character, but because it *is given*. It is by the reference of our series to the real, as it appears directly within this point of contact, or indirectly in the element continuous with this point, that these series become exclusive. We perhaps may be allowed to express this otherwise by saying, it is only the 'this' which is real, and ideas will suffice so far as 'thisness', but can never give 'this'. It is perhaps a hard saying, and announces difficulties we shall need both courage and patience to contend with.

§ 23. Everything that is given us, all psychical events, be they [65] sensations, or images, or reflections, or feeling, or ideas, or emotions—every possible phenomenon that can be present—both is 'this' and has 'thisness'. But its stamp of uniqueness and singularity comes to it from the former and not from the latter. If we distinguish the aspects of existence and content[11][16] (Chapter I,[g] § 4), and put on the one side *that* anything is, and on the other side *what* it is, then the thisness falls within the content, but the this does not fall there. It is the mere sign of my immediate relation, my direct encounter in sensible presentation with the real world. I will not here ask how 'this' is related to existence, how

---

[11][16] 'Content' or 'quality' means here anything distinguishable so as to be for us a content or quality. In saying that the 'this' does not fall within the 'what', we must add that it does not fall in the 'that' either. For each of these is an abstraction. Again, where a quality is unique, it ceases to be so if you take it as distinct from its 'that'—for, if so, there may be another instance.

---

[g] 'The General Nature of Judgement', repr. above, Part I, Ch. i.

far it holds of the actual fact, and how far only of the mere appearance; whether it *is* or is only *for me*. Apart from that, at least so much is certain, that we find uniqueness in our contact with the real, and that we do not find it anywhere else. The singularity which comes with presentation and is what we call 'this', is not a *quality* of that which is given.

But thisness on the other hand does belong to the content, and is the general character of every appearance in space or time. Thisness, if we like, we may call particularity. Everything that is given us is given, in the first place, surrounded and immersed in a complex detail of innumerable relations to other phenomena in space or time. In its internal quality we find again a distinction of aspects, which we always can carry to a certain length, and can never be sure we have quite exhausted. And the internal relations of its component elements in space or time are again indefinite. We are never at the end of them. This detail appears to come to us on compulsion; we seem throughout to perceive it as it is, and in no sense to make or even to alter it. And this detail it is which constitutes thisness.[12]

[66]   But such particularity in space or time, such an exclusive nature, after all, is only a *general* character. It falls in the content and does not give the existence. It marks the sort but it misses the thing. In abstraction from the this it is merely ideal, and, apart from the this, ideas as we know can not reach to uniqueness. No amount of thisness which an event possesses will exclude the existence of self-same events in other like series. Such exclusiveness falls all within the description, and that which is only of this description is simply such and can not be this.

---

[12] The apprehension of this character, it may be objected, takes time, and, if any time for observation is given, the product, for all we know, has been altered. But this difficulty occurs in all observation. We everywhere assume, first, that things are not different unless we can discriminate them. And we assume, in the second place, our ability to distinguish a change in ourselves from a change in the object. We assume that more of the same object is observed, unless we have reason either to suppose that our fancy has wandered away from that object, or that the object itself has undergone a change. I do not here ask if these assumptions are valid. But I may remark in passing, that the doubt if in introspection we examine a present, or only a past state of mind, should change its form. It should not take the two as exclusive here, unless it faces the same problem elsewhere. For the observation of external phenomena labours under the identical difficulty. If an internal fact can not possibly be *both* present *and* past, then an external fact must be likewise restricted. The two kinds of observation are not essentially different. External facts are not absolutely fixed, nor are internal facts in absolute flux.

In every judgement, where we analyze the given, and where as the subject we place the term 'this', it is not an idea which is really the subject. In using 'this' we do *use* an idea, and that idea is and must be universal; but what we *mean*, and fail to express, is our reference to the object which is given as unique.

§ 24. And here we encounter an awkward question. The reader possibly may be willing to accept our account of thisness. He may agree that, so far as in our use of the term we mean mere relativity in space or time, in other words particularity, we do not at all go beyond the content. And he may allow the consequence that we have so an idea which is only universal. But in using 'this', he may go on to object that we have in addition *another* idea. We have the idea of immediate contact with the presented reality; and it is that idea which is signified by 'this', and which qualifies the idea which stands as the subject of our analytic judgement.

We answer, Assuredly, if such were the case, the reference to fact would inevitably and always fall outside the judgement. Once again we should be floating in the air, and never be more than hypothetical. But the question raised need not so be dismissed, for it leads to an interesting if subtle reflection. The idea [67] of 'this', unlike most ideas, can not be used as a symbol in judgement.

It is certain, in the first place, that we have the idea. Indeed we could scarcely deny that we had it, unless in so doing we actually used it. Beside the idea of exclusion in a series, which is mere thisness, we have also the idea of my immediate sensible relation to reality, and, if so, we have 'this'. We are able to abstract an idea of presence from that direct presentation which is never absent; and presence, though it does not fall within the content, though we can hardly call it a quality of the appearance, yet is recognized as the same amid a change of content, is separable from it, and makes a difference to it. Thus ideally fixed 'this' becomes an universal among other universals.

§ 25. But, despite the likeness, it is very different from an ordinary idea. Ideas, we shall remember, are used as symbols (Chap. I[h]). In my idea of a 'horse' we have (i) the existence of an image in my head, (ii) its whole content, and (iii) its meaning. In other

[h] 'The General Nature of Judgement', repr. above, Part I, Ch. 1.

words we may always distinguish (i) that it is, and (ii) what it is, and (iii) what it signifies. The two first of these aspects belong to it as a fact. The third is the universal which does not belong to it, but is thought of without a relation to its existence, and in actual judgement is referred away to some other subject.

The idea of 'this' has a striking difference. Distinguished as an aspect of presented reality, when we call it up we take any perception or feeling that is given, and, attending to the aspect of presence within it, recognize that as the meaning of our term. We contemplate it ideally, without any reference to the content of that which is actually before us.

But how shall we fare when, attempting a judgement, we attribute the adjective we have so cut loose to *another* substantive? It is here we are stopped. For any judgement so made we discover must be false. The other fact can not be presented without *ipso facto* altering the given. It degrades our given to one element within a larger presentation, or else it wholly removes it from existence. The given disappears and with itself carries our idea away. We are now unable to predicate the idea, since we no [68] longer possess it, or if we still have it, then what supports it excludes that other fact to which we wish to refer it.

§ 26. To repeat the above, the presented instance of reality is unique. By discrimination we are able to fix that uniqueness in the shape of an idea. We thereupon try to make it the idea of something else. But, for the idea to be true of something else, that something else must be present and unique. We have then either two unique presentations, or one must disappear. If the first one goes, the idea goes with it. If the last one goes, there is now no fact for the idea to be referred to. In either case there can be no judgement. The idea, we see, is not the *true* idea of anything other than its own reality. It is a sign which, *if we judge*, can signify nothing except itself. To be least alone then when most alone, and to enjoy the delights of solitude together, are phrases which have a very good sense; but, taken in their bare and literal meaning, they would exemplify the contradiction we have here before us.

Between the fact and the idea of the 'this' in judgement, there can be no practical difference. The idea of this would be falsely used, unless what it marks were actually presented. But in that case we should be trying to use a sign, when we have before us the fact which is signified. We can use the idea so far as to recognize the fact before us as a fact which is 'this'; but such a use does not go beyond the given. It affirms of the subject a predicate without which the subject disappears. It implies discrimination within the fact in which, since the aspect discriminated is not separable from the given, that given with its aspect still remains as the subject. So that the addition of the idea adds nothing to the subject. And if again it were possible to import the idea from the content of *another* fact, the operation would be uncalled for and quite inoperative.

And it is not possible. It would be, as we have seen, the attempt to have before us two unique facts at once. What we mean by 'this' is the exclusive focus of presentation which lights up its content, and it is of that singular content that we use the idea. And to treat that idea as a meaning which could be true elsewhere, would be to bring into our focus another content. But since both must be unique, as well as the same, a dilemma arises which we need not draw out.

§ 27. And if 'this' be used in a different sense, if it does not [69] mark the presence of the whole sensible detail that falls within the focus; if it is used for that which I specially attend to, the result will be the same. If I make A my object to the exclusion of all others, then this special relation to myself must be false, if used of any other. If applied to A it can not possibly also be applied to B.

'But,' it may be said, 'I exclusively attend to both. A and B are both elements within the given "this", and hence I can predicate "this" of either. I can transfer the idea, which I find is true of one, and use it as a predicate which is true of the other. And so, after all, the idea of "this" will be used symbolically.' I am afraid of losing the main question in subtleties, but I must reply by pointing out a confusion. Since A and B are both taken together, you can not exclusively deal with each separately. So much is now clear. But, on the other hand, if you take each by itself as a mere element in the 'this', then you can not predicate 'this' of *either*. Both will *belong to* the 'this', but neither will *be* that to which they belong. They will be presented, but neither by itself will *be* the unique presentation. They will not have the 'this' in common, but the 'this' will have them. It will be their common substantive which will share its own exclusive nature with nothing.

I hardly think that by further intricacies we shall make more clear what can not be made obvious. If anything in the above has been grasped by the reader, I trust to have shown that the use of 'this', as a symbol in judgement, is not only impossible, but that, if it existed, it would be wholly nugatory.[13]

[70] § 28. We escape from ideas, and from mere universals, by a reference to the real which appears in perception. It is thus our assertion attains the uniqueness without which it would not correspond to the fact. And analytic judgements, it may seem, are thus secured to us. But now, when we return to the question we asked in § 19, and when we pass to judgements that are synthetic, and extend to spaces and times not falling within the radius of direct presentation, we seem at first sight to be no better off. What we have gained, it may now appear, has been at the expense of everything beyond. The series of all our spaces and times will now have to be referred to the one unique point of contact with reality. It is only so that their content can be stamped with the mark of fact. But it seems impossible to establish this relation.

The content of these synthetic assertions we know is universal. It may be true of innumerable other series. This unsubstantial chain, if left to itself, does not touch the ground in any one point. On the other hand, the given source of reality refuses, it seems, to have anything to do with these floating threads. Their symbolic content can not be directly attributed to the presentation, because it is irreconcilable with the content of that. And, if we can not have another presentation, where is the fact in connection with which our universals can attain reality?

§ 29. We must turn in our difficulty to a result we got from a

---

[13] 'This' is not the only idea which can never be true as a symbol. I will not ask to what extent 'this' means 'for me', but what has been said of 'this' will hold in the main of 'I', 'me' and 'mine'. But there are difficulties here which we can not discuss. We may remark in passing that, for the purposes of metaphysics, it would be necessary to find all those ideas whose content appears not able to be used as the adjective of something else. This would bear on the so-called 'ontological proof'. For the ideas of uniqueness &c., vid. infr. §§ 38, 39.[14{19}]

[14{19}] The one idea, so far as positive, is that of reality, or experience, as immediate. Under this one main head of immediacy fall the 'now', 'here', and 'mine'. It is under the last of these that we are concerned with Attention.

But in the present volume I certainly did not always mean by 'presentation' the outward or even the inward perception of an object. The reader, I fear, must be on his guard throughout against what is perhaps a careless use of this term.

former discussion.[15]{20} We saw that the real, which appears in perception, is not identical with the real just *as* it appears there. If the real must be 'this', must encounter us directly, we cannot conclude that the 'this' we take is all the real, or that nothing is real beyond the 'this'. It is impossible, perhaps, to get directly at reality, except in the content of one presentation: we may never see it, so to speak, but through a hole. But what we see of it may make us certain that, beyond this hole, it exists indefinitely. If by 'this' we understand unique appearance, then, as 'this' was not any part of the content, so neither is it any quality of the real, in such a sense as to shut up the real within that quality. It would belong to metaphysics to discuss this further, and we must here be content with a crude result. The real is what appears to me. The appearance is not generic but unique. But the real itself is *not* unique, in the sense in which its appearance is so.[16]{21}   [71]

The reality we divined to be self-existent, substantial, and individual; but, as it appears within a presentation, it is none of these. The content throughout is infected with relativity, and, adjectival itself, the whole of its elements are also adjectival. Though given as fact every part is given as existing by reference to something else. The mere perpetual disappearance in time of the given appearance is itself the negation of its claim to self-existence. And again, if we take it while it appears, its limits, so to speak, are never secured from the inroads of unreality. In space or in time its outside is made fact solely by relation to what is beyond. Living by relation to what it excludes, it transcends its limits to join another element, and invites that element with its own boundaries. But with edges ragged and wavering, that flow outward and inward unstably, it already is lost. It is adjectival on what is beyond itself. Nor within itself has it any stability. There is no solid point of either time or space. Each atom is merely a collection of atoms, and those atoms again are not things but relations of elements that vanish. And when asked what is ultimate, and can stand as an individual, you can answer nothing.

[15]{20} 'Former discussion.' See § 10 foll.
[16]{21} Reality is unique (*a*) negatively and (*b*) positively. The given 'this' also offers itself as unique. But an examination shows that we have here but appearance. The 'this', through its content, negates itself as unique, and is seen to involve transcendence and ideality.

The real can not be identical with the content that appears in presentation. It for ever transcends it, and gives us a title to make search elsewhere.

§ 30. The endeavour to find the completeness of the real, which we feel can not exist except as an individual, will lead us first to Synthetic judgements of time and space. But, before we proceed, we may pause for a moment, to reflect on the general nature of the attempt. If the reality is self-existent, self-contained, and complete, it needs, one would think, no great effort of reason to perceive that this character is not to be found in a mere series of phenomena. It is one thing to seek the reality *in* that series; it is quite another thing to try to find it *as* the series. A completed series in time or space can not possibly exist. It is the well-known phantasm of the spurious infinite, a useful fiction, it may be, for certain purposes and at certain levels of thought, but none the [72] less a phantasm which, until it is recognized, stops the way of all true philosophic thought. It emerges often in the school of 'experience', in its Logic and again in its Hedonistic Ethics, where it begets and will continue to beget chimaeras. We shall meet it again in the present chapter, but must return to our search for reality within a series of phenomena, a search not yet degraded to a pursuit of phantasms, but carrying in itself the root of illusion.

§ 31. The real then itself transcends the presentation, and invites us to follow it beyond that which is given. On the other hand, we seem to find contact with reality and to touch ground nowhere, so to speak, outside the presented. How then is a content to be referred to the real, if it can not be referred to the real as perceived? We must answer that the content is referred *indirectly*. It is not attributed to the given as such; but, by establishing its connection with what is presented, it is attributed to the real which appears in that given. Though it is not and can not be found in presentation, it is true because it is predicated of the reality, and unique because it is fixed in relation with immediate perception. The ideal world of spaces beyond the sensible space, and of times not present but past and future, fastens itself on to the actual world by fastening itself to the quality of the immediate this. In a single word continuity of content is taken to show identity of element.

§ 32. But such continuity, and the consequent extension of the 'this' as given, depend, like every other ideal construction, on identity. An inference always, we shall see hereafter, stands on the identity of indiscernibles.[i] Sameness of quality proves real sameness. . . . And the identity here has a double form. (i) In the first place the symbolical content must have 'thisness'. (ii) In the second place it must share some point with the 'this'.

To explain, (i) the idea we are to connect with perception must be the idea of something in space or some event in time. It must have the character of particularity, the general idea of indefinite detail and endless relation. We know by this that it is of the same sort as the content of the given. The description of both is one and the same. They both have 'thisness', and therefore their element *may be* identical.

(ii) But, so far as we have gone, we still are left in the world of [73] universals, which *may* or *might* touch the ground in some place and meet the fact which appears in perception, but which do not certainly *do* thus. We wish, on the one side, to pass beyond presented content, and, on the other side, to connect with this content an ideal series; and we seek for a link by which to fasten them together.

That link is found by establishing a point which is the same in both, and is the same because its quality is the same. The 'this' contains a complex of detail, either times or spaces (or both) in series, which we may call *c. d. e. f.* The idea, on its side, contains a series of particulars *a. b. c. d.* The identity of *c. d.* in each extends the perception *c. d. e. f.* by the ideal spaces or times *a. b.*, and the whole is given by synthetical construction as a single fact *a. b. c. d. e. f.* The whole series now is referred to the real, and by the connection with unique presentation, has become a series of events or spaces, itself unique and the same as no other series in the world. It is thus by inference that we transcend the given through synthetic judgements. . . .

§ 38. We now perhaps are able to say what it is we mean by [77] the idea of an individual (or, we had better say, of a particular) fact. We saw the futility of seeking to find this in the proper names of persons, for what they stand for is never confined to a

[i] This is a reference to what Bradley calls the Principle of Identity or the Axiom of the Identity of Indiscernibles: 'What is true in one context is true in another' (*PL* 143). He takes it to be equivalent to '[W]hat *seems* the same *is* the same' (*PL* 288).

single event. The idea of particularity implies two elements. We must first have a content qualified by 'thisness', and we must add to that content the general idea of reference to the reality. In other words a particular must first be represented in a series; this gives us the first element. But so far we do not get beyond mere 'thisness'; the members are exclusive, within the series, but the whole collection is not unique. To get the complete idea of a particular fact we must make our series, so to speak, *externally* exclusive as well and thus particular. And we do not do this till we qualify it by the idea of reference to our unique reality.

If we *actually* attributed the series to reality, we not only should have got the idea that we wanted, but also more.[17]{28} We should have judged that our idea was true in fact. And in this case we do not wish to go so far. We desire to have the idea of uniqueness, but not to assert the reality of the idea.

We possess, as we have seen (§ 24) in the idea of 'this', the idea of immediate contact with the real, and it is this idea we must add to our series. When we think of the series both as a whole, and as touching the real in a point of presentation, we have thought of it then as truly particular. But there we must stop. For if we went on to judge our idea to be true, we should have to find it a special place in the unique series which extends perception. And we saw that to use the idea of 'this' as the symbol of another content in judgement, was quite impossible. So long, however, as we abstain from judgement, we can attach the aspect of 'this' to a content other than that which is really presented.

[78] This is what we mean by the idea of a particular. There is a difference when we come to an individual person. Our idea is there particular, since it has limits within a particular series. But it also involves a real identity persisting throughout a change of events. And so it falls outside the class of mere synthetic judgements.

§ 39. Uniqueness is merely the negative side of the idea of 'this'. A content is unique when, although of a sort (and that means regarded from the aspect of content) it nevertheless is the same as no other, is the only one there is of its sort. Uniqueness implies the idea of a series,[18]{29} and is then relative or absolute.

---

[17]{28} 'If we *actually* &c.' We do and must 'attribute the series to reality', though not to reality as present.

[18]{29} 'Implies the idea of a series.' This is very doubtful.

It is relative when the series, which contains the element which excludes the others, is itself *not* unique. In any universe our fancy constructs, a thing may be unique but only unique within that universe. We have, on the other hand, absolute uniqueness when the series is connected with direct presentation. In that case the relations within the series fix against each other the elements it holds, and nothing can be fact without its appearing in that one series. But the real subject, which, in predicating uniqueness, excludes any other event of the kind, we must remember, is not the particular event as such and taken by itself. It is rather the real which appears in that particular and so excludes others. We have here a negative existential judgement. . . .

§ 40. After meeting many difficulties, some of which, I trust, may have been overcome, we have finished our account of the second division of singular judgements. We must pass to the third, the assertions not confined to an event or a number of events in time (§ 7). But, before we proceed, let us pause for a moment, and, however dangerous the experiment may be, let us try to put before our very eyes a synthetic judgement. Let us call before our mind some series of pictures, like Hogarth's Progress of the harlot or rake; but let us also imagine something beside. One picture in the series must *be* the reality, the actual person in a real room, and on the walls of this real room must be hung the series of earlier and later pictures. By virtue of the sameness in the quality of the man, as he is in the room and is in the pictures, we, neglecting the appearance in particular frames, arrange the whole series as *his* past and future. We transcend in this way the visible room and the presented scene, and view the real life of [79] the person extending itself as a series in time.

But the man in the real room that we see, is body and bones and breath and blood, while his past and future, if we mean by reality a sensible fact, are nothing in the world but glass and wood and paint and canvas. It is the same with all our future and past. The events of memory and of anticipation are facts now in our minds, but they no more *are* the reality they represent than paint and canvas are a throbbing heart. No doubt they stand for reality, and we flatter ourselves that, if they can not be fact, at least they are true. True indeed they may be if truth means a natural and inevitable way of representing the real. But if by their truth we understand more than this; if we say that the reality *is* as it appears in our ideal construction, and that actually there *exists* a series of facts past present and future—I am afraid that truth, if we came to examine it, would change into false-hood. It would be false if measured by the test of perception, and it may be, if tried by another standard, it would be falser still.

§ 41. The life of a man can not be presented in any one scene, and our very illustration has gone farther than we thought. That life is not even a mere succession of serial events, but contains (so we think of it) a something the same, a real identity which appears in all, but which is not any, nor even every, event. We find ourselves brought to the third main class of singular judge-ments, and are speaking of a subject which is not an event. These judgements are separated into two divisions, according as the individual with which they deal is related to some given period of time, or not to any time in particular.

III. (i) In the history of a man or nation we have a content referred to the real, but to the real as it appears throughout one certain part of that series which is determined by relation to given perception. (ii) In the second division we must place any judgements we make about the Universe or God or the soul, if we take the soul to be eternal. Our ideas are here identified with the real that we find in perception, but they do not[j] attach them-selves to any one part of the phenomenal series. It may be said, of course, that such judgements are illusory. But, as we saw, that conclusion, if true, could only be established by a metaphysical enquiry we have no place for. The judgements exist, and logic can do nothing else but recognize them.

[80]

This third and last class of singular judgements is distinct from the others. Its essence is that its ultimate subject is not the real, as it appears in the 'this' or in any one event in the series. But the distinction is to a certain extent unstable. Just as analytic judgements are always tending to become synthetic, so here it is impossible to separate sharply the first division of this class from synthetic judgements. On the one hand the continuity of the ele-ment of time strictly excludes a mere serial character. In every judgement about events we unknowingly are asserting the exist-ence of an identity. On the other hand an individual living in a series seems naturally to belong to that class of judgement which

---

[j] We have deleted a second occurrence of the word 'not' here.

constructs a series. Since, however, when an individual is concerned, we explicitly recognize something real, enduring throughout the changes of events, it is better perhaps to keep up a distinction which in principle must be admitted to fluctuate. The example of an individual person took us from analytic to synthetic judgements. And it has served again to carry us on further.

§ 42.[19]{33} We have now considered all the three classes of singular judgements, and have seen in what way they attribute an idea to the real which appears. We have already anticipated the account to be given of Existential judgements, and may deal with them rapidly. Confining ourselves here to those which are affirmative, we can say at once that the subject in all of them is the ultimate reality, either (*a*) as it appears in some part of the series determined by the 'this', or (*b*) as it underlies the whole series of phenomena. When I say 'A exists,' or 'A is real,' the content A is in truth the predicate. We use it to qualify existence or reality, in one of the two senses we have now mentioned.

The enquiry into existential propositions reduces to absurdity the notion that judgement consists in ideas. If we add to the adjectival idea of A another adjectival idea of reality, then, failing wholly in reference to fact, we fall entirely short of judge- [81] ment. But this is not all. The idea of reality, like the idea of 'this', is not an ordinary symbolic content, to be used without any regard to its existence. The idea of what is real, or of that which exists, is found as an element in that actual reality and actual existence which we encounter directly. It can not in judgement be removed from this, and be transplanted away to *another* reality. We have here the same obstacle which met us before (§§ 25-7). The idea cannot be predicated of anything except its own reality. For, to get the idea, you must take it by a distinction from what is given. If you then make it a predicate of anything not given, you have a collision, and your judgement disappears. But if, on the other hand, you predicate it of that which actually is given, your procedure is idle. Why employ an

---

[19]{33} §§ 42, 43. The division into (*a*) and (*b*), in § 42, is clearly wrong, if only because it omits all the worlds of events which fall outside my 'real' world. See Note 3{3}.

Instead of using 'existence' as one with 'reality', it is far better, I think, to limit it to the sphere of events. But, if so, though all judgements will be 'real', certainly not all will be 'existential'.

idea to assert reality when you have the fact, and when your ideal synthesis is a mere analysis of this given reality, and attributed in the end to that as subject? 'Real' is clearly the adjective of 'reality', and we know no reality but what appears in presentation. The idea then, to be true, must be true of that reality. But, if so, we must have the subject before us in the shape of fact, and, if we did not, the idea would at once become false. For a more detailed discussion we may refer to §§ 25–7.

Nor would it repay us here to examine the somewhat surprising view which Herbart has advocated (vid. § 75). Our enquiries in this chapter should have prepared us for the result that the ultimate subject is never an idea, and that the idea of existence is never a true predicate. The subject, in the end, is always reality, which is qualified by adjectives of ideal content.

§ 43. We cannot say there is a class of existential judgements, for all singular judgements have by this time been shown to be existential. And, with this conclusion, we may pass beyond them to another branch of affirmative judgements. In these we no longer have to do with any particular facts or in any sense with separate individuals. They are universal in the sense of transcending what is singular. They are not 'concrete' but 'abstract', since, leaving things, they assert about qualities, alone or in synthesis. In this respect, we may remark in passing, there is no real [82] difference between the 'general' and the 'abstract'; for, taken in comparison with the particular thing, the general idea is a mere abstraction.

§ 44. We have reached the common type of universal judgement; and the point in this which we notice at once, is that every such judgement is concerned with adjectivals. They assert a connection between elements of content, and say nothing about the place of those elements in the series of events. In 'Equilateral triangles are equiangular' all I affirm is that with one set of qualities you will have the other set, but I make no assertion about where and when. And 'Mammals are warm-blooded' does not tell me anything about this or that mammal. It merely assures me that, finding one attribute, I shall find the other.

The fact that is asserted in an abstract judgement is not the existence of the subject or predicate (§ 6), but simply the connection between the two. And this connection rests on a supposal.

The abstract universal, 'A is B,' means no more than 'given A, in that case B,' or 'if A, then B.' In short, such judgements are always hypothetical and can never be categorical. And the proper terms by which to introduce them are 'given', or 'if', or 'whenever', or 'where', or 'any', or 'whatever'. We should beware of 'all'.

§ 45. For the use of 'all', we have seen above (§ 6), is most misleading and dangerous. It encourages that tendency to understand the universal in the sense of a collection, which has led to so many mistaken consequences. We shall glance elsewhere at that extraordinary teaching on the subject of quantity, in which the traditional logic delights. And we shall see hereafter, when we come to inference, the absurd incompetence of the *dictum de omni*.[k] For our present purpose we need criticize no further the attempt to understand the 'all' collectively. Even if that use were justifiable in itself, it would be irrelevant; for a judgement where 'all' means a real collection of actual cases, belongs to a class we have already disposed of. If 'all' signifies a number of individual facts, the judgement is concerned with actual particulars. And so it obviously is but one form of the singular judgement. 'All A is B,' will be an abbreviated method of setting forth that this A is B, and that A is B, and the other A is B, and so on until the lot is exhausted. Such judgements fall clearly under the head of singular. [83]

But, when this class is banished to the preceding category,

---

[k] The *dictum de omni* is derived from Aristotle's *Prior Analytics* 24ᵇ26: 'And we say that one term is predicated of all of another, whenever nothing can be found of which the other term cannot be asserted: "to be predicated of none" must be understood in the same way' (*The Complete Works of Aristotle*, rev. Oxford trans., ed. Jonathan Barnes (Princeton, NJ: Princeton University Press, 1984)). The *dictum de omni* is the definition of 'predicated of all' found in the first part of the quotation. The *dictum de nullo* is the definition of 'predicated of none' found in the second part. Despite this derivation these dicta were stated in a variety of ways. Frequently they were combined as the *dictum de omni et nullo*. In many medieval and modern expositions of traditional logic, this dictum was held to be the supreme rule of reasoning applicable to all syllogisms and, ultimately, to all arguments. For example, Richard Whately (*Elements of Logic*, 2nd edn. (London: J. Mawan, 1827), 88–9) states the *dictum de omni et nullo* as follows: 'whatever is predicated of a term distributed, whether affirmatively or negatively, may be predicated in like manner of everything contained under it'. He explains it by means of the 'syllogism' 'All tyrants deserve death. Caesar was a tyrant. *Therefore* he deserved death.' 'Deserves death' is predicated of 'all tyrants' taken distributively and 'Caesar' is contained under 'all tyrants'. It follows from the application of the dictum that 'deserves death' may be predicated of 'Caesar'.

have we any universal judgements left us? We can not doubt
that; for there are judgements which do not assert the existence
of particular cases. We come at once upon the judgements that
connect adjectival elements, and that say nothing about the series
of phenomena. These abstract universals are always hypothetical
and never categorical.[20] . . .

[85]   § 48. Such universal judgements are all hypothetical, and with
this conclusion we are landed once more in our former difficulties
(§ 6). Judgement, we saw, always meant to be true, and truth
must mean to be true of fact. But here we encounter judgements
which seem not to be about fact. For a hypothetical judgement
must deal with a supposal. It appears to assert a necessary connection, which holds between ideas within my head but not outside it. But, if so, it can not be a judgement at all; while on the
other hand it plainly does assert and can be true or false.

We are not able to rest in this conclusion, and yet we can not
take back our premises. Let us then try to look more closely at
the problem, and ask more narrowly what is involved in these
judgements. And, in the first place, we can not expect to succeed
until we know what a supposal is.

A supposition, in the first place, is known to be ideal, and
known perhaps to diverge from fact. At a low stage of mind,
where everything is fact . . . it could not exist. For the supposed
must be known as an ideal content, and, in addition, it has to be
retained before the mind without a judgement. It is not referred
as an adjective, either positively or negatively, to the real. In
other words reality is not qualified either by the attribution or
the exclusion of it. But though it does not judge, a supposition is
intellectual, for (as such) it excludes desire and emotion. And
again it is more than mere imagination, for it is fixed by attention and preserves, or should preserve, its identity of content. . . .
It certainly is all this, and yet this is not all. For to think of a
chimaera is not quite the same thing as to *suppose* a chimaera.

[86]   A supposition means thinking for a particular end, and in a
special way. It is not a mere attending to a certain meaning, or
an analysis of its elements. It has a reference to the real world,

------

[20] We may here remark that, taking 'A is B' to mean 'the things that are A are
the things that are B,' the judgement must be singular, if an existing set of things
be denoted, and will be universal and abstract if possible things are included as
well.

and it involves a desire to see what happens. We may illustrate perhaps from other usages. 'Say it is so for argument's sake,' 'Treat it as this and then you will see,' are much the same as, 'Suppose it to be so.' A supposal is, in short, an ideal experiment.[21]{40} It is the application of a content to the real, with a view to see what the consequence is, and with a tacit reservation

[21]{40} 'Ideal experiment.' But (*a*) we must remember that there are no *mere* ideas. Every idea is referred to its own world as there real and true, and as, so far, not merely 'in my head'. And (*b*) the 'reality', to which my idea is opposed, is not necessarily 'fact' in the sense of belonging to my 'real world'. It itself may be 'imaginary', though here, as against my idea, it is taken as real.

Having then an idea, or rather a truth, holding in one region, we may be said to apply this to another region of reality with a view to observe the result. This other reality, as we have it, repels our idea, or admits its opposite, and hence, taken on one side, the result is doubt. But on the other side it is a judgement made subject to an x. We assert, that is, not S—M—P, but S(x)—M—P. M—P, we say, is true, but, as to S—M, we have not got that actually, and, further, we do not know what qualification of S is involved in the reality of S—M.

We can, I think, easily see [the] psychological nature and origin [of the logical meaning of 'If'], if we take the case of means (M) to an end desired, a certain alteration, that is, of a given fact (S). I may have one or more ideas of these means, but there is something in S, *as I have it*, which repels them all. I, however, retain them because they are (*a*) relevant and interesting, and also (*b*) possible. They contain, that is, some of the conditions of S, as that is to be altered, and I do not know that there really are counter-conditions in S itself. On the other side I do not know, and I will not assume, that S does *not* contain these. Hence I refrain from action, and assert S—M—P subject to a doubt as to S—M. I hold, in other words, S(x)—M—P as true. And here x means (*a*) that further conditions are involved, and that (*b*) as to the nature and effect of these I am more or less ignorant.

The supposed (to pass to another point) is in one aspect (M—P) quite certain and actual. It is in connection with S (as known) that M—P is but possible. And I may add that, where S itself is taken as possible only, the supposed is here *doubly* possible. But, essentially and always, what is supposed is taken as possible.

This statement may seem at first to be in conflict with plain facts, such as the example given on p. 87 (cf. *Essays on Truth and Reality* ['On Floating Ideas and the Imaginary', repr. below], pp. [229–47]). I may be told that possibility is here certainly excluded. I would on the other side, however, ask the reader to reflect whether certainty is not contrary to the very meaning of 'If'. And, since to my mind that point is clear, I conclude that any appearance to the contrary rests on what may be called linguistic or rhetorical artifice. I actually, that is, assert or deny some real connection, and so far there is no 'If'. But, for some unstated reason, I desire at the same time to suggest that things throughout might have been otherwise. And I convey at once my undoubting judgement and my doubtful suggestion by licentiously applying 'if' to the undiscriminated compound. 'The destruction of the barometer (§ 50) caused the absence of warning—*and* it need not have been so.' And 'since you are well (which you might not have been)' is the double meaning conveyed in 'si vales bene est'. We may notice further in this connection that it is common to refute an asserted S—P by showing it as true *only* if the impossible is supposed.

that no actual judgement has taken place. The supposed is treated as if it were real, in order to see how the real behaves when qualified thus in a certain manner.

You might say it is the adding the idea of existence to a given thought, while you abstain from judgement. But that I do not think would be satisfactory. For it is not the mere *idea* of existence that is used. What we use is the real that is always in immediate contact with our minds, and which in a variety of judgements we already have qualified by a certain content. And it is to this that we bring up another idea, in order to see what result will come of it.

§ 49. So far there is neither truth not falsehood, for we have not judged. The operation, we may say, is so far 'subjective'. It is all our own doing, and all of it holds inside our heads, and not at all outside. The real is not qualified by the attribute we apply to it. But, so soon as we judge, we have truth or falsehood, and the real is at once concerned in the matter. The connection of the consequence, of the 'then' with the 'if', of the result of our experiment with its conditions, is the fact that is asserted, and that is true or false of the reality itself.

But the question is *how*. You do not assert the existence of the ideal content you suppose, and you do not assert the existence of the consequence. And you can not assert the existence of the connection, for how can a connection remain as a fact when no facts are connected? 'If you only had been silent you would have passed for a philosopher.'[1] But you were not silent, you were not thought a philosopher, and one was not, and could not possibly *be*, a result of the other. If the real must be qualified by the connection of the two, it seems that it will not be qualified at all. [87] Neither condition, nor result, nor relation can be ascribed to it; and yet we *must* ascribe something, for we judge. But what can it be?

§ 50. When I go to a man with a fictitious case, and lay before him a question of conduct, and when he replies to me, 'I should act in this way, and not in the other way,' I may come from him with some knowledge of fact. But the fact is not the invented position, nor yet the hypothetical course of action, nor the imaginary relation between the two. The fact is the quality in the

---

[1] This appears to be a reference to Boethius, *The Consolation of Philosophy*, book 2, prose 7.

man's disposition.[22]{[41]} It has answered to a trial in a certain way. But the test was a fiction, and the answer is no fact, and the man is not qualified by one or the other. It is *his* latent character that is disclosed by the experiment.

It is so with all hypothetical judgement. The fact that is affirmed as an adjective of the real, and on which depends the truth or falsehood, does not explicitly appear in the judgement. Neither conditions nor result of the ideal experiment are taken to be true. What is affirmed is the mere ground of the connection; not the actual existing behaviour of the real, but a latent quality of its disposition, a quality which has appeared in the experiment, but the existence of which does not depend on that experiment. 'If you had not destroyed our barometer, it would now forewarn us.' In this judgement we assert the existence in reality of such circumstances, and such a general law of nature, as would, *if we suppose* some conditions present, produce a certain result. But assuredly those conditions and their result are not predicated, nor do we even hint that they are real. They themselves and their connection are both impossible. It is the diminution of pressure and the law of its effect, which we affirm of the actual world before us. And of course that law is resolvable further (§ 52).

§ 51. In all judgement the truth seems none of our making. We perhaps need not judge, but, if we judge, we lose all our liberty. In our relation to the real we feel under compulsion (§ 4). In a categoric judgement the elements themselves are not dependent on our choice. Whatever we may think or say, they exist. But, in a hypothetic judgement, there is no compulsion as regards the elements. The second, indeed, depends on the first, but the first is arbitrary. It depends on my choice. I may apply it to the real, or [88] not, as I please; and I am free to withdraw the application I have made. And, when the condition goes, the result goes too. The compulsion extends no further than the connection, and yet it

---

[22]{[41]} 'The fact is the quality in the man's disposition.' (i) It is so *here*, but even here a 'disposition' apart from any circumstances is an impossible abstraction. Further (ii), if 'disposition' is used to explain 'conditional', then obviously, since the very meaning of 'disposition' involves a standing 'if', the explanation is circular. (iii) The objection to 'quality' is that it seems merely to repeat (what we knew before) that things are so; and to admit (if we add 'latent') that we do not know *how* (Cf. *Appearance and Reality* ['Degrees of Truth and Reality,' repr. below], pp. [183–200]).

does not extend to the connection as such. The relation of the elements in a hypothetical judgement is not an actual attribute of the real, for that relation itself is arbitrary. It need not be true outside the experiment. The fact which existed before the experiment, and remains true after it, and in no way depends on it, is neither the elements, nor the relation between them, but it is a quality. It is the ground of the sequence that *is* true of the real, and it is this ground which exerts compulsion. . . .

§ 53. We have seen that, what hypothetical judgements assert, is simply the quality which is the ground of the consequence. [89] And all abstract universals, we have seen, are hypothetical. It may here be asked, Are the two things one? Are all hypothetical judgements thus universal?

This might for a moment appear to be doubtful, since the real, to which application is made, is at times an individual. And for the purposes of this, and the following section, I will give some examples; 'If God is just the wicked will be punished,' 'Had I a toothache I should be wretched,' 'If there were a candle in this room it would be light,' 'If it is now six o'clock we shall have dinner in an hour,' 'If this man has taken that dose, he will be dead in twenty minutes.' It may surprise some readers to hear that these judgements are as universal as 'All men are mortal': but I think we shall find that such is the case.

In the first place it is certain that in none of these judgements is the subject taken to be actually real. We do not say above that a just God exists, or that I have a toothache; we only suppose it. The subject is supposed, and, if we consider further, we shall find that subject is nothing more than an ideal content, and that what is asserted is not anything beside a connection of adjectives. The 'that', the 'this', the 'I', the 'now', do not really pass into the supposition. They are the point of reality to which we apply our ideal experiment, but they themselves are in no case *supposed*. More or less of their content is used in the hypothesis, and passes into the subject. But, apart from themselves, their content can not possibly be called individual. . . .

[90] § 56. We have found, thus far, that all abstract judgements are hypothetical, and in this connection we have endeavoured to show what a supposition is, and to lay bare that occult affirmation as to real, which is made in every hypothetical judgement. Singular judgements we have already discussed, and we

found that, be they analytic or synthetic, they all at first sight seem categorical. They do not merely attribute to the real a latent quality, which manifests itself in an unreal relation, but they qualify the real by the actual content which appears in the judgement. It is not the mere connection, but the very elements which they declare to exist.

We have still remaining another kind of judgement (§ 7), but, before we proceed, it is better to consider the result we have arrived at. That result perhaps may call for revision, and it is possible that the claim of the singular judgement to a categoric position may not maintain itself.

Chapter 2 (*continued*)

[91] § 57. What is the position in which we now find ourselves? We began with the presumption that a judgement, if true, must be true of reality. On the other hand we found that every abstract universal judgement was but hypothetical. We have endeavoured to reconcile these conflicting views by showing in what way, and to what extent, a conditional judgement asserts of the fact. But singular judgements stand apart, and have claimed to be wholly categorical, and true of the reality; and hence they demand a position above that given to universal judgements. We must now scrutinize this pretension. We must still defer all notice of those individual judgements which transcend the series of events in time. Confining ourselves to judgements about the phenomenal series, let us proceed to ask, Are they categorical? Do they truly and indeed rank higher, and closer to the real world, than those universal judgements which we found were hypothetical? We shall perhaps do well to prepare our minds for an unwelcome conclusion.

In passing from the singular to the universal judgement, we seem to have been passing away from reality. Instead of a series of actual phenomena connected with the point of present perception, we have but a junction of mere adjectivals, the existence of which we do not venture to affirm. In the one case we have what seem solid facts; in the other we have nothing but a latent quality, the mere name of which makes us feel uneasy. We have not quite lost our hold of the real, but we seem to have left it a long way off. We keep our connection by an impalpable thread with a veiled and somewhat ambiguous object.

But our thoughts may perhaps take a different colour, if we look around us in the region we have come to. However strange it may seem to us at first, yet our journey towards shadows and away from the facts has brought us at last to the world of sci-
[92] ence. The end of science, we all have been taught, is the discovery of *laws*; and a law is nothing but a hypothetical judgement. It is a proposition which asserts a synthesis of adjectivals. It is uni-

versal and abstract. And it does not assert the existence of either of the elements it connects. It may *imply* (§ 6), but such an implication is not essential. In mathematics, for instance, the truth of our statement is absolutely independent of the existence of either subject or predicate. In physics or chemistry the truth does not depend on the actual existence at the present moment of the elements and their relation. If it did so, the law might be true at one instant and false at the next. When the physiologist, again, tells us that strychnine has a certain effect on nerve centres, he does not wait to enunciate his law until he is sure that some dose of strychnine is operating in the world; nor does he hasten to recall it as soon as he has lost that assurance. It would be no advantage to dwell upon this point. It may be regarded now as a certain result, that the strict expression for all universal laws must begin with an 'if', and go on with a 'then'.

§ 58. And from this we may draw a certain presumption. If the singular judgement is nearer the fact, and if, in leaving it, we have actually receded from reality, yet at least in science that is not felt to be the case. And there is another presumption which may help to strengthen us. In common life we all experience the tendency to pass from one single case to some other instance. We take what is true at one time and place to be always true at all times and places. We generalize from a single example. We may deplore this tendency as an ineradicable vice of the unphilosophic mind, or we may recognize it as the inevitable condition of all experience, and the *sine qua non* of every possible inference. . . . But in either case, let us recognize it or deplore it, we still do not feel the passage we have made as an *attempt* to go from the stronger to the weaker, from that which is more true to that which is less. And yet, without doubt, it is a transition away from the individual to the universal and hypothetical.

§ 59. But a matter of this sort is not settled by presumptions. There are prejudices, it may be, that operate both ways. And we may be told, on behalf of the singular judgement, that it is *the fact* that these judgements are categorical. For they do assert the actual existence of their adjectival content, and, attributing to the real an explicit quality, they are truer than any hypothetical judgement, if indeed they are not the *only* true judgements. Such, we take it, is the claim of the singular judgement, and it can not be denied that its claim in one respect is very well founded. It [93]

does *assert* the existence of its content, and does affirm directly of
the real. But the answer we must make is that, although it does
so assert and affirm, yet, when we leave the popular view and
look more closely at the truth of things, the assertion and
affirmation which it makes are *false*, and the claim it puts forward rests on a mistake. We must subject the pretensions of the
singular judgement to an examination which we think may prove
fatal.

§ 60. We need spend no time on the synthetic judgement. In
transcending what is given by actual perception, we without any
doubt make use of an inference. A synthesis of adjectives is connected with the present by virtue of the identity of a point of
content. By itself this synthesis is merely universal, and is therefore hypothetical. It becomes categoric solely by relation to that
which is given, and hence the whole weight of the assertion rests
on the analytic judgement. If that is saved, it will then be time to
discuss its extension; but if, on the other hand, the analytic be
lost, it carries with it the synthetic judgement.

§ 61. Let us turn at once to the judgements which assert within
what is given in present perception. These seem categorical
because they content themselves with the analysis of the given,
and predicate of the real nothing but a content that is directly
presented. And hence it appears that the elements of these judgements must actually exist. An ideal content is attributed to the
real, which that very real does now present to me. I am sure that
nothing else is attributed. I am sure that I do not make any
inference, and that I do not generalize. And how then can my
assertion fail to be true? How, if true, can it fail to be categorical?

We maintain, on the other hand, that analytic judgements of
[94] sense are all false. There are more ways than one of saying the
thing that is not true. It is not always necessary to go beyond the
facts. It is often more than enough to come short of them. And it
is precisely this coming short of the fact, and stating a part as if
it were the whole, which makes the falseness of the analytic
judgement.

§ 62. The fact, which is given us, is the total complex of qualities and relations which appear to sense. But what we assert of
this given fact is, and can be, nothing but an ideal content. And
it is evident at once that the idea we use can not possibly exhaust

the full particulars of what we have before us. A description, we all know, can not ever reach to a complete account of the manifold shades, and the sensuous wealth of one entire moment of direct presentation. As soon as we judge, we are forced to analyze, and forced to distinguish. We must separate some elements of the given from others. We sunder and divide what appears to us as a sensible whole. It is never more than an arbitrary selection which goes into the judgement. We say 'There is a wolf,' or 'This tree is green'; but such poor abstractions, such mere bare meanings, are much less than the wolf and the tree which we see; and they fall even more short of the full particulars, the mass of inward and outward setting, from which we separate the wolf and the tree. If the real as it appears is $X = a \; b \; c \; d \; e \; f \; g \; h$, then our judgement is nothing but $X = a$, or $X = a\text{-}b$. But $a\text{-}b$ by itself has never been given, and is not what appears. It was *in* the fact and we have taken it out. It was *of* the fact and we have given it independence. We have separated, divided, abridged, dissected, we have mutilated the given.[23] And we have done this arbitrarily: we have selected what we chose. But, if this is so, and if every analytic judgement must inevitably so alter the fact, how can it any longer lay claim to truth?

§ 63. No doubt we shall be told, 'This is idle subtlety. The judgement does not copy the whole perception, but why should it do so? What it does say, and does reproduce, at all events is there. Fact is fact, and given is given. They do not cease to be such because something beside themselves exists. To maintain that "There is a wolf" is false, because an abstract wolf is not given entirely by itself, is preposterous and ridiculous.'

And I am afraid that with some readers this will end the discussion. But to those who are willing to venture further, I would suggest as encouragement that a thing may seem ludicrous, not because it is at all absurd in itself, but because it conflicts with hardened prejudice. And it is a prejudice of this kind that we have now encountered. [95]

§ 64. It is a very common and most ruinous superstition to suppose that analysis is no alteration, and that, whenever we distinguish, we have at once to do with divisible existence. It is an immense assumption to conclude, when a fact comes to us as a

[23] Cf. here Lotze's admirable chapter, *Logik* [2nd edn. (Leipzig: Hirzel, 1880)], II. VIII. [English trans. ed. Bernard Bosanquet (Oxford: Clarendon Press, 1887)].

whole, that some parts of it may exist without any sort of regard
for the rest. Such naive assurance of the outward reality of all
mental distinctions, such touching confidence in the crudest identity of thought and existence, is worthy of the school which so
loudly appeals to the name of Experience. Boldly stated by
Hume[m] . . . this cardinal principle of error and delusion has
passed into the traditional practice of the school, and is believed
too deeply to be discussed or now recognized. The protestations
of fidelity to fact have been somewhat obtrusive, but self-
righteous innocence and blatant virtue have served once more
here to cover the commission of the decried offence in its dead-
liest form. If it is true in any sense (and I will not deny it) that
thought in the end is the measure of things, yet at least this is
false, that the divisions we make within a whole all answer to elements whose existence does *not* depend on the rest. It is wholly
unjustifiable to take up a complex, to do any work we please
upon it by analysis, and then simply predicate as an adjective of
the given these results of our abstraction. These products were
never there as such, and in saying, as we do, that as such they
are there, we falsify the fact. You can not always apply in actual
experience that coarse notion of the whole as the sum of its parts
into which the school of 'experience' so delights to torture phenomena. If it is wrong in physiology to predicate the results, that
are reached by dissection, simply and as such of the living body,
it is here infinitely more wrong. The whole that is given us is a
continuous mass of perception and feeling; and to say of this
whole, that any one element would be what it is there, when
[96]   apart from the rest, is a very grave assertion. We might have supposed it not quite self-evident, and that it was possible to deny it
without open absurdity.

§ 65. I should like to digress so far as to adduce two examples
of error, which follow from the mistake we are now considering.
When we ask 'What is the *composition* of Mind,' we break up
that state, which comes to us as a whole, into units of feeling.
But since it is clear that these units by themselves are not all the
'composition', we are forced to recognize the existence of rela-

---

[m] At this point Bradley refers to a later passage in *PL* (pp. 301–2), where he
quotes David Hume, *A Treatise of Human Nature* (Oxford: Clarendon Press,
1888; 2nd edn. 1978), 636: 'All our distinct perceptions are distinct existences, and
. . . the mind never perceives any real connection among distinct existences.'

tions. But this does not stagger us. We push on with the conceptions we have brought to the work, and which of course can not
be false, and we say, Oh yes, we have here some more units, naturally not quite the same as the others, and—*voilà tout*. But
when a sceptical reader, whose mind has been warped by a
different education, attempts to form an idea of what is meant,
he is somewhat at a loss. If units have to exist together, they
must stand in relation to one another; and, if these relations are
also units, it would seem that the second class must also stand in
relation to the first. If A and B are feelings, and if C their relation is another feeling, you must either suppose that component
parts can exist without standing in relation with one another, or
else that there is a *fresh* relation between C and AB. Let this be
D, and once more we are launched on the infinite process of
finding a relation between D and C—AB; and so on for ever. If
relations are facts that exist *between* facts, then what comes
between the relations and the other facts? The real truth is that
the units on one side, and on the other side the relation existing
between them, are nothing actual.[24][50] They are fictions of the
mind, mere distinctions within a single reality, which a common
delusion erroneously takes for independent facts. If we believe
the assurance of a distinguished Professor,[25] this burning faith in
the absurd and the impossible, which was once the privilege and
the boast of theology, can now not be acquired anywhere outside
the sacred precincts of the laboratory. I am afraid it is difficult to
adopt such an optimistic conclusion.

§ 66. And perhaps I may be pardoned if, by another illustra-   [97]
tion, I venture to show how entirely the mind which is purified
by science can think in accordance with orthodox Christianity. In
the religious consciousness God and Man are elements that are
given to us in connection. But, reflecting on experience, we make
distinctions, and proceed as above to harden these results of
analysis into units. We thus have God as an unit on one side,

---

[24][50] 'The real truth . . . actual.' This is the doctrine for which I have now for
so many years contended. Relations exist only in and through a whole which can
not in the end be resolved into relations and terms. 'And', 'together' and
'between', are all in the end senseless apart from such a whole. The opposite view
is maintained (as I understand) by Mr. Russell, and was perhaps at last tacitly
adopted by Prof. Royce. But, for myself, I am unable to find that Mr. Russell has
ever really faced this question.

[25] Vid. [Thomas Henry] Huxley, *Hume* [London: Macmillan, 1879], pp. 52, 69.

and Man as an unit on the other: and then we are puzzled about
their relation. The relation of course must be *another* unit, and
we go on to find that we should like something *else*, to mediate
once more, and go between this product and what we had at
first. We fall at once into the infinite process, and, having taken
up with polytheism, the length we go is not a matter of principle.

§ 67. To return to the analytic judgement. When I say 'There is a
wolf,' the real fact is a particular wolf, not like any other, in relation to this particular environment and to my internal self, which
is present in a particular condition of feeling emotion and
thought. Again, when I say 'I have a toothache,' the fact once
more is a particular ache in a certain tooth, together with all my
perceptions and feelings at that given moment. The question is,
when I take in my judgement one fragment of the whole, have I
got the right to predicate this of the real, and to assert 'It, *as it is*,
is a fact of sense'? Now I am not urging that the analytic judgement is in *no* sense true. I am saying that, if you take it as asserting the existence of its content as given fact, your procedure is
unwarranted. And I ask, on what principle do you claim the right
of selecting what you please from the presented whole and treating that fragment as an actual quality? It certainly *does* not exist
by itself, and how do you know that, when put by itself, it *could*
be a quality of *this* reality? The sensible phenomenon is what it is,
and is all that it is; and anything less than itself must surely be
something *else*. A fraction of the truth, here as often elsewhere,
becomes entire falsehood, because it is used to qualify the whole.

§ 68. The analytic judgement is not true *per se*. It can not
stand by itself. Asserting, as it does, of the particular presentation, it must always suppose a further content, which falls outside that fraction it affirms. What it says is true, if true at all,
because of something else. The fact it states is really fact only in
relation to the rest of the context, and only because of the rest of
that context. It is not true except under that condition. So we
have a judgement which is really conditioned, and which is false
if you take it as categorical. To make it both categorical and
true, you must get the condition inside the judgement. You must
take up the given as it really appears, without omission, unaltered, and unmutilated. And this is impossible.

§ 69. For ideas are not adequate to sensible perception, and, beyond this obstacle, there are further difficulties. The real, which appears within the given, can not possibly be confined to it. Within the limit of its outer edges its character gives rise to the infinite process in space and time. Seeking there for the simple, at the end of our search we still are confronted by the composite and relative. And the outer edges themselves are fluent. They pass for ever in time and space into that which is outside them. It is true that the actual light we see falls only upon a limited area; but the continuity of the element, the integrity of the context, forbids us to say that this illuminated section by itself is real. The reference of the content to something other than itself lies deep within its internal nature. It proclaims itself to be adjectival, to be relative to the outside; and we violate its essence if we try to assert it as having existence entirely in its own right. Space and time have been said to be 'principles of individuation'. It would be truer to say they are principles of relativity. They extend the real just as much as they confine it.

I do not mean that past and future *are* actually given, and that they come within the circle of presentation. I mean that, *although* they can not be given, the given would be destroyed by their absence. If real with them, it would not be given; and, given without them, it is for ever incomplete and therefore unreal. The presented content is, in short, not compatible with its own presentation. It involves a contradiction, and might at once on that ground be declared to be unreal. But it is better here to allow it free course, and to suffer it to develop by an impossible consequence its inherent unsoundness.

§ 70. We say that you can not ascribe to the real one part of [99] what is given in present perception. And now we must go further. Even if you could predicate the whole present content, yet still you would fail unless you asserted also both the past and the future. You can not assume (or I, at least, do not know your right to assume) that the present exists independent of the past, and that, taking up one fragment of the whole extension, you may treat this part as self-subsistent, as something that owes nothing to its connection with the rest. If your judgement is to be true as well as categorical, you must get the conditions entirely within it. And here the conditions are the whole extent of spaces and times which are required to make the given complete. The difficulty is insuperable. It is not merely that ideas can not copy facts of sense. It is not merely that our understandings are limited, that we do not know the whole of the series, and that our powers are inadequate to apprehend so large an object. No possible mind could represent to itself the completed series of space and time; since, for that to happen, the infinite process must have come to an end, and be realized in a finite result. And this can not be. It is not merely inconceivable psychologically; it is metaphysically impossible.

§ 71. Our analytical judgements are hence all either false or conditioned. 'But *conditioned*,' I may be told, 'is a doubtful phrase. After all it is not the same as hypothetical. A thing is conditio*nal* on account of a supposal, but on the other hand it is conditio*ned* by a fact. We have here the difference between "if" and "because". When a statement is true in consequence of the truth of another statement, they both are categorical.' I quite admit the importance of the distinction . . . But I deny its relevancy for our present purpose.

The objection rests on the following contention. 'Admitted that in the series of phenomena every element is relative to the rest and is because of something else, yet for all that the judgement may be categorical. The something else, though we are unable to bring it within the judgement, though we can not in the end ever know it at all and realize it in thought, is, for all that, fact. And, this being so, the statement is true; since it rests in the end, not at all on an "if" but upon a "because", which, although unknown, is none the less real. Let the analytic judgement admit its relativity, let it own its adjectival and dependent character, and it surely saves itself and remains categorical.'

[100]

But even this claim it is impossible to admit. I will not raise a difficulty about the 'because' which is never realized, and the fact which can never be brought before the mind. My objection is more fatal. In the present case there *is* no because,[26{54}] and there *is* no fact.

We are fastened to a chain, and we wish to know if we are really secure. What ought we to do? Is it of much use to say, 'This link we are tied to is certainly solid, and it is fast to the

---

[26{54}] 'There is no because,' i.e. of the character which you assume and require. The argument here is, in my opinion, sound, but it is perhaps better put as follows. The condition, on which the judgement holds, is unknown, and it admits also the opposite of what is asserted. The judgement therefore, in its present form, is at once both true and false.

next, which seems very strong and holds firmly to the next; beyond this we can not see more than a certain moderate distance, but, so far as we know, it all holds together'? The practical man would first of all ask, 'Where can I find the last link of my chain? When I know that is fast, and not hung in the air, it is time enough to inspect the connection.' But the chain is such that every link begets, as soon as we come to it, a new one; and, ascending in our search, at each remove we are still no nearer the last link of all, on which everything depends. The series of phenomena is so infected with relativity, that, while it is itself, it can never be made absolute. Its existence refers itself to what is beyond, and, did it not do so, it would cease to exist. A last fact, a final link, is not merely a thing which we can not know, but a thing which could not possibly be real. Our chain by its nature can not have a support. Its essence excludes a fastening at the end. We do not merely fear that it hangs in the air, but we know it must do so. And when the end is unsupported, all the rest is unsupported. Hence our conditio*ned* truth is only conditio*nal*. It avowedly depends on what is not fact, and it is not categorically true. Not standing by itself, it hangs from a supposition; or perhaps a still worse destiny awaits it, it hangs from nothing and falls altogether.

§ 72. It will be said, of course, that this is mere metaphysics. Given is given, and fact is fact. Nay we ourselves distinguished above the individual from the hypothetic judgement, on the ground that the former went to perception, and that we found [101] there existing the elements it asserted. Such a plain distinction should not be ignored, because it disappears in an over-subtle atmosphere. But I do not wish to take back this distinction. It is valid at a certain level of thought; and, for the ordinary purposes of logical enquiry, individual judgements, both synthetic and analytic, may conveniently be taken as categorical, and in this sense opposed to universal judgements.

But, when we go further into the principles of logic, and are forced to consider how these classes of judgement stand to one another, we are certain to go wrong, if we have not raised such questions as the above. It is not enough to know that we have a ground of distinction. We must ask if it is a *true* ground. Is it anything more than a point to reckon from? Is it also fact? Does the light of presence, which falls on a content, guarantee its

truthfulness even if we copy? Are the presented phenomenon,
and series of phenomena, actual realities? And, we have seen,
they are not so. The given in sense, if we could seize it in judgement, would still disappoint us. It is not self-existent and is therefore unreal, and the reality transcends it, first in the infinite
process of phenomena, and then altogether. The real, which (as
we say) appears in perception, is neither a phenomenon nor a
series of phenomena.

§ 73. It may be said 'This is only the product of reflection. If
we are content to take the facts as they come to us, if we will
only leave them just as we feel them, they never disappoint us.
They neither hang by these airy threads from the past, nor perish
internally in a vanishing network of never-ending relations
between illusory units. The real, as it simply comes to us in sense,
has nothing of all this. It is one with itself, individual and complete, absolute and categorical.' We are not here concerned to
controvert this statement. We are not called on to ask if anything
that is given is given apart from intellectual modification, if there
is any product we can observe and watch, with which we have
not already interfered. We have no motive here to raise such an
issue; nor again do we rejoice in that infatuation for intellect,
and contempt for feeling, which is supposed to qualify the
[102] competent metaphysician. Nor will we pause to argue that frus-
trated feeling itself heads the revolt against the truth of sense. It
was a baffled heart that first raised the suspicion of a cheated
head.

You may say, if you like, that the real just as we feel it is
true.[27][56] But, if so, then *all* judgements are surely false, and
your singular judgement goes with the rest. For our present purpose we may admit your assertion, but, if it is meant as an objection, we answer it by asking the question, What then? Who is it
who says this? Who counts himself so free from the sin of
reflection as to throw this stone? Some man no doubt who has
not an idea of the consequences of his saying; some writer whose
pages are filled with bad analysis and dogmatic metaphysics;
some thinker whose passion for 'experience' is mere prejudice in
favour of his own one-sided theory, and whose loyal regard for

---

[27][56] 'You may say &c.' It is of course the English empiricist of 1883 who is
being addressed here. As to how far the criticism is now out of date, the reader
must judge for himself.

the sensible fact means inability to distinguish it from that first result of a crude reflection in which he sticks.

For the present we may assume, what metaphysics would discuss, that phenomena are what we can not help thinking them *in the end*, and that the *last* result of our thought is true, or all the truth we have. It is not the beginning but the end of reflection which is valid of the real; or we are such at least that our minds are unable to decide for aught else. And we have seen that our thinking about the real, if we remain at the level of the analytic judgement, will not stand criticism. The result of our later and, we are forced to believe, our better reflection is conviction that at least this judgement is not true. To assert as a quality of the real either the whole or part of the series of phenomena, is to make a false assertion.

§ 74. The reality is given and is present to sense; but you can not, as we saw (§ 11), convert this proposition, and say, Whatever is present and given is, as such, real. The present is not merely that section of the phenomena in space and time which it manifests to us. It is not simply the same as its appearance. Presence is our contact with actual reality; and the reception of the elements of sensuous perception as existing facts is one kind of contact, but it is not the only kind.

In hypothetical judgements there is a sense in which the real is given; for we feel its presence in the connection of the elements, [103] and we ascribe the ground to the real as its quality. Hypothetical judgements in the end must rest on direct presentation, though from that presentation we do not take the elements and receive them as fact. It is merely their synthesis which holds good of the real (§ 50), and it is in our perception of the ground of that synthesis that we come into present contact with reality. I will not ask if this contact is more direct than that which supports the analytical judgement. But at all events we may say it is truer; since truth is what is true of the ultimate real. A supersensible ultimate quality is not much to assert, but at all events the assertion seems not false.[28]{59} On the other hand the categoric

---

[28]{59} 'The assertion seems not false.' On the other side, since it depends on an unknown condition, and since therefore its opposite also is possible, it has not absolute truth. In this point, and so far, it is like the 'analytical judgement of sense'. On the other hand it is higher and truer because, and so far as, its condition is less unknown and less dependent on mere 'matter of fact'.

affirmation of the analytic judgement of sense we know is not true. The content it asserts we know is not real. And, taken in this sense, there remains no hope for the individual judgement.

§ 75. There is no hope for it at all, till it abates its pretensions, till it gives up its claims to superiority over the hypothetic judgement, and is willing to allow that it itself is no more than conditional. But it does not yet know the degradation that awaits it. It may say, 'It is true that I am not categorical. My content is conditioned, and the "because" has turned round in my hands into "if". But at least I am superior to the abstract hypothetical. For in that the elements are not even asserted to have reality, whereas, subject to the condition of the rest of the series, I at least assert my content to be fact. So far at least I affirm existence and maintain my position.'

But this claim is illusory, for if the individual judgement becomes in this way hypothetical, it does not assert that its content has *any* existence. If it did it would contradict itself, and I will endeavour to explain this.

The content *a—b* in the categoric judgement was directly ascribed to real existence. The abstract universal judgement *a—b* does not ascribe either *a* or *b* or their connection to the real;[29]{60} it merely ascribes a quality *x*. The question now is Can you save the categoric *a—b* by turning it into a hypothetical in which *a—b* is still asserted of existence, though under a condition,—or must it become the universal *a—b* which ignores existence? In the latter case it would simply mean, 'Given *a*, then *b*.' But in the former it [104] would run, 'Given something *else*, then *a—b* exists.' This illusory claim is not very pretentious, but I wish to show that it is suicidal.

Drobisch (*Logik*[n], § 56), following Herbart (I. 106), translates the judgement, 'P exists,' into 'If anything exists anywhere, then P exists.' I consider this translation to be incorrect; for it covertly assumes that something does exist, and hence is in substance still categorical. And if we apply this translation to the facts of sense, then what is really supposed is the completed series of other phenomena, and the translation must run thus, 'If *everything else*

---

[29]{60} 'Does not ascribe . . . real.' This, we have seen (Note 3{3}) is wrong. But, if 'existence' meant my 'real world' of events, it could stand. On the 'quality' see Note 21{40}.

---

[n] Moritz Wilhelm Drobisch, *Neue Darstellung der Logik*, 4th edn. (Leipzig: Leopold Voss, 1875).

exists, then P exists.' But the assertion is now suicidal, for 'everything else', we have seen above (§ 70), can never be a real fact. The hypothetical assertion of existence[30{61}] is therefore made dependent on a condition which can not exist. Now it is not true that the consequence of a false hypothesis must be false; but it certainly is true, when an impossible ground is laid down as the sole condition of existence, that in a roundabout way existence is denied. The individual judgement, we saw, was false when taken categorically. And now, we see, when taken hypothetically, instead of asserting it rather denies, or at least suggests that denial may be true.

§ 76. The only hope for the singular judgement lies in complete renunciation. It must admit that the abstract, although hypothetical, is more true than itself is. It must ask for a place in the same class of judgement and be content to take the lowest room there. It must cease to predicate its elements of the real, and must confine itself to asserting their connection as adjectives generally, and apart from particular existence. Instead of meaning by 'Here is a wolf,' or 'This tree is green,' that 'wolf' and 'green tree' are real facts, it must affirm the general connection of wolf with elements of the environment, and of 'green' with 'tree'. And it must do this in an abstract sense, without any reference to the particular fact. In a low and rudimentary form it thus tends to become a scientific law, and, entirely giving up its original claims, it now sets its foot on the ladder of truth.

§ 77. But it remains upon the very lowest round. Every judgement of perception is in a sense universal, and, if it were not so, it could never be used as the basis of inference. The statement goes beyond the particular case, and involves a connection of [105] adjectives which is true without respect to 'this' 'here' and 'now'. If you take it as ascribing its ideal content to *this* reality, it no doubt is singular, but, if you take it as asserting a synthesis *inside* that ideal content, it transcends perception; for anywhere else with the same conditions the same result would hold. The synthesis is true, not here and now, but universally.

[30{61}] If 'existence' (Notes 3{3} and 18{29}) means my 'real world', then to say of anything that its existence is implied in there being such a world, is, so far, unconditional assertion. But on the other hand, so far as this world itself is not absolutely real and true, the assertion becomes, so far, merely relative, and dependent on an unknown condition. If you could say that P, as such, is implied in the real, that would make P true absolutely.

And yet its truth remains most rudimentary, for the connection of adjectives is immersed in matter. The content is full of indefinite relations, and, in the first vague form which our statements assume, we are sure on the one hand to take into the assertion elements which have nothing to do with the synthesis, and, on the other hand, to leave out something which really helps to constitute its necessity. We say for example, 'This body putrefies'; but it does not putrefy because it is this body. The real connection is far more abstract. And again on the other hand it would not putrefy simply because of anything that *it* is, and without foreign influence. In the one case we add irrelevant details, and in the other we leave out an essential factor. In the one case we say, 'The real is such that, given abc, then d will follow,' when the connection is really nothing but a—d. In the other case we say, 'The connection is a—b,' when a is not enough to necessitate b, and the true form of synthesis is a (c)—b. Measured by a standard of scientific accuracy, the first forms of our truths must always be false. They say too little, or too much, or both; and our upward progress must consist in correcting them by removing irrelevancies and filling up the essential.[31]

§ 78. The practice of science confirms the result to which our long analysis has brought us; for what is once true for science is true for ever. Its object is not to record that complex of sensible phenomena, which from moment to moment perception presents to us. It desires to get a connection of content, to be able to say, Given this or that element, and something else universally holds good. It endeavours to discover those abstract elements in their full completeness, and to arrange the lower under the higher. [106] Recurring to a term we used before, we may say its aim is to purge out 'thisness', to reconstruct the given as ideal syntheses of abstract adjectives. Science from the first is a process of idealization; and experiment, Hegel has long ago told us, is an idealizing instrument, for it sublimates fact into general truths.

Both in common life and in science alike, a judgement is at once applied to fresh cases. It is from the first an universal truth. If it really were particular and wholly confined to the case it appears in, it might just as well have never existed, for it could

---

[31] For explanation and illustration I must refer to Lotze's admirable chapter cited above [in Note 23].

not be used. A mere particular judgement does not really exist, and, if it did exist, would be utterly worthless. . . .

§ 79. It is time that we collected what result has come from these painful enquiries. If we consider the ultimate truth of assertions, then, so far as we have gone, the categorical judgement in its first crude form has entirely disappeared. The distinction between individual and universal, categorical and hypothetical, has been quite broken through. All judgements are categorical, for they all do affirm about the reality, and assert the existence of a quality in that. Again, all are hypothetical, for not one of them can ascribe to real existence its elements as such. All are individual, since the real which supports that quality which forms the ground of synthesis, is itself substantial. Again all are universal, since the synthesis they affirm holds out of and beyond the particular appearance. They are every one abstract, for they disregard context, they leave out the environment of the sensible complex, and they substantiate adjectives. And yet all are concrete, for they none of them are true of anything else than that individual reality which appears in the sensuous wealth of presentation.

§ 80. But, if we remain at a lower point of view, if we agree not to scrutinize the truth of judgements, and if we allow assertions as to particular fact to remain in the character which they claim for themselves, in that case our result will be somewhat different.[32{65}] Abstract judgements will all be hypothetical, but the judgements that analyze what is given in perception will all be categorical. Synthetic judgements about times or spaces beyond perception will come in the middle. They involve an inference on the strength of an universal, and so far they must have a hypothetical character. They again involve an awkward assumption, for you can go to them only through the identity of an element in the several contents of a perception and an idea. As however, on the strength of this assumption, the universal is brought into connection with the given, the 'if' is so turned into a 'because', and the synthetic judgement may be called categorical. The two classes, so far, will on one side be assertions about [107]

[32{65}] The division made in § 80 is (we have seen) indefensible, if only because the 'imaginary' is left out. See Note 18. And for the 'awkward assumption' cf. § 32.

particular fact and on the other side abstract or adjectival assertions. The latter are hypothetical, and the first categorical.

§ 81. We have all this time omitted to consider that class of
judgement which makes an assertion about an individual which is
not a phenomenon in space or time (§ 41). Is it possible that here
we have at last a judgement which is not in any sense hypothetical? Can one of these directly predicate of the individual real an
attribute which really and truly belongs to it? May we find here a
statement which asserts the actual existence of its elements, and
which is not false? Can truth categorical be finally discovered in
some such judgement as 'The self is real,' or 'Phenomena are
nothing beyond the appearance of soul to soul'? It would seem to
us strange indeed if this were so, and yet after all perhaps it is
our minds that are really estranged.

But we can not here attempt to answer these questions. We
can only reply when asked where truth categorical dwells, 'Either
here or nowhere.'

Introduction to The Negative Judgement

The third chapter of *The Principles of Logic*, 'The Negative Judgement', is an application of Bradley's general view of the nature of judgement to the specific case of negative judgements. Bradley applies this general view in the preliminary form in which he states it in 'The General Nature of Judgement' rather than in the considerably deepened form of 'The Categorical and Hypothetical Forms of Judgement'. His concern is to explain how negative judgements contain an ideal content which is predicated of reality.

After summarizing his view in §1, Bradley devotes the rest of this chapter to a defence of two theses that support it. The first thesis, defended in §§2–6, is that negative judgements stand on a different level of reflection from affirmative judgements. By this Bradley means that negative judgements portray what they deny as something that has a truth-value. This is analogous to the way in which negation is represented as a truth-functional operator in sentential logic. Bradley explains this claim in §§2–3 and elaborates it in §§4–6 by contrasting it with three claims about negative judgements that he rejects.

The second thesis, defended in §§7, 12, and 15–20, is that negative judgements presuppose a positive ground. This is a denial of any view that takes negative judgements to be true or false irrespective of their relation to any other judgements. It further specifies that at least one of these other judgements must be affirmative. Bradley explains this claim briefly in §7 and applies it to different kinds of negative judgements in §12. In §§15–19 he attempts to clarify it further by arguing that the positive ground that a negative judgement presupposes is, in the terminology of the logical tradition, the contrary, not the contradictory. Bradley concludes the chapter in §20 by suggesting that his view of negative judgements has metaphysical implications. Bradley's view of negative judgements plays a crucial role in his metaphysics, a fact to which he makes no reference in this chapter. (Its role in his metaphysics is explained in 'The General Nature of Reality', [121–2], reprinted below.)

J.A.

3[1]{1}

The Negative Judgement

§ 1. After the long discussion of the preceding chapter, we are so [114] familiar with the general character of judgement that we can afford to deal rapidly with particular applications. Like every other variety, the negative judgement depends on the real which appears in perception. In the end it consists in the declared refusal of that subject[2]{2} to accept an ideal content. The suggestion of the real as qualified and determined in a certain way, and the exclusion of that suggestion by its application to actual reality, is the proper essence of the negative judgement.

§ 2. Though denial, as we shall see, can not be reduced to or derived from affirmation, yet it would probably be wrong to consider the two as co-ordinate species. It is not merely as we shall see lower down (§ 7), that negation presupposes a positive ground. It stands at a different level of reflection. For in affirmative judgement we are able to attribute the content directly to the real itself. To have an idea, or a synthesis of ideas, and to refer this as a quality to the fact that appears in presentation, was all that we wanted. But, in negative judgement,[3]{3} this very reference of content to reality must itself be an idea. Given X the fact, and an idea a—b, you may at once attribute a—b to X; but you can not deny a—b of X, so long as you have merely X and a—b. For, in order to deny, you must have the suggestion of an affirmative relation. The idea of X, as qualified by a—b, which we may write $x\,(a$—$b)$, is the ideal content which X repels, and is what we deny in our negative judgement.

Repr. from PL, book I, 'Judgement'.

[1]{1} This chapter contains some serious errors.

[2]{2} 'That subject,' i.e., as in one with a selected determination. See Chapter I ['The General Nature of Judgement', repr. above, Part I, Ch. I], §§ 11 and 12.

[3]{3} The abstraction of the idea from all 'reference' is not defensible. See on Chap. I [ibid.], § 10. There is always some region in which an idea is real. It is only where the perceived world is taken as the one real object, that other worlds are merely 'subjective'.

It may be said, no doubt, that in affirmative judgement the real subject is always idealized. We select from the whole that appears in presentation, and mean an element that we do not mention . . . When we point to a tree and apply the word 'green', it may be urged that the subject is just as ideal as when the same object [115] rejects the offered suggestion 'yellow'. But this would ignore an important difference. The tree, in its presented unity with reality, can accept at once the suggested quality. I am not always forced to suspend my decision, to wait and consider the whole as ideal, to ask in the first place, Is the tree green? and then decide that the tree is a green tree. But in the negative judgement where 'yellow' is denied, the positive relation of 'yellow' to the tree must precede the exclusion of that relation. The judgement can never anticipate the question. I must always be placed at that stage of reflection which sometimes I avoid in affirmative judgement.

§ 3. And this distinction becomes obvious, if we go back to origins and consider the early development of each kind. The primitive basis of affirmation is the coalescence of idea with perception. But mere non-coalescence of an idea with perception is a good deal further removed from negation. It is not the mere presence of an unreferred idea, nor its unobserved difference, but it is the failure to refer it, or identify it, which is the foundation of our first denial. The exclusion by presented fact of an idea, which attempted to qualify it, is what denial starts from. What negation must begin with is the attempt on reality, the baffled approach of a qualification. And in the consciousness of this attempt is implied not only the suggestion that is made, but the subject to which that suggestion is offered. Thus in the scale of reflection negation stands higher than mere affirmation. It is in one sense more ideal, and it comes into existence at a later stage of the development of the soul.

§ 4. But the perception of this truth must not lead us into error. We must never say that negation is the denial of an existing judgement. For judgement, as we know, implies belief; and it is not the case that what we deny we must once have believed. And again, since belief and disbelief are incompatible, the negative judgement would in this way be made to depend on an element which, alike by its existence or its disappearance, would remove the negation itself. What we deny is not the reference of the idea to actual fact. It is the mere idea of the fact, as so qualified, which negation excludes; it repels the suggested synthe- [116] sis,[4{4}] not the real judgement.

§ 5. From this we may pass to a counterpart error. If it is a mistake to say that an affirmative judgement is presupposed in denial, it is no less a mistake to hold that the predicate alone is affected, and that negation itself is a kind of affirmation. We shall hereafter recognize the truth which this doctrine embodies, but, in the form it here assumes, we can not accept it. The exclusion by fact of an approaching quality is a process which calls for its own special expression. And when we are asked to simplify matters by substituting 'A is Not-B' for 'A is not B,' we find an obvious difficulty. In order to know that A accepts Not-B, must we not already have somehow learnt that A excludes B? And, if so, we reduce negation to affirmation by first of all denying, and then asserting that we have denied,—a process which no doubt is quite legitimate, but is scarcely reduction or simplification.

§ 6. There is a further objection we shall state hereafter (§ 16) to the use of Not-B as an independent predicate. But at present we must turn to clear the ground of another error. We may be told that negation 'affects only the copula'; and it is necessary first to ask what this means. If it means what it says, we may dismiss it at once, since the copula may be wanting. If the copula is not there when I positively say 'Wolf', so also it is absent when I negatively say 'No wolf'. But, if what is meant is that denial and assertion are two sorts of judgement, which stand on a level, then the statement once again needs correction. It is perfectly true that these two different sorts of judgement exist. The affirmative judgement qualifies a subject by the attribution of a quality, and the negative judgement qualifies a subject by the explicit rejection of that same quality. We have thus two kinds of asserted relation. But the mistake arises when we place them on a level. It is not only true that, as a condition of denial, we must have already a suggested synthesis, but there is in addition another objection. The truth of the negative may be seen in the end to lie in the affirmation of a positive quality; and hence assertion and denial cannot stand on one level. In 'A is not B' the real fact is a character x belonging to A, and which is incompatible with B. The

---

[4{4}] The 'suggested synthesis' (here and lower down) needs correction in the sense of the foregoing Note.

[117] basis of negation is really the assertion of *a quality that excludes*
(*x*). It is not, as we saw, the mere assertion of the quality of
exclusion (Not-B).

§ 7. Every negation must have a ground, and this ground is
positive. It is that quality *x* in the subject which is incompatible
with the suggested idea. A is not B because A is such that, if it
were B, it would cease to be itself. Its quality would be altered if
it accepted B; and it is by virtue of this quality, which B would
destroy, that A maintains itself and rejects the suggestion. In
other words its quality *x* and B are discrepant. And we can not
deny B without affirming in A the pre-existence of this discrepant
quality.

But in negative judgement *x* is not made explicit. We do not
say what there is in A which makes B incompatible. We often, if
asked, should be unable to point out and to distinguish this
latent hindrance; and in certain cases no effort we could make
would enable us to do this. If B is accepted, A loses its character;
and in these cases we know no more. The ground is not merely
unstated but is unknown. . . .

[120] § 12. The various kinds of negative judgement follow closely
the varieties of affirmation. The immediate subject may be part
of the content of present perception ('This stone is not wet'); or
it may be found in some part of the series of space, or again of
time, which we do not perceive ('Marseilles is not the capital of
France,' 'It did not freeze last night'). Again what is denied may
be a general connection ('A metal need not be heavier than
water'). In this last case it is of course the unexpressed quality at
the base of the hypothesis (Chap. II[a] § 50) which the real
excludes.[5{11}] But, in all negative judgement, the ultimate subject
is the reality that comes to us in presentation. We affirm in all
alike that the quality of the real excludes an ideal content that is
offered. And so every judgement, positive or negative, is in the
end existential.

In existential judgement, as we saw before (Chap. II.[b] § 42),
the apparent is not the actual subject. Let us take such a denial

---

[5{11}] 'The unexpressed quality.' See on Chap. II ['The Categorical and
Hypothetical Forms of Judgement'], § 50.

---

[a] 'The Categorical and Hypothetical Forms of Judgement', repr. above, Part I,
Ch. 2.
[b] Ibid.

as 'Chimaeras are non-existent.' 'Chimaeras' is here ostensibly the subject, but is really the predicate. It is the quality of harbouring chimaeras which is denied of the nature of things. And we deny this because, if chimaeras existed, we should have to alter our view of the world. In some cases that view, no doubt, can be altered, but, so long as we hold it, we are bound to refuse all predicates it excludes. The positive quality of the ultimate
· reality may remain occult or be made explicit, but this, and nothing else, lies always at the base of a negative judgement. . . .

§ 15. To resume, logical negation always contradicts, but never [122] asserts the existence of the contradictory. To say 'A is not B' is merely the same as to deny that 'A is B,' or to assert that 'A is B' is false. And, since it can not go beyond this result, a mere denial of B can never assert that the contradictory Not-B is real. The fact it does assert is the existence of an opposite incompati- [123] ble quality, either in the immediate or ultimate subject. This is the reason why the suggested A—B is contradicted; and it is only because this something else is true, that the statement A—B is rejected as false. But then this positive ground, which is the basis of negation, is not *contradictory*. It is merely discrepant, opposite, incompatible. It is only *contrary*. In logical negation the denial and the fact can never be the same.

§ 16. The contradictory idea, if we take it in a merely negative form, must be banished from logic. If Not-A were solely the negation of A, it would be an assertion without a quality, and would be a denial without anything positive to serve as its ground. A something that is only not something else, is a relation that terminates in an impalpable void, a reflection thrown upon empty space. It is a mere nonentity which can not be real. And, if such were the sense of the dialectical method (as it must be confessed its detractors have had much cause to suppose),[6{16}] that sense would, strictly speaking, be nonsense. It is impossible for anything to be *only* Not-A. It is impossible to realize Not-A in thought. It is less than nothing, for nothing itself is not wholly negative. Nothing at least is empty thought, and that means at least my thinking emptily. Nothing means nothing else but failure. And failure is impossible unless something fails; but Not-A would be impersonal failure itself.

[6{16}] 'Much cause' should perhaps be 'some cause'.

Not-A must be more than a bare negation. It must also be positive. It is a general name for any quality which, when you make it a predicate of A, or joint predicate with A,[7]{[17]} removes A from existence. The contradictory idea is the universal idea of the discrepant or contrary. In this form it must keep its place in logic. It is a general name for any hypothetical discrepant; but we must never for a moment allow ourselves to think of it as the collection of discrepants.

§ 17. Denial or contradiction is not the same thing as the assertion of the contrary; but in the end it can rest on nothing else.[8]{[18]} The contrary however which denial asserts, is never explicit. In 'A is not B' the discrepant ground is wholly unspecified. The basis of contradiction may be the assertion A— [124] C or A—D, C and D being contraries of B. But again it may perhaps be nothing of the sort. We may reject A—B, not in the least on the ground of A, but because A itself is excluded from reality. The ultimate real may be the subject which has some quality discrepant with A—B. For contradiction rests on an undetermined contrary. It does not tell us what quality of the subject excludes the predicate. It leaves us in doubt if the subject itself is not excluded. Something there is which repels the suggestion; and that is all we know. Sokrates may be not sick because he is well, or because there is now no such thing as Sokrates.

§ 18. Between acceptance and rejection there is no middle-point, and so contradiction is always dual. There is but one Not-B. But contrary opposition is indefinitely plural. The number of qualities that are discrepant or incompatible with A, can not be determined by a general rule. It is possible of course to define a contrary in some sense which will limit the use of the term; but for logical purposes this customary restriction is nothing but lumber. In logic the contrary should be simply the discrepant.

---

[7]{[17]} 'Or joint predicate.' In a sense it never is anything but a joint predicate. See *Appearance and Reality*, Appendix, Note A ['Contradiction, and the Contrary', repr. below, pp. 213–25].

[8]{[18]} The main point is this, that denial means exclusion from and by the real. *Mere* denial, however, rests on *abstract* exclusion, which, as abstract, is really nothing. Actually the real excludes because the real is qualified incompatibly, and may be so in a variety of senses, the whole of which variety is ignored by the abstract ideal.

Nothing is gained by trying to keep up an effete tradition. If a technical distinction can not be called necessary, it is better to have done with it.

§ 19. Contradiction is thus a 'subjective' process, which rests on an unnamed discrepant quality. It can not claim 'objective' reality; and since its base is undetermined, it is hopelessly involved in ambiguity. In 'A is not B' you know indeed what it is you deny, but you do not say what it is you affirm. It may be a quality in the nature of things which is incompatible with A, or again with B. Or again it may be either a general character of A itself which makes B impossible, or it may be some particular predicate C. That 'a round square is three-cornered,' or that 'happiness lies in an infinite quantity,' may at once be denied. We know a round square, or an infinite number, are not in accordance with the nature of things. But 'virtue is quadrangular,' or 'is mere self-seeking,' we deny again because virtue has no existence in space, and has another quality which is opposite to selfishness.

'The King of Utopia died on Tuesday' may be safely contradicted. And yet the denial must remain ambiguous. The ground may be that there is no such place, or it never had a king, or he [125] still is living, or, though he is dead, yet he died on Monday. This doubtful character can never be removed from the contradiction. It is the rejection of an idea, on account of some side of real fact which is implied but occult.

§ 20. We may conclude this chapter by setting before ourselves a useful rule. I think most of us know that one can not affirm without also in effect denying something. In a complex universe the predicate you assert is certain to exclude some other quality, and this you may fairly be taken to deny. But another pitfall, if not so open, yet no less real, I think that some of us are quite unaware of. Our sober thinkers, our discreet Agnostics, our diffident admirers of the phenomenal region—I wonder if ever any of them see how they compromise themselves with that little word *'only'*. How is it that they dream there is something else underneath appearance, and first suspect that what meets the eye veils something hidden? But our survey of negation has taught us the secret, that nothing in the world can ever be denied except on the strength of positive knowledge. I hardly know if I am right in introducing suggestive ideas into simple minds; but yet I must end with the rule I spoke of. We can not deny without also affirming; and it is of the very last importance, whenever we deny, to get as clear an idea as we can of the positive ground our denial rests on.

PART II

Metaphysics

Introduction to the Argument of Bradley's Metaphysics

Appearance and Reality is divided into book I and book II. The argument of Bradley's metaphysics, as it is presented there, falls into two stages: a sceptical stage in book I and a constructive stage in book II. This introduction follows the structure of *Appearance and Reality* but also aims to relate Bradley's argument to particular chapters in his *Essays on Truth and Reality*.

Book I: The Sceptical Argument

The sceptical argument rests on the claim that contradictions inevitably occur in the development of any system of communicable knowledge (what Bradley calls 'relational' knowledge) because the form of unconditional predicative thought is intrinsically self-contradictory. (See e.g. *ETR*, ch. VIII, 'Coherence and Contradiction', below, Part II, sect. 2, Ch. 6.)

In book I of *Appearance and Reality* (chs. iv–xii) Bradley exemplifies contradictions that can be seen to be implicit in our thinking with respect to space, time, movement, causation, activity, and the self. He accepts that the principle of non-contradiction provides a necessary condition of any thinkable content possessing absolute truth (*AR* 120, below, pp. 132–5). He therefore concludes that the judgemental systems in terms of which we identify positions of things in time and space, movements, causes, and so on cannot be taken to possess absolute truth. Or to put it equivalently: the systems of objects which in our everyday and scientific thinking we identify in terms of the ideas of time, space, cause, and so on cannot *within metaphysics* be taken to be ultimately real. They can only be taken to be more or less inadequate *appearances* of reality.[a]

The fundamental premiss for this sceptical position is argued for in

---

[a] Bradley in general uses the term 'reality' in contrast to 'appearance'. Any object or system of objects that could possibly be identified in a linguistically communicable content of consciousness (Bradley argues within his metaphysics) must be regarded as a more or less inadequate *appearance* of reality. Somewhat misleadingly he occasionally uses the expression '*special* reality', or simply 'a reality', synonymously with this usage of 'appearance'. When, in the context of metaphysics, he wishes to concentrate attention on the ultimate nature of reality—as a whole and as opposed to how reality appears when it is known, more or less inadequately and partially, in terms of the various 'special' systems of communicable thought possessed by human beings—Bradley is prone to capitalize the 'R' and use the term 'Reality'. Hence any putative characterization of the ultimate nature of Reality will aim to give the nature of, what Bradley also refers to as, the Absolute.

chapters ii and iii of *Appearance and Reality* (below, Part II, Sect. 1, Chs. 2 and 3). In these chapters Bradley considers a set of formal concepts which structure all our communicable thinking: namely, the ideas of thing, quality, and relation. These concepts will be exercised whenever we think anything which is expressible in terms of declarative sentences employing grammatically substantival and adjectival terms. We can thus see them as determining the general form of our predicative thought and thus as constituting a set of categories analogous to Kant's. However, Bradley argues that the exercise of these categories, although essential to the formulation of truths, inevitably leads to contradictions. So the contradictions which in *Appearance and Reality*, chapters iv–x he exemplifies in our thinking about time, space, movement, causation, and so on are, on Bradley's view, to be seen as having their source in the contradictory nature of predicative thought as such. So at the end of chapter iii Bradley can say 'The reader who has followed and has grasped the principle of this chapter, will have little need to spend time upon those [in book I] which succeed it' (*AR* 29, below, p. 131).

It is difficult to do justice to chapters ii and iii of *Appearance and Reality*. It is certainly impossible to do them justice if Bradley's regress arguments against relations are treated in isolation from his main concern in those chapters. The best way of understanding the nature of his concern is to view it from within the history of philosophy and see it as analogous to that which faced Russell and Wittgenstein when, within the context of their versions of logical atomism, they sought to delineate the form of an atomic proposition.[b] The difference is that on Bradley's view there can be no question of delineating such a form correctly since the very notion of an unconditional predication is incoherent.

Bradley refers to the problem as 'the problem of inherence' (*AR* 19, below, p. 122; 27, below, p. 130) or, alternatively, the problem of the

[b] Cf. B. Russell, An Enquiry into Meaning and Truth (Harmondsworth: Penguin, 1962), 92, where Russell says: 'One is tempted to regard 'this is red' as a subject–predicate proposition; but if one does so, one finds that "this" becomes a substance, an unknowable something in which predicates inhere, but which, nevertheless, is not identical with the sum of its predicates. . . . I wish to suggest that "this is red" is not a subject–predicate proposition, but is of the form "redness is here"; that "red" is a name, not a predicate; and that what would commonly be called a "thing" is nothing but a bundle of coexisting qualities such as redness, hardness, etc.'. Cf. also B. Russell, 'Logical Atomism', in *Logic and Knowledge,* ed. R. C. Marsh (London: Allen & Unwin, 1956), 323–43. This was written in 1924 and Russell indicates how seriously he still took Bradley's arguments concerning internal and external relations. It shows clearly that Russell always saw Bradley as a serious competitor in the same field—in what has come to be called the philosophy of logic. Cf. Ronald K. Tacelli's 'Cook Wilson as Critic of Bradley', *History of Philosophy Quarterly*, 8/2 (1991), 199–205, for a lucid defence of Bradley's arguments.

meaning of 'is' (*AR* 16, below, p. 119) when we predicate categorically, or unconditionally, of one thing, e.g. a lump of sugar, a conjunction of different things, e.g. hardness, whiteness, sweetness. The problem fundamentally is: How can we think, without contradiction, of one thing as being *unconditionally* many different things? To think of *R* as being unconditionally *a* is to think of it as being such that there is nothing else whatsoever that could be the case or not the case in regard to *R*, or in regard to anything other than *R*, that could affect the truth-value of '*Ra*'. But that, Bradley maintains, is equivalent to asserting that *R* is simply a. (See e.g. *ETR* 228, below, pp. 317–18.) But if so it follows that strictly speaking we could not, without contradiction, assert unconditionally of one thing, *R*, that it is *a* and *b* and *c* etc. given that *a* is not *b* and nor is it *c* etc. (*AR* 16, below, p. 119).

It might seem that the problem can be avoided by construing *R* 'phenomenalistically', as Russell did at one time, and taking it not as a logical subject that *has* qualities predicable of it but as itself simply a collection of *nameable* qualia *a, b, c* etc. On this analysis, the subject, as that in which qualities inhere, disappears, and the thing itself becomes nothing more than a set of designatable qualia coexisting in a certain relationship: the particular thing becomes a *relational complex*.

But Bradley argues that this simply pushes the problem back a stage. The qualia themselves now take on the role of logical subjects (*AR* 16–17, below, pp. 119–20) and then the question of how the relations by which the qualia are interrelated within the complex unity stand to those qualia must be faced.

If the postulated relations are treated, like the qualia, as nameable things capable of independent existence then obviously a vicious regress arises: the relations themselves will have to be related in some designatable way to the qualia and so on *ad infinitum* (*AR* 17–18, below, pp. 119–20). But if, to avoid this regress, the relations are not construed as nameable and independently real but are taken to be predicated of their terms (i.e. predicated of the nameable constituents of the complex unity) then the original problem of inherence simply reappears in a modified form (*AR* 17, below, pp. 119–20) and another regress—equally vicious—confronts the analysis (*AR* 26–7, below, pp. 128–9).

If we take the relations to be predicable (given that not all the relations could conceivably be resolved into the interrelated qualia constitutive of a complex, or vice versa (*AR* 25–6, below, pp. 127–8)) Bradley argues that any interrelated qualium will have to be construed as having a dual character. One part of the character of any such qualium will have to be posited as the *internal* foundation of its having certain relations that it has, but another part will have to be posited as the *external* result of its having certain relations that it has. But then either (1) the qualium will now have to be treated as a logical subject in which two qualities inhere and the old problem recurs yet again, or (2), if the phenomenalistic analysis is persisted with, each qualium will itself have to be treated as constituted of interrelated qualia, and so on *ad infinitum*. (*AR* 26–7, below, pp. 128–9.)

Hence, vicious regresses face a phenomenalistic analysis either if the relations are taken to be wholly external to their interrelated qualia, or if they are taken to be founded partly in the natures of their terms. Thus a phenomenalistic analysis of the notion of a thing *qua* subject of qualities and relations can provide no solution to the problem of inherence.

No matter how philosophers strive to achieve a theoretical understanding of the predicative 'is', Bradley maintains, they inevitably arrive back at the old dilemma: 'If you predicate what is different, you ascribe to the subject what it is *not*; and if you predicate what is *not* different, you say nothing at all'[c] (*AR* 17, below, p. 120).

Thus Bradley maintains that this dilemma is intrinsic to the form of unconditional predication. He therefore concludes, like Russell and Wittgenstein, that the verbal forms of our actual unconditional predications must in fact be misleading as to the character of the judgements they express. However, Bradley draws a conclusion from this which is totally opposed to that of the logical atomists. Bradley argues that if the form of an unconditional predication is incoherent it could not be the case that the truth-values of our everyday complex judgements are ultimately determined by a bedrock of unconditionally statable facts. No unconditionally assertible propositions of the kind posited in logical atomism could conceivably lie at the foundations of our knowledge of reality. Our belief systems must, therefore, be in that sense foundationless. As Bradley expresses it, our judgements are not merely conditioned by conditions unknown to us; they must without exception be irreducibly condition*al*. (See *PL*, ch. ii, §§ 68–71, above, Part I, Ch. 2; also *ETR* 226–33, below, pp. 316–32.)

Thus on Bradley's view the quest for categorical subject–predicate assertions which are unconditionally true is inevitably abortive. Knowledge and truth must be sought not by searching for an illusory

---

[c] Wittgenstein's picture theory of meaning might be seen as an attempt to avoid Bradley's dilemma. The picture theory attempts to provide a schema for determinate propositional meaning by avoiding the traditional subject–predicate asymmetry. According to the picture theory in the context of an atomic proposition a concatenation of simple objects will be asserted as existing. No object is predicated of any other object. Objects are concatenated in states of affairs like the links of a chain—hence no links are needed to interrelate the links (cf. *Tractatus Logico-Philosophicus*, § 2.03). But simple objects themselves must have both formal (internal) and material (external) properties and, Bradley would argue, are thereby subject to 'internal fission'.

foundation of incorrigible truths but by bringing progressively more and more of the unknown conditions of our ostensibly unconditional judgements explicitly and coherently into the ideal contents of those judgements. This in practice will amount to placing our judgements within belief systems of progressively more comprehensive scope. (Cf. Part II, Sect. 2, Chs. 5 and 6 below.) This process can be seen as exemplified when disparate areas of knowledge are brought into intelligible connection within the special sciences. On Bradley's view of judgement and truth *as a matter of necessity* the wider the range of data that a belief system can bring into intelligible connection, i.e. the more comprehensive the system, the greater will be the degree of its truth. It is at this point that the fundamental difference between Bradley's logic, with its coherence theory of truth, and that of atomism, with its correspondence theory, can be located. According to the latter account—given the posited contingency and logical independence of (i.e. the unconditionality of) the ultimate atomic bases of our knowledge—any system of propositions expressive of our knowledge or belief, no matter how extensive and coherent, could as a matter of logical possibility be utterly false. It follows equally, for the atomist, as Russell in fact argued against the coherence theory, that a purely fictional story could as a matter of logical possibility be more coherent and comprehensive than the historical truth. For Bradley, give his rejection of the possibility of irreducibly unconditional propositions, true or false, both these suppositions would be inconceivable.[d] (Cf. *ETR* 113–16, below, pp. 259–61; 231–3, below, pp. 319–21; but see also *PL* 685–6.)

Once we come to see that the intellect, on pain of contradiction, cannot properly rest content in any of its unconditionally asserted predications, but must always seek to establish the unknown conditions of those predications, Bradley maintains that we will be able to appreciate that the apparently independent demands for coherence and for comprehensiveness constitute two integral aspects of a single criterion of truth: what Bradley calls 'the principle of system' (cf. e.g. *ETR* 202–3, below, pp. 296–7; 241–2, below, p. 322).

However, if we accept this view of truth then we are faced with two

---

[d] However, it is important to appreciate that on Bradley's view no special science is to be construed as having privileged metaphysical status. Nor, in general, are the special sciences to be seen as necessarily having epistemological superiority over other judgemental systems in terms of which we think and act, e.g. those connected with historical thought, morality, religious belief, etc. We are in fact faced with irrevocably disparate systems of thought, and the a priori idea of, say, contemporary physics being more comprehensive in scope than, for example, some system of morality, or religion, is absurd. The great value of the modern sciences lies in the fact that, like the arts and history, they represent unparalleled spiritual achievements.

consequences which, it would seem, have serious consequences for the possibility of metaphysics.

Firstly, no matter how systematic our knowledge might become we will always, at any given stage, be confronted with some facts which will demand for their description assertions which are unconditional with respect to their form and *as such* self-contradictory. Hence no matter how comprehensive a system of belief might become the objects knowable in terms of it could constitute, so far as metaphysics is concerned, only a more or less inadequate appearance of reality.

Secondly, given that all our judgements are irreducibly conditional, so that in any judgement there will always be unknown conditions of the judgement's truth waiting to be brought explicitly into the ideal content of the judgement, there will be no absolute distinction between a judgement and its correlative system of belief. And given that a system of belief can only possess a degree of truth and never be absolutely true it will follow that no judgement isolated from a system can be absolutely true either. (Cf. *ETR* 232–3, below, pp. 321–2.)

Given these conclusions it would seem that, in so far as it seeks absolute truth concerning the ultimate nature of reality as a whole, metaphysical knowledge must be impossible.

Book II: The Constructive Metaphysics

However, Bradley does not stop with this sceptical conclusion. The basis for the constructive stage of his metaphysics is laid in the first three chapters of book II of *Appearance and Reality* (chs. xiii and xiv, 'The General Nature of Reality', and ch. xv, 'Thought and Reality'; below, Part II, Sect. 1, Chs. 4–6). His argument again has a logical foundation. It rests on the view of negation argued for in the *Principles of Logic* (ch. iii, 'The Negative Judgement', above, Part I, Ch. 3) and this view connects once again with Bradley's rejection of the possibility of unconditionally true and unconditionally false propositions.

Bradley rejects as impossible what he calls 'bare negation' (*AR* 121–2, below, pp. 133–5). According to the concept of bare negation a negative proposition, p, can be true independently of its relation to any affirmative proposition whatsoever, apart from p. If 'not-p' is true it could be true simply and solely in virtue of the non-existence of the fact described by the affirmative proposition 'p'. This conception of negation clearly requires the possibility of the very sort of unconditionally true, or false, propositional content that Bradley maintains is contradictory. If absolutely unconditional truths and falsehoods are impossible, so also is bare negation.

Bradley's alternative account of negation proceeds as follows. As a corollary of his rejection of unconditional truths and falsehoods Bradley maintains that our thought is to be construed as predicated of reality in more or less comprehensive and evolving systems of logically related ideal contents (see e.g. *ETR* 230, below, p. 319). Within the context of such ideal constructions particular subjects of our judgements will be thought of as exhibiting particular determinations of determinable properties and relations (cf. *AR* 19, below, pp. 121–2). Hence, thinking in terms of a particular example of such a judgemental system, if it is true that a certain point on the cover of a book, known to exist in fact, is *not* red then we can infer that it must be some one out of a disjunction of other colour possibilities. It must be some colour, say, green, which is incompatible with its being red. Its being green will be the positive ground on which the truth of the negative judgement ('It is not red') rests: it will be what makes the negative judgement true. (Cf. *PL*, ch. iii, §§ 6–8, above, part I, Ch. 3.)

So on this view of negation, for any true negative judgement not-p, there must always be some fact describable by means of a true affirmative judgement, q, logically contrary to p, which provides the positive ground, or truth-condition, of not-p and the falsity-condition of p. The positive grounds of many of our true negative judgements will remain unknown to us but, nevertheless, Bradley insists, any true negation must have a positive ground.

Taking this to be a general feature of negative judgements Bradley then proceeds to argue in the following way. We cannot deny, or even doubt, the principle of non-contradiction: i.e. the principle that, for any reality R, and for any attribute a, R cannot be unconditionally both a and not-a. If R could be unconditionally both a and not-a, the act of denial, and the state of doubt, would lose their significance (*AR* 120, below, p. 132). The principle itself therefore cannot be coherently denied or doubted. We must therefore admit that reality as it is in its ultimate nature cannot be represented adequately in terms of any system of ideal contents that contains contradictions.

Given this, and given that any true negation must rest on a positive ground, Bradley maintains that we can conclude that reality must in its ultimate nature be a *consistent* system of existence (*AR* 123, below, pp. 134–5). But, as Bradley notes, the question now is of the meaning of 'consistency' in this context. It cannot mean the property defined within the special science of formal logic: the property possessed by sets of propositions when they are capable of being true together. Reality itself cannot be any set of ideal contents (cf. *PL* 45–6, above, pp. 34–6), consistent or otherwise. Bradley therefore designates the property which excludes the possibility of reality being represented adequately in any ideal construction containing contradictions, 'harmony'. Reality must be a harmonious system of existence. But the property of harmony at this stage must be understood simply formally: simply as a property x which is the positive ground of the judgement that reality cannot contradict itself.

In addition Bradley maintains that we can know two further things of a general kind with respect to the nature of reality as such.

First, we can know that to assert the existence of a reality of either a Kantian or a Cartesian sort, externally related to human consciousness, is contradictory (*AR*, Appendix, pp. 492–3, below, pp. 210–11; *AR* 158–60, below, pp. 165–8; *ETR* 113–17, below, pp. 259–62). It would be like, as Bradley puts it, saying 'Since all my faculties are totally confined to my garden, I cannot tell if the roses next door are in flower' (*AR* 111). Thus reality cannot coherently be postulated as external to possible experience or knowledge. Nor, on the other hand, can any appearances be allowed to fall outside reality *as an all comprehending whole*. Therefore we can conclude that the ultimate character of reality must be such as somehow to include all diverse and conflicting phenomena transformed into a harmonious form (*AR* 123, below, p. 135; 213, below, p. 178).

Secondly, and this is simply a corollary of the argument of *Appearance and Reality*, chapters ii and iii, we can know that reality could not in, for example, either a Cartesian or a Leibnizian or a Russellian manner, consist in a plurality of independent self-subsistent subjects of predication. The metaphysical notion of a self-subsistent being is that of something that as a matter of logical possibility could have existed, with its nature unchanged, in isolation from everything else that happens in fact to exist. Hence for a universe consisting of a plurality of genuine individuals to be possible it would have to be possible, in principle, to know with complete adequacy any given part without reference to any other part of the universe. In other words it would have to be possible for there to be a less than totally comprehensive system of belief that was logically consistent. But this is precisely what, Bradley argues, is impossible (*ETR* 233, below, pp. 321–2). Hence, ontological pluralism must be rejected.

We can know, therefore, that the universe as a whole must be the sole genuinely individual existent. But, again, the universe could not be *single* in our usual sense of the term: reality could not be one in the sense of that term according to which 'one' is applied to a thing of some general sort. Reality, in the sense of all that there is, cannot be thought of as a thing of a general sort of which there could be other instances.

So Bradley concludes: 'The universe is one in the sense that its differences exist harmoniously within one whole, beyond which there is nothing' (*AR* 127, below, p. 139).

Bradley then asks if it is possible to give a degree of material content to this simply formal outline. He argues that it is possible and that reality in its ultimate nature must *be* sentient experience (cf. *AR* 127–30, below, pp. 139–41). After what seems like a Berkeleian thought experiment, he says: 'Anything, in no sense felt or perceived, becomes to me quite unmeaning. And as I cannot try to think of it without realizing either that I am not thinking at all, or that I am thinking of it against my will as being experienced, I am driven to the conclusion that for me experience is the same as reality' (*AR* 128, below, p. 140).

This might seem to involve a direct appeal to Berkeley's contention that to suppose that there exist, in addition to perceiving subjects themselves, things that are unperceived is incoherent.[e] But it is clear that Bradley does not intend, in any straightforward way, to employ this argument since almost immediately he goes on to say: '[I]f, seeking for reality, we go to experience, what we certainly do *not* find is a subject or an object . . . What we discover rather is a whole in which distinctions can be made, but in which divisions do not exist' (*AR* 128, below, p. 140).

The notion of experience that Bradley is referring to here must be that of a 'finite centre' of immediate experience (cf. *ETR* 410–12, below, pp. 326–8). It must be the centre of experience which *ex hypothesi* will be the locus of any particular sentient being's immediate cognitive contact with reality and that from within which all possible objects, both mental and physical, inner and outer, of his thoughts and thought-impregnated experiences will be distinguished. This in itself is a theoretical philosophical notion. And it is difficult to see that it could have the significance for metaphysics that Bradley claims it to have independently of his scepticism with respect to the metaphysical adequacy of communicable thought.

Moreover, if for the moment we ignore the question of the metaphysical inadequacy of our communicable thought, it is clear that in contexts outside metaphysics Bradley would find no special difficulty in our thinking of objects as existing independently of human sentience. For example, it is clearly internal to the idea of our real world of fact (cf. *ETR* 46–8, below, pp. 244–6) that the objects of human beings' waking sense-perceptions exist independently of those perceptions. Again, as a result of developments in the natural sciences (and remember that for Bradley there is no question but that these developments give us in varying degrees quite genuine knowledge) we are constrained to think of the earth as having existed long before the emergence of sentience. It is only

---

[e] Cf. J. L. Mackie, *Problems from Locke* (Oxford: Clarendon Press, 1976), 53–4, for a critique of Berkeley's argument which would hardly touch Bradley's.

when such partial ways of thinking of reality are taken to be metaphysically adequate that, on Bradley's view, they give rise to utter error (*AR* 250–1). So, for Bradley, there is no simple Berkeleian argument, independently of the view of thought delineated in *The Principles of Logic* and the arguments of book I of *Appearance and Reality*, to an idealist metaphysics.

Also, as implied earlier, Bradley's notion of immediate experience is not to be confused with the notion according to which experience is thought of as a causal input of 'sensory data' from spatial objects. For one thing, for Bradley, sentient experience includes not only perception but also the 'presented facts' of thinking and volition, in addition to bodily sensations, pleasant and unpleasant (cf. *AR* 140, below), pp. 150–1). Thus sentient experience will include not merely the perceptions associated with the functioning of the special organs of sense but the immediate experiences that a sentient being will in general enjoy, and suffer, in both the practical and theoretical pursuits of his life.

Further, we might note, Bradley would reject the identity theorists' attempted identification of immediate experiences with particular brain states describable in terms of the ideal constructions of physiologists.[f] Bradley contends that no coherent way of thinking of reality as a whole could 'conjure away' those experiences which we are acquainted with in living our everyday lives (e.g. *AR* 150, below, pp. 159–60). We know what such experiences are like *immediately* in living our lives.[g] Such experiences could not conceivably be taken to be identical with any of the merely thinkable objects identifiable in the general terms of the abstract linguistically communicable constructions of physiologists (cf. *AR* 150, below, p. 159). Immediate experience must be seen as the irreducibly individual basis *from* which all our ideal constructions, scientific and otherwise, are predicated of reality and thus, at the same time, as providing our immediate, pre-theoretical, cognitive contact with reality.

So, for Bradley, there is no question of a physicalist reduction of sentient experience being intelligible. But on the other hand it would be equally incoherent to portray, as the subjective idealist does, the objects we know as spatially extended as dependent for their existence on our inner states. Our selves as temporally extended subjects, just as much as material bodies existing in space, will be objects of ideal constructions.

---

[f] Cf. the Russellian version of the identity theory formulated in 'Logical Atomism', where Russell says: 'a mind is a track of sets of compresent events in a region of space-time where there is matter which is peculiarly liable to form habits . . . Thus a mind and a brain are not really distinct' (*Logic and Knowledge* 343).
[g] Cf. T. Nagel, 'What is it Like to be a Bat?', in *Mortal Questions* (Cambridge: Cambridge University Press, 1983), 165 ff.; also Timothy Sprigge, 'Final Causes', *Proceedings of the Aristotelian Society*, supp. vol. 45 (1971), 166–8.

They will be particular objects distinguishable in relational thoughts predicated of reality against the background of, and from within, a finite centre of immediate experience (cf. *ETR* 410–12, below, pp. 326–8). Hence, given the inherent metaphysical inadequacy of communicable thought, our selves as souls with more or less determinate histories of inner states cannot be taken to be constitutive of ultimate reality any more than material bodies can.[h]

It is at this point that a crucial step can be seen to be made in Bradley's metaphysics. If we grant (1) the force of Bradley's arguments establishing the unreality, metaphysically speaking, of the objects of our ideal constructions in general, inner or outer, (2) the force of his constructive metaphysical argument establishing the formal structure of reality as a genuine individual, utterly harmonious system, somehow embracing all finite beings as modes through which it exists, and (3) the metaphysical irreducibility of immediate experience, it would seem to follow that reality itself could be nothing beyond a genuinely individual immediate experience in which the conflicting demands of the various sides, theoretical and practical, of our natures as sentient beings are brought into a perfect fulfilment.

Thus we arrive at Bradley's characterization of the Absolute: of the individual 'divined' in *The Principles of Logic* as the ultimate logical subject of any predication that could be true or false. And finally we are in a position to appreciate the central features of Bradley's account of the relation between thought and reality which, as he put it in the Appendix to *Appearance and Reality* 'contains the main thesis of this work'. (Cf. *AR*, Appendix introduction, pp. 492–3, below, p. 211; *AR* 158–60, below, pp. 165–8; *ETR* 112–15, below, pp. 258–60.)

1. The criterion of truth, with its integral aspects of coherence and comprehensiveness, is (unlike in the correspondence or copy theory) internal to the activity of thinking itself.[i] Increasing system is a character that the intellect recognizes in the very experience of thinking as always desirable.

2. But at the same time thought, or truth, can become aware of its

---

[h] However, Bradley does argue that in so far as a soul's behavioural habits will be a function of its own peculiar history it will be 'itself its own laws' in a way that a merely material body, governed by strictly universal mechanistic laws, will not. A soul will therefore tend to be self-dependent and, thus far, will approach more nearly the ideal of a truly self-subsistent being. Thus a soul can, in an intelligible sense, be regarded as less unreal than a material body. (Cf. AR 312–16.)

[i] Cf. 'In order to tell whether a picture is true or false we must compare it with reality' (*Tractatus Logico-Philosophicus* § 2.223). But, given the picturing is the only conceivable mode of representing reality, it is not clear how this comparing could be carried out. Our systems of thought could be 'internally' consistent but totally false.

own intrinsic incoherence. It can thus know that it must, in virtue of its relational form, fail in fulfilling the desire it can recognize as internal to its own nature.

3. Moreover thought can, through coming to appreciate the individuality of the logical subject of its predications, see that its own psychical existence can ultimately be nothing other than a mode of that unique individual's existence and, as such, be identical with it.

4. Finally thought can frame an idea of what it would have to become if it were to satisfy completely the desire internal to its own nature. In order to achieve utterly comprehensive knowledge it would have to lose its relational nature ('commit suicide') and thus become an *immediate*, supra-relational, mode of cognition in an utterly harmonious identity with the ultimate logical subject of its relational predications (i.e. with reality).

Of course, as merely finite beings, we could not hope to know what such an all-comprehending, supra-relational, experience would be like or, even less, explain why or how it manifests itself in finite centres of experience (cf. e.g. *AR* 162, below, p. 169). But we can understand that it is only by the increasingly systematic exercise of relational thought that we can transcend the *lower* immediacy of animal sentience and achieve increasing harmony and satisfaction in the various sides of our lives as self-conscious beings (*ETR* 219–22, below pp. 312–13). Thus it is possible to conceive of our thought-impregnated, and space- and time-bound lives (1) as being capable of moving in thought and action towards the utterly harmonious, and *higher*, immediacy of experience constituting the Absolute and (2) at the same time as being, in metaphysical strictness, simply modes through which, under the forms of time and space, the Absolute realizes its all-embracing, and timeless, perfection.

G.S.

SECTION I

Appearance and Reality

Appearance and Reality was first published in 1893. In our Introduction we have attempted to describe in outline the structure of Bradley's metaphysical argument and we have selected texts to exemplify that structure. As a result we have had to omit much of considerable interest and much for which Bradley is well known. We have not included from book I of *Appearance and Reality* any of those chapters in which Bradley illustrates in detail how linguistically communicable thought, as exercised in relation to space and time, motion, causation, activity, and the self, leads to contradictions. Nor, on the other hand, have we included (except for Ch. 7, 'Error') any of those chapters from book II in which Bradley demonstrates in detail that his metaphysical account of the ultimate nature of reality is compatible with the existence of the main categories of phenomena and with the facts of our everyday human experiences (e.g. with the existence of evil and goodness, temporal and spatial appearance, the particularity and egocentricity of our experiences, other people, nature as the object of natural science, and the distinction between body and soul).

G.S.

Metaphysics: Its Aim and Justification

We may agree, perhaps, to understand by metaphysics an [1] attempt to know reality as against mere appearance, or the study of first principles or ultimate truths, or again the effort to comprehend the universe, not simply piecemeal or by fragments, but somehow as a whole. . . .

The question . . . is not whether we are to reflect and ponder [3] on ultimate truth—for perhaps most of us do that, and are not likely to cease. The question is merely as to the way in which this should be done. And the claim of metaphysics is surely not unreasonable. Metaphysics takes its stand on this side of human nature, this desire to think about and comprehend reality. And it merely asserts that, if the attempt is to be made, it should be done as thoroughly as our nature permits. There is no claim on its part to supersede other functions of the human mind; but it protests that, if we are to think, we should sometimes try to think properly. And the opponent of metaphysics, it appears to me, is driven to a dilemma. He must either condemn all reflection on the essence of things—and, if so, he breaks, or, rather, tries to [4] break, with part of the highest side of human nature—or else he allows us to think, but not to think strictly. . . . I certainly do not suppose that it would be good for every one to study metaphysics, and I cannot express any opinion as to the number of persons who should do so. But I think it quite necessary, even on the view that this study can produce no positive results, that it should still be pursued. There is, so far as I can see, no other certain way of protecting ourselves against dogmatic superstition. Our orthodox theology on the one side, and our commonplace materialism on the other side (it is natural to take these as prominent instances), vanish like ghosts before the daylight of free sceptical inquiry. I do not mean, of course, to condemn

Repr. from *AR*, Introduction.

wholly either of these beliefs; but I am sure that either, when taken seriously, is the mutilation of our nature. Neither, as experience has amply shown, can now survive in the mind which has thought sincerely on first principles; and it seems desirable that there should be such a refuge for the man who burns to think consistently, and yet is too good to become a slave, either to [5] stupid fanaticism or dishonest sophistry. That is one reason why I think that metaphysics, even if it end in total scepticism, should be studied by a certain number of persons.

And there is a further reason which, with myself perhaps, has even more weight. All of us, I presume, more or less, are led beyond the region of ordinary facts. Some in one way and some in others, we seem to touch and have communion with what is beyond the visible world. In various manners we find something higher, which both supports and humbles, both chastens and transports us. And, with certain persons, the intellectual effort to understand the universe is a principal way of thus experiencing the Deity. No one, probably, who has not felt this, however differently he might describe it, has ever cared much for metaphysics. And, wherever it has been felt strongly, it has been its own justification. The man whose nature is such that by one path alone his chief desire will reach consummation, will try to find it on that path, whatever it may be, and whatever the world thinks of it; and, if he does not, he is contemptible. Self-sacrifice is too often the 'great sacrifice' of trade, the giving cheap what is worth nothing. To know what one wants, and to scruple at no means that will get it, may be a harder self-surrender. And this appears to be another reason for some persons pursuing the study of ultimate truth.

And that is why, lastly, existing philosophies cannot answer the purpose. For whether there is progress or not, at all events there is change; and the changed minds of each generation will require a difference in what has to satisfy their intellect. Hence there seems as much reason for new philosophy as there is for new poetry. In each case the fresh production is usually much inferior to something already in existence; and yet it answers a purpose if it appeals more personally to the reader. What is really worse may serve better to promote, in certain respects and in a certain generation, the exercise of our best functions. And that is why, so long as we alter, we shall always want, and shall always have, new metaphysics. . . .

2

Substantive and Adjective

We find the world's contents grouped into things and their quali- [16] ties. The substantive and adjective is a time-honoured distinction and arrangement of facts, with a view to understand them and to arrive at reality. I must briefly point out the failure of this method, if regarded as a serious attempt at theory.

We may take the familiar instance of a lump of sugar. This is a thing, and it has properties, adjectives which qualify it. It is, for example, white, and hard, and sweet. The sugar, we say, *is* all that; but what the *is* can really mean seems doubtful. A thing is not any one of its qualities, if you take that quality by itself; if 'sweet' were the same as 'simply sweet', the thing would clearly be not sweet. And, again, in so far as sugar is sweet it is not white or hard; for these properties are all distinct. Nor, again, can the thing be all its properties, if you take them each sever-ally. Sugar is obviously not mere whiteness, mere hardness, and mere sweetness; for its reality lies somehow in its unity. But if, on the other hand, we inquire what there can be in the thing beside its several qualities, we are baffled once more. We can discover no real unity existing outside these qualities, or, again, existing within them.

But it is our emphasis, perhaps, on the aspect of unity which has caused this confusion. Sugar is, of course, not the mere plu-rality of its different adjectives; but why should it be more than its properties in relation? When 'white', 'hard', 'sweet', and the rest coexist in a certain way, that is surely the secret of the thing. The qualities are, and are in relation. But here, as before, when we leave phrases we wander among puzzles. 'Sweet', 'white', and 'hard' seem now the subjects about which we are saying some- [17] thing. We certainly do not predicate one of the other; for, if we attempt to identify them, they at once resist. They are in this

Repr. from *AR*, ch. ii.

wholly incompatible, and, so far, quite contrary. Apparently, then, a relation is to be asserted of each. One quality, *A*, is in relation with another quality, *B*. But what are we to understand here by *is*? We do not mean that 'in relation with *B*' *is A*, and yet we assert that *A is* 'in relation with *B*'. In the same way *C* is called 'before *D*', and *E* is spoken of as *being* 'to the right of *F*'. We say all this, but from the interpretation, then 'before *D*' *is C*, and 'to the right of *F*' *is E*, we recoil in horror. No, we should reply, the relation is not identical with the thing. It is only a sort of attribute which inheres or belongs. The word to use, when we are pressed, should not be *is*, but only *has*. But this reply comes to very little. The whole question is evidently as to the meaning of *has*; and, apart from metaphors not taken seriously, there appears really to be no answer. And we seem unable to clear ourselves from the old dilemma, If you predicate what is *different*, you ascribe to the subject what it is *not*; and if you predicate what is *not* different, you say nothing at all.

Driven forward, we must attempt to modify our statement. We must assert the relation now, not of one term, but of both. *A* and *B* are identical in such a point, and in such another point they differ; or, again, they are so situated in space or in time. And thus we avoid *is*, and keep to *are*. But, seriously, that does not look like the explanation of a difficulty; it looks more like trifling with phrases. For, if you mean that *A* and *B*, taken each severally, even 'have' this relation, you are asserting what is false. But if you mean that *A* and *B* in such a relation are so related, you appear to mean nothing. For here, as before, if the predicate makes no difference, it is idle; but, if it makes the subject other than it is, it is false.

But let us attempt another exit from this bewildering circle. Let us abstain from making the relation an attribute of the related, [18] and let us make it more or less independent. 'There is a relation *C*, in which *A* and *B* stand; and it appears with both of them.' But here again we have made no progress. The relation *C* has been admitted different from *A* and *B*, and no longer is predicated of them. Something, however, seems to be said of this relation *C*, and said, again, of *A* and *B*. And this something is not to be the ascription of one to the other. If so, it would appear to be another relation, *D*, in which *C*, on one side, and, on the other side, *A* and *B*, stand. But such a makeshift leads at once to the infinite process. The new relation D can be predicated in no way of C, or of A and B; and hence we must have recourse to a fresh relation, E, which comes between D and whatever we had before. But this must lead to another, F; and so on, indefinitely. Thus the problem is not solved by taking relations as independently real. For, if so, the qualities and their relation fall entirely apart, and then we have said nothing. Or we have to make a new relation between the old relation and the terms; which, when it is made, does not help us. It either itself demands a new relation, and so on without end, or it leaves us where we were, entangled in difficulties.

The attempt to resolve the thing into properties, each a real thing, taken somehow together with independent relations, has proved an obvious failure. And we are forced to see, when we reflect, that a relation standing alongside of its terms is a delusion. If it is to be real, it must be so somehow at the expense of the terms, or, at least, must be something which appears in them or to which they belong. A relation between A and B implies really a substantial foundation within them. This foundation, if we say that A is like to B, is the identity X which holds these differences together. And so with space and time—everywhere there must be a whole embracing what is related, or there would be no differences and no relation. It seems as if a reality possessed differences, A and B, incompatible with one another and also with itself. And so in order, without contradiction, to retain its various properties, this whole consents to wear the form of relations between them. And this is why qualities are found to be [19] some incompatible and some compatible. They are all different, and, on the other hand, because belonging to one whole, are all forced to come together. And it is only where they come together distantly by the help of a relation, that they cease to conflict. On the other hand, where a thing fails to set up a relation between its properties, they are contrary at once. Thus colours and smells live together at peace in the reality; for the thing divides itself, and so leaves them merely side by side within itself. But colour collides with colour, because their special identity drives them together. And here again, if the identity becomes relational by help of space, they are outside one another, and are peaceful once more. The 'contrary', in short, consists of differences possessed by that which cannot find the relation which serves to couple them apart. It is marriage attempted without a *modus vivendi.* But where the whole, relaxing its unity, takes the form of an arrangement, there is co-existence with concord.

I have set out the above mainly because of the light which it throws upon the nature of the 'contrary'[a]. It affords no solution of our problem of inherence. It tells us how we are forced to arrange things in a certain manner, but it does not justify that arrangement. The thing avoids contradiction by its disappearance into relations, and by its admission of the adjectives to a standing of their own. But it avoids contradiction by a kind of suicide. It can give no rational account of the relations and the terms which it adopts, and it cannot recover the real unity, without which it is nothing. The whole device is a clear makeshift. It consists in saying to the outside world, 'I am the owner of these my adjectives', and to the properties, 'I am but a relation, which leaves you your liberty'. And to itself and for itself it is the futile pretence to have both characters at once. Such an arrangement may work, but the theoretical problem is not solved.

The immediate unity, in which facts come to us, has been broken up by experience, and later by reflection. The thing with its [20] adjectives is a device for enjoying at once both variety and concord. But the distinctions, once made, fall apart from the thing, and away from one another. And our attempt to understand their relations brought us round merely to a unity, which confesses itself a pretence, or else falls back upon the old undivided substance, which admits of no relations. We shall see the hopelessness of its dilemma more clearly when we have examined how relation stands to quality. But this demands another chapter.

I will, in conclusion, dispose very briefly of a possible suggestion. The distinctions taken in the thing are to be held only, it may be urged, as the ways in which *we* regard it. The thing itself maintains its unity, and the aspects of adjective and substantive are only *our* points of view. Hence they do no injury to the real. But this defence is futile, since the question is how without error we may think of reality. If then your collection of points of view is a defensible way of so thinking, by all means apply it to the thing, and make an end of our puzzle. Otherwise the thing, without the points of view, appears to have no character at all, and

---

[a] For contrary see 'Contradictory, and Contrary' repr. in Appendix, below.

they, without the thing, to possess no reality—even if they could be made compatible among themselves, the one with the other. In short, this distinction, drawn between the fact and our manner of regarding it, only serves to double the original confusion. There will now be an inconsistency in my mind as well as in the thing; and, far from helping, the one will but aggravate the other.

3

Relation and Quality

[21] It must have become evident that the problem, discussed in the last chapter, really turns on the respective natures of quality and relation. And the reader may have anticipated the conclusion we are now to reach. The arrangement of given facts into relations and qualities may be necessary in practice, but it is theoretically unintelligible. The reality, so characterized, is not true reality, but is appearance.

And it can hardly be maintained that this character calls for no understanding—that it is a unique way of being which the reality possesses, and which we have got merely to receive. For it most evidently has ceased to be something quite immediate. It contains aspects now distinguished and taken as differences, and which tend, so far as we see, to a further separation. And, if the reality really has a way of uniting these in harmony, that way assuredly is not manifest at first sight. On our own side those distinctions which even consciously we make may possibly in some way give the truth about reality. But, so long as we fail to justify them and to make them intelligible to ourselves, we are bound, so far, to set them down as mere appearance.

The object of this chapter is to show that the very essence of these ideas is infected and contradicts itself. Our conclusion briefly will be this. Relation presupposes quality, and quality relation. Each can be something neither together with, nor apart from, the other; and the vicious circle in which they turn is not the truth about reality.

1. Qualities are nothing without relations. In trying to exhibit the truth of this statement, I will lay no weight on a considerable mass of evidence. This, furnished by psychology, would attempt to show how qualities are variable by changes of relation. The differences we perceive in many cases seem to have been so cre-

Repr. from *AR*, ch. iii.

ated. But I will not appeal to such an argument, since I do not see [22]
that it could prove wholly the non-existence of original and independent qualities. And the line of proof through the necessity of
contrast for perception has, in my opinion, been carried beyond
logical limits. Hence, though these considerations have without
doubt an important bearing on our problem, I prefer here to disregard them. And I do not think that they are necessary.

We may proceed better to our conclusion in the following way.
You can never, we may argue, find qualities without relations.
Whenever you take them so, they are made so, and continue so,
by an operation which itself implies relation. Their plurality gets
for us all its meaning through relations; and to suppose it otherwise in reality is wholly indefensible. I will draw this out in
greater detail.

To find qualities without relations is surely impossible. In the
field of consciousness, even when we abstract from the relations
of identity and difference, they are never independent. One is
together with, and related to, one other, at the least—in fact,
always to more than one. Nor will an appeal to a lower and
undistinguished state of mind, where in one feeling are many
aspects, assist us in any way. I admit the existence of such states
without any relation, but I wholly deny there the presence of
qualities. For if these felt aspects, while merely felt, are to be
called qualities proper, they are so only for the observation of an
outside observer. And then for him they are given *as* aspects—
that is, together with relations. In short, if you go back to mere
unbroken feeling, you have no relations and no qualities. But if
you come to what is distinct, you get relations at once.

I presume we shall be answered in this way. Even though, we
shall be told, qualities proper cannot be discovered apart from
relations, that is no real disproof of their separate existence. For
we are well able to distinguish them and to consider them by
themselves. And for this perception certainly an operation of our
minds is required. So far, therefore, as you say, what is different
must be distinct, and, in consequence, related. But this relation [23]
does not really belong to the reality. The relation has existence
only for us, and as a way of our getting to know. But the distinction, for all that, is based upon differences in the actual; and
these remain when our relations have fallen away or have been
removed.

But such an answer depends on the separation of product from process, and this separation seems indefensible. The qualities, as distinct, are always made so by an action which is admitted to imply relation. They are made so, and, what is more, they are emphatically kept so. And you cannot ever get your product standing apart from its process. Will you say, the process is not essential? But that is a conclusion to be proved, and it is monstrous to assume it. Will you try to prove it by analogy? It is possible for many purposes to accept and employ the existence of processes and relations which do not affect specially the inner nature of objects. But the very possibility of so distinguishing in the end between inner and outer, and of setting up the inner as absolutely independent of all relation, is here in question. Mental operations such as comparison, which presuppose in the compared qualities already existing, could in no case prove that these qualities depend on no relations at all. But I cannot believe that this is a matter to be decided by analogy, for the whole case is briefly this. There is an operation which, removing one part of what is given, presents the other part in abstraction. This result is never to be found anywhere apart from a persisting abstraction. And, if we have no further information, I can find no excuse for setting up the result as being fact without the process. The burden lies wholly on the assertor, and he fails entirely to support it. The argument that in perception one quality must be given first and before others, and therefore cannot be relative, is hardly worth mentioning. What is more natural than for qualities always to have come to us in some conjunction, and never alone?

[24] We may go further. Not only is the ignoring of the process a thing quite indefensible—even if it blundered into truth—but there is evidence that it gives falsehood. For the result bears internally the character of the process. The manyness of the qualities cannot, in short, be reconciled with their simplicity. Their plurality depends on relation, and, without that relation, they are not distinct. But, if not distinct, then not different, and therefore not qualities.

I am not urging that quality without difference is in every sense impossible. For all I know, creatures may exist whose life consists, for themselves, in one unbroken simple feeling; and the arguments urged against such a possibility in my judgement come short. And, if you want to call this feeling a quality, by all means gratify your desire. But then remember that the whole point is quite irrelevant. For no one is contending whether the universe is or is not a quality in this sense; but the question is entirely as to qualities. And a universe confined to one feeling would not only not be qualities, but it would fail even to be one quality, as different from others and as distinct from relations. Our question is really whether relation is essential to differences.

We have seen that in fact the two are never found apart. We have seen that the separation by abstraction is no proof of real separateness. And now we have to urge, in short, that any separateness implies separation, and so relation, and is therefore, when made absolute, a self-discrepancy. For consider, the qualities *A* and *B* are to be different from each other; and, if so, that difference must fall somewhere. If it falls, in any degree or to any extent, outside *A* or *B*, we have relation at once. But, on the other hand, how can difference and otherness fall inside? If we have in *A* any such otherness, then inside *A* we must distinguish its own quality and its otherness. And if so, then the unsolved problem breaks out inside each quality, and separates each into two qualities in relation. In brief, diversity without relation seems a word without meaning. And it is no answer to urge that plurality proper is not in question here. I am convinced of the opposite, but by all means, if you will, let us confine ourselves to [25] distinctness and difference. I rest my argument upon this, that if there are no differences, there are no qualities, since all must fall into one. But, if there is any difference, then that implies a relation. Without a relation it has no meaning; it is a mere word, and not a thought; and no one would take it for a thought if he did not, in spite of his protests, import relation into it. And this is the point on which all seems to turn, Is it possible to think of qualities without thinking of distinct characters? Is it possible to think of these without some relation between them, either explicit, or else unconsciously supplied by the mind that tries only to apprehend? Have qualities without relation any meaning for thought? For myself, I am sure that they have none.

And I find a confirmation in the issue of the most thorough attempt to build a system on this ground. There it is not too much to say that all the content of the universe becomes something very like an impossible illusion. The Reals are secluded and simple, simple beyond belief if they never suspect that they are not so.[1] But our fruitful life, on the other hand, seems due to their persistence in imaginary recovery from unimaginable perversion. And they remain guiltless of all real share in these ambiguous connections, which seem to make the world. They are above it, and fixed like stars in the firmament—if there only were a firmament.

2. We have found that qualities, taken without relations, have no intelligible meaning. Unfortunately, taken together with them, they are equally unintelligible. They cannot, in the first place, be wholly resolved into the relations. You may urge, indeed, that without distinction no difference is left; but, for all that, the differences will not disappear into the distinction. They must come to it, more or less, and they cannot wholly be made by it. I still insist that for thought what is not relative is nothing. But I urge, on the other hand, that nothings cannot be related, and that to turn qualities in relation into mere relations is impossible. Since [26] the fact seems constituted by both, you may urge, if you please, that either one of them constitutes it. But if you mean that the other is not wanted, and that relations can somehow make the terms upon which they seem to stand, then, for my mind, your meaning is quite unintelligible. So far as I can see, relations must depend upon terms, just as much as terms upon relations. And the partial failure, now manifest, of the Dialectic Method seems connected with some misapprehension on this point.

Hence the qualities must be, and must *also* be related. But there is hence a diversity which falls inside each quality. Each has a double character, as both supporting and as being made by the relation. It may be taken as at once condition and result, and the question is as to how it can combine this variety. For it must combine the diversity, and yet it fails to do so. A is both made, and is not made, what it is by relation; and these different aspects are not each the other, nor again is either A. If we call its diverse aspects a and α, then A is partly each of these. As a it is the difference on which distinction is based, while as α it is the distinctness that results from connection. A is really both somehow together as A $(a—\alpha)$. But (as we saw in ['Substantive and Adjective' repr. above])[a] *without* the use of a relation it is impos-

---

[1] The Reals to which I am alluding here are Herbart's.

[a] Cf. the argument on pp. 119–23.

sible to predicate this variety of *A*. And, on the other hand, *with* an internal relation *A*'s unity disappears, and its contents are dissipated in an endless process of distinction. *A* at first becomes *a* in relation with α but these terms themselves fall hopelessly asunder. We have got, against our will, not a mere aspect, but a new quality *a*, which itself stands in a relation; and hence (as we saw before with *A*) its content must be manifold. As going into the relation it itself is a^2, and as resulting from the relation in itself is $α^2$. And it combines, and yet cannot combine, these adjectives. We, in brief, are led by a principle of fission which conducts us to no end. Every quality in relation has, in consequence, a diversity within its own nature, and this diversity cannot immediately be asserted of the quality. Hence the quality must exchange its unity for an internal relation. But, thus set free, the diverse [27] aspects, because each something in relation, must each be something also beyond. This diversity is fatal to the internal unity of each; and it demands a new relation, and so on without limit. In short, qualities in a relation have turned out as unintelligible as were qualities without one. The problem from both sides has baffled us.

3. We may briefly reach the same dilemma from the side of relations. They are nothing intelligible, either with or without their qualities. In the first place, a relation without terms seems mere verbiage; and terms appear, therefore, to be something beyond their relation. At least, for myself, a relation which somehow precipitates terms which were not there before, or a relation which can get on somehow without terms, and with no differences beyond the mere ends of a line of connection, is really a phrase without meaning. It is, to my mind, a false abstraction, and a thing which loudly contradicts itself; and I fear that I am obliged to leave the matter so. As I am left without information, and can discover with my own ears no trace of harmony, I am forced to conclude to a partial deafness in others. And hence a relation, we must say, without qualities is nothing.

But how the relation can stand to the qualities is, of the other side, unintelligible. If it is nothing to the qualities, then they are not related at all; and, if so, as we saw, they have ceased to be qualities, and their relation is a nonentity. But if it is to be something to them, then clearly we now shall require a *new* connecting relation. For the relation hardly can be the mere adjective of one

or both of its terms; or, at least, as such it seems indefensible.[2]
And, being something itself, if it does not itself bear a relation to
[28] the terms, in what intelligible way will it succeed in being anything to them? But here again we are hurried off into the eddy of
a hopeless process, since we are forced to go on finding new relations without end. The links are united by a link, and this bond
of union is a link which also has two ends; and these require
each a fresh link to connect them with the old. The problem is to
find how the relation can stand to its qualities; and this problem
is insoluble. If you take the connection as a solid thing, you have
got to show, and you cannot show, how the other solids are
joined to it. And, if you take it as a kind of medium or unsubstantial atmosphere, it is a connection no longer. You find, in
this case, that the whole question of the relation of the qualities
(for they certainly in some way *are* related) arises now outside it,
in precisely the same form as before. The original relation, in
short, has become a nonentity, but, in becoming this, it has
removed no element of the problem.

I will bring this chapter to an end. It would be easy, and yet
profitless, to spin out its argument with ramifications and
refinements. And for me to attempt to anticipate the reader's
objections would probably be useless. I have stated the case, and
I must leave it. The conclusion to which I am brought is that a
relational way of thought—any one that moves by the machinery
of terms and relations—must give appearance, and not truth. It
is a makeshift, a device, a mere practical compromise, most necessary, but in the end most indefensible. We have to take reality
as many, and to take it as one, and to avoid contradiction. We
want to divide it, or to take it, when we please, as indivisible; to
go as far as we desire in either of these directions, and to stop
when that suits us. And we succeed, but succeed merely by shut-
ting the eye, which if left open would condemn us; or by a perpetual oscillation and a shifting of the ground, so as to turn our
back upon the aspect we desire to ignore. But when these incon-

---

[2] The relation is not the adjective of one term, for, if so, it does not relate. Nor
for the same reason is it the adjective of each term taken apart, for then again
there is no relation between them. Nor is the relation their common property, for
then what keeps them apart? They are now not two terms at all, because not separate. And within this new whole, in any case, the problem of inherence would
break out in an aggravated form. But it seems unnecessary to work this all out in
detail.

sistencies are forced together, as in metaphysics they must be, the result is an open and staring discrepancy. And we cannot attribute this to reality; while, if we try to take it on ourselves, we have changed one evil for two. Our intellect, then, has been [29] condemned to confusion and bankruptcy, and the reality has been left outside uncomprehended. Or rather, what is worse, it has been stripped bare of all distinction and quality. It is left naked and without a character, and we are covered with confusion.

The reader who has followed and has grasped the principle of this chapter, will have little need to spend his time upon those which succeed it.[b] He will have seen that our experience, where relational, is not true; and he will have condemned, almost without a hearing, the great mass of phenomena. . . .

[b] Presumably Bradley intends this to apply simply to the chapters within book I of *AR*. The argument in book II, which yields a positive metaphysical conclusion, requires an additional principle.

4

The General Nature of Reality

[119] At the beginning of our inquiry into the nature of the real we encounter, of course, a general doubt or denial. To know the truth, we shall be told, is impossible, or is, at all events, wholly impracticable. We cannot have positive knowledge about first principles; and, if we could possess it, we should not know when actually we had got it. What is denied is, in short, the existence of a criterion. . . .

[120]   Is there an absolute criterion? This question, to my mind, is answered by a second question: How otherwise should we be able to say anything at all about appearance? For through the last Book, the reader will remember, we were for the most part criticizing. We were judging phenomena and were condemning them, and throughout we proceeded as if the self-contradictory could not be real. But this was surely to have and to apply an absolute criterion. For consider: you can scarcely propose to be quite passive when presented with statements about reality. You can hardly take the position of admitting any and every nonsense to be truth, truth absolute and entire, at least so far as you know. For, if you think at all so as to discriminate between truth and falsehood, you will find that you cannot accept open self-contradiction. Hence to think is to judge, and to judge is to criticize, and to criticize is to use a criterion of reality. And surely to doubt this would be mere blindness or confused self-deception. But, if so, it is clear that, in rejecting the inconsistent as appearance, we are applying a positive knowledge of the ultimate nature of things. Ultimate reality is such that it does not contradict itself; here is an absolute criterion. And it is proved absolute by the fact that, either in endeavouring to deny it, or even in attempting to doubt it, we tacitly assume its validity.

One of these essays in delusion may be noticed briefly in pass-

Repr. from *AR*, ch. xiii.

ing. We may be told that our criterion has been developed by experience, and that therefore at least it may not be absolute. But why anything should be weaker for having been developed is, in the first place, not obvious. And, in the second place, the whole doubt, when understood, destroys itself. For the alleged origin of our criterion is delivered to us by knowledge which rests throughout on its application as an absolute test. And what can be more irrational than to try to prove that a principle is doubtful, when the proof through every step rests on its unconditional truth? It would, of course, not be irrational to take one's stand on this cri- [121] terion, to use it to produce a conclusion hostile to itself, and to urge that therefore our whole knowledge is self-destructive, since it essentially drives us to what we cannot accept. But this is not the result which our supposed objector has in view, or would welcome. He makes no attempt to show in general that a psychological growth is in any way hostile to metaphysical validity. And he is not prepared to give up his own psychological knowledge, which knowledge plainly is ruined if the criterion is *not* absolute. The doubt is seen, when we reflect, to be founded on that which it endeavours to question. And it has but blindly borne witness to the absolute certainty of our knowledge about reality.

Thus we possess a criterion, and our criterion is supreme. I do not mean to deny that we might have several standards, giving us sundry pieces of information about the nature of things. But, be that as it may, we still have an over-ruling test of truth, and the various standards (if they exist) are certainly subordinate. This at once becomes evident, for we cannot refuse to bring such standards together, and to ask if they agree. Or, at least, if a doubt is suggested as to their consistency, each with itself and with the rest, we are compelled, so to speak, to assume jurisdiction. And if they were guilty of self-contradiction, when examined or compared, we should condemn them as appearance. But we could not do that if they were not subject to one tribunal. And hence, as we find nothing not subordinate to the test of self-consistency, we are forced to set that down as supreme and absolute.

But it may be said that this supplies us with no real information. If we think, then certainly we are not allowed to be inconsistent, and it is admitted that this test is unconditional and absolute. But it will be urged that, for knowledge about any matter, we require something more than a bare negation. The ultimate reality (we are agreed) does not permit self-contradiction, but a prohibition or an absence (we shall be told) by itself [122] does not amount to positive knowledge. The denial of inconsistency, therefore, does not predicate any positive quality. But such an objection is untenable. It may go so far as to assert that a bare denial is possible, that we may reject a predicate though we stand on no positive basis, and though there is nothing special which serves to reject. This error has been refuted in my *Principles of Logic*[a] and I do not propose to discuss it here. I will pass to another sense in which the objection may seem more plausible. The criterion, it may be urged, in itself is doubtless positive; but, for our knowledge and in effect, is merely negative. And it gives us therefore no information at all about reality, for, although knowledge is there, it cannot be brought out. The criterion is a basis, which serves as the foundation of denial; but, since this basis cannot be exposed, we are but able to stand on it and unable to see it. And it hence, in effect, tells us nothing, though there are assertions which it does not allow us to venture on. This objection, when stated in such a form, may seem plausible, and there is a sense in which I am prepared to admit that it is valid. If by the nature of reality we understand its full nature, I am not contending that this in a complete form is knowable. But that is very far from being the point here at issue. For the objection denies that we have a standard which gives *any* positive knowledge, *any* information, complete or incomplete, about the genuine reality. And this denial assuredly is mistaken.

The objection admits that we know what reality *does*, but it refuses to allow us any understanding of what reality *is*. The standard (it is agreed) both exists and possesses a positive character, and it is agreed that this character rejects inconsistency. It is admitted that we know this, and the point at issue is whether such knowledge supplies any positive information. And to my mind this question seems not hard to answer. For I cannot see how, when I observe a thing at work, I am to stand there and to [123] insist that I know nothing of its nature. I fail to perceive how a function is nothing at all, or how it does not positively qualify that to which I attribute it. To know only so much, I admit, may very possibly be useless; it may leave us without the information

---

[a] Cf. 'The Negative Judgement', repr. above, Part I, Ch. 3.

which we desire most to obtain; but, for all that, it is not total ignorance.

Our standard denies inconsistency, and therefore asserts consistency. If we can be sure that the inconsistent is unreal, we must, logically, be just as sure that the reality is consistent. The question is solely as to the meaning to be given to consistency. We have now seen that it is not the bare exclusion of discord, for that is merely our abstraction, and is otherwise nothing. And our result, so far, is this. Reality is known to possess a positive character, but this character is at present determined only as that which excludes contradiction.

But we may make a further advance. . . . [A]ll appearance must belong to reality. For what appears is, and whatever is cannot fall outside the real. And we may now combine this result with the conclusion just reached. We may say that everything, which appears, is somehow real in such a way as to be self-consistent. The character of the real is to possess everything phenomenal in a harmonious form.

I will repeat the same truth in other words. Reality is one in this sense that it has a positive nature exclusive of discord, a nature which must hold throughout everything that is to be real. Its diversity can be diverse only so far as not to clash, and what seems otherwise anywhere cannot be real. And, from the other side, everything which appears must be real. Appearance must belong to reality, and it must therefore be concordant and other than it seems. The bewildering mass of phenomenal diversity must hence somehow be at unity and self-consistent; for it cannot be elsewhere than in reality, and reality excludes discord. Or again we may put it so: the real is individual. It is one in the sense that its positive character embraces all differences in an inclusive harmony. And this knowledge, poor as it may be, is certainly more than bare negation or simple ignorance. So far as it [124] goes, it gives us positive news about absolute reality.

Let us try to carry this conclusion a step further on. We know that the real is one; but its oneness so far, is ambiguous. Is it one system, possessing diversity as an adjective; or is its consistency, on the other hand, an attribute of independent realities? We have to ask, in short, if a plurality of reals is possible, and if these can merely coexist so as not to be discrepant? Such a plurality would mean a number of beings not dependent on each other. On the one hand they would possess somehow the phenomenal diversity, for that possession, we have seen, is essential. And, on the other hand, they would be free from external disturbance and from inner discrepancy. After the inquiries of our First Book[b] the possibility of such reals hardly calls for discussion. For the internal states of each give rise to hopeless difficulties. And, in the second place, the plurality of the reals cannot be reconciled with their independence. I will briefly resume the arguments which force us to this latter result.

If the Many are supposed to be without internal quality, each would forthwith become nothing, and we must therefore take each as being internally somewhat. And, if they are to be plural, they must be a diversity somehow coexisting together. Any attempt again to take their togetherness as unessential seems to end in the unmeaning. We have no knowledge of a plural diversity, nor can we attach any sense to it, if we do not have it somehow as one. And, if we abstract from this unity, we have also therewith abstracted from the plurality, and are left with mere being.

Can we then have a plurality of independent reals which merely coexist? No, for absolute independence and coexistence are incompatible. Absolute independence is an idea which consists merely in one-sided abstraction. It is made by an attempted division of the aspect of several existence from the aspect of relatedness; and these aspects, whether in fact or thought, are really indivisible.

[125] If we take the diversity of our reals to be such as we discover in feeling and at a stage where relations do not exist, that diversity is never found except as one integral character of an undivided whole. And if we forcibly abstract from that unity, then together with feeling we have destroyed the diversity of feeling. We are left not with plurality, but with mere being, or, if you prefer it, with nothing. Coexistence in feeling is hence an instance and a proof not of self-sufficiency, but of dependence, and beside this it would add a further difficulty. If the nature of our reals is the diversity found at a stage below relations, how are we to dispose of the mass of relational appearance? For that exists, and

---

[b] Cf. 'Substantive and Adjective' and 'Relation and Quality', repr. above, Part II, Sect. 1, Chs. 2 and 3.

existing it must somehow qualify the world, a world the reality of which is discovered only at a level other than its own. Such a position would seem not easy to justify.

Thus a mode of togetherness such as we can verify in feeling destroys the independence of our reals. And they will fare no better if we seek to find their coexistence elsewhere. For any other verifiable way of togetherness must involve relations, and they are fatal to self-sufficiency. Relations, we saw, are a development of and from the felt totality. They inadequately express, and they still imply in the background that unity apart from which the diversity is nothing. Relations are unmeaning except within and on the basis of a substantial whole, and related terms, if made absolute, are forthwith destroyed. Plurality and relatedness are but features and aspects of a unity.

If the relations in which the reals somehow stand are viewed as essential, that, as soon as we understand it, involves at once the internal relativity of the reals. And any attempt to maintain the relations as merely external must fail. For if, wrongly and for argument's sake, we admit processes and arrangements which do not qualify their terms, yet such arrangements, if admitted, are at any rate not ultimate. The terms would be prior and independent only with regard to *these* arrangements, and they would remain relative otherwise, and vitally dependent on some whole. And severed from this unity, the terms perish by the very stroke which aims to set them up as absolute. [126]

The reals therefore cannot be self-existent, and, if self-existent, yet taken as the world they would end in inconsistency. For the relations, because they exist, must somehow qualify the world. The relations then must externally qualify the sole and self-contained reality, and that seems self-contradictory or meaningless.[1] and if it is urged that a plurality of independent beings may be unintelligible, but that after all some unintelligible facts must be

---

[1] To this brief statement we might add other fatal objections. There is the question of the reals' interaction and of the general order of the world. Here, whether we affirm or deny, we turn in a maze. The fact of knowledge plunges us again in a dilemma. If we do not know that the Many are, we cannot affirm them. But the knowledge of the Many seems compatible with the self-existence neither of what knows nor of what is known. Finally, if the relations are admitted to an existence somehow alongside of the reals, the sole reality of the reals is given up. The relations themselves have now become a second kind of real thing. But the connection between these new reals and the old ones, whether we deny or affirm it, leads to insoluble problems.

affirmed—the answer is obvious. An unintelligible fact may be admitted so far as, first, it is a fact, and so far as, secondly, it has a meaning which does not contradict itself internally or make self-discrepant our view of the world. But the alleged independence of the reals is no fact, but a theoretical construction; and, so far as it has a meaning, that meaning contradicts itself, and issues in chaos. A reality of this kind may safely be taken as unreal.

We cannot therefore maintain a plurality save as dependent on the relations in which it stands. Or if desiring to avoid relations we fall back on the diversity given in feeling, the result is the same. The plurality then sinks to become merely an integral aspect in a single substantial unity, and the reals have vanished.

5

The General Nature of Reality (cont.)

Our result so far is this. Everything phenomenal is somehow real; and the absolute must at least be as rich as the relative. And, further, the Absolute is not many; there are no independent reals. The universe is one in this sense that its differences exist harmoniously within one whole, beyond which there is nothing. Hence the Absolute is, so far, an individual and a system, but, if we stop here, it remains but formal and abstract. Can we then, the question is, say anything about the concrete nature of the system?

Certainly, I think, this is possible. When we ask as to the matter which fills up the empty outline, we can reply in one word, that this matter is experience. And experience means something much the same as given and present fact. We perceive, on reflection, that to be real, or even barely to exist, must be to fall within sentience. Sentient experience, in short, is reality, and what is not this is not real. We may say, in other words, that there is no being or fact outside of that which is commonly called psychical existence. Feeling, thought, and volition (any groups under which we class psychical phenomena) are all the material of existence, and there is no other material, actual or even possible. This result in its general form seems evident at once; and, however serious a step we now seem to have taken, there would be no advantage at this point in discussing it at length. For the test in the main lies ready to our hand, and the decision rests on the manner in which it is applied. I will state the case briefly thus. Find any piece of existence, take up anything that any one could possibly call a fact, or could in any sense assert to have being, and then judge if it does not consist in sentient experience. Try to discover any sense in which you can still continue to speak of it, when all perception and

Repr. from *AR*, ch. xiv.

[128] feeling have been removed; or point out any fragment of its matter, any aspect of its being, which is not derived from and is not still relative to this source. When the experiment is made strictly, I can myself conceive of nothing else than the experienced. Anything, in no sense felt or perceived, becomes to me quite unmeaning. And as I cannot try to think of it without realizing either that I am not thinking at all, or that I am thinking of it against my will as being experienced, I am driven to the conclusion that for me experience is the same as reality. The fact that falls elsewhere seems, in my mind, to be a mere word and a failure, or else an attempt at self-contradiction. It is a vicious abstraction whose existence is meaningless nonsense, and is therefore not possible.

This conclusion is open, of course, to grave objection, and must in its consequences give rise to serious difficulties. I will not attempt to anticipate the discussion of these, but before passing on, will try to obviate a dangerous mistake. For, in asserting that the real is nothing but experience, I may be understood to endorse a common error. I may be taken first to divide the percipient subject from the universe; and then, resting on that subject, as on a thing actual by itself, I may be supposed to urge that it cannot transcend its own states. Such an argument would lead to impossible results, and would stand on a foundation of faulty abstraction. To set up the subject as real independently of the whole, and to make the whole into experience in the sense of an adjective of that subject, seems to me indefensible. And when I contend that reality must be sentient, my conclusion almost consists in the denial of this fundamental error. For if, seeking for reality, we go to experience, what we certainly do *not* find is a subject or an object, or indeed any other thing whatever, standing separate and on its own bottom. What we discover rather is a whole in which distinctions can be made, but in which divisions do not exist. And this is the point on which I insist, and it is the very ground on which I stand, when I urge that reality is sentient experience. I mean that to be real is to be indissolubly one thing with sentience. It is to be something which comes as a feature [129] and aspect within one whole of feeling, something which, except as an integral element of such sentience, has no meaning at all. And what I repudiate is the separation of feeling from the felt, or of the desired from desire, or of what is thought from thinking, or the division—I might add—of anything from anything else. Nothing is ever so presented as real by itself, or can be argued so to exist without demonstrable fallacy. And in asserting that the reality is experience, I rest throughout on this foundation. You cannot find fact unless in unity with sentience, and one cannot in the end be divided from the other, either actually or in idea. But to be utterly indivisible from feeling or perception, to be an integral element in a whole which is experienced, this surely is itself to *be* experience. Being and reality are, in brief, one thing with sentience; they can neither be opposed to, nor even in the end distinguished from it.

I am well aware that this statement stands in need of explanation and defence. This will, I hope, be supplied by succeeding chapters, and I think it better for the present to attempt to go forward. Our conclusion, so far, will be this, that the Absolute is one system, and that its contents are nothing but sentient experience. It will hence be a single and all-inclusive experience, which embraces every partial diversity in concord. For it cannot be less than appearance, and hence no feeling or thought, of any kind, can fall outside its limits. And if it is more than any feeling or thought which we know, it must still remain more of the same nature. It cannot pass into another region beyond what falls under the general head of sentience. For to assert that possibility would be in the end to use words without a meaning. We can entertain no such suggestion except as self-contradictory, and as therefore impossible.

This conclusion will, I trust, at the end of my work bring more conviction to the reader; for we shall find that it is the one view which will harmonize all facts. And the objections brought against it, when it and they are once properly defined, will prove untenable. But our general result is at present seriously defective; [130] and we must now attempt to indicate and remedy its failure in principle.

What we have secured, up to this point, may be called mere theoretical consistency. The Absolute holds all possible content in an individual experience where no contradiction can remain. And it seems, at first sight, as if this theoretical perfection could exist together with practical defect and misery. For apparently, so far as we have gone, an experience might be harmonious, in such a

way at least as not to contradict itself, and yet might result on
the whole in a balance of suffering. Now no one can genuinely
believe that sheer misery, however self-consistent, is good and
desirable. And the question is whether in this way our conclusion
is wrecked.

There may be those possibly who here would join issue at
once. They might perhaps wish to contend that the objection is
irrelevant, since pain is no evil. I shall discuss the general question of good and evil in a subsequent chapter, and will merely
say here that for myself I cannot stand upon the ground that
pain is no evil. I admit, or rather I would assert, that a result, if
it fails to satisfy our whole nature, comes short of perfection.
And I could not rest tranquilly in a truth if I were compelled to
regard it as hateful. While unable, that is, to deny it, I should,
rightly or wrongly, insist that the inquiry was not yet closed, and
that the result was but partial. And if metaphysics is to stand, it
must, I think, take account of all sides of our being. I do not
mean that every one of our desires must be met by a promise of
particular satisfaction; for that would be absurd and utterly
impossible. But if the main tendencies of our nature do not reach
consummation in the Absolute, we cannot believe that we have
attained to perfection and truth. And we shall have to consider
later on what desires must be taken as radical and fundamental.
But here we have seen that our conclusion, so far, has a serious
defect, and the question is whether this defect can be directly
remedied. We have been resting on the theoretical standard
[131]   which guarantees that Reality is a self-consistent system. Have
we a practical standard which now can assure us that this system
will satisfy our desire for perfect good? An affirmative answer
seems plausible, but I do not think it would be true. Without any
doubt we possess a practical standard; but that does not seem to
me to yield a conclusion about reality, or it will not give us at
least directly the result we are seeking. I will attempt briefly to
explain in what way it comes short.

That a practical end and criterion exists I shall assume, and
I will deal with its nature more fully hereafter. . . . I may say
for the present that, taken in the abstract, the practical standard
seems to be the same as what is used for theory. It is individuality, the harmonious or consistent existence of our contents; an
existence, further, which cannot be limited, because, if so, it

would contradict itself internally (Chapters xx and xxiv[a]). Nor need I separate myself at this stage from the intelligent Hedonist, since, in my judgement, practical perfection will carry a balance of pleasure. These points I shall have to discuss, and for the present am content to assume them provisionally and vaguely. Now taking the practical end as individuality, or as clear pleasure, or rather as both in one, the question is whether this end is known to be realized in the Absolute, and, if so, upon what foundation such knowledge can rest. It apparently cannot be drawn directly from the theoretical criterion, and the question is whether the practical standard can supply it. I will explain why I believe that this cannot be the case.

I will first deal briefly with the 'ontological' argument. The essential nature of this will, I hope, be more clear to us hereafter (Chapter xxiv[b]) and I will here merely point out why it fails to give us help. This argument might be stated in several forms, but the main point is very simple. We have the idea of perfection— there is no doubt as to that—and the question is whether perfection also actually exists. Now the ontological view urges that the fact of the idea proves the fact of the reality; or, to put it otherwise, it argues that, unless perfection existed, you could not have it in idea, which is agreed to be the case. I shall not discuss at [132] present the general validity of this argument, but will confine myself to denying its applicability. For, if an idea has been manufactured and is composed of elements taken up from more than one source, then the result of manufacture need not as a whole exist out of my thought, however much that is the case with its separate elements. Thus we might admit that, in one sense, perfection or completeness would not be present in idea unless also it were real. We might admit this, and yet we might deny the same conclusion with respect to *practical* perfection. For the perfection that is real might simply be theoretical. It might mean system so far as system is mere theoretical harmony and does *not* imply pleasure. And the element of pleasure, taken up from elsewhere, may then have been added in our minds to this valid idea. But, if so, the addition may be incongrous, incompatible, and really, if we knew it, contradictory. Pleasure and system perhaps are in truth a false compound, an appearance which exists, as

[a] Repr. below, Part II, Sect. 1, Chs. 8 and 9.
[b] Not repr. in this volume.

such, only in our heads; just as would be the case if we thought, for example, of a perfect finite being. Hence the ontological argument cannot prove the existence of practical perfection;[1] and let us go on to inquire if any other proof exists.

It is in some ways natural to suppose that the practical end somehow postulates its existence as a fact. But a more careful examination tends to dissipate this idea. The moral end, it is clear, is not pronounced by morality to have actual existence. This is quite plain, and it would be easier to contend that morality even postulates the opposite. Certainly, as we shall perceive hereafter, the religious consciousness does imply the reality of that object, which also is its goal. But a religion whose object is perfect will be founded on inconsistency, even more than is the case with mere morality. For such a religion, if it implies the existence of its ideal, implies at the same time a feature which is [133] quite incompatible. This we shall discuss in a later chapter, and all that I will urge here is that the religious consciousness cannot prove that perfection really exists. For it is not true that in all religions the object is perfection; nor, where it is so, does religion possess any right to dictate to or to dominate over thought. It does not follow that a belief must be admitted to be true, because, given a certain influence, it is practically irresistible. There is a tendency in religion to take the ideal as existing; and this tendency sways our minds and, under certain conditions, may amount to compulsion. But it does not, therefore, and merely for this reason, give us truth, and we may recall other experience which forces us to doubt. A man, for instance, may love a woman whom, when he soberly considers, he cannot think true, and yet, in the intoxication of her presence, may give up his whole mind to the suggestions of blind passion. But in all cases, that alone is really valid for the intellect, which in a calm moment the mere intellect is incapable of doubting. It is only that which for thought is compulsory and irresistible—only that which thought must assert in attempting to deny it—which is a valid foundation for metaphysical truth.

'But how', I may be asked, 'can you justify this superiority of the intellect, this predominance of thought? On what foundation,

---

[1] Notice that I do not distinguish as yet between 'existence' and 'reality' [i.e. between existence in a given world, e.g. in our real spatio-temporal series, and Reality construed as the ultimate subject of all judgement, true and false].

if on any, does such a despotism rest? For there seems no special force in the intellectual axiom if you regard it impartially. Nay, if you consider the question without bias, and if you reflect on the nature of axioms in general, you may be brought to a wholly different conclusion. For *all* axioms, as a matter of fact, are practical. They all depend upon the will. They none of them in the end can amount to more than the impulse to behave in a certain way. And they cannot express more than this impulse, together with the impossibility of satisfaction unless it is complied with. And hence, the intellect, far from possessing a right to predominate, is simply one instance and one symptom of practical compulsion. Or (to put the case more psychologically) the intellect is merely one result of the general working of pleasure and pain. It [134] is even subordinate, and therefore its attempt at despotism is founded on baseless pretensions.'

Now, apart from its dubious psychological setting, I can admit the general truth contained in this objection. The theoretical axiom is the statement of an impulse to act in a certain manner. When that impulse is not satisfied there ensues disquiet and movement in a certain direction, until such a character is given to the result as contents the impulse and produces rest. And the expression of this fundamental principle of action is what we call an axiom. Take, for example, the law of avoiding contradiction. When two elements will not remain quietly together but collide and struggle, we cannot rest satisfied with that state. Our impulse is to alter it, and, on the theoretical side, to bring the content to a shape where without collision the variety is thought as one. And this inability to rest otherwise, and this tendency to alter in a certain way and direction, is, when reflected on and made explicit, our axiom and our intellectual standard.

'But is not this', I may be asked further, 'a surrender of your position? Does not this admit that the criterion used for theory is merely a practical impulse, a tendency to movement from one side of our being? And, if so, how can the intellectual standard be predominant?' But it is necessary here to distinguish. The whole question turns on the difference between the several impulses of our being. You may call the intellect, if you like, a mere tendency to movement, but you must remember that it is a movement of a very special kind. I shall enter more fully into the nature of thinking hereafter, but the crucial point may be stated at once. In thought the standard, you may say, amounts merely to 'act so'; but then 'act so' means 'think so', and 'think so' means 'it is'. And the psychological origin and base of this movement, and of this inability to act otherwise, may be anything you please; for that is all utterly irrelevant to the metaphysical issue. Thinking is the attempt to satisfy a special impulse, and the attempt implies an assumption about reality. You may avoid the assumption so far as you decline to think, but, if you sit down to the game, there is only one way of playing. In order to think at all you must subject yourself to a standard, a standard which implies an absolute knowledge of reality; and while you doubt this, you accept it, and obey while you rebel. You may urge that thought, after all, is inconsistent, because appearance is not got rid of but merely shelved. That is another question which will engage us in a future chapter, and here may be dismissed. For in any case thinking means the acceptance of a certain standard, and that standard, in any case, is an assumption as to the character of reality.

[135]

'But why', it may be objected, 'is this assumption better than what holds for practice? Why is the theoretical to be superior to the practical end?' I have never said that this is so. Only here, that is in metaphysics, I must be allowed to reply, we are acting theoretically. We are occupied specially, and are therefore subject to special conditions; and the theoretical standard within theory must surely be absolute. We have no right to listen to morality when it rushes in blindly. 'Act so,' urges morality, that is *'be* so or be dissatisfied'. But if I am dissatisfied, still apparently I may be none the less real. 'Act so,' replies speculation, that is, *'think* so or be dissatisfied; and if you do not think so, what you think is certainly not real.' And these two commands do not seem to be directly connected. If I am theoretically not satisfied, then what appears must in reality be otherwise; but, if I am dissatisfied practically, the same conclusion does not hold. Thus the two satisfactions are not the same, nor does there appear to be a straight way from the one to the other. Or consider again the same question from a different side. Morality seemed anxious to dictate to metaphysics, but is it prepared to accept a corresponding dictation? If it were to hear that the real world is quite other than its ideal, and if it were unable theoretically to shake this result, would morality acquiesce? Would it not, on the other hand, regardless of this, still maintain its own ground? Facts may *be* as you say, but none the less they should not be so, and something else *ought* to be. Morality, I think, would take this line, [136] and, if so, it should accept a like attitude in theory. It must not dictate as to what facts are, while it refuses to admit dictation as to what they should be.

Certainly, to any one who believes in the unity of our nature, a one-sided satisfaction will remain incredible. And such a consideration to my mind carries very great weight. But to stand on one side of our nature, and to argue from that directly to the other side, seems illegitimate. I will not here ask how far morality is consistent with itself in demanding complete harmony . . . What seems clear is that, in wishing to dictate to mere theory, it is abandoning its own position and is courting foreign occupation. And it is misled mainly by a failure to observe essential distinctions. 'Be so' does not mean always 'think so', and 'think so', in its main signification, certainly does not mean 'be so'. Their difference is the difference between 'you ought' and 'it is'—and I can see no direct road from the one to the other. If a theory could be made by the will, that would have to satisfy the will, and, if it did not, it would be false. But since metaphysics is mere theory, and since theory from its nature must be made by the intellect, it is here the intellect alone which has to be satisfied. Doubtless a conclusion which fails to content all the sides of my nature leaves *me* dissatisfied. But I see no direct way of passing from 'this does not satisfy my nature' to 'therefore it is false'. For false is the same as theoretically untenable, and we are supposing a case where mere theory has been satisfied, and where the result has in consequence been taken as true. And, so far as I see, we must admit that, *if* the intellect is contented, the question is settled. For we may feel as we please about the intellectual conclusion, but we cannot, on such external ground, protest that it is false.

Hence if we understand by perfection a state of harmony with pleasure, there is no direct way of showing that reality is perfect. For, so far as the intellectual standard at present seems to go, we might have harmony with pain and with partial dissatisfaction. [137] But I think the case is much altered when we consider it otherwise, and when we ask if on another ground such harmony is possible. The intellect is not to be dictated to; that conclusion is irrefragable. But is it certain, on the other hand, that the mere intellect can be self-satisfied, if other elements of our nature remain not contented? Or must we not think rather that indirectly any partial discontent will bring unrest and imperfection into the intellect itself? If this is so, then to suppose any imperfection in the Absolute is inadmissible. To fail in any way would introduce a discord into perception itself. And hence, since we have found that, taken perceptively, reality is harmonious, it must be harmonious altogether, and must satisfy our whole nature. Let us see if on this line we can make an advance.

If the Absolute is to be theoretically harmonious, its elements must not collide. Idea must not disagree with sensation, nor must sensations clash. In every case, that is, the struggle must not be a mere struggle. There must be a unity which it subserves, and a whole, taken in which it is a struggle no longer. How this resolution is possible we may be able to see partly in our subsequent chapters, but for the present I would insist merely that somehow it must exist. Since reality is harmonious, the struggle of diverse elements, sensations or ideas, barely to qualify the self-same point must be precluded. But, if idea must not clash with sensation, then there cannot in the Absolute be unsatisfied desire or any practical unrest. For in these there is clearly an ideal element not concordant with presentation but struggling against it, and, if you remove this discordance, then with it all unsatisfied desire is gone. In order for such a desire, in even its lowest form, to persist, there must (so far as I can see) be an idea qualifying diversely a sensation and fixed for the moment in discord. And any such state is not compatible with theoretical harmony.

But this result perhaps has ignored an outstanding possibility. Unsatisfied desires might, as such, not exist in the Absolute, and [138] yet seemingly there might remain a clear balance of pain. For, in the first place, it is not proved that all pain must arise from an unresolved struggle; and it may be contended, in the second place, that possibly the discord might be resolved, and yet, so far as we know, the pain might remain. In a painful struggle it may be urged that the pain can be real, though the struggle is apparent. For we shall see, when we discuss error (Chapter xvi[c]) how

---

[c] Repr. below, Part II, Sect. 1, Ch. 7.

discordant elements may be neutralized in a wider complex. We shall find how, in that system, they can take on a different arrangement, and so result in harmony. And the question here as to unsatisfied desires will be this. Can they not be merged in a whole, so as to lose their character of discordance, and thus cease to be desires, while their pain none the less survives in reality? If so, that whole, after all, would be imperfect. For, while possessor of harmony, it still might be sunk in misery, or might suffer at least with a balance of pain. This objection is serious, and it calls for some discussion here. I shall have to deal with it once more in our concluding chapter.

I feel at this point our want of knowledge with regard to the conditions of pleasure and pain. It is a tenable view, one at least which can hardly be refuted, that pain is caused, or conditioned, by an unresolved collision. Now, if this really is the case, then, given harmony, a balance of pain is impossible. Pain, of course, is a fact, and no fact can be conjured away from the universe; but the question here is entirely as to a *balance* of pain. Now it is common experience that in mixed states pain may be neutralized by pleasure in such a way that the balance is decidedly pleasant. And hence it is possible that in the universe as a whole we may have a balance of pleasure, and in the total result no residue of pain. This is possible, and *if* an unresolved conflict and discord is essential to pain, it is much more than possible. Since the reality is harmonious, and since harmony excludes the conditions which are requisite for a balance of pain, that balance is impossible. I will urge this so far as to raise a very grave doubt. I question our [139] right even to suppose a state of pain in the Absolute.

And this doubt becomes more grave when we consider another point. When we pass from the conditions to the effects of painful feeling, we are on surer ground. For in our experience the result of pain is disquietude and unrest. Its main action is to set up change, and to prevent stability. There is authority, I am aware, for a different view, but, so far as I see, that view cannot be reconciled with facts. This effect of pain has here a most important bearing. Assume that in the Absolute there is a balance of pleasure, and all is consistent. For the pains can condition those processes which, as processes, disappear in the life of the whole; and these pains can be neutralized by an overplus of pleasure. But if you suppose, on the other hand, a balance of pain, the difficulty becomes at once insuperable. We have postulated a state of harmony, and, together with that, the very condition of instability and discord. We have in the Absolute, on one side, a state of things where the elements cannot jar, and where in particular idea does not conflict with presentation. But with pain on the other side we have introduced a main-spring of change and unrest, and we thus produce necessarily an idea not in harmony with existence. And this idea of a better and of a non-existing condition of things must directly destroy theoretical rest. But, if so, such an idea must be called impossible. There is no pain on the whole, and in the Absolute our whole nature must find satisfaction. For otherwise there is no theoretical harmony, and that harmony we saw must certainly exist. I shall ask in our last chapter if there is a way of avoiding this conclusion, but for the present we seem bound to accept it as true. We must not admit the possibility of an Absolute perfect in apprehension yet resting tranquilly in pain. The question as to actual evidence of defect in the universe will be discussed in Chapter xvii;[d] and our position so far is this. We cannot argue directly that all sides of our nature must be satisfied, but indirectly we are led to the same result. For we are forced to assume theoretical satisfaction; and [140] to suppose that existing one-sidedly, and together with practical discomfort, appears inadmissible. Such a state is a possibility which seems to contradict itself. It is a supposition to which, if we cannot find any ground in its favour, we have no right. For the present at least it is better to set it down as inconceivable.

And hence, for the present at least, we must believe that reality satisfies our whole being. Our main wants—for truth and life, and for beauty and goodness—must all find satisfaction. And we have seen that this consummation must somehow be experience, and be individual. Every element of the universe, sensation, feeling, thought and will, must be included within one comprehensive sentience. And the question which now occurs is whether really we have a positive idea of such sentience. Do we at all know what we mean when we say that it is actual?

Fully to realize the existence of the Absolute is for finite beings impossible. In order thus to know we should have to be, and

---

[d] Not repr. in this volume.

then *we* should not exist. This result is certain, and all attempts to avoid it are illusory. But then the whole question turns on the sense in which we are to understand 'knowing'. What is impossible is to construct absolute life in its detail, to have the specific experience in which it consists. But to gain an idea of its main features—an idea true so far as it goes, though abstract and incomplete—is a different endeavour. And it is a task, so far as I see, in which we may succeed. For these main features, to some extent, are within our own experience; and again the idea of their combination is, in the abstract, quite intelligible. And surely no more than this is wanted for a knowledge of the Absolute. It is a knowledge which of course differs enormously from the fact. But it is true, for all that, while it respects its own limits; and it seems fully attainable by the finite intellect.

I will end this chapter by briefly mentioning the sources of such knowledge. First, in mere feeling, or immediate presenta- [141] tion, we have the experience of a whole . . . This whole contains diversity, and, on the other hand, is not parted by relations. Such an experience, we must admit, is most imperfect and unstable, and its inconsistencies lead us at once to transcend it. Indeed, we hardly possess it as more than that which we are in the act of losing. But it serves to suggest to us the general idea of a total experience, where will and thought and feeling may all once more be one. Further, this same unity, felt below distinctions, shows itself later in a kind of hostility against them. We find it in the efforts made both by theory and practice, each to complete itself and so to pass into the other. And, again, the relational form, as we saw, pointed everywhere to a unity. It implies a substantial totality beyond relations and above them, a whole endeavouring without success to realize itself in their detail. Further, the ideas of goodness, and of the beautiful, suggest in different ways the same result. They more or less involve the experience of a whole beyond relations though full of diversity. Now, if we gather (as we can) such considerations into one, they will assuredly supply us with a positive idea. We gain from them the knowledge of a unity which transcends and yet contains every manifold appearance. They supply not an experience but an abstract idea, an idea which we make by uniting given elements. And the mode of union, once more in the abstract, is actually given. Thus we know what is meant by an experience, which embraces all divisions, and yet somehow possesses the direct nature of feeling. We can form the general idea of an absolute experience in which phenomenal distinctions are merged, a whole become immediate at a higher stage without losing any richness. Our complete inability to understand this concrete unity in detail is no good ground for our declining to entertain it. Such a ground would be irrational, and its principle could hardly everywhere be adhered to. But if we can realize at all the general features of the Absolute, if we can see that somehow they come together in a

[142] way known vaguely and in the abstract, our result is certain. Our conclusion, so far as it goes, is real knowledge of the Absolute, positive knowledge built on experience, and inevitable when we try to think consistently. We shall realize its nature more clearly when we have confronted it with a series of objections and difficulties. If our result will hold against them all, we shall be able to urge that in reason we are bound to think it true.

6

Thought and Reality

In the present chapter I will try to state briefly the main essence [143] of thought, and to justify its distinction from actual existence. It is only by misunderstanding that we find difficulty in taking thought to be something less than reality.

If we take up anything considered real, no matter what it is, we find in it two aspects. There are always two things we can say about it; and, if we cannot say both, we have not got reality. There is a 'what' and a 'that', an existence and a content, and the two are inseparable. That anything should be, and should yet be nothing in particular, or that a quality should not qualify and give a character to anything, is obviously impossible. If we try to get the 'that' by itself, we do not get it, for either we have it qualified, or else we fail utterly. If we try to get the 'what' by itself, we find at once that it is not all. It points to something beyond, and cannot exist by itself and as a bare adjective. Neither of these aspects, if you isolate it, can be taken as real, or indeed in that case is itself any longer. They are distinguishable only and are not divisible.

And yet thought seems essentially to consist in their division. For thought is clearly, to some extent at least, ideal. Without an idea there is no thinking, and an idea implies the separation of content from existence. It is a 'what' which, so far as it is a mere [144] idea, clearly *is* not, and if it also *were*, could, so far, not be called ideal. For ideality lies in the disjoining of quality from being. Hence the common view, which identifies image and idea, is fundamentally in error. For an image is a fact, just as real as any sensation; it merely a fact of another kind and it is not one whit more ideal. But an idea is any part of the content of a fact so far as that works out of immediate unity with its existence. And an idea's factual existence may consist in a sensation or

Repr. from *AR*, ch. xv.

perception, just as well as in an image. The main point and the essence is that some feature in the 'what' of a given fact should be alienated from its 'that' so far as to work beyond it, or at all events loose from it. Such a movement is ideality, and, where it is absent, there is nothing ideal.

We can understand this most clearly if we consider the nature of judgement, for there we find thought in its completed form. In judgement an idea is predicated of a reality. Now, in the first place, what is predicated is not a mental image. It is not a fact inside my head which the judgement wishes to attach to another fact outside. The predicate is a mere 'what', a mere feature of content, which is used to qualify further the 'that' of the subject. And this predicate is divorced from its psychical existence in my head, and is used without any regard to its being there. When I say 'this horse is a mammal', it is surely absurd to suppose that I am harnessing my mental state to the beast between the shafts. Judgement adds an adjective to reality, and this adjective is an idea, because it is a quality made loose from its own existence, and is working free from its implication with that. And, even when a fact is merely analysed—when the predicate appears not to go beyond its own subject, or to have been imported divorced from another fact outside—our account still holds good. For here obviously our synthesis is a reunion of the distinguished, and it implies a separation, which, though it is overridden, is never unmade. The predicate is a content which has been made loose from its own immediate existence and is used in divorce [145] from that first unity. And, again, as predicated, it is applied without regard to its own being as abstracted and in my head. If this were not so, there would be no judgement; for neither distinction nor predication would have taken place. But again, if it is so, then once more here we discover an idea.

And in the second place, when we turn to the subject of the judgement, we clearly find the other aspect, in other words, the 'that'. Just as in 'this horse is a mammal' the predicate was *not* a fact, so most assuredly the subject is an actual existence. And the same thing holds good with every judgement. No one ever *means* to assert about anything but reality, or to do anything but qualify a 'that' by a 'what'. And, without dwelling on a point which I have worked out elsewhere,[1] I will notice a source of possible

[1] *Principles of Logic*, book I [The General Nature of Judgement' and 'The

mistake. 'The subject, at all events,' I may be told, 'is in no case a *mere* "that". It is never bare reality, or existence without character.' And to this I fully assent. I agree that the subject which we *mean*—even before the judgement is complete, and while still we are holding its elements apart—is more than a mere 'that'. But then this is not the point. The point is whether with every judgement we do not find an aspect of existence, absent from the predicate but present in the subject, and whether in the synthesis of these aspects we have not got the essence of judgement. And for myself I see no way of avoiding this conclusion. Judgement is essentially the re-union of two sides, 'what' and 'that', provisionally estranged. But it is the alienation of these aspects in which thought's ideality consists.

Truth is the object of thinking, and the aim of truth is to qualify existence ideally. Its end, that is, is to give a character to reality in which it can rest. Truth is the predication of such content as, when predicated, is harmonious, and removes inconsistency and with it unrest. And because the given reality is never consistent, thought is compelled to take the road of indefinite expansion. If thought were successful, it would have a predicate consistent in itself and agreeing entirely with the subject. But, on the other hand, the predicate must be always ideal. It must, that is, be a 'what' not in unity with its own 'that', and therefore, in and by itself, devoid of existence. Hence, so far as in thought this alienation is not made good, thought can never be more than merely ideal. [146]

I shall very soon proceed to dwell on this last consideration, but will first of all call attention to a most important point. There exists a notion that ideality is something outside of facts, something imported into them, or imposed as a sort of layer above them; and we talk as if facts, when let alone, were in no sense ideal. But any such notion is illusory. For facts which are not ideal, and which show no looseness of content from existence, seem hardly actual. They would be found, if anywhere, in feelings without internal lapse, and with a content wholly single. But if we keep to fact which is given, this changes in our hands, and it compels us to perceive inconsistency of content. And then this content cannot be referred merely to its given 'that', but is

Categorical and Hypothetical Forms of Judgement', repr. above, Part I, Chs. 1 and 2].

forced beyond it, and is made to qualify something outside. But, if so, in the simplest change we have at once ideality—the use of content in separation from its actual existence. . . . For the content of the given is for ever relative to something not given, and the nature of its 'what' is hence essentially to transcend its 'that'. This we may call the ideality of the given finite. It is not manufactured by thought, but thought itself is its development and product. The essential nature of the finite is that everywhere, as it presents itself, its character should slide beyond the limits of its existence.

And truth, as we have seen, is the effort to heal this disease, as it were, homoeopathically. Thought has to accept, without reserve, the ideality of the 'given', its want of consistency and its self-transcendence. And by pushing this self-transcendence to the uttermost point, thought attempts to find there consummation and rest. The subject, on the one hand, is expanded until it is no [147] longer what is given. It becomes the whole universe, which presents itself and which appears in each given moment with but part of its reality. It grows into an all-inclusive whole, existing somewhere and somehow, if we only could perceive it. But on the other hand, in qualifying this reality, thought consents to a partial abnegation. It has to recognize the division of the 'what' from the 'that', and it cannot so join these aspects as to get rid of mere ideas and arrive at actual reality. For it is in and by ideas only that thought moves and has life. The content it applies to the reality has, as applied, no genuine existence. It is an adjective divorced from its 'that', and never in judgement, even when the judgement is complete, restored to solid unity. Thus the truth belongs to existence, but it does not as such exist. It is a character which indeed reality possesses, but a character which, as truth and as ideal, has been set loose from existence; and it is never rejoined to it in such a way as to come together singly and *make* fact. Hence, truth shows a dissection and never an actual life. Its predicate can never be equivalent to its subject. And if it became so, and if its adjectives could be at once self-consistent and re-welded to existence, it would not be truth any longer. It would have then passed into another and a higher reality.

And I will now deal with the misapprehension to which I referred, and the consideration of which may, I trust, help us forward.

There is an erroneous idea that, if reality is more than thought, thought itself is, at least, quite unable to say so. To assert the existence of anything in any sense beyond thought suggests, to some minds, the doctrine of the Thing-in-itself. And of the Thing-in-itself we know . . . that if it existed we could not know of it; and, again, so far as we know of it, we know that it does not exist. The attempt to apprehend this Other in succeeding would be suicide, and in suicide could not reach anything beyond total failure. Now, though I have urged this result, I wish to keep [148] it within rational limits, and I dissent wholly from the corollary that nothing more than thought exists. But to think of anything which can exist quite outside of thought I agree is impossible. If thought is one element in a whole, you cannot argue from this ground that the remainder of such a whole must stand apart and independent. From this ground, in short, you can make no inference to a Thing-in-itself. And there is no impossibility in thought's existing as an element, and no self-contradiction in its own judgement that it is less than the universe.

We have seen that anything real has two aspects, existence and character, and that thought always must work within this distinction. Thought, in its actual processes and results, cannot transcend the dualism of the 'that' and the 'what'. I do not mean that in no sense is thought beyond this dualism, or that thought is satisfied with it and has no desire for something better. But taking judgement to be completed thought, I mean that in no judgement are the subject and predicate the same. In every judgement the genuine subject is reality, which goes beyond the predicate and of which the predicate is an adjective. And I would urge first that, in desiring to transcend this distinction, thought is aiming at suicide. We have seen that in judgement we find always the distinction of fact and truth, of idea and reality. Truth and thought are not the thing itself, but are of it and about it. Thought predicates an ideal content of a subject, which idea is not the same as fact, for in it existence and meaning are necessarily divorced. And the subject, again, is neither the mere 'what' of the predicate, nor is it any other mere 'what'. Nor, even if it is proposed to take up a whole with both its aspects, and to predicate the ideal character of its own proper subject, will that proposal assist us. For if the subject is the same as the predicate, why trouble oneself to judge? But if it is not the same, then what is it, and how is it different? Either then there is no judgement at all, and but a pretence of thinking without thought, or there is a [149] judgement, but its subject is more than the predicate, and is a 'that' beyond a mere 'what'. The subject, I would repeat, is never *mere* reality, or bare existence without character. The subject, doubtless, has unspecified content which is not stated in the predicate. For judgement is the differentiation of a complex whole, and hence always is analysis and synthesis in one. It separates an element from, and restores it to, the concrete basis; and this basis of necessity is richer than the mere element by itself. But then this is not the question which concerns us here. That question is whether, in any judgement which really says anything, there is not in the subject an aspect of existence which is absent from the bare predicate. And it seems clear that this question must be answered in the affirmative. And if it is urged that the subject itself, being in thought, can therefore not fall beyond, I must ask for more accuracy; for 'partly beyond' appears compatible with 'partly within'. And, leaving prepositions to themselves, I must recall the real issue. For I do not deny that reality *is* an object of thought; I deny that it is barely and *merely* so. If you rest here on a distinction between thought and its object, that opens a further question to which I shall return (pp. 153-4[a]). But if you admit that in asserting reality to fall within thought, you meant that in reality there is nothing beyond what is made thought's object, your position is untenable. Reflect upon any judgement as long as you please, operate upon the subject of it to any extent which you desire, but then (when you have finished) make an actual judgement. And when that is made, see if you do not discover, beyond the content of your thought, a subject of which it is true, and which it does not comprehend. You will find that the object of thought in the end must be ideal, and that there is no idea which, as such, contains its own existence. The 'that' of the actual subject will for ever give a something which is not a mere idea, something which is different from any truth, something which makes such a difference to your thinking, that without it you have not even thought completely.

[150]   'But', it may be answered, 'the thought you speak of is thought that is not perfect. Where thought is perfect there is no discrep-

---

[a] See below, pp. 161-2.

ancy between subject and predicate. A harmonious system of content predicating itself, a subject self-conscious in that system of content, this is what thought should mean. And here the division of existence and character is quite healed up. If such completion is not actual, it is possible, and the possibility is enough.' But it is not even possible, I must persist, if it really is unmeaning. And once more I must urge the former dilemma. If there is no judgement, there is no thought; and if there is no difference, there is no judgement, nor any self-consciousness. But if, on the other hand, there is a difference, then the subject is beyond the predicated content.

Still a mere denial, I admit, is not quite satisfactory. Let us then suppose that the dualism inherent in thought has been transcended. Let us assume that existence is no longer different from truth, and let us see where this takes us. It takes us straight to thought's suicide. A system of content is going to swallow up our reality; but in our reality we have the fact of sensible experience, immediate presentation with its colouring of pleasure and pain. Now I presume there is no question of conjuring this fact away; but how it is to be exhibited as an element in a system of thought-content, is a problem not soluble. Thought is relational and discursive, and, if it ceases to be this, it commits suicide; and yet, if it remains thus, how does it contain immediate presentation? Let us suppose the impossible accomplished; let us imagine a harmonious system of ideal contents united by relations, and reflecting itself in self-conscious harmony. This is to be reality, all reality; and there is nothing outside it. The delights and pains of the flesh, the agonies and raptures of the soul, these are fragmentary meteors fallen from thought's harmonious system. But these burning experiences—how in any sense can they be mere pieces of thought's heaven? For, if the fall is real, there is a world outside thought's region, and, if the fall is apparent, then human error itself is not included there. Heaven, in brief, must either not be heaven, or else not all reality. Without a metaphor, feeling [151] belongs to perfect thought, or it does not. If it does not, there is at once a side of existence beyond thought. But if it does belong, then thought is different from thought discursive and relational. To make it include immediate experience, its character must be transformed. It must cease to predicate, it must get beyond mere relations, it must reach something other than truth. Thought, in a word, must have been absorbed into a fuller experience. Now such an experience may be called thought, if you choose to use that word. But if any one else prefers another term, such as feeling or will, he would be equally justified. For the result is a whole state which both includes and goes beyond each element; and to speak of it as simply one of them seems playing with phrases. For (I must repeat it) when thought begins to be more than relational, it ceases to be mere thinking. A basis, from which the relation is thrown out and into which it returns, is something not exhausted by that relation. It will, in short, be an existence which is not mere truth. Thus, in reaching a whole which can contain every aspect within it, thought must absorb what divides it from feeling and will. But when these all have come together, then, since none of them can perish, they must be merged in a whole in which they are harmonious. But that whole assuredly is not simply *one* of its aspects. And the question is *not* whether the universe is in any sense intelligible. The question is whether, if you thought it and understood it, there would be no difference left between your thought and the thing. And, supposing that to have happened, the question is then whether thought has not changed its nature.

Let us try to realize more distinctly what this supposed consummation would involve. Since both truth and fact are to be there, nothing must be lost, and in the Absolute we must keep every item of our experience. We cannot have less, but, on the other hand, we may have much more; and this more may so supplement the elements of our actual experience that in the whole they may become transformed. But to reach a mode of apprehen-
[152] sion, which is quite identical with reality, surely predicate and subject, and subject and object, and in short the whole relational form, must be merged. The Absolute does not want, I presume, to make eyes at itself in a mirror, or, like a squirrel in a cage, to revolve the circle of its perfections. Such processes must be dissolved in something not poorer but richer than themselves. And feeling and will must also be transmuted in this whole, into which thought has entered. Such a whole state would possess in a superior form that immediacy which we find (more or less) in feeling; and in this whole all divisions would be healed up. It would be experience entire, containing all elements in harmony.

Thought would be present as a higher intuition; will would be there where the ideal had become reality; and beauty and pleasure and feeling would live on in this total fulfilment. Every flame of passion, chaste or carnal, would still burn in the Absolute unquenched and unabridged, a note absorbed in the harmony of its higher bliss. We cannot imagine, I admit, how in detail this can be. But if truth and fact are to be one, then in some such way thought must reach its consummation. But in that consummation thought has certainly been so transformed, that to go on calling it thought seems indefensible.

I have tried to show first that, in the proper sense of thought, thought and fact are not the same. I have urged, in the second place, that, if their identity is worked out, thought ends in a reality which swallows up its character. I will ask next whether thought's advocates can find a barrier to their client's happy suicide.

They might urge, first, that our consummation is the Thing-in-itself, and that it makes thought know what essentially is not knowable. But this objection forgets that our whole is not anything but sentient experience. And it forgets that, even when we understand by 'thought' its strict discursive form, our reality does not exist apart from this. Emphatically the Absolute is nothing if taken apart from any single one of its elements. But the Thing-in-itself, on the other hand, must exist apart.

Let us pass to another objection against our view. We may be [153] told that the End, because it is that which thought aims at, is therefore itself (mere) thought. This assumes that thought cannot desire a consummation in which it is lost. But does not the river run into the sea, and the self lose itself in love? And further, as good a claim for predominance might be made on behalf of will, and again on behalf of beauty and sensation and pleasure. Where all elements reach their end in the Absolute, that end can belong to no one severally. We may illustrate this principle by the case of morality. That essentially desires an end which is not merely moral because it is super-moral. Nay, even personality itself, our whole individual life and striving, tends to something beyond mere personality. Of course, the Absolute has personality, but it fortunately possesses so much more, that to call it personal would be as absurd as to ask if it is moral.

But in self-consciousness, I may be told, we actually experience a state where truth and being are identical; and here, at all events, thinking is not different from reality. But . . . no such state exists. There is no self-consciousness in which the object is the same as the subject, none in which what is perceived exhausts the whole self. In self-consciousness a part or element, or again a general aspect or character, becomes distinct from the whole mass and stands over against the felt background. But the background is never exhausted by this object, and it never could be so. An experiment should convince any man that in self-consciousness what he feels cannot wholly come before him. It can be exhausted, if at all, only by a long series of observations, and the summed result of these observations cannot be experienced as a fact. Such a result cannot ever be verified as quite true at any particular given moment. In short consciousness implies discrimination of an element from the felt mass, and a consciousness that should discriminate every element at once is psychologically impossible. And this impossibility, if it became actual, would still leave us held in a dilemma. For there is either no difference, and therefore no distinction, and no consciousness; or there is a distinction, and therefore a difference between object and reality. But surely, if self-consciousness is appealed to, it is evident that at any moment I am more than the self which I can think of. How far everything in feeling may be called intelligible, is not the question here. But what is felt cannot be understood so that its truth and its existence become the same. And, if that were possible, yet such a process would certainly not be thinking.

[154]

In thinking the subject which thinks is more than thought. And that is why we can imagine that in thinking we find all reality. But in the same way the whole reality can as well be found in feeling or in volition. Each is one element in the whole, or the whole in one of its aspects; and hence, when you get an aspect or element, you have the whole with it. But because, given one aspect (whichever it may be), we find the whole universe, to conclude that in the universe there is nothing beyond this single aspect, seems quite irrational.

But the reader may agree that no one really can believe that mere thought includes everything. The difficulty lies, he may urge, in *maintaining* the opposite. Since in philosophy we must think, how is it possible to transcend thought without a self-contradiction? For theory can reflect on, and pronounce about, all things, and in reflecting on them it therefore includes them. So that to maintain in thought an Other is by the same act to destroy its otherness, and to persist is to contradict oneself. While admitting that thought cannot satisfy us as to reality's falling wholly within its limits, we may be told that, so long as we think, we must ignore this admission. And the question is, therefore, whether philosophy does not end in sheer scepticism—in the necessity, that is, of asserting what it is no less induced to deny. The problem is serious, and I will now attempt to exhibit its solution.

We maintain an Other than mere thought. Now in what sense do we hold this? Thought being a judgement, we say that the [155] predicate is never the same as the subject; for the subject is reality presented as 'this' (we must not say as *mere* 'this'). You can certainly abstract from presentation its character of 'thisness', or its confused relatedness; and you can also abstract the feature of presentation. Of these you can make ideas,[2] for there is nothing which you cannot think of. But you find that these ideas are not the same as the subject of which you must predicate them. You can think of the subject, but you cannot get rid of it, or substitute mere thought-content for it. In other words, in practice thought always is found with, and appears to demand, an Other.

Now the question is whether this leads to self-contradiction. If thought asserted the existence of any content which was not an actual or possible object of thought—certainly that assertion in my judgement would contradict itself. But the Other which I maintain, is not any such content, nor is it another separated 'what', nor in any case do I suggest that it lies outside intelligence. Everything, all will and feeling, is an object for thought, and must be called intelligible. This is certain; but, if so, what becomes of the Other? If we fall back on the mere 'that', thatness itself seems a distinction made by thought. And we have to face this difficulty: If the Other exists, it must be something; and if it is nothing, it certainly does not exist.

Let us take an actual judgement and examine the subject there with a view to find our Other. In this we at once meet with a complication. We always have more content in the presented

[2] *Principles of Logic*, [§§ 21–7, repr. above, Part I, Ch. 2].

subject than in the predicate, and it is hence harder to realize what, beside this overplus of content, the subject possesses. However, passing this by, we can find in the subject two special characters. There is first (*a*) sensuous infinitude, and (*b*) in the second place there is immediacy.

(*a*) The presented subject has a detail which is unlimited. By this I do not mean that the actual plurality of its features exceeds [156] a finite number. I mean that its detail always goes beyond itself, and is indefinitely relative to something outside.[3] In its given content it has relations which do not terminate within that content; and its existence therefore is not exhausted by itself, as we ever can have it. If I may use the metaphor, it has always edges which are ragged in such a way as to imply another existence from which it has been torn, and without which it really does not exist. Thus the content of the subject strives, we may say, unsuccessfully towards an all-inclusive whole. Now the predicate, on its side, is itself not free from endlessness. For its content, abstracted and finite, necessarily depends on relation to what is beyond. But it lacks the sensible and compulsory detail of the subject. It is not given as one thing with an actual but indefinite context. And thus, at least ostensibly, the predicate is hostile to endlessness.

(*b*) This is one difference, and the second consists in immediacy. The subject claims the character of a single self-subsistent being. In it the aspects of 'what' and 'that' are not taken as divorced, but it is given with its content as forming one integral whole. The 'what' is not sundered from the 'that', and turned from fact into truth. It is not predicated as the adjective of another 'that', or even of its own. And this character of immediacy is plainly not consistent with endlessness. They are, in truth, each an imperfect appearance of individuality. But the subject clearly possesses both these discrepant features, while the predicate no less clearly should be without them. For the predicate seeks also for individuality but by a different road.

Now, if we take the subject to have these two characters which are absent from the predicate, and if the desire of thought implies removal of that which makes predicate and subject differ—we

---

[3] This sensible 'infinite' is the same as the finite, which we just saw was in its essence 'ideal'.

begin to perceive the nature of our Other. And we may see at once what is required in order to extinguish its otherness. Subject and predicate alike must accept reformation. The ideal content of [157] the predicate must be made consistent with immediate individuality; and, on its side, the subject must be changed so as to become consistent with itself. It must become a self-subsistent, and that means an all-inclusive, individual. But these reforms are impossible. The subject must pass into the judgement, and it becomes infected with the relational form. The self-dependence and immediacy, which it claims, are not possessed by its content. Hence in the attempted self-assertion this content drives the subject beyond actual limits, and so begets a process which is infinite and cannot be exhausted. Thus thought's attempt wholly to absorb the subject must fail. It fails because it cannot reform the subject so as to include and exhaust its content. And, in the second place, thought fails because it cannot reform itself. For, if *per impossibile* the exhausted content were comprised within a predicate, that predicate still could not bear the character of immediacy. I will dwell for a little on both points.

Let us consider first the subject that is presented. It is a confused whole that, so far as we make it an object, passes into a congeries of qualities and relations. And thought desires to transform this congeries into a system. But, to understand the subject, we have at once to pass outside it in time, and again also in space. On the other hand these external relations do not end, and from their own nature they cannot end. Exhaustion is not merely impracticable, it is essentially impossible. And this obstacle would be enough; but this is not all. Inside the qualities, which we took first as solid end-points of the relations, an infinite process breaks out. In order to understand, we are forced to distinguish to the end, and we never get to that which is itself apart from distinction. Or we may put the difficulty otherwise thus. We can neither take the terms with their relations as a whole that is self-evident, that stands by itself, and that calls for no further account; nor, on the other side, when we distinguish, can we avoid the endless search for the relation between the relation and its terms.[4]

Thus thought cannot get the content into a harmonious [158]

---

[4] For this see ['Relation and Quality', repr. above, Part II, Sect. 1, Ch. 3].

system. And in the next place, even if it did so, that system would not *be* the subject. It would either be a maze of relations, a maze with a plan, of which for ever we made the circuit; or otherwise it would wholly lose the relational form. Our impossible process, in the first place, would assuredly have truth distinguished from its reality. For it could avoid this only by coming to us bodily and all at once, and, further, by suppressing entirely any distinction between subject and predicate. But, if in this way thought became immediate, it would lose its own character. It would be a system of relations no longer, but would have become an individual experience. And the Other would certainly have been absorbed, but thought itself no less would have been swallowed up and resolved into an Other.

Thought's relational content can never be the same as the subject, either as that subject appears or as it really is. The reality that is presented is taken up by thought in a form not adequate to its nature, and beyond which its nature must appear as an Other. But, to come at last in full view of the solution of our problem, this nature also is the nature which thought wants for itself. It is the character which even mere thinking desires to possess, and which in all its aspects exists within thought already, though in an incomplete form. And our main result is briefly this. The end, which would satisfy mere truth-seeking, would do so just because it had the features possessed by reality. It would have to be an immediate, self-dependent, all-inclusive individual. But, in reaching this perfection, and in the act of reaching it, thought would lose its own character. Thought does desire such individuality, that is precisely what it aims at. But individuality, on the other hand, cannot be gained while we are confined to relations.

Still we may be told that we are far from the solution of our problem. The fact of thought's desiring a foreign perfection, we may hear, is precisely the old difficulty. If thought desires this, [159] then it is no Other, for we desire only what we know. The object of thought's desire cannot, hence, be a foreign object; for what is an object is, therefore, *not* foreign. But we reply that we have penetrated below the surface of any such dilemma. Thought desires for its content the character which makes reality. These features, if realized, would destroy mere thought; and hence they are an Other beyond thought. But thought, nevertheless, can desire them, because its content has them already in an incomplete form. And in desire for the completion of what one has there is no contradiction. Here is the solution of our difficulty.

The relational form is a compromise on which thought stands, and which it develops. It is an attempt to unite differences which have broken out of the felt totality.[5] Differences forced together by an underlying identity, and a compromise between the plurality and the unity—this is the essence of relation. But the differences remain independent, for they cannot be made to resolve themselves into their own relation. For, if so, they would perish, and their relation would perish with them. Or, otherwise, their outstanding plurality would still remain unreconciled with their unity, and so within the relation would beget the infinite process. The relation, on the other side, does not exist beyond the terms; for, in that case, itself would be a new term which would aggravate the distraction. But again, it cannot lose itself within the terms; for, if so, where is their common unity and their relation? They would in this case not be related, but would fall apart. Thus the whole relational perception joins various characters. It has the feature of immediacy and self-dependence; for the terms are given to it and not constituted by it. It possesses again the character of plurality. And as representing the primitive felt whole, it has once more the character of a comprehending unity—a unity, however, not constituted by the differences, but added from without. And, even against its wish, it has further a restless infinitude; for such infinitude is the very result of its practical compromise. And thought desires, retaining these features, to reduce them to harmony. It aims at an all-[160] inclusive whole, not in conflict with its elements, and at elements subordinate to a self-dependent whole. Hence neither the aspect of unity, nor of plurality, nor of both these features in one, is really foreign to thought. There is nothing foreign that thought wants in desiring to be a whole, to comprehend everything, and yet to include and be superior to discord. But, on the other hand, such a completion, as we have seen, would prove destructive; such an end would emphatically make an end of mere thought. It would bring the ideal content into a form which would *be* reality itself, and where mere truth and mere thought would certainly

---

[5] For this see ['Relation and Quality', repr. above, Part II, Sect. 1, Ch. 3].

perish. Thought seeks to possess in its object that whole character of which it already owns the separate features. These features it cannot combine satisfactorily, though it has the idea, and even the partial experience, of their complete combination. And, if the object were made perfect, it would forthwith *become* reality, but would cease forthwith to be an object. It is this completion of thought beyond thought which remains for ever an Other. Thought can form the idea of an apprehension, something like feeling in directness, which contains all the character sought by its relational efforts. Thought can understand that, to reach its goal, it must get beyond relations. Yet in its nature it can find no other working means of progress. Hence it perceives that somehow this relational side of its nature must be merged and must include somehow the other side. Such a fusion would compel thought to lose and to transcend its proper self. And the nature of this fusion thought can apprehend in vague generality, but not in detail; and it can see the reason why a detailed apprehension is impossible. Such anticipated self-transcendence *is* an Other; but to assert that Other is *not* a self-contradiction.

Hence in our Absolute thought can find its Other without inconsistency. The entire reality will be merely the object thought out, but thought out in such a way that mere thinking is absorbed. This same reality will be feeling that is satisfied completely. In its direct experience we get restored with interest every feature lost by the disruption of our primitive felt whole. We possess the immediacy and the strength of simple apprehension, no longer forced by its own inconsistencies to pass into the infinite process. And again volition, if willed out, becomes our Absolute. For we reach there the identity of idea and reality, not too poor but too rich for division of its elements. Feeling, thought, and volition have all defects which suggest something higher. But in that higher unity no fraction of anything is lost. For each one-sided aspect, to gain itself, blends with that which seemed opposite, and the product of this fusion keeps the riches of all. The one reality, we may say from our human point of view, was present in each aspect in a form which does not satisfy. To work out its full nature it has sunk itself into these differences. But in each it longs for that absolute self-fruition which comes only when the self bursts its limits and blends with another finite self. This desire of each element for a perfection which implies fusion with

[161]

others, is not self-contradictory. It is rather an effort to remove a present state of inconsistency, to remain in which would indeed be fixed self-contradiction.

Now, if it is objected that such an Absolute is the Thing-in-itself, I must doubt if the objector can understand. How a whole which comprehends everything can deserve that title is past my conjecture. And, if I am told that the differences are lost in this whole, and yet the differences *are*, and must therefore be left out-side—I must reply to this charge by a counter-charge of thought-less confusion. For the differences are not lost, but are all contained in the whole. The fact that *more* is included there than these several, isolated, differences hardly proves that these differences are not there at all. When an element is joined to another in a whole of experience, then, on the whole, and for the whole, their mere specialities need not exist; but, none the less, each element in its own partial experience may retain its own speciality. 'Yes; but these partial experiences', I may be told, 'will at all events fall outside the whole.' Surely no such consequence follows. The self-consciousness of the part, its consciousness of itself [162] even in opposition to the whole—all will be contained within the one absorbing experience. For this will embrace all self-consciousness harmonized, though, as such, transmuted and sup-pressed. We cannot possibly construe, I admit, such an experi-ence to ourselves. We cannot imagine how in detail its outline is filled up. But to say that it is real, and that it unites certain gen-eral characters within the living system of one undivided appre-hension, is within our power. The assertion of this Absolute's reality I hope in the sequel to justify. Here (if I have not failed) I have shown that, at least from the point of view of thinking, it is free from self-contradiction. The justification for thought of an Other may help both to explain and to bury the Thing-in-itself.

7

Error

[164] A general doctrine is not destroyed by what we fail to understand. It is destroyed only by that which we actually do understand, and can show to be inconsistent and discrepant with the theory adopted.

    And this is the real issue here. Error and evil are no disproof of our absolute experience so long as we merely fail to see how in detail it comprehends them. They are a disproof when their nature is understood in such a way as to collide with the Absolute. And the question is whether this understanding of them is correct. . . . I will begin first with Error.

Error is without any question a dangerous subject, and the chief difficulty is as follows. We cannot, on the one hand, accept anything between non-existence and reality, while, on the other hand, error obstinately refuses to be either. It persistently attempts to maintain a third position, which appears nowhere to [165] exist, and yet somehow is occupied. In false appearance there is something attributed to the real which does not belong to it. But if the appearance is not real, then it is not false appearance, because it is nothing. On the other hand, if it is false, it must therefore be true reality, for it is something which is. And this dilemma at first sight seems insoluble. Or, to put it otherwise, an appearance, which is, must fall somewhere. But error, because it is false, cannot belong to the Absolute; and, again, it cannot appertain to the finite subject, because that, with all its contents, cannot fall outside the Absolute; at least, if it did, it would be nothing. And so error has no home, it has no place in existence; and yet, for all that, it exists. And for this reason it has occasioned much doubt and difficulty.

    For Psychology and for Logic the problem is much easier.

Repr. from *AR*, ch. xvi.

Error can be identified with wrong inference, and can be compared on one side with a typical model; while, on the other side, we can show by what steps it originates. But these inquiries, however interesting, would not much assist us, and we must endeavour here to face the problem more directly. We must take our stand on the distinction between idea and reality.

Error is the same as false appearance, or (if the reader objects to this) it is at any rate one kind of false appearance. Now appearance is content not at one with its existence, a 'what' loosened from its 'that'. And in this sense we have seen that every truth is appearance, since in it we have divorce of quality from being (pp. 143-4[a]). The idea which is true is the adjective of reality so far as its content goes. It, so far, is restored, and belongs, to existence. But an idea has also another side, its own private being as something which is and happens. And an idea, as content, is alienated from this its own existence as an event. Even where you take a presented whole, and predicate one or more features, our account still holds good. For the content predicated has now become alien to its existence. On the one side it has not been left in simple unity with the whole, nor again is it predicated so far as changed from a mere feature into another and [166] separate fact. In 'sugar is sweet' the sweetness asserted of the sugar is *not* the sweetness so far as divided from it, and turned into a second thing in our minds. This thing has its own being there, and to predicate it, as such, of the sugar would clearly be absurd. In respect of its own existence the idea is therefore always a mere appearance. But this character of divorce from its private reality becomes usually still more patent, where the idea is not taken from presentation but supplied by reproduction. Wherever the predicate is seen to be supplied from an image, the existence of that image can be seen at once *not* to be the predicate. It is something clearly left outside of the judgement and quite disregarded.[2]

Appearance then will be the looseness of character from being, the distinction of immediate oneness into two sides, a 'that' and a 'what'. And this looseness tends further to harden into fracture and into the separation of two sundered existences. Appearance

---

[2] [Cf. 'Thought and Reality', repr. above, Part II, Sect. I, Ch. 6.]

[a] See above, pp. 153-4.

will be truth when a content, made alien to its own being, is related to some fact which accepts its qualification. The true idea is appearance in respect of its own being as fact and event, but is reality in connection with other being which it qualifies. Error, on the other hand, is content made loose from its own reality, and related to a reality with which it is discrepant. It is the rejection of an idea by existence which is not the existence of the idea as made loose. It is the repulse by a substantive of a liberated adjective.[3] Thus it is an appearance which not only appears, but is false. It is in other words the collision of a mere idea with reality.

There are serious problems with regard both to error and truth, and the distinction between them, which challenge our scrutiny. I think it better however to defer these to later chapters. I will therefore limit here the inquiry, so far as is possible, and [167] will consider two main questions. Error is content neither at one with its own being, nor otherwise allowed to be an adjective of the real. If so, we must ask (1) why it cannot be accepted by reality, and (2) how it still actually can belong to reality; for we have seen that this last conclusion is necessary.

1. Error is rejected by reality because that is harmonious, and is taken necessarily to be so, while error, on the other hand, is self-contradictory. I do not mean that it is a content merely not at one (if that were possible) with its own mere being.[4] I mean that its inner character, as ideal, is itself discordant and self-discrepant. But I should prefer not to call error a *predicate* which contradicts itself. For that might be taken as a statement that the contradiction already is present in the mere predicate, *before* judgement is attempted; and this, if defensible, would be misleading. Error is the qualification of a reality in such a way that in the result it has an inconsistent content, which for that reason is rejected. Where existence has a 'what' colliding within itself, there the predication of this 'what' is an erroneous judgement. If a reality is self-consistent, and its further determination has introduced discord, there the addition is the mistake, and the reality is unaffected. It is unaffected, however, solely on the assumption that its own nature in no way suggested and called in the discor-

---

[3] Whether the adjective has been liberated from this substantive or from another makes no difference.

[4] In the end no finite predicate or subject can possibly be harmonious.

dant. For otherwise the whole result is infected with falseness, and the reality could never have been pure from discrepancy.[5]

It will perhaps tend to make clearer this general view of error if I defend it against some possible objections. Error is supposed by some persons to be a departure from experience, or from what is given merely. It is again taken sometimes as the confusion of internal image with outward sensation. But any such views are of course most superficial. Quite apart from the difficulty of finding anything merely given, and the impossibility of always using actual present sensation as a test of truth—without noticing the strange prejudice that outward sensations are never false, and the dull blindness which fails to realize that the 'inward' is a fact just as solid as the 'outward'—we may dismiss the whole objection. For, if the given has a content which is not harmonious, then, no matter in what sense we like to take 'given', that content is not real. And any attempt, either to deny this, or to maintain that in the given there is never discrepancy, may be left to itself. But I will go on to consider the same view as it wears a more plausible form. 'We do not', I may be told, 'add or take away predicates simply at our pleasure. We do not, so long as this arbitrary result does not visibly contradict itself, consider it true.' And I have not said that we should do this.

Outside known truth and error we may, of course, have simple ignorance. An assertion, that is, must in every case be right or be wrong; but, for us and for the present, it may not yet be either. Still, on the other hand, we do know that, *if* the statement is an error, it will be so because its content collides internally. 'But this' (an objector may reply) 'is really not the case. Take the statement that at a certain time an event did, or did not, happen. This would be erroneous because of disagreement with fact, and not always because it is inconsistent with itself.' Still I must insist that we have some further reason for condemning this want of correspondence with fact. For why, apart from such a reason, should either we or the fact make an objection to this defect? Suppose that when William has been hung, I assert that it was John. My assertion will then be false, because the reality does not admit of both events, and because William is certain. And if so,

[168]

---

[5] The doctrine here is stated subject to correction in ['Degrees of Truth and Reality', repr. below. Part II, Sect. 1, Ch. 10]. No finite predicate or subject can really be self-consistent.

then after all my error surely will consist in giving to the real a
self-discrepant content. For otherwise, when John is suggested, I
could not reject the idea. I could only say that certainly it was
William, and might also, for all that I knew, be John too. But in
our actual practice we proceed thus: since 'both John *and*
William' forms a discordant content, that statement is in error—
[169] here to the extent of John.[6] In the same way, if where no man is
you insist on John's presence, then, without discussing here the
nature of the privative judgement, we can understand the mistake. You are trying to force on the reality something which
would make it inconsistent, and which therefore is erroneous. But
it would be alike easy and idle to pursue the subject further; and
I must trust that, to the reader who reflects, our main conclusion
is already made good. Error is qualification by the self-
discrepant. We must not, if we take the predicate in its usual
sense, in all cases place the contradiction within that. But where
discrepancy is found in the result of qualification, it is there that
we have error. And I will now pass to the second main problem
of this chapter.

2. The question is about the relation of error to the Absolute.
How is it possible for false appearance to take its place within
reality? We have to some extent perceived in what error consists,
but we still are confronted by our original problem. Qualification
by the self-discrepant exists as a fact, and yet how can it be real?
The self-contradiction in the content both belongs, and is unable
to belong, to reality. The elements related, and their synthesis,
and their reference to existence—these are things not to be got
rid of. You may condemn them, but your condemnation cannot
act as a spell to abolish them wholly. If they were not there, you
could not judge them, and then you judge them not to be; or you
pronounce them apparently somehow to exist without really
existing. What is the exit from this puzzle?

There is no way but in accepting the whole mass of fact, and
in then attempting to correct it and make it good. Error *is* truth,
it is partial truth, that is false only because partial and left
incomplete. The Absolute *has* without subtraction all those quali-

---

[6] I do not here touch the question why John is sacrificed rather than William
(or both). On this see ['Degrees of Truth and Reality', repr. below, Part II, Sect.
1, Ch. 9].

ties, and it has every arrangement which we seem to confer upon it by our mere mistake. The only mistake lies in our failure to [170] give also the complement. The reality owns the discordance and the discrepancy of false appearance; but it possesses also much else in which this jarring character is swallowed up and is dissolved in fuller harmony. I do not mean that by a mere rearrangement of the matter which is given to *us*, *we* could remove its contradictions. For, being limited, we cannot apprehend all the details of the whole. And we must remember that every old arrangement, condemned as erroneous, itself forms part of that detail. To know all the elements of the universe, with all the conjunctions of those elements, good and bad, is impossible for finite minds. And hence obviously we are unable throughout to reconstruct our discrepancies. But we can comprehend in general what we cannot see exhibited in detail. We cannot understand how in the Absolute a rich harmony embraces every special discord. But, on the other hand, we may be sure that this result is reached; and we can even gain an imperfect view of the effective principle. I will try to explain this latter statement.

There is only one way to get rid of contradiction, and that way is by dissolution. Instead of one subject distracted, we get a larger subject with distinctions, and so the tension is removed. We have at first A, which possesses the qualities c and b, inconsistent adjectives which collide; and we go on to produce harmony by making a distinction within this subject. That was really not mere A, but either a complex within A, or (rather here) a wider whole in which A is included. The real subject is A + D; and this subject contains the contradiction made harmless by division, since A is c and D is b. This is the general principle, and I will attempt here to apply it in particular. Let us suppose the reality to be X ($a\ b\ c\ d\ e\ f\ g\ \ldots$), and that we are able only to get partial views of this reality. Let us first take such a view as 'X ($a\ b$) is b'. This (rightly or wrongly) we should probably call a true view. For the content b does plainly belong to the subject; and, further, the appearance also—in other words, the separation of b in the predicate—can partly be explained. For, answering to [171] this separation, we postulate now *another* adjective in the subject; let us call it β. The 'thatness', the psychical existence of the predicate, which at first was neglected, has now also itself been included in the subject. We may hence write the subject as X ($a\ b$

β); and in this way we seem to avoid contradiction. Let us go further on the same line, and, having dealt with a truth, pass next to an error. Take the subject once more as X (*a b c d e* . . .), and let us now say 'X (*a b*) is *d*'. This is false, because *d* is not present in the subject, and so we have a collision. But the collision is resolved if we take the subject, not as mere X (*a b*), but more widely as X (*a b c d*). In this case the predicate *d* becomes applicable. Thus the error consisted in the reference to *d* of *a b*; as it might have consisted in like manner in the reference of *a b* to *c*, or again of *c* to *d*. All of these exist in the subject, and the reality possesses with each both its 'what' and its 'that'. But not content with a provisional separation of these indissoluble aspects, not satisfied (as in true appearance) to have *a*α, *b*β, and *d*δ—forms which may typify distinctions that bring no discord into the qualities—we have gone on further into error. We have not only loosened 'what' from 'that', and so have made appearance; but we have in each case then bestowed the 'what' on a wrong quality within the real subject. We have crossed the threads of the connection between our 'whats' and our 'thats', and have thus caused collision, a collision which disappears when things are taken as a whole. . . .

[172]   But our account, it will fairly be objected, is untenable because incomplete. For error is *not* merely negative. The content, isolated and so discordant, is after all held together in a positive discord. And so the elements may exist, and their relations to their subjects may all be there in the Absolute, together with the complements which make them all true, and yet the problem is not solved. For the point of error, when all is said, lies in this very insistence on the partial and discrepant, and this discordant emphasis will fall outside of every possible rearrangement. I admit this objection, and I endorse it. The problem of error cannot be solved by an enlarged scheme of relations. Each misarrangement cannot be taken up wholly as an element in the compensations of a harmonious mechanism. For there is a positive sense and a specific character which marks each appearance, and this will still fall outside. Hence, while all that appears somehow is, all has not been accounted for by any rearrangement.

But on the other side the Absolute is not, and cannot be thought as, any scheme of relations. If we keep to these, there is no harmonious unity in the whole. The Absolute is beyond a mere arrangement, however well compensated, though an arrangement is assuredly one aspect of its being. Reality, consists, as we saw, in a higher experience, superior to the distinctions which it includes and overrides. And, with this, the last objection to the transformation of error has lost its basis. The one-sided emphasis of error, its isolation as positive and as not dissoluble in a wider [173] connection—this again will contribute, we know not how, to the harmony of the Absolute. It will be another detail, which, together with every 'what' and 'that' and their relations, will be absorbed into the whole and will subserve its perfection.

On this view there still are problems as to error and truth which we must deal with hereafter. But the main dilemma as to false appearance has, I think, been solved. That both exists and is, as such, not real. Its arrangement becomes true in a wider rearrangement of 'what' and of 'that'. Error is truth when it is supplemented. And its positive isolation also is reducible, and exists as a mere element within the whole. Error is, but is not barely what it takes itself to be. And its mere one-sidedness again is but a partial emphasis, a note of insistence which contributes, we know not how, to greater energy of life. And, if so, the whole problem has, so far, been disposed of.

Now that this solution cannot be verified, in the sense of being made out in detail, is not an admission on my part. It is rather a doctrine which I assert and desire to insist on. It is impossible for us to show, in the case of every error, how in the whole it is made good. It is impossible, even apart from detail, to realize how the relational form is in general absorbed. But, upon the other hand, I deny that our solution is either unintelligible or impossible. And possibility here is all that we want. For we have seen that the Absolute *must be* a harmonious system. We have first perceived this in general, and here specially, in the case of error, we have been engaged in a reply to an alleged negative instance. Our opponent's case has been this, that the nature of error makes our harmony impossible. And we have shown, on the other side, that he possesses no such knowledge. We have pointed out that it is at least possible for errors to correct themselves, and, as such, to disappear in a higher experience. But, if so, we *must* affirm that they are thus absorbed and made good. For what is *possible*, and what a general principle compels us to say *must be*, that certainly *is*.

8

Recapitulation

[213] It may be well at this point perhaps to look back on the ground which we have traversed. In our First Book we examined some ways of regarding reality, and we found that each of them contained fatal inconsistency. Upon this we forthwith denied that, as such, they could be real. But upon reflection we perceived that our denial must rest upon positive knowledge. It can only be because we know, that we venture to condemn. Reality therefore, we are sure, has a positive character, which rejects mere appearance and is incompatible with discord. On the other hand it cannot be a something apart, a position qualified in no way save as negative of phenomena. For that leaves phenomena still contradictory, while it contains in its essence the contradiction of a something which actually is nothing. The Reality, therefore, must be One, not as excluding diversity, but as somehow including it in such a way as to transform its character. There is plainly not anything which can fall outside of the Real. That must be qualified by every part of every predicate which it rejects; but it has such qualities as counterbalance one another's failings. It has a super-abundance in which all partial discrepancies are resolved and remain as higher concord.

And we found that this Absolute is experience, because that is really what we mean when we predicate or speak of anything. It is not one-sided experience, as mere volition or mere thought; but it is a whole superior to and embracing all incomplete forms of life. This whole must be immediate like feeling, but not, like feeling, immediate at a level below distinction and relation. The Absolute is immediate as holding and transcending these differences. And because it cannot contradict itself, and does not suffer a division of idea from existence, it has therefore a balance of pleasure over pain. In every sense it is perfect.

Repr. from *AR*, ch. xx.

Then we went on to inquire if various forms of the finite [214] would take a place within this Absolute. We insisted that nothing can be lost, and yet that everything must be made good, so as to minister to harmony. And we laid stress on the fact that the *how* was inexplicable. To perceive the solution in detail is not possible for our knowledge. But, on the other hand, we urged that such an explanation is not necessary. We have a general principle which seems certain. The only question is whether any form of the finite is a negative instance which serves to overthrow this principle. Is there anything which tends to show that our Absolute is not possible? And, so far as we have gone, we have discovered as yet nothing. We have at present not any right to a doubt about the Absolute. We have got no shred of reason for denying that it is possible. But, if it is possible, that is all we need seek for. For already we have a principle upon which it is necessary; and therefore it is certain.

In the following chapters I shall still pursue the same line of argument. I shall inquire if there is anything which declines to take its place within the system of our universe. And, if there is nothing that is found to stand out and to conflict, or to import discord when admitted, our conclusion will be attained. But I will first add a few remarks on the ideas of Individuality and Perfection.

We have seen that these characters imply a negation of the discordant and discrepant, and a doubt, perhaps, may have arisen about their positive aspect. Are they positive at all? When we predicate them, do we assert or do we only deny? Can it be maintained that these ideas are negative simply? It might be urged against us that reality means barely non-appearance, and that unity is the naked denial of plurality. And in the same way individuality might be taken as the barren absence of discord and of dissipation. Perfection, again, would but deny that we are compelled to go further, or might signify merely the failure of unrest and of pain. Such a doubt has received, I think, a solution beforehand, but I will point out once more its cardinal mistake.

In the first place a mere negation is unmeaning (pp. 121-2[a]). [215] To deny, except from a basis of positive assumption, is quite

[a] See above, pp. 133-4.

impossible. And a bare negative idea, if we could have it, would be a relation without a term. Hence some positive basis must underlie these negations which we have mentioned. And, in the second place, we must remember that what is denied is, none the less, somehow predicated of our Absolute. It is indeed because of this that we have called it individual and perfect.

1. It is, first, plain that at least the idea of affirmative being supports the denial of discrepancy and unrest. Being, if we use the term in a restricted sense, is not positively definable. It will be the same as the most general sense of experience. It is different from reality, if that, again, is strictly used. Reality (proper) implies a foregone distinction of content from existence, a separation which is overcome. Being (proper), on the other hand, is immediate, and at a level below distinctions; though I have not thought it necessary always to employ these terms in a confined meaning. However, in its general sense of experience, being underlies the ideas of individuality and perfection. And these, at least so far, must be positive.

2. And, in the second place, each of them is positively determined by what it excludes. The aspect of diversity belongs to the essence of the individual, and is affirmatively contained in it. The unity excludes what is diverse, so far only as that attempts to be anything by itself, and to maintain isolation. And the individual is the return of this apparent opposite with all its wealth into a richer whole. How in detail this is accomplished I repeat that we do not know; but we are capable, notwithstanding, of forming the idea of such a positive union (Chapters xiv and xxvii[b]). Feeling supplies us with a low and imperfect example of an immediate whole. And, taking this together with the idea of qualification by the rejected, and together with the idea of [216] unknown qualities which come in to help—we arrive at individuality. And, though depending on negation, such a synthesis is positive.

And, in a different way, the same account is valid of the Perfect. That does not mean a being which, in regard to unrest and painful struggle, is a simple blank. It means the identity of idea and existence, attended also by pleasure. Now, so far as pleasure goes, that certainly is not negative. But pleasure is far

[b] See above, Part II, Sect. 1, Ch. 5, and below, Ch. 10.

from being the only positive element in perfection. The unrest and striving, the opposition of fact to idea, and the movement towards an end—these features are not left outside of that Whole which is consummate. For all the content, which the struggle has generated, is brought home and is laid to rest undiminished in the perfect. The idea of a being qualified somehow, without any alienation of its 'what' from its 'that'—a being at the same time fully possessed of all hostile distinctions, and the richer for their strife—this is a positive idea. And it can be realized in its outline, though certainly not in detail.

I will advert in conclusion to an objection drawn from a common mistake. Quantity is often introduced into the idea of perfection. For the perfect seems to be that beyond which we cannot go, and this tends naturally to take the form of an infinite number. But, since any real number must be finite, we are at once involved here in a hopeless contradiction. And I think it necessary to say no more on this evident illusion; but will pass on to the objection which may be urged against our view of the perfect. If the perfect is the concordant, then no growth of its area or increase of its pleasantness could make it more complete. We thus, apparently, might have the smallest being as perfect as the largest; and this seems paradoxical. But the paradox really, I should say, exists only through misunderstanding. For we are accustomed to beings whose nature is always and essentially defective. And so we suppose in our smaller perfect a condition of want, or at least of defect; and this condition is diminished by alteration in quantity. But, where a being is really perfect, our supposition would be absurd. Or, again, we imagine first a crea- [217] ture complete in itself, and by the side of it we place a larger completion. Then unconsciously we take the greater to be, in some way, apprehended by the smaller; and, with this, naturally the lesser being becomes by contrast defective. But what we fail to observe is that such a being can no longer be perfect. For an idea which is not fact has been placed by us within it; and that idea at once involves a collision of elements, and by consequence also a loss of perfection. And thus a paradox has been made by our misunderstanding. We assumed completion, and then surreptitiously added a condition which destroyed it. And this, so far, was a mere error.

But the error may direct our attention to a truth. It leads us to ask if two perfections, great and small, can possibly exist side by side. And we must answer in the negative. If we take perfection in its full sense, we cannot suppose two such perfect existences. And this is not because one surpasses the other in size; for that is wholly irrelevant. It is because finite existence and perfection are incompatible. A being, short of the Whole, but existing within it, is essentially related to that which is not-itself. Its inmost being is, and must be, infected by the external. Within its content there are relations which do not terminate inside. And it is clear at once that, in such a case, the ideal and the real can never be at one. But their disunion is precisely what we mean by imperfection. And thus incompleteness, and unrest, and unsatisfied ideality, are the lot of the finite. There is nothing which, to speak properly, is individual or perfect, except only the Absolute.

9

Degrees of Truth and Reality

We [have] reached the question of degrees in Truth and Reality, and we must now endeavour to make clear what is contained in that idea.[1] An attempt to do this, thoroughly and in detail, would carry us too far. To show how the world, physical and spiritual, realizes by various stages and degrees the one absolute principle, would involve a system of metaphysics. And such a system I am not undertaking to construct. I am endeavouring merely to get a sound general view of Reality, and to defend it against a number of difficulties and objections. But, for this, it is essential to explain and to justify the predicates of higher and lower. While dealing with this point, I shall develop further the position which we have already assigned to Thought (Chapters xv and xvi[a]).

The Absolute, considered as such, has of course no degrees; for it is perfect, and there can be no more or less in perfection (Chapter xx[b]). Such predicates belong to, and have a meaning only in the world of appearance. We may be reminded, indeed, that the same absoluteness seems also possessed by existence in time. For a thing either may have a place there, or may have none, but it cannot inhabit any interval between presence and absence. This view would assume that existence in time is Reality; and in practice, and for some purposes, that is admissible. But, besides being false, the assumption tends naturally to pass beyond itself. For, if a thing may not exist less or more, it must certainly more or less occupy existence. It may usurp ground by its direct presence, but again, further, by its influence and relative importance. Thus we should find it difficult, in the

Repr. from *AR*, ch. xxiv.

[1] I may mention that in this chapter I am, perhaps even more than elsewhere, indebted to Hegel.

---

[a] See above, Part II, Sect. 1, Chs. 6 and 7.
[b] See above, Part II, Sect. 2, Ch. 8.

end, to say exactly what we understand by 'having' existence. We should even find a paradox in the assertion, that everything alike *has* existence to precisely the same degree.

[319]   But here, in metaphysics, we have long ago passed beyond this one-sided point of view. On one hand the series of temporal facts has been perceived to consist in ideal construction. It is ideal, not indeed wholly . . . but still essentially. And such a series is but appearance; it is not absolute, but relative; and, like all other appearance, it admits the distinction of more and less. On the other hand, we have seen that truth, which again itself is appearance, both unconsciously and deliberately diverges from this rude essay. And, without considering further the exploded claim set up by temporal fact, we may deal generally with the question of degrees in reality and truth.

We have already perceived the main nature of the process of thinking.[2] Thought essentially consists in the separation of the 'what' from the 'that'. It may be said to accept this dissolution as its effective principle. Thus it renounces all attempt to *make* fact, and it confines itself to content. But by embracing this separation, and by urging this independent development to its extreme, thought indirectly endeavours to restore the broken whole. It seeks to find an arrangement of ideas, self-consistent and complete; and by this predicate it has to qualify and make good the Reality. And, as we have seen, its attempt would in the end be suicidal. Truth should mean what it stands for, and should stand for what it means; but these two aspects in the end prove incompatible. There is still a difference, unremoved, between the subject and the predicate, a difference which, while it persists, shows a failure in thought, but which, if removed, would wholly destroy the special essence of thinking.

We may put this otherwise by laying down that any categorical judgement must be false. The subject and the predicate, in the end, cannot either *be* the other. If however we stop short of this goal, our judgement has failed to reach truth; while, if we attained it, the terms and their relation would have ceased. And hence all our judgements, to be true, must become conditional.

[320] The predicate, that is, does not hold unless by the help of some-

[2] [Cf. 'Thought and Reality' and 'Error', repr. above, Part II, Sect. 1, Chs. 6 and 7.]

thing else. And this 'something else' cannot be stated, so as to fall inside even a new and conditional predicate.[3]

It is however better, I am now persuaded, not to say that every judgement is hypothetical.[4] The word, it is clear, may introduce irrelevant ideas. Judgements are conditional in this sense, that what they affirm is incomplete. It cannot be attributed to Reality, as such, and before its necessary complement is added. And, in addition, this complement in the end remains unknown. But while it remains unknown, we obviously cannot tell how, if present, it would act upon and alter our predicate. For to suppose that its presence would make no difference is plainly absurd, while the precise nature of the difference falls outside our knowledge. But, if so, this unknown modification of our predicate may, in various degrees, destroy its special character. The content in fact might so be altered, be so redistributed and blended, as utterly to be transformed. And, in brief, the predicate may, taken as such, be more or less completely untrue. Thus we really always have asserted subject to, and at the mercy of, the unknown.[5] And hence our judgement, always but to a varying extent, must in the end be called conditional.

But with this we have arrived at the meeting-ground of error and truth. There will be no truth which is entirely true, just as [321] there will be no error which is totally false. With all alike, if taken strictly, it will be a question of amount, and will be a matter of more or less. Our thoughts certainly, for some purposes, may be taken as wholly false, or again as quite accurate; but truth and error, measured by the Absolute, must each be subject always to degree. Our judgements, in a word, can never reach as far as perfect truth, and must be content merely to enjoy more or less of *Validity*. I do not simply mean by this term that, for working purposes, our judgements are admissible and will pass. I mean that less or more they actually possess the character and type of absolute truth and reality. They can take the place of the Real to various extents, because containing in themselves less or

---

[3] I may, perhaps, refer here to my *Principles of Logic*. Even metaphysical statements about the Absolute, I would add, are not strictly categorical.

[4] This term often implies the reality of temporal existence, and is also, apart from that, objectionable. See Mr. Bosanquet's admirable *Logic*, i, Chapter vi.

[5] Hence in the end we must be held to have asserted the unknown. It is however better *not* to call this the predication of an unknown quality [cf. 'The Categorical and Hypothetical Forms of Judgement', repr. above, Part I, Ch. 2].

more of its nature. They are its representatives, worse or better, in proportion as they present us with truth affected by greater or less derangement. Our judgements hold good, in short, just so far as they agree with, and do not diverge from, the real standard. We may put it otherwise by saying that truths are true, according as it would take less or more to convert them into reality.

We have perceived, so far, that truth is relative and always imperfect. We have next to see that, though failing of perfection, all thought is to some degree true. On the one hand it falls short of, and on the other hand at the same time, it realizes the standard. But we must begin by inquiring what this standard is.

Perfection of truth and of reality has in the end the same character. It consists in positive, self-subsisting individuality; and I have endeavoured to show in Chapter xx,[b] what individuality means. Assuming that the reader has recalled the main points of that discussion, I will point out the two ways in which individuality appears. Truth must exhibit the mark of internal harmony, or, again, the mark of expansion and all-inclusiveness. And these two characteristics are diverse aspects of a single principle. That which contradicts itself, in the first place, jars, because the whole, immanent within it, drives its parts into collision. And the way to find [322] harmony, as we have seen, is to redistribute these discrepancies in a wider arrangement. But, in the second place, harmony is incompatible with restriction and finitude. For that which is not all-inclusive must by virtue of its essence internally disagree; and, if we reflect, the reason of this becomes plain. That which exists in a whole has external relations. Whatever it fails to include within its own nature, must be related to it by the whole, and related externally. Now these extrinsic relations, on the one hand, fall outside of itself, but, upon the other hand, cannot do so. For a relation must at both ends affect, and pass into, the being of its terms. And hence the inner essence of what is finite itself both is, and is not, the relations which limit it. Its nature is hence incurably relative, passing, that is, beyond itself, and importing, again, into its own core a mass of foreign connections. Thus to be defined from without is, in principle, to be distracted within. And, the smaller the element, the more wide is this dissipation of its essence—a dissipation too thorough to be deep, or to support the title of an intestine

b Repr. above, Part II, Sect. I, Ch. 8.

division.[6] But, on the contrary, the expansion of the element should increase harmony, for it should bring these external relations within the inner substance. By growth the element becomes, more and more, a consistent individual, containing in itself its own nature; and it forms, more and more, a whole inclusive of discrepancies and reducing them to system. The two aspects, of extension and harmony, are thus in principle one, though (as we shall see later) for our practice they in some degree fall apart. And we must be content, for the present, to use them independently.

Hence to be more or less true, and to be more or less real, is to be separated by an interval, smaller or greater, from all-inclusiveness or self-consistency. Of two given appearances the one more wide, or more harmonious, is more real. It approaches [323] nearer to a single, all-containing, individuality. To remedy its imperfections, in other words, we should have to make a smaller alteration. The truth and the fact, which, to be converted into the Absolute, would require less rearrangement and addition, is more real and truer. And this is what we mean by degrees of reality and truth. To possess more the character of reality, and to contain within oneself a greater amount of the real, are two expressions for the same thing.

And the principle on which false appearance can be converted into truth . . . consists, as we saw, in supplementation and in rearrangement . . . A total error would mean the attribution of a content to Reality, which, even when redistributed and dissolved, could still not be assimilated. And no such extreme case seems possible. An error can be total only in this sense that, when it is turned into truth, its particular nature will have vanished, and its actual self be destroyed. But this we must allow, again, to happen with the lower kinds of truth. There cannot for metaphysics be, in short, any hard and absolute distinction between truths and falsehoods. With each assertion the question is, how much will be left of that assertion, if we suppose it to have been converted into ultimate truth? Out of everything that makes its special nature as the predication of this adjective, how much, if

---

[6] It may seem a paradox to speak of the distraction, say, of a material particle. But try to state what that *is*, without bringing into it what it is *not*. Its distraction, of course, is not felt. But the point is that self-alienation is here too extreme for any feeling, or any self, to exist.

anything, will survive? And the amount of survival in each case, as we have already seen, gives the degree of reality and truth.

But it may perhaps be objected that there are judgements without any real meaning, and that there are mere thoughts, which do not even pretend to attribute anything to Reality. And, with these, it will be urged that there can no longer remain the least degree of truth. They may, hence, be adjectives of the Real, but are not judgements about it. The discussion of this objection falls, perhaps, outside the main scope of my work, but I should like briefly to point out that it rests on a mistake. In the first place every judgement, whether positive or negative, and however frivolous its character, makes an assertion about Reality.[7] And the content asserted cannot, as we have seen, be altogether an error, though its ultimate truth may quite transform its original meaning. And, in the second place, every kind of thought implies a judgement, in this sense that it ideally qualifies Reality. To question, or to doubt, or to suggest, or to entertain a mere idea, is not explicitly to judge. So much is certain and obvious. But, when we inquire further into what these states necessarily imply, our conclusion must be otherwise. If we use judgement for the reference, however unconscious and indefinite, of thought to reality, then without exception to think must be, in some sense, to judge. Thought in its earliest stage immediately modifies a direct sensible presentation; and, although, on one side, the qualification becomes conditional, and although the reality, on the other side, becomes partly non-sensuous, thought's main character is still preserved. The reference to reality may be, in various degrees, undefined and at large. The ideal content may be applied subject to more or less transformation; its struggling and conditional character may escape our notice, or may again be realized with less or more consciousness. But to hold a thought, so to speak, in the air, without a relation of any kind to the Real, in any of its aspects of spheres, we should find in the end to be impossible.[8]

This statement, I am aware, may seem largely paradoxical. The

[7] I may refer the reader here to my *Principles of Logic*, or, rather, to Mr. Bosanquet's *Logic*, which is, in many points, a great advance on my own work, I have, to a slight extent, modified my views on Judgement. [Cf. 'On Floating Ideas and the Imaginary', repr. below, Part II, Sect. 2, Ch. 1.]

[8] See Mr. Bosanquet's *Logic*, Introduction, and the same author's *Knowledge and Reality*, pp. 148–55.

merely imaginary, I may be told, is not referred to reality. It may, on the contrary, be even with consciousness held apart. But, on further reflection, we should find that our general account will hold good. The imaginary always is regarded as an adjective of the real. But, in referring it, (*a*) we distinguish, with more or less [325] consciousness, the regions to which it is, and to which it is not, applicable. And (*b*) we are aware, in different degrees, of the amount of supplementation and rearrangement, which our idea would require before it reached truth. These are two aspects of the same principle, and I will deal briefly with each.

(*a*) With regard to the first point we must recall the want of unity in the world, as it comes within each of us. The universe we certainly feel is one, but that does not prevent it from appearing divided, and in separate spheres and regions. And between these diverse provinces of our life there may be no visible connection. In art, in morality and religion, in trade or politics, or again in some theoretical pursuit, it is a commonplace that the individual may have a world of his own. Or he may rather have several worlds without rational unity, conjoined merely by coexistence in his own personality. And this separation and disconnectedness (we may fail to observe) is, in some degree, normal. It would be impossible that any man should have a world, the various provinces of which were quite rationally connected, or appeared always in system. But, if so, no one, in accepting or rejecting ideas, can always know the precise sense in which he affirms or denies. He means, from time to time, by reality some one region of the Real, which habitually he fails to distinguish and define. And the attempt at distinction would but lead him to total bewilderment. The real world, perhaps consciously, may be identified with the spatial system which we construct. This is 'actual fact', and everything else may be set apart as mere thought, or as mere imagination or feeling, all equally unreal. But, if so, against our wills these banished regions, nevertheless, present themselves as the *worlds* of feeling, imagination, and thought. However little we desire it, these form, in effect, actual constituent factors in our real universe. And the ideas, belonging to these several fields, certainly cannot be entertained without an identification, however vague, of each with its department of the Real. We treat the imaginary as existing somehow in some world, or in some by- [326] world, of the imagination. And, in spite of our denial, all such worlds are for us inevitably the appearances of that whole which we feel to be a single Reality.

And, even when we consider the extreme cases of command and of wish, our conclusion is unshaken. A desire is not a judgement, but still in a sense it implies one. It might, indeed, appear that what is ordered or desired is, by its essence, divorced from all actual reality. But this first impression would be erroneous. All negation, we must remember, is relative. The idea, rejected by reality, is none the less predicable, when its subject is altered. And it is predicable again, when (what comes to the same thing) itself is modified. Neglecting this latter refinement, we may point out how our account will hold good in the case of desire. The content wished for certainly in one sense is absent from reality; and the idea, we must be able to say, does *not* exist. But real existence, on the other hand, has been taken here in a limited meaning. And hence, outside that region of fact which repels the idea, it can, at the same time, be affirmatively referred to reality. It is this reference indeed which, we may say, makes the contradiction of desire intolerable. That which I desire is not consciously assumed to exist, but still vaguely, somehow and in some strange region, it is felt to be there; and, because it is there, its non-appearance excites painful tension. Pursuing this subject we should find that, in every case in the end, to be thought of is to be entertained as, and so judged to be, real.

(*b*) And this leads us to the second point. We have seen that every idea, however imaginary, is, in a sense, referred to reality. But we saw also that, with regard to the various meanings of the real subject, and the diverse provinces and regions in which it appears, we are all, more or less, unconscious. This same want of consciousness, in varying amounts, is visible also in our way of applying the predicate.[9] Every idea can be made the true adjective of reality, but, on the other hand (as we have seen), every idea must be altered. More or less, they all require a supplementation

[327]

---

[9] As was before remarked, these two points, in the end, are the same. Since the various worlds, in which reality appears, cannot each stand alone, but must condition one the other, hence that which is predicated categorically of one world, will none the less be conditional, when applied to the whole. And, from the other side, a conditional predicate of the whole will become categorical, if made the adjective of a subject which is limited and therefore is conditional. These ways of regarding the matter, in the end, are but one way. And, in the end, there is no difference between conditional and conditioned.

and rearrangement. But of this necessity, and, of the amount of it, we may be totally unaware. We commonly use ideas with no clear notion as to how far they are conditional, and are incapable of being predicated downright of reality. To the suppositions implied in our statements we usually are blind; or the precise extent of them is, at all events, not distinctly realized. This is a subject upon which it might be interesting to enlarge, but I have perhaps already said enough to make good our result. However little it may appear so, to think is always, in effect, to judge. And all judgements we have found to be more or less true, and in different degrees to depart from, and to realize, the standard. With this we may return from what has been, perhaps, to some extent a digression.

Our single standard, as we saw above, wears various aspects, and I will now proceed briefly to exemplify its detail. (*a*) If we take, first, an appearance in time, and desire to estimate the amount of its reality, we have, on one side, to consider its harmoniousness. We have to ask, that is, how far, before its contents can take their place as an adjective of the Real, they would require rearrangement. We have to inquire how far, in other words, these contents are, or are not, self-consistent and systematic. And then, on the other side, we must have regard to the extent of time, or space, or both, which our appearance occupies.[10] Other things being equal, [328] whatever spreads more widely in space, or again lasts longer in time, is therefore more real. But (*b*), beside events, it is necessary to take account of laws. These are more and less abstract or concrete, and here our standard in its application will once more diverge. The abstract truths, for example, of mathematics on one side, and, on the other side, the more concrete connections of life or mind, will each set up a varying claim. The first are more remote from fact, more empty and incapable of self-existence, and they are therefore less true. But the second, on the other hand, are narrower, and on this account more false, since clearly they pervade, and hold good over, a less extent of reality. Or, from the other side, the law which is more abstract contradicts itself more, because it is determined by exclusion from a wider area. Again the generalization nearer sense, being fuller of irrelevancy, will,

---

[10] The intensity of the appearance can be referred, I think, to two heads, (i) that of extent, and (ii) that of effectiveness. But the influence of a thing outside of its own limits will fall under an aspect to be mentioned lower down (pp. 195–6).

looked at from this point of view, be more internally discordant. In brief, whether the system and the true individual is sought in temporal existence, or in the realm standing above events, the standard still is the same. And it is applied always under the double form of inclusiveness and harmony. To be deficient in either of these aspects is to fall short of perfection; and, in the end, any deficiency implies failure in both aspects alike.

And we shall find that our account still holds good when we pass on to consider higher appearances of the universe. It would be a poor world which consisted merely of phenomenal events, and of the laws that somehow reign above them. And in our everyday life we soon transcend this unnatural divorce between principle and fact. (*c*) We reckon an event to be important in proportion to its effectiveness, so far as its being, that is, spreads in influence beyond the area of its private limits. It is obvious that here the two features, of self-sufficiency and self-transcendence, are already discrepant. We reach a higher stage where some existence embodies, or in any way presents in itself, a law and a principle. However, in the mere example and instance of a universal truth, the fact and the law are still essentially alien to each other, and the defective character of their union is plainly visible. Our standard moves us on towards an individual with laws of its own, and to laws which form the vital substance of a single existence. And an imperfect appearance of this character we were compelled in our last chapter[c] to recognize in the individual habits of the soul. Further in the beauty which presents us with a realized type, we find another form of the union of fact with principle. And, passing from this to conscious life, we are called on still for further uses and fresh applications of our standard. In the will of the individual, or of the community, so far as adequately carried out and expressing itself in outward fact, we have a new claim to harmonious and self-included reality. And we have to consider in each case the consistency, together with the range and area, of the principle, and the degree up to which it has mastered and passed into existence. And we should find ourselves led on from this, by partial defect, to higher levels of being. We should arrive at the personal relation of the individual to ends theoretical and practical, ends which call for realization, but which from their nature cannot be realized in a finite personality. And,

[329]

---

[c] *AR*, ch. xxiii, 'Body and Soul'.

once more here, our standard must be called in when we endeavour, as we must, to form a comparative estimate. For, apart from the success or failure of the individual's will, these ideas of ultimate goodness and reality themselves possess, of course, very different values. And we have to measure the amount of discordancy and limitation, which fixes the place to be assigned, in each case, to these various appearances of the Absolute.

To some of these provinces of life I shall have to return in later chapters. But there are several points to which, at present, I would draw attention. I would repeat, first, that I am not undertaking to set out completely the different aspects of the world; nor am I trying to arrange these according to their comparative degrees of reality and truth. A serious attempt to perform this would have to be made by any rational system of first principles, but in this work I am dealing solely with some main features of things. However, in the second place, there is a consideration which I would urge to the reader. With any view of the world which confines known reality to existence in time, and which limits truth to the attempt to reproduce somehow the series of events—with any view for which merely a thing exists, or barely does not exist, and for which an idea is false, or else is true— how is it possible to be just to the various orders of appearance? For, if we are consistent, we shall send the mass of our chief human interests away to some unreal limbo of undistinguished degradation. And, if we are not consistent, yet how can we proceed rationally without an intellectual standard? And I think we are driven to this alternative. We must either be incapable of saying one word on the relative importance of things; we can tell nothing of the comparative meaning, and place in the world, owned by art, science, religion, social life or morality; we are wholly ignorant as to the degrees of truth and reality which these possess, and we cannot even say that for the universe any one of them has any significance, makes any degree of difference, or matters at all. Either this, or else our one-sided view must be revolutionized. But, so far as I see, it can be revolutionized only in one of two ways. We may accept a view of truth and reality such as I have been endeavouring to indicate, or we must boldly subordinate everything to the test of feeling. I do not mean that, beside our former inadequate ideal of truth, we should set up,

[330]

also and alongside, an independent standard of worth. For this expedient, first, would leave no clear sense to 'degrees of truth' or 'of reality'; and, in the second place, practically our two standards would tend everywhere to clash. They would collide hopelessly without appeal to any unity above them. Of some religious belief, for example, or of some aesthetic representation, we might be compelled to exclaim, 'How wholly false, and yet how superior to truth, and how much more to us than any possible reality!' And of some successful and wide-embracing theory we might remark that it was absolutely true and utterly despicable, or of some physical facts, perhaps, that they deserved no kind of attention. Such a separation of worth from reality and truth would mutilate our nature, and could end only in irrational compromise or oscillation. But this shifting attitude, though common in life, seems here inadmissible; and it was not this that I meant by a subordination to feeling. I pointed to something less possible, but very much more consistent. It would imply the setting up of feeling in some form as an absolute test, not only of value but also of truth and reality. Here, if we took feeling as our end, and identified it with pleasure, we might assert of some fact, no matter how palpable, This is absolutely nothing; or, because it makes for pain, it is even worse, and is therefore even less than nothing. Or because some truth, however obvious, seemed in our opinion not favourable to the increase of pleasure, we should have to treat it at once as sheer falsehood and error. And by such an attitude, however impracticable, we should have at least *tried* to introduce some sort of unity and meaning into our world.[11]

But if to make mere feeling our one standard is in the end impossible, if we cannot rest in the intolerable confusion of a double test and control, nor can relapse into the narrowness, and the inconsistency, of our old mutilated view—we must take courage to accept the other revolution. We must reject wholly the idea that known reality consists in a series of events, external or inward, and that truth merely is correspondence with such a form of existence. We must allow to every appearance alike its

[331]

---

[11] Such an attitude, beside being impracticable, would however still be internally inconsistent. It breaks down in the position which it gives to truth. The understanding, so far as used to judge of the tendencies of things, is still partly independent. We either then are forced back, as before, to a double standard, or we have to make mere feeling the judge also with regard to these tendencies. And this is clearly to end in mere momentary caprice, and in anarchy.

own degree of reality, if not also of truth, and we must every [332] where estimate this degree by the application of our single standard. I am not here attempting even (as I have said) to make this estimate in general; and, in detail, I admit that we might find cases where rational comparison seems hopeless. But our failure in this respect would justify no doubt about our principle. It would be solely through our ignorance and our deficiency that the standard ever could be inapplicable. And, at the cost of repetition, I may be permitted to dwell briefly on this head.

Our standard is Reality in the form of self-existence; and this, given plurality and relations, means an individual system. Now we have shown that no perfect system can possibly be finite, because any limitation from the outside infects the inner content with dependence on what is alien. And hence the marks of harmony and expansion are two aspects of one principle. With regard to harmony (other things remaining the same), that which has extended over and absorbed a greater area of the external, will internally be less divided.[12] And the more an element is consistent, the more ground, other things being equal, is it likely to cover. And if we forget this truth, in the case of what is either abstracted for thought or is isolated for sense, we can recall it by predicating these fragments, as such, of the Universe. We are then forced to perceive both the inconsistency of our predicates, and the large extent of outer supplement which we must add, if we wish to make them true. Hence the amount of either wideness or consistency gives the degree of reality and also of truth. Or, regarding the same thing from the other side, you may estimate by what is lacking. You may measure the reality of anything by the relative amount of transformation, which would follow if its defects were made good. The more an appearance, in being corrected, is transmuted and destroyed, the less reality can such an appearance contain; or, to put it otherwise, the less genuinely [333] does it represent the Real. And on this principle we succeeded in attaching a clear sense to that nebulous phrase 'Validity'.

And this standard, in principle at least, is applicable to every kind of subject-matter. For everything, directly or indirectly, and with a greater or less preservation of its internal unity, has a rela-

---

[12] The reader must not forget here that the inconsistency and distraction, which cannot be felt, is *therefore* the greatest (pp. 186–7). Feeling is itself a unity and a solution, however incomplete.

tive space in Reality. For instance, the mere intensity of a pleasure or pain, beside its occupancy of consciousness, has also an
outer sphere or halo of effects. And in some low sense these
effects make a part of, or at least belong to, its being. And with
facts of perception their extent both in time, and also in space,
obviously gives us a point of comparison between them. If,
again, we take an abstract truth, which, as such, nowhere has
existence, we can consider the comparative area of its working
influence. And, if we were inclined to feel a doubt as to the reality of such principles, we might correct ourselves thus. Imagine
everything which they represent removed from the universe, and
then attempt to maintain that this removal makes no real
difference. And, as we proceed further, a social system, conscious
in its personal members of a will carried out, submits itself naturally to our test. We must notice here the higher development of
concrete internal unity. For we find an individuality, subordinat-
ing to itself outward fact, though not, as such, properly visible
within it. This superiority to mere appearance in the temporal
series is carried to a higher degree as we advance into the worlds
of religion, speculation, and art. The inward principle may here
become far wider, and have an intenser unity of its own; but, on
the side of temporal existence, it cannot possibly exhibit itself as
such. The higher the principle, and the more vitally it, so to
speak, possesses the soul of things, so much the wider in proportion must be that sphere of events which in the end it controls.
But, just for this reason, such a principle cannot be handled or
seen, nor is it in any way given to outward or inward perception.
[334] It is only the meaner realities which can ever be so revealed, and
which are able to be verified as sensible facts.

And it is only a standard such as ours which can assign its proper
rank to sense-presentation. It is solely by accepting such a test that
we are able to avoid two gross and opposite mistakes. There is a
view which takes, or attempts to take, sense-perception as the one
known reality. And there is a view which endeavours, on the other
side, to consider appearance in time as something indifferent. It
tries to find reality in the world of insensible thought. Both mistakes lead, in the end, to a like false result, and both imply, and
are rooted in, the same principle of error. In the end each would
force us to embrace as complete reality a meagre and mutilated

fraction, which is therefore also, and in consequence, internally discrepant. And each is based upon one and the same error about the nature of things. We have seen that the separation of the real into idea and existence is a division admissible only within the world of appearance. In the Absolute every such distinction must be merged and disappears. But the disappearance of each aspect, we insisted also, meant the satisfaction of its claims in full. And hence, though how in detail we were unable to point out, either side must come together with its opposite in the Whole. There thought and sense alike find each its complement in the other. The principle that reality can wholly consist in one of these two sides of appearance, we therefore reject as a fundamental error.

Let us consider more closely the two delusions which have branched from this stem. The first of these, perceiving that the series of events is essential, concludes from this ground that mere sense, either outward or inward, is the one reality. Or, if it stops short of this, it still argues that to be real is to be, as such, perceptible. Because, that is, appearance in the temporal series is found necessary for reality—a premiss which is true—an unconscious passage is made, from this truth, to a vicious conclusion. To appear is construed to imply appearance always, so to speak, [335] in person. And nothing is allowed to be real, unless it can be given bodily, and can be revealed, within one piece of the series. But this conclusion is radically erroneous. No perception ever, as we have seen clearly, has a character contained within itself. In order to be fact at all, each presentation must exhibit ideality, or in other words transcendence of self; and that which appears at any one moment, is, as such, self-contradictory. And, from the other side, the less a character is able, as such, to appear—the less its necessary manifestation can be narrowed in time or in space—so much the more is it capable of both expansion and inner harmony. But these two features, as we saw, are the marks of reality.

And the second of the mistakes is like the first. Appearance, once more, is falsely identified with presentation, as such, to sense; and a wrong conclusion is, once more, drawn from this basis. But the error now proceeds in an opposite direction. Because the highest principles are, obviously and plainly, not perceptible by sense, they are taken to inhabit and to have their being in the world of pure thought. And this other region, with more or less consistency, is held to constitute the sole reality. But here, if excluded wholly from the serial flow of events, this world of thought is limited externally and is internally discordant; while, if, further, we attempt to qualify the universe by our mere ideal abstract, and to attach this content to the Reality which appears in perception, the confusion becomes more obvious. Since the sense-appearance has been given up, as alien to truth, it has been in consequence set free, and is entirely insubordinate. And its concrete character now evidently determines, and infects from the outside, whatever mere thought we are endeavouring to predicate of the Real. But the union in all perception of thought with sense, the co-presence everywhere in all appearances of fact with ideality—this is the one foundation of truth. And, when we added to this the saving distinction that to have existence need not mean to exist,[d] and that to be realized in time is not always to be visible by any sense, we have made ourselves secure against

[336] the worst of errors. From this we are soon led to our principle of degrees in truth and reality. Our world and our life need then no longer be made up arbitrarily. They need not be compounded of the two hemispheres of fact and fancy. Nor need the Absolute reveal itself indiscriminately in a chaos where comparison and value are absent. We can assign a rational meaning to the distinctions of higher and lower. And we have grown convinced that, while not to appear is to be unreal, and while the fuller appearance marks the fuller reality, our principle, with but so much, is only half stated. For comparative ability to exist, individually and as such, within the region of sense, is a sign everywhere, so far as it goes, of degradation in the scale of being.

Or, dealing with the question somewhat less abstractly, we may attempt otherwise to indicate the true position of temporal existence. This, as we have seen, is not reality, but it is, on the other hand, in our experience one essential factor. And to suppose that mere thought without facts could either be real, or could reach to truth, is evidently absurd. The series of events is, without doubt, necessary for our knowledge,[13] since this series supplies the one source of all ideal content. We may say, roughly and with

---

[d] The distinction that Bradley alludes to here is, it seems, that between having existence of some sort or other, and existing in *our real world*, i.e. being locatable in the time-series identifiable as containing one's waking sense-perceptions and their indexically demonstrable objects.

[13] The series, in its proper character, is, of course, an ideal construction. But we may disregard that here.

sufficient accuracy, that there is nothing in thought, whether it be matter or relations, except that which is derived from perception. And, in the second place, it is only by starting from the presented basis that we construct our system of phenomena in space and time. We certainly perceived . . . that any such constructed unity was but relative, imperfect, and partial. But, none the less, a building up of the sense-world from the ground of actual presentation is a condition of all our knowledge. It is not true that everything, even if temporal, has a place in *our* one 'real' order of space or time. But, indirectly or directly, every known element must be connected with its sequence of events, and, at least in some sense, must show itself even there. The test of truth after [337] all, we may say, lies in presented fact.

We should here try to avoid a serious mistake. Without existence we have perceived that thought is incomplete; but this does not mean that, without existence, mere thought in itself is complete fully, and that existence to this superadds an alien but necessary completion. For we have found in principle that, if anything were perfect, it would not gain by an addition made from the outside. And, here in particular, thought's first object, in its pursuit of actual fact, is precisely the enlarging and making harmonious of its own ideal content. And the reason for this, as soon as we consider it, is obvious. The dollar, merely thought of or imagined, is comparatively abstract and void of properties. But the dollar, verified in space, has got its place in, and is determined by, an enormous construction of things. And to suppose that the concrete context of these relations in no sense qualifies its inner content, or that this qualification is a matter of indifference to thought, is quite indefensible.

A mere thought would mean an ideal content held apart from existence. But (as we have learnt) to hold a thought is always somehow, even against our will, to refer it to the Real. Hence our mere idea, now standing in relation with the Real, is related also to the phenomenal system of events in time. It is related to them, but without any connexion with the internal order and arrangements of their system. But this means that our mere idea is determined by that system entirely from the outside. And it will therefore itself be permeated internally, and so destroyed by the contingency forced into its content through these chaotic relations. Considered from this side, a thought, if it actually were bare, would stand at a level lower than the, so-called, chance facts of sense. For in the latter we have, at least, *some* internal connexion with the context, and already a fixed relation of universals, however impure.

All reality must be revealed in the world of events; and that is most real which, within such an order or orders, finds least foreign [338] to itself. Hence, if *other things remain equal*, a definite place in, and connection with, the temporal system gives increase of reality. For thus the relations to other elements, which must in any case determine, determine, at least to some extent, internally. And thus the imaginary, so far, must be poorer than the perceptible fact; or, in other words, it is compulsorily qualified by a wider area of alien and destructive relations. I have emphasized 'if other things remain equal', for this restriction is important. There is imagination which is higher, and more true, and most emphatically more real, than any single fact of sense. And this brings us back to our old distinction. Every truth must appear, and must subordinate existence; but this appearance is not the same thing as to be present, properly and as such, within given limits of sense-perception. With the general principles of science we may perhaps see this at once. And again, with regard to the necessary appearances of art or religion, the same conclusion is evident. The eternal experience, in every case, fails to enter into the series of space or of time; or it enters that series improperly, and with a show which in various ways contradicts its essence. To be nearer the central heart of things is to dominate the extremities more widely; but it is not to appear there except incompletely and partially through a sign, an unsubstantial and a fugitive mode of expression. Nothing anywhere, not even the realized and solid moral will, can either be quite real, as it exists in time, or can quite appear in its own essential character. But still the ultimate Reality, where all appearance as such is merged, is in the end the actual identity of idea and existence. And, throughout our world, whatever is individual is more real and true; for it contains within its own limits a wider region of the Absolute, and it possesses more intensely the type of self-sufficiency. Or, to put it otherwise, the interval between such an element and the Absolute is smaller. We should require less alteration, less destruction of its own special nature, in order to make this higher element completely real. . . .

10

Ultimate Doubts

There are certain truths about the Absolute, which, for the pre- [480] sent at least,[1] we can regard as unconditional. In this point they can be taken to differ in kind from all subordinate truths, for with the latter it is a question only of more or less fallibility. They are all liable to a possible intellectual correction, and the amount of this possibility cannot be certainly known. Our power of abstraction varies widely with different regions of knowledge, but no finite truth (however reached) can be considered as secure. Error with all of them is a matter of probability, and a matter of degree. And those are relatively true and strong which more nearly approach to perfection.

It is this perfection which is our measure. Our criterion is individuality, or the idea of complete system; and above, in Chapter xxiv,[a] we have already explained its nature. And I venture to think that about the main principle there is no great difficulty. Difficulty is felt more when we proceed to apply it in detail. We saw that the principles of internal harmony and of widest extent in the end are the same, for they are divergent aspects of the one idea of concrete unity. But for a discussion of such points the [481] reader must return to our former chapter.

A thing is more real as its opposite is more inconceivable. This is part of the truth. But, on the other hand, the opposite is more inconceivable, or more impossible, *because* the thing itself is more real and more probable and more true. The test (I would repeat it once more here) in its essence is positive. The stronger, the more systematic and more fully organized, a body of knowledge becomes, so much the more impossible becomes that which in any point conflicts with it. Or, from the other side, we may resume our doctrine thus. The greater the amount of knowledge

Repr. from *AR*, ch. xxvii.

[1] For a further statement see below.

[a] Repr. above, Part II, Sect. 1, Ch. 9.

which an idea or fact would, directly or indirectly, subvert, so much the more probably is it false and impossible and inconceivable. And there may be finite truths, with which error—and I mean by error here liability to intellectual correction—is most improbable. The chance may fairly be treated as too small to be worth considering. Yet after all it exists.

Finite truths are all conditional, because they all must depend on the unknown. But this unknown—the reader must bear in mind—is merely relative. Itself is subordinate to, and is included in, our absolute knowledge; and its nature, in general, is certainly not unknown. For, if it is anything at all, it is experience, and an element in the one Experience. Our ignorance, at the mercy of which all the finite lies, is not ignorance absolute. It covers and contains more than we are able to know, but this 'more' is known beforehand to be still of the self-same sort. And we must [482] now pass from the special consideration of finite truth.[2]

It is time to re-examine a distinction which we laid down above. We found that some knowledge was absolute, and that, in contrast with this, all finite truth was but conditional. But, when we examine it more closely, this difference seems hard to maintain. For how can truth be true absolutely, if there remains a gulf between itself and reality? Now in any truth about Reality the

---

[2] It is impossible here to deal fully with the question how, in case of a discrepancy, we are able to correct our knowledge. We are forced indefinitely to enlarge experience, because, as it is, being finite it cannot be harmonious. Then we find a collision between some fact or idea, on the one hand, and, on the other hand, some body of recognized truth. Now the self-contradictory cannot be true; and the question is how to rearrange it so as to make it harmonious. What is it in any given case, we have to ask, which has to be sacrificed? The conflict itself may perhaps be apparent only. A mere accident may have been taken for what is essential, and, with the correction of this mistake, the whole collision may cease. Or the fresh idea may be found to be untenable. It contains an error, and is therefore broken up and resolved; or, if that is not possible, it may be provisionally set on one side and disregarded. This last course is however feasible only if we assume that our original knowledge is so strong as to stand fast and unshaken. But the opposite of this may be the case. It may be our former knowledge which, on its side, has to give way, and must be modified and overruled by the fresh experience. But, last of all, there is a further possibility which remains. Neither of our conflicting pieces of knowledge may be able to stand as true. Each may be true enough to satisfy and to serve, for some purposes, and at a certain level; and yet both, viewed from above, can be seen to be conflicting errors. Both must therefore be resolved to the point required, and must be rearranged as elements in a wider whole. Separation of the accidents from the essence must here be carried on until the essence itself is more or less dissolved. I have no space to explain, or to attempt to illustrate, this general statement.

word 'about' is too significant. There remains always something outside, and other than, the predicate. And, because of this which is outside, the predicate, in the end, may be called conditional. In brief, the difference between subject and predicate, a difference essential to truth, is not accounted for.[3] It depends on something not included within the judgement itself, an element outlying and, therefore, in a sense unknown. The type and the essence, in other words, can never reach the reality. The essence realized, we may say, is too much to be truth, and, unrealized and abstract, it is assuredly too little to be real. Even absolute truth in the end seems thus to turn out erroneous.

And it must be admitted that, in the end, no possible truth is [483] quite true. It is a partial and inadequate translation of that which it professes to give bodily. And this internal discrepancy belongs irremovably to truth's proper character. Still the difference drawn between absolute and finite truth must none the less be upheld. For the former, in a word, is not *intellectually* corrigible. There is no intellectual alteration which could possibly, as general truth, bring it nearer to ultimate Reality. We have seen that any suggestion of this kind is but self-destructive, that any doubt on this point is literally senseless. Absolute truth is corrected only by passing outside the intellect. It is modified only by taking in the remaining aspects of experience. But in this passage the proper nature of truth is, of course, transformed and perishes.

Any finite truth, on the other side, remains subject to intellectual correction. It is incomplete not merely as being confined by its general nature, as truth, within one partial aspect of the Whole. It is incomplete as having within its own intellectual world a space falling outside it. There is truth, actual or possible, which is over against it, and which can stand outside it as an Other. But with absolute truth there is no intellectual outside. There is no competing predicate which could conceivably qualify its subject, and which could come in to condition and to limit its assertion. Absolute knowledge may be conditional, if you please; but its condition is not any *other* truth, whether actual or possible.

The doctrine, which I am endeavouring to state, is really sim-

---

[3] The essential inconsistency of truth may, perhaps, be best stated thus. If there is any difference between *what it means* and *what it stands for*, then truth is clearly not realized. But, if there is no such difference, then truth has ceased to exist.

ple. Truth is one aspect of experience, and is therefore made imperfect and limited by what it fails to include. So far as it is absolute, it does however give the general type and character of all that possibly can be true or real. And the universe in this general character is known completely. It is not known, and it never can be known, in all its details. It is not known, and it never, as a whole, can be known, in such a sense that knowledge would be the same as experience or reality. For knowledge and truth—if we suppose them to possess that identity—would have been, [484] therewith, absorbed and transmuted. But on the other hand the universe does not exist, and it cannot possibly exist, as truth or knowledge, in such a way as not to be contained and included in the truth we call absolute. For, to repeat it once more, such a possibility is self-destructive. We may perhaps say that, if *per impossibile* this could be possible, we at least could not possibly entertain the idea of it. For such an idea, in being entertained, vanishes into its opposite or into nonsense. Absolute truth is error only if you expect from it more than mere general knowledge. It is abstract,[4] and fails to supply its own subordinate details. It is one-sided, and cannot give bodily all sides of the Whole. But on the other side nothing, so far as it goes, can fall outside it. It is utterly all-inclusive and contains beforehand all that could ever be set against it. For nothing can be set against it, which does not become intellectual, and itself enter as a vassal into the kingdom of truth. Thus, even when you go beyond it, you can never advance outside it. When you take in more, you are condemned to take in more of the self-same sort. The universe, as truth, in other words preserves one character, and of that character we possess infallible knowledge.

And, if we view the matter from another side, there is no opposition between Reality and truth. Reality, to be complete, must take in and absorb this partial aspect of itself. And truth itself would not be complete, until it took in and included all aspects of the universe. Thus, in passing beyond itself and in

---

[4] It is not abstract in the way in which we have seen that all finite truth is abstract. That was precarious intellectually, since, more or less, it left other truth outside and over against it. It was thus always one piece among other pieces of the world of truth. It could be added to, intellectually, so as to be transformed. Absolute truth, on the other hand, cannot be altered by the addition of any truth. There is no possible truth which does not fall under it as one of its own details. Unless you presuppose it, in short, no other truth remains truth at all.

abolishing the difference between its subject and predicate, it does but carry out the demands of its proper nature. But I may perhaps hope, that this conclusion has been sufficiently secured . . . To repeat—in its general character Reality is present in knowledge and truth, that absolute truth which is distinguished and brought out by metaphysics. But this general character of Reality is not Reality itself, and again it is not more than the general character even of truth and knowledge. Still, so far as there is any truth and any knowledge at all, this character is absolute. Truth is conditional, but it cannot be intellectually transcended. To fill in its conditions would be to pass into a whole beyond mere intellect. [485]

The conclusion which we have reached, I trust, the outcome of no mere compromise, makes a claim to reconcile extremes. Whether it is to be called Realism or Idealism I do not know, and I have not cared to inquire. It neither puts ideas and thought first, nor again does it permit us to assert that anything else by itself is more real. Truth is the whole world in one aspect, an aspect supreme in philosophy, and yet even in philosophy conscious of its own incompleteness. So far again as our conclusion has claimed infallibility, it has come, I think, into no collision with the better kind of common sense. That metaphysics should approve itself to common sense is indeed out of the question. For neither in its processes nor in its results can it expect, or even hope, to be generally intelligible. But it is no light thing, except for the thoughtless, to advocate metaphysical results which, if they *were* understood by common sense, would at once be rejected. I do not mean that on subordinate points, such as the personality of the Deity or a continuance of the individual after death—points on which there is not any general consent in the world—philosophy is bound to adopt one particular view. I mean that to arrange the elements of our nature in such a way that the system made, when understood, strikes the mind as one-sided, is enough of itself to inspire hesitation and doubt. On this head at least, our main result is, I hope, satisfactory. The absolute knowledge that we have claimed is no more than an outline. It is knowledge which seems sufficient, on one side, to secure the chief interests of our nature, and it abstains, on the other side, from pretensions which all must feel are not human.

[486] We insist that all Reality must keep a certain character. The whole of its contents must be experience, they must come together into one system, and this unity itself must be experience. It must include and must harmonize every possible fragment of appearance. Anything which in any sense can be more than and beyond what we possess, must still inevitably be more of the self-same kind. We persist in this conclusion, and we urge that, so far as it goes, it amounts to absolute knowledge. But this conclusion on the other side, I have pointed out, does not go very far. It leaves us free to admit that what we know is, after all, nothing in proportion to the world of our ignorance. We do not know what other modes of experience may exist, or, in comparison with ours, how many they may be. We do not know, except in vague outline, what the Unity is, or, at all, why it appears in our particular forms of plurality. We can even understand that such knowledge is impossible, and we have found the reason why it is so. For truth can know only, we may say, so far as itself is. And the union of all sides of our nature would not leave them, in any case, as they are. Truth, when made adequate to Reality, would be so supplemented as to have become something else— something other than truth, and something for us unattainable. We have thus left due space for the exercise of doubt and wonder. We admit the healthy scepticism for which all knowledge in a sense is vanity, which feels in its heart that science is a poor thing if measured by the wealth of the real universe. We justify the natural wonder which delights to stray beyond our daylight world, and to follow paths that lead into half-known half-unknowable regions. Our conclusion, in brief, has explained and has confirmed the irresistible impression that all is beyond us.

Everything is error, but everything is not illusion. It is error where, and in so far as, our ideas are not the same as reality. It is illusion where, and in so far as, this difference turns to a conflict in our nature. Where experience, inward or outward, clashes with our views, where there arises thus disorder, confu-
[487] sion, and pain, we may speak of illusion. It is the course of events in collision with the set of our ideas. Now error, in the sense of one-sided and partial truth, is necessary to our being. Indeed nothing else, so to speak, could be relative to our needs, nothing else could answer the purpose of truth. And to suit the divergent aspects of our inconsistent finite lives, a variety of error

in the shape of diverse partial truths is required. And, if things could be otherwise, then, so far as we see, finite life would be impossible. Therefore we must have error present always, and this presence entails some amount of illusion. Finite beings, themselves not self-consistent, have to realize their various aspects in the chance-world of temporal events. And hence ideas and existence cannot precisely correspond, while the want of this correspondence must to some extent mean illusion. There are finite souls, we must admit sadly, to whom, on the whole, life has proved a disappointment and cheat. There is perhaps no one to whom, at certain moments and in some respect, this conclusion has not come home. But that, in general and in the main, life is illusory cannot be rationally maintained. And if, in general and in the rough, our ideas are answered by events, that is all surely which, as finite beings, we have a right to expect. We must reply then, that, though illusions exist here and there, the whole is not an illusion. We are not concerned to gain an absolute experience which for us, emphatically, could be nothing. We want to know, in effect, whether the universe is concealed behind appearances, and is making a sport of us. What we find here truer and more beautiful and better and higher—are these things really so, or in reality may they be all quite otherwise? Our standard, in other words, is it a false appearance not owned by the universe? And to this, in general, we may make an unhesitating reply. There is no reality at all anywhere except in appearance, and in our appearance we can discover the main nature of reality. This nature cannot be exhausted, but it can be known in abstract. And it is, really and indeed, this general character of the very universe itself which distinguishes for us the relative worth of [488] appearances. We make mistakes, but still we use the essential nature of the world as our own criterion of value and reality. Higher, truer, more beautiful, better and more real—these, on the whole, count in the universe as they count for us. And existence, on the whole, must correspond with our ideas. For, on the whole, higher means for us a greater amount of that one Reality, outside of which all appearance is absolutely nothing.

It costs little to find that in the end Reality is inscrutable. It is easy to perceive that any appearance, not being the Reality, in a sense is fallacious. These truths, such as they are, are within the reach of any and every man. It is a simple matter to conclude further, perhaps, that the Real sits apart, that it keeps state by itself and does not descend into phenomena. Or it is as cheap, again, to take up another side of the same error. The Reality is viewed perhaps as immanent in all its appearances, in such a way that it is, alike and equally, present in all. Everything is so worthless on one hand, so divine on the other, that nothing can be viler or can be more sublime than anything else. It is against both sides of this mistake, it is against this empty transcendence and this shallow Pantheism, that our pages may be called one sustained polemic. The positive relation of every appearance as an adjective to Reality, and the presence of Reality among its appearances in different degrees and with diverse values—this double truth we have found to be the centre of philosophy. It is because the Absolute is no sundered abstraction but has a positive character, it is because this Absolute itself is positively present in all appearance, that appearances themselves can possess true differences of value. And, apart from this foundation, in the end we are left without a solid criterion of worth or of truth or reality. This conclusion—the necessity on one side for a standard, and the impossibility of reaching it without a positive knowledge of the Absolute—I would venture to press upon any intelligent worshipper of the Unknown.

[489]   The Reality itself is nothing at all apart from appearances. It is in the end nonsense to talk of realities—or of anything else—to which appearances could appear, or between which they somehow could hang as relations. Such realities (we have seen) would themselves be appearances or nothing. For there is no way of qualifying the Real except by appearances, and outside the Real there remains no space in which appearances could live. Reality appears in its appearances, and they are its revelation; and otherwise they also could be nothing whatever. The Reality comes into knowledge, and, the more we know of anything, the more in one way is Reality present within us. The Reality is our criterion of worse and better, of ugliness and beauty, of true and false, and of real and unreal. It in brief decides between, and gives a general meaning to, higher and lower. It is because of this criterion that appearances differ in worth; and, without it, lowest and highest would, for all we know, count the same in the universe. And Reality is one Experience, self-pervading and superior to

mere relations. Its character is the opposite of that fabled extreme which is barely mechanical, and it is, in the end, the sole perfect realization of spirit. We may fairly close this work then by insisting that Reality is spiritual. There is a great saying of Hegel's, a saying too well known, and one which without some explanation I should not like to endorse. But I will end with something not very different, something perhaps more certainly the essential message of Hegel. Outside of spirit there is not, and there cannot be, any reality, and, the more that anything is spiritual, so much the more is it veritably real.

APPENDIX

Introduction: The Dilemma of the Relation of Thought to Reality

[491] I. With regard to the arrangement of my work I offer no defence. It was not in my power to write a systematic treatise, and, that being so, I thought the way I took was as good as any other. The order of the book seemed to myself a matter of no great importance. So far as I can see, whatever way I had taken the result would have been the same, and I must doubt if any other way would have been better for most readers. . . .

II. The actual starting-point and basis of this work is an assumption about truth and reality. I have assumed that the object of metaphysics is to find a general view which will satisfy the intellect, and I have assumed that whatever succeeds in doing this is real and true, and that whatever fails is neither. This is a doctrine which, so far as I see, can neither be proved nor ques-
[492] tioned. The proof or the question, it seems to me, must imply the truth of the doctrine, and, if that is not assumed, both vanish. . . .

III. But with this we come against the great problem of the relation of Thought to Reality. For if we decline (as I think wrongly) to affirm that all truth is thought, yet we certainly cannot deny this of a great deal of truth, and we can hardly deny that truth satisfies the intellect. But, if so, truth therefore, as we have seen, is real. And to hold that truth is real, not because it is true but because also it is something else, seems untenable; for, if so, the something else left outside would make incomplete and would hence falsify the truth. But then, on the other hand, can thought, however complete, be the same as reality, the same altogether, I mean, and with no difference between them? This is a question to which I could never give an affirmative reply. . . .

But with this we are left, it appears, in a dilemma. There is a

Repr. from *AR*. This Appendix was added by Bradley to the 2nd end., 1897, as a reply to his critics.

difference between on the one side truth or thought (it will be convenient now to identify these), and on the other side reality. But to assert this difference seems impossible without somehow transcending thought or bringing the difference into thought, and these phrases seem meaningless. Thus reality appears to be an Other different from truth and yet not able to be truly taken as different; and this dilemma to myself was long a main cause of perplexity and doubt. We indeed do something to solve it by the identification of being or reality with experience or with sentience [493] in its widest meaning. This step I have taken without hesitation, and I will not add a further defence of it here. . . . But this step by itself leaves us far from the desired solution of our dilemma; for between facts of experience and the thought of them and the truth about them the difference still remains, and the difficulty which attaches to this difference.

The solution of this dilemma offered in Chapter xv[a] is, I believe, the only solution possible. It contains the main thesis of this work, views opposed to that thesis remaining, it seems to me, caught in and destroyed by the dilemma. And we must notice two main features in this doctrine. It contends on one side that truth or thought essentially does not satisfy its own claims, that it demands to be, and so far already is, something which completely it cannot be. Hence if thought carried out its own nature, it both would and would not have passed beyond itself and become also an Other. And in the second place this self-completion of thought, by inclusion of the aspects opposed to mere thinking, would be what we mean by reality, and by reality we can mean no more than this. The criticisms on this doctrine which I have seen, do not appear to me to rest on any serious inquiry either as to what the demands of thought really are, or what their satisfaction involves. But if to satisfy the intellect is to be true and real, such a question must be fundamental.

IV. With the solution of this problem about truth comes the whole view of Reality. Reality is above thought and above every partial aspect of being, but it includes them all. Each of these completes itself by uniting with the rest, and so makes the perfection of the whole. And this whole is experience, for anything other than experience is meaningless. Now anything that in any

---

[a] Repr. above, Part II, Sect. I, Ch. 6.

sense 'is', qualifies the absolute reality and so is real. But on the other hand, because everything, to complete itself and to satisfy its own claims, must pass beyond itself, nothing in the end is real except the Absolute. Everything else is appearance; it is that the character of which goes beyond its own existence, is inconsistent with it and transcends it. And viewed intellectually appearance is error. But the remedy lies in supplementation by inclusion of that which is both outside and yet essential, and in the Absolute this remedy is perfected. There is no mere appearance or utter chance or absolute error, but all is relative. And the degree of reality is [494] measured by the amount of supplementation required in each case, and by the extent to which the completion of anything entails its own destruction as such.

V. But this Absolute, it has been objected, is a mere blank or else unintelligible. Certainly it is unintelligible if that means that you cannot understand its detail, and that throughout its structure constantly in particular you are able to answer the question, Why or How. And that it is not in this sense intelligible I have clearly laid down. But as to its main character we must return a different reply. We start from the diversity in unity which is given in feeling, and we develop this internally by the principle of self-completion beyond self, until we reach the idea of an all-inclusive and supra-relational experience. This idea, it seems to me, is in the abstract intelligible and positive, and so once more is the principle by which it is reached; and the criticism which takes these as mere negations rests, I think, on misunderstanding. The criticism which really desires to be effective ought, I should say, to show that my view of the starting-point is untenable, and the principle of development, together with its result, unsound, and such criticism I have not yet seen. But with regard to what is unintelligible and inexplicable we must surely distinguish. A theory may contain what is unintelligible, so long as it really contains it; and not to know how a thing can be is no disproof of our knowing that it both must be and is. The whole question is whether we have a general principle under which the details can and must fall, or whether, on the other hand, the details fall outside or are negative instances which serve to upset the principle. Now I have argued in detail that there are no facts which fall outside the principle or really are negative instances; and hence, because the principle is undeniable, the facts both must and can comply with it, and therefore they do so. And given a knowledge of 'how' in general, a mere ignorance of 'how' in detail is permissible and harmless. This argument in its general character is, I presume, quite familiar even to those critics who seem to have been surprised by it; and the application of it here is, so far as I see, legitimate and necessary. And for that application I must refer to the body of the work.

VI. With regard to the unity of the Absolute we know that the Absolute must be one, because anything experienced is experi- [495] enced in or as a whole, and because anything like independent plurality or external relations cannot satisfy the intellect. And it fails to satisfy the intellect because it is a self-contradiction. Again for the same reason the Absolute is one system in the very highest sense of that term, any lower sense being unreal because in the end self-contradictory. . . .

Note A. Contradiction, and the Contrary

If we are asked 'What is contrary or contradictory?' (I do not [500] find it necessary here to distinguish between these), the more we consider the more difficult we find it to answer. 'A thing cannot be or do two opposites at once and in the same respect'—this reply at first sight may seem clear, but on reflection may threaten us with an unmeaning circle. For what are 'opposites' except the adjectives which the thing cannot so combine? Hence we have said no more than that we in fact find predicates which in fact will not go together, and our further introduction of their 'opposite' nature seems to add nothing. 'Opposites will not unite, and their apparent union is mere appearance.' But the mere appearance really perhaps lies in their intrinsic opposition. And if one arrangement has made them opposite, a wider arrangement may perhaps unmake their opposition, and may include them all at once and harmoniously. Are, in short, opposites really opposite [501] at all, or are they, after all, merely different? Let us attempt to take them in this latter character.

'A thing cannot without an internal distinction be . . . two

First pub. in *Mind*, NS 5 (1896); repr. with omissions in *AR*. Repr. here from *AR*.

different things, and differences cannot belong to the same thing in the same point unless in that point there is diversity. The appearance of such a union may be fact, but is for thought a contradiction.' This is the thesis which to me seems to contain the truth about the contrary, and I will now try to recommend this thesis to the reader.

The thesis in the first place does not imply that the end which we seek is tautology. Thought most certainly does not demand mere sameness, which to it would be nothing. A bare tautology (Hegel has taught us this, and I wish we could all learn it) is not even so much as a poor truth or a thin truth. It is not a truth in any way, in any sense, or at all. Thought involves analysis and synthesis, and if the Law of Contradiction forbade diversity, it would forbid thinking altogether. And with this too necessary warning I will turn to the other side of the difficulty. Thought cannot do without differences, but on the other hand it cannot make them. And, as it cannot make them, so it cannot receive them merely from the outside and ready-made. Thought demands to go *proprio motu*, or, what is the same thing, with a ground and reason. Now to pass from *A* to *B*, if the ground remains external, is for thought to pass with no ground at all. But if, again, the external fact of *A*'s and *B*'s conjunction is offered as a reason, then that conjunction itself creates the same difficulty. For thought's analysis can respect nothing, nor is there any principle by which at a certain point it should arrest itself or be arrested. Every distinguishable aspect becomes therefore for thought a diverse element to be brought to unity. Hence thought can no more pass without a reason from *A* or from *B* to its conjunction, than before it could pass groundlessly from *A* to *B*. The transition, being offered as a mere datum, or effected as a mere fact, is not thought's own self-movement. Or in other words, because for thought no ground can be merely external, the passage is groundless. Thus *A* and *B* and their conjunction are, like atoms, pushed in from the outside by chance or fate; and what is thought to do with them but either make or accept an arrangement which to it is wanton and without reason—or, having no reason for anything else, attempt against reason to identify them simply?

'This is not so,' I shall be told, 'and the whole case is otherwise. There are certain ultimate complexes given to us as facts, [502]   and these ultimates, as they are given, thought simply takes up as principles and employs them to explain the detail of the world. And with this process thought is satisfied.' To me such a doctrine is quite erroneous. For these ultimates (*a*) cannot make the world intelligible, and again (*b*) they are not given, and (*c*) in themselves they are self-contradictory, and not truth but appearance.

Certainly for practice we have to work with appearance and with relative untruths, and without these things the sciences of course would not exist. There is, I suppose, here no question about all this, and all this is irrelevant. The question here is whether with so much as this the intellect can be satisfied, or whether on the other hand it does not find in the end defect and self-contradiction. Consider first (*a*) the failure of what is called 'explanation'. The principles taken up are not merely in themselves not rational, but, being limited, they remain external to the facts to be explained. The diversities therefore will only *fall*, or rather must be *brought*, under the principle. They do not come out of it, nor of themselves do they bring themselves under it. The explanation therefore in the end does but conjoin aliens inexplicably. The obvious instance is the mechanical interpretation of the world. Even if here the principles were rational intrinsically, as surely they are not, they express but one portion of a complex whole. The rest therefore, even when and where it has been 'brought under' the principles, is but conjoined with them externally and for no known reason. Hence in the explanation there is in the end neither self-evidence nor any 'because' except that brutally things come so.

'But in any case,' I may hear, 'these complexes are given and do not contradict themselves,' and let us take these points in their order. (*b*) The transition from *A* to *B*, the inherence of *b* and *c* as adjectives in *A*, the union of discretion and continuity in time and space—'such things are facts', it is said. 'They are given to an intellect which is satisfied to accept and to employ them.' They may be facts, I reply, in some sense of that word, but to say that, as such and in and by themselves, they are given is erroneous. What is given is a presented whole, a sensuous total in which these characters are found; and beyond and beside these characters there is always given something else. And to urge 'but at any rate these characters are there,' is surely futile. For certainly they are not, when there, as they are when you by an abstraction have taken them out. Your contention is that certain

ultimate conjunctions of elements are given. And I reply that no
such *bare* conjunction is or possibly can be given. For the back-
[503]   ground is present, and the background and the conjunction are, I
submit, alike integral aspects of the fact. The background therefore must be taken as a condition of the conjunction's existence,
and the intellect must assert the conjunction subject in this way
to a condition. The conjunction is hence not bare but dependent,
and it is really a connection mediated by something falling outside it. A thing, for example, with its adjectives can never be simply given. It is given integrally with a mass of other features, and
when it is affirmed of Reality it is affirmed of Reality qualified by
this presented background. And this Reality (to go further) is
and must be qualified also by what transcends any one presentation. Hence the mere complex, alleged to be given to the intellect,
is really a selection made by or accepted by that intellect. An
abstraction cuts away a mass of environing particulars, and offers
the residue bare, as something given and to be accepted free from
supporting conditions. And for working purposes such an artifice
is natural and necessary, but to offer it as ultimate fact seems to
me to be monstrous. We have an intellectual product, to be logically justified, if indeed that could be possible, and most certainly
we have not a genuine datum.

At this point we may lay down an important result. The intellect cannot be reduced to choose between accepting an irrational
conjunction or rejecting something given. For the intellect can
always accept the conjunction not as bare but as a connection,
the bond of which is at present unknown. It is taken therefore as
by itself appearance which is less or more false in proportion as
the unknown conditions, if filled in, less or more would swamp
and transform it. The intellect therefore while rejecting whatever
is alien to itself, if offered as absolute, can accept the inconsistent
if taken as subject to conditions. Beside absolute truth there is
relative truth, useful opinion, and validity, and to this latter
world belong so-called non-rational facts.[1]

[504]   (*c*) And any mere conjunction, I go on to urge, is for thought
self-contradictory. Thought, I may perhaps assume, implies

---

[1] I use 'validity' much in the sense in which it was made current, I believe, by
Lotze, and in which it has been said, I presume, with some truth, partly to coincide with δόξα [opinion]. For my own purposes . . . what is self-contradictory
may also for me be valid.[a] . . .

analysis and synthesis and distinction in unity. Further the mere conjunction offered to thought cannot be set apart itself as something sacred, but may itself properly and indeed must become thought's object. There will be a passage therefore from one element in this conjunction to its other element or elements. And on the other hand, by its own nature, thought must hold these in unity. But, in a bare conjunction, starting with *A* thought will externally be driven to *B*, and seeking to unite these it will find no ground of union. Thought can of itself supply no internal bond by which to hold them together, nor has it any internal diversity by which to maintain them apart. It must therefore seek barely to identify them, though they are different, or somehow to unite both diversities where it has no ground of distinction and union. And this does not mean that the connection is merely unknown and may be affirmed as unknown, and also, supposing it were known, as rational. For, if so, the conjunction would at once not be bare, and it is as bare that it is offered and not as conditional. But, if on the other hand it remains bare, then thought to affirm it must unite diversities without any internal distinction, and the attempt to do this is precisely what contradiction means.

'But', I shall be told, 'you misrepresent the case. What is offered is not the elements apart, nor the elements plus an external bond, but the elements together and in conjunction.' Yes, I reply, but the question is how thought can think what is offered. If thought in its own nature possessed a 'together', a 'between', and an 'all at once', then in its own intrinsic passage, or at least somehow in its own way and manner, it could reaffirm the external conjunction. But if these sensible bonds of union fall outside the inner nature of thought, just as much as do the sensible terms which they outwardly conjoin—the case surely is different. Then forced to distinguish and unable to conjoin by its own proper

---

ᵃ Lotze uses the term 'validity' as a primitive term for a particular kind of reality. According to Lotze, to say that something is real is to affirm it, even though different realities are affirmed in irreducibly different ways. Events occur, relations hold, things exist or have being. Strictly speaking, ideas are dated events which occur in minds. However, it is possible to abstract the content of an idea from its occurrence and to affirm its reality. To do so is to assert that it has validity. For further discussion, see Hermann Lotze, *Logic*, ii (Oxford: Clarendon Press, 1888), 208–10. 'Doxa' is a term used in Greek philosophy for opinion. Plato, for example, contrasts doxa with both knowledge and ignorance at *Republic* 476e–480a.

nature, or with a reason, thought is confronted by elements that
[505] strive to come together without a way of union. The sensible
conjunctions remain for thought mere other elements in the congeries, themselves failing in connection and external to others.
And, on the other hand, driven to unite without internal distinction thought finds in this attempt a self-contradiction. You may
exclaim against thought's failure, and in this to some degree I am
with you; but the fact remains thus. Thought cannot accept tautology and yet demands unity in diversity. But your offered conjunctions on the other side are for it no connections or ways of
union. They are themselves merely other external things to be
connected. And so thought, knowing what it wants, refuses to
accept something different, something which for it is appearance,
a self-inconsistent attempt at reality and truth. It is idle from the
outside to say to thought, 'Well, unite but do not identify'. How
can thought unite except so far as in itself it has a mode of
union? To unite without an internal ground of connection and
distinction is to strive to bring together barely in the same point,
and that is self-contradiction.

Things are not contrary because they are opposite, for things
by themselves are not opposite. And things are not contrary
because they are diverse, for the world as a fact holds diversity in
unity. Things are self-contrary when, and just so far as, they
appear as bare conjunctions, when in order to think them you
would have to predicate differences without an internal ground of
connection and distinction, when, in other words, you would
have to unite diversities simply, and that means in the same
point. This is what contradiction means, or I at least have been
able to find no other meaning. For a mere 'together', a bare conjunction in space or time, is for thought unsatisfactory and in the
end impossible. It depends for its existence on our neglecting to
reflect, or on our purposely abstaining, so far as it is concerned,
from analysis and thought. But any such working arrangement,
however valid, is but provisional. On the other hand, we have
found that no intrinsical opposites exist, but that contraries, in a
sense, are made. Hence in the end nothing is contrary nor is
there any insoluble contradiction. Contradictions exist so far only
as internal distinction seems impossible, only so far as diversities
are attached to one unyielding point assumed, tacitly or
expressly, to be incapable of internal diversity or external com-

plement. But any such fixture is an abstraction, useful perhaps, but in the end appearance. And thus, where we find contradiction, there is something limited and untrue which invites us to transcend it.

Standing contradictions appear where the subject is narrowed artificially, and where diversity in the identity is taken as excluded. A thing cannot be at once in two places if in the 'at [506] once' there is no lapse, nor can one place have two bodies at once if both claim it in their character as extended. The soul cannot affirm and deny at a single time, unless (as some perhaps rightly hold) the self itself may be divided. And, to speak in general, the more narrowly we take the subject, and the less internal ground for diversity it contains, the more it threatens us with standing or insoluble contradictions. But, we may add, so much the more abstractedness and less truth does such a subject possess. We may instance the presence of 'disparate' qualities, such as white, hard and hot, in a single thing. The 'thing' is presented as one feature of an indefinite complex, and it is affirmed as predicate of a reality transcending what is given. It is hence capable in all ways of indefinite addition to its apparent character. And to deny that in the 'real thing' can be an internal diversity and ground of distinction seems quite irrational. But so far as for convenience or from thoughtlessness the denial is made, and the real thing is identified with our mutilated and abstract view of the thing—so far the disparate qualities logically clash and become contradictory.[2]

The Law of Contradiction tells us that we must not simply identify the diverse, since their union involves a ground of distinction. So far as this ground is rightly or wrongly excluded, the Law forbids us to predicate diversities. Where the ground is merely not explicit or remains unknown, our assertion of any complex is provisional and contingent. It may be valid and good, but it is an incomplete appearance of the real, and its truth is relative. Yet, while it offers itself as but contingent truth and as more or less incomplete appearance, the Law of Contradiction has nothing against it. But abstracted and irrational conjunctions taken by themselves as reality and truth, in short 'facts' as they are accepted by too many philosophers, the Law must condemn.

---

[2] Of course the real thing or the reality of the thing may turn out to be something very different from the thing as we first take it up.

And about the truth of this Law, so far as it applies, there is in my opinion no question. The question will be rather as to how far the Law applies and how far therefore it is true.

But before we conclude, there is a matter we may do well to consider. In this attempt to attribute diversity and to avoid contradiction what in the end would satisfy the intellect supposing that it could be got? This question, I venture to think, is too often ignored. Too often a writer will criticize and condemn some view [507] as being that which the mind cannot accept, when he apparently has never asked himself what it is that would satisfy the intellect, or even whether the intellect could endure his own implied alternative. What in the end then, let us ask, would content the intellect?

While the diversities are external to each other and to their union, ultimate satisfaction is impossible. There must, as we have seen, be an identity and in that identity a ground of distinction and connection. But that ground, if external to the elements into which the conjunction must be analyzed, becomes for the intellect a fresh element, and it itself calls for synthesis in a fresh point of unity. But hereon, because in the intellect no intrinsic connections were found, ensues the infinite process. Is there a remedy for this evil?

The remedy might lie here. If the diversities were complementary aspects of a process of connection and distinction, the process not being external to the elements or again a foreign compulsion of the intellect, but itself the intellect's own *proprius motus*, the case would be altered. Each aspect would of itself be a transition to the other aspect, a transition intrinsic and natural at once to itself and to the intellect. And the Whole would be a self-evident analysis and synthesis of the intellect itself by itself. Synthesis here has ceased to be mere synthesis and has become self-completion, and analysis, no longer mere analysis, is self-explication. And the question how or why the many are one and the one is many here loses its meaning. There is no why or how beside the self-evident process, and towards its own differences this whole is at once their how and their why, their being, substance, and system, their reason, ground, and principle of diversity and unity.

Has the Law of Contradiction anything here to condemn? It

seems to me it has nothing. The identity of which diversities are predicated is in no case simple. There is no point which is not itself internally the transition to its complement, and there is no unity which fails in internal diversity and ground of distinction. In short 'the identity of opposites', far from conflicting with the Law of Contradiction, may claim to be the one view which satisfies its demands, the only theory which everywhere refuses to accept a standing contradiction.[3] And if all that we find were in the end such a self-evident and self-complete whole, containing in itself as constituent processes the detail of the Universe, so far as I see the intellect would receive satisfaction in full. But for myself, unable to verify a solution of this kind, connections in the end must remain in part mere syntheses, the putting together [508] of differences external to one another and to that which couples them. And against my intellectual world the Law of Contradiction has therefore claims nowhere satisfied in full. And since, on the other hand, the intellect insists that these demands must be and are met, I am led to hold that they are met in and by a whole beyond the mere intellect. And in the intellect itself I seem to find an inner want and defect and a demand thus to pass itself beyond itself. And against this conclusion I have not yet seen any tenable objection.

The view which to me appears to be true is briefly this. That abstract identity should satisfy the intellect, even in part, is wholly impossible. On the other hand I cannot say that to me any principle or principles of diversity in unity are self-evident. The existence of a single content (I will not call it a quality) which should be simple experience and being in one is to me not in itself impossible intrinsically. If I may speak mythologically I am not sure that, if no diversity were given, the intellect of itself could invent it or would even demand it. But, since diversity is there as a fact, any such hypothesis seems illegitimate. As a fact and given we have in feeling diversity and unity in one whole, a whole implicit and not yet broken up into terms and relations. This immediate union of the one and many is an 'ultimate fact' from which we start; and to hold that feeling, because immediate, must be simple and without diversity is, in my view, a doctrine

---

[3] On this and other points I would refer to Mr. McTaggart's excellent work on *Hegelian Dialectic*. [John McTaggart Ellis McTaggart, *Studies in the Hegelian Dialectic* (Cambridge: Cambridge University Press, 1896).]

quite untenable.[4] That I myself should have been taken as committed to this doctrine is to me, I must be allowed to add, really surprising. But feeling, if an ultimate fact, is not true ultimately or real. Even of itself it is self-transcendent and transitory. And, when we try to think its unity, then, as we have seen, we end in failure. For thought in its own nature has no 'together' and is forced to move by way of terms and relations, and the unity of these remains in the end external and, because external, inconsistent. But the conclusion I would recommend is no vain attempt either to accept bare identity or to relapse into a stage before thinking begins. Self-existence and self-identity are to be found, I would urge, in a whole beyond thought, a whole to which thought points and in which it is included, but which is known only in abstract character and could not be verified in its detail.

[509]   And since I have been taken to build on assumptions which I am unable to recognize, I will here repeat what it is that I have assumed. I have assumed first that truth has to satisfy the intellect, and that what does not do this is neither true nor real. This assumption I can defend only by showing that any would-be objector assumes it also. And I start from the root-idea of being or experience, which is at once positive and ultimate. Then I certainly do not go on to assume about being that it must be self-contained, simple or what not?—but I proceed in another manner. I take up certain facts or truths (call them what you please) that I find are offered me, and I care very little what it is I take up. These facts or truths, as they are offered, I find my intellect rejects, and I go on to discover why it rejects them. It is because they contradict themselves. They offer, that is, a complex of diversities conjoined in a way which does not satisfy my intellect, a way which it feels is not its way and which it cannot repeat as its own, a way which for it results in mere collision. For, to be satisfied, my intellect must understand, and it cannot understand by taking a congeries, if I may say so, in the lump. My intellect may for certain purposes, to use an old figure, swallow mysteries unchewed, but unchewed it is unable in the end to stomach and digest them. It has not, as some opponents of Hegel would seem to assume, any such strange faculty of sensuous intu-

---

[4] Feeling is certainly *not* 'un-differentiated' if that means that it contains no diverse aspects. I would take the opportunity to state that this view as to feeling is so far from being novel that I owe it, certainly in the main, to Hegel's psychology.

ition. On the contrary my intellect is discursive, and to understand it must go from one point to another, and in the end also must go by a movement which it feels satisfies its nature. Thus, to understand a complex *AB*, I must begin with *A* or *B*. And beginning, say, with *A*, if I then merely *find B*, I have either lost *A* or I have got beside *A* something else, and in neither case have I understood. For my intellect cannot simply unite a diversity, nor has it in itself any form or way of togetherness, and you gain nothing if beside *A* and *B* you offer me their conjunction in fact. For to my intellect that is no more than another external element. And 'facts', once for all, are for my intellect not true unless they satisfy it. And, so far as they are not true, then, as they are offered, they are not reality.

From this I conclude that what is real must be self-contained and self-subsistent and not qualified from the outside. For an external qualification is a mere conjunction, and that, we have seen, is for the intellect an attempt of diversities simply to identify themselves, and such an attempt is what we mean by self-contradiction. Hence whatever is real must be qualified from itself, and that means that, so far as it is real, it must be self-contained and self-subsistent. And, since diversities exist, they must [510] therefore somehow be true and real; and since, to be understood and to be true and real, they must be united, hence they must be true and real in such a way that from *A* or *B* the intellect can pass to its further qualification without an external determination of either. But this means that *A* and *B* are united, each from its own nature, in a whole which is the nature of both alike. And hence it follows that in the end there is nothing real but a whole of this kind.[5]

From the other side—Why do I hold reality to be a self-contained and self-consistent individual? It is because otherwise, if I admit an external determination and a qualification by an other,

---

[5] And hence it follows also that every 'part' of this whole must be internally defective and (when thought) contradictory. For otherwise how from one to others and the rest could there be any internal passage? And without such a passage and with but an external junction or bond, could there be any system or whole at all which would satisfy the intellect, and could be taken as real or possible? I at least have given my reason for answering this question in the negative. We may even, forgetting other points of view, say of the world,

> Thus every part is full of vice,
> Yet the whole mass a paradise.

I am left with a conjunction, and that for the intellect is a self-contradiction. On the other hand the real cannot be simple, because, to be understood, it must somehow be taken with and be qualified by the diversity which is a fact. The diversity therefore must fall within and be subordinate to a self-determined whole, an individual system, and any other determination is incompatible with reality. These ideas may be mistaken, but to my mind they do not seem to be obscure, nor again are they novel. But if I may judge from the way in which some critics have taken them, they must involve some great obscurity or difficulty. But, not apprehending this, I am unfortunately unable to discuss it.[6]

We have found that nothing in itself is opposite and refuses to unite. Everything again is opposite if brought together into a point which owns no internal diversity. Every bare conjunction is [511] therefore contradictory when taken up by thought, because thought in its nature is incapable of conjunction and has no way of mere 'together'. On the other side no such conjunction is or possibly could be given. It is itself a mere abstraction, useful perhaps and so legitimate and so far valid, but taken otherwise to be condemned as the main root of error.

Contradiction is appearance, everywhere removable by distinction and by further supplement, and removed actually, if not in and by the mere intellect, by the whole which transcends it. On the other hand contradiction, or rather what becomes such, as soon as it is thought out, is everywhere necessary. Facts and views partial and one-sided, incomplete and so incoherent—things that offer themselves as characters of a Reality which they cannot express, and which present in them moves them to jar with and to pass beyond themselves—in a word *appearances* are the stuff of which the Universe is made. If we take them in their proper character we shall be prone neither to overestimate nor to slight them.

---

[6] The Law of Identity, I may be allowed to note in this connection, is the denial that truth, if true, is alterable from the outside. For, if so, it would become either itself conjoined with its own absence, or itself conjoined with a positive other; and either alternative (to take them here as alternatives), we have seen, is self-contradictory. Hence any mere context cannot modify a truth so far as it is true. It merely adds, we must say, something more which leaves the truth itself unaffected. Truth cannot be modified, in other words, except from within. This of course opens a problem, for truth seems on the one hand to be abstract, as truth, and so incomplete, and on the other hand, if true, to be self-contained and even self-existent.

We have now seen the nature of incompatibles or contraries. There are no native contraries, and we have found no reason to entertain such an idea. Things are contrary when, being diverse, they strive to be united in one point which in itself does not admit of internal diversity. And for the intellect any bare conjunction is an attempt of this sort. The intellect has in its nature no principle of mere togetherness, and the intellect again can accept nothing which is alien to itself. A foreign togetherness of elements is for the intellect, therefore, but one offered external element the more. And, since the intellect demands a unity, every distinguishable aspect of a 'together' must be brought into one. And if in this unity no internal connection of diversity natural to the intellect can be found, we are left with a diversity belonging to and conjoined in one undistinguished point. And this is contradiction, and contradiction in the end we found was this and nothing but this. On the other hand we urged that bare irrational conjunctions are not given as facts. Every perceived complex is a selection from an indefinite background, and, when judged as real, it is predicated both of this background and of the Reality which transcends it. Hence in this background and beyond it lies, we may believe, the reason and the internal connection of all we take as a mere external 'together'. Conjunction and contradiction in short is but our defect, our one-sidedness, and our abstraction, and it is appearance and not Reality. But the reason we have to assume may in detail be not accessible to our intellect.

SECTION 2

Essays on Truth and Reality

Essays on Truth and Reality was published in 1914. It is a collection of papers some of which were previously unpublished but most of which had appeared in *Mind*. They represent Bradley's mature thought and are in general intended to clarify and expound views adopted in *The Principles of Logic* and *Appearance and Reality*. An exception with respect to the latter purpose is 'On Our Fear of Death and Desire for Immortality', which shows Bradley at his analytical best and presages some recent discussions of personal identity. We have reproduced our selections in the order of their appearance in *Essays on Truth and Reality*. This was not the chronological order of their writing.

G.S.

On Floating Ideas and the Imaginary

This article is important as the source of a central criticism that Bradley himself levelled against the first edition of *The Principles of Logic*. The main thesis of the article is expressed in the claim: 'The difference between my world of fact and my other worlds is important and necessary, but the exaggerated value we often tend to attach to it is really illusory' (*ETR*, 49, below, p. 247) Bradley admits that he himself in *The Principles of Logic* appeared to attach just such an exaggerated value to the difference (cf. e.g. *PL* 39 n. 13, above, p. 26; 110 n. 40, above, p. 69).

In the first section Bradley rejects as an acceptable basis for metaphysics the view according to which reality is to be identified with *our world of fact*: that is, is to be identified with the spatio-temporal system of objects that I can think of at *this* moment as containing my present perceptions, my body and the objects I can draw attention to by pointing and using sentences containing demonstratives like 'this', 'here', 'now'. For a start, Bradley argues, our idea of this world is unclear and inconsistent with respect to the actual existence of the past and future. Moreover, it cannot easily be thought of as containing imaginary objects, or moral values, or abstract entities, or the facts of art, science, religion, and so on. Such things must, in an adequate metaphysics, somehow be accommodated within reality (*ETR* 30, below, pp. 232–3).

He suggests that a better basis for a metaphysics, and one more in keeping with psychological fact, is provided by the view that (1) the whole universe construed as containing both one's self and what is not one's self will be immediately felt as being in some sense a single totality, but (2) against the background of this immediate and largely implicit experience of unity there will be, for the normal adult human being, an indefinite multiplicity of more or less disparate worlds distinguishable as objects of thought and thought-impregnated experiences (*ETR* 31, below, pp. 233–4).

Coinciding with this contention Bradley argues that, from a logical point of view, any use of ideas—even those used in imagining things in fiction, or in framing the contents of questions or commands or

'On Floating Ideas and the Imaginary' was first pub. in *Mind*, NS 15 (1906). Repr. here from *ETR*, ch. iii.

denials—must be construed as involving the predication of those ideas of reality. Thus Bradley contends that the ideal contents that I exercise in such acts, although they will not in general be predicated of any objects in my real world of fact, will nevertheless represent situations as obtaining in thinkable worlds distinguishable from that world. Thus, to put it in Bradley's terminology, ideas used in such contexts cannot be taken to float *absolutely*. I will take them to float *relatively* to some particular thinkable world (e.g. to my real world of fact, or to the world of Mr Pickwick, or whatever) which is currently the special subject of my thoughts, but they will nevertheless necessarily characterize some other thinkable world (*ETR* 32–41, below, pp. 234–41).

In the second section Bradley is concerned (1) with the nature of the imaginary in general (cf. *ETR* 46–7, below, pp. 244–5) and (2) to argue (against Kant, for example) that the difference between an imaginary object and real object of a given kind must be construed as one of *content* (*ETR* 42–3, below, pp. 241–2).

Even though the ideal construction in terms of which we ordinarily think of our real world of fact is an unclear and inconsistent one, Bradley maintains that nevertheless our world of fact has a special kind of priority: it is, we take it, the sole locus of genuinely historical human action, and it is only in virtue of a positive exclusion from our real world of fact that we can in the first instance distinguish systems of objects as merely imaginary (*ETR* 47, below, pp. 245–6). Our real world of fact, as an object of my thought at any moment, will be distinguished in terms of an ideal construction that I refer to reality from my point of contact with it in immediate experience and thus it will be distinguished on the basis of a unique felt content or quality: 'on that of which I am aware when I say "this myself which is now"' (ibid.). In the end without reference to this content I could not distinguish imaginary worlds from my real of fact and thus without this difference of content the distinction between imaginary and real would vanish (*ETR* 47–8, below, pp. 245–7). Only in so far as we abstract from that difference of content (and, for example, talk about an imaginary and a real shilling *simply* as shillings) can imaginary and real objects be taken to be identical in content (*ETR* 48–9, below, pp. 246–7).

G.S.

In this chapter[1] I shall attempt to deal briefly with several sub- [28]
jects or perhaps aspects of one subject. My aim throughout is to
advocate the same main conclusion, but no satisfactory treatment
of the questions opened is possible within these limits. The first
discussion will be about the existence of floating ideas, the next
will examine the difference in content between the 'real' and the
'imaginary' . . . The conclusion to be urged or suggested in each
case is that a hard division between the real and the imaginary is
not tenable. The true nature and criterion of reality must hence
be sought and found elsewhere.

I. I will take first the question as to floating ideas. . . . Every
idea[2] essentially qualifies reality, but no idea on the other hand
does this simply and bodily. Every idea has its own existence as a
fact, and with this side of its being it, as an idea and so far, does
not qualify reality. Its essence, we may say, lies in ignoring or in
discounting this side of itself. And thus everywhere truth and
ideas have a double aspect. But every idea, used as an idea, must
so far attach itself as an adjective to the real, and hence in the
end there will be no such thing as an idea which merely floats.

This conclusion is very commonly rejected as false. Its falsehood is at times even silently assumed against those who maintain its truth. And certainly at first sight any such doctrine seems
open to grave objection. 'An idea', it may be said, 'always, if you
please, refers in some sense to the real world, and always, if you
please, neglects or discounts its own private existence, if, that is,
it possesses any. But on the other hand there are ideas which
plainly do not qualify the real. When an idea is taken as false it
may even be repelled and denied. And, apart from this, ideas
may be recognized as merely imaginary, and, taken in this character, they float suspended above the real world. The same thing
happens wherever we deal with questions, with ideal experiments,
and again with those suggestions which we merely entertain without pronouncing on their truth. And how, when you do not
know that an idea is true, or when you even know that it is not

---

[1] The first two divisions of this chapter may be taken as a commentary on various parts of my book *Appearance and Reality*. See especially ['Degrees of Truth
and Reality', 183–200 above]. [This chapter originally had three divisions. Only
the first two are reprinted here.]
[2] This holds even of the idea of 'nothing'.

true, can you say in such a case that the idea qualifies reality? In such cases the idea, it is plain, can do no more than float.' There is force in this objection, and with myself, I admit, the objection at one time more or less prevailed.[3] I will now, however, attempt to show briefly that it rests upon misconception.

[30]   The misconception is in short a false assumption as to the limits of the real world. Reality is identified with the world of actual fact, and outside of this world floats the unsubstantial realm of the imaginary. And actual fact, when we inquire, is in the end the world which is continuous with my body. It is the construction which in my waking hours[4] I build round this centre. My body, taken in one with my present feelings and with the context which in space and time I can connect with this basis, is regarded by me as actual fact while all else is unreal. Thus my dreams are facts so far as they take their place as events in the real series, while the contents of my dreams are not real since they cannot so be ordered. The real world on this view is a group and series of actual events, and the test in the end is continuous connection with my felt waking body. This is the doctrine which consciously or unconsciously underlies our common view as to the actual world. And it is this doctrine, I think, which usually is asserted or implied when the existence of mere floating ideas seems plausible.

I do not purpose here to discuss formally the truth and consistency of this view of reality's limits.[5] The doctrine is in trouble at once with regard to the actual existence of past and future. It fails wholly to explain the position given to the sphere of general

---

[3] *Principles of Logic*, pp. [19–20]. There are, besides, various more or less objectionable expressions used in the account of ideas which is given there. So far as I know, these expressions have not been used by me since, though I hardly understand how a careful reader of the volume could be deceived by them. The term 'sign' or 'symbol', for instance, implies strictly, I suppose, the recognized individual existence of the sign. And obviously with an idea this aspect may be absent. There are other expressions also which, if you take them literally, are certainly false, and also inconsistent with what may be called the general doctrine of the book. But I hope that the statements as to ideas, which I have made several times since 1883, are less misleading. I should have added that, from the first and throughout, Prof. Bosanquet has consistently advocated the true doctrine. The debt which philosophy owes to him here has not been adequately recognized.

[4] In the end in my present waking moment. The point is further discussed later in this chapter.

[5] The foundation of this view is exposed in the second part of the present chapter.

and of abstract ideas. And to say that, when confronted with the facts of the spiritual world, with art and science, morality and religion, it proves inadequate, is to use a weak expression. The truth is that no one except for certain purposes really believes in such a view, and that no one for other purposes can fail, however unawares, to reject it. And, without pausing to consider any possible attempts at defence, I will proceed to offer another view which seems at least more in accordance with fact.

Every man's world, the whole world, I mean, in which his self [31] also is included, is one, and it comes to his mind as one universe. It necessarily does so even when he maintains that it truly is but plural. But this unity is perhaps for most men no more than an underlying felt whole. There is, we may say, an implicit sense rather than an explicit object, but none the less the unity is experienced as real. On the other hand above this felt totality there is for the average man an indefinite number of worlds, worlds all more or less real but all, so far as appears, more or less independent. There are the facts perceived by the outer senses, and there is the inner realm of ideas and intimate feelings and passing moods. And these regions more or less may correspond, but they do not correspond wholly. Then there is my present actual world, and the ambiguous existence of what has been and is about to be. There are the worlds of duty and of religious truth, which on the one side penetrate and on the other side transcend the common visible facts. And there are the regions of hope, desire and dream, madness and drunkenness and error, all 'unreal', if you please, but all counting as elements in the total of reality. The various worlds of politics, commerce, invention, trade and manufacture, all again have their places. Above the sensible sphere rises the intellectual province of truth and science, and, more or less apart from this, the whole realm of the higher imagination. Both in poetry and in general fiction, and throughout the entire region of the arts and of artistic perception, we encounter reality. Things are here in various ways for us incontestable, valid and 'true', while in another sense of the word 'truth' these things could not be called true. But this multiplicity of our worlds may perhaps be taken as a fact which is now recognized.[6] The diversity and even the division of our various worlds is indefinite and

[6] Cf. Prof. James's *Psychology*, chap. xxi. [William James, *The Principles of Psychology* (London: Macmillan, n.d.).]

in a sense is endless. And, without entering further into detail, I
[32] will state at once how this diversity bears on our problem.
Because there are many worlds, the idea which floats suspended
above one of them is attached to another. There are in short
floating ideas, but not ideas which float absolutely. Every idea on
the contrary is an adjective which qualifies a real world, and it is
loose only when you take it in relation to another sphere of
reality.

On the one side the whole Universe or the Absolute Reality is
the subject to which in the end every idea is attached. On the
other side (and this is the side on which we have to dwell here)
the reality qualified by an idea depends always on a distinction.
The subject in a judgement is never Reality in the fullest sense. It
is reality taken, or meant to be taken, under certain conditions
and limits. It is reality in short understood in a special sense.[7]
And hence when an idea floats above, and is even repelled by,
one region of the world, there is available always another region
in which it inheres and to which as an adjective it is attached.
And everywhere, where we seem to find ideas which float
absolutely, we can discover the ground to which really they are
fixed.

I will go on to point this out in a variety of instances, but,
before proceeding, I must lay stress on an important distinction.
If 'judgement' is used in its ordinary sense of explicit judgement,
where we have a distinct predicate and subject taken one as
applied to the other, then it certainly is true that apart from
judgement we have ideas. And if the issue is raised thus, and if
not to be so predicated means to float, then inevitably we shall
be forced to believe in floating ideas. For in doubt and in denial,
to take obvious instances, we should find the evidence that they
exist. But the issue, if so raised, I must go on to urge, is raised
wrongly. We have not to choose everywhere between an idea
[33] which is predicated and an idea which simply floats. On the contrary, an ideal content can qualify and be attached to a subject
apart from any predication in the proper sense or any explicit
judgement. And by virtue of such an attachment the ideas which
relatively float are everywhere from another point held captive.

---

[7] It is not possible for me to attempt here to explain and justify the above. I
may perhaps in passing point out that, if the subject were the entire reality, no
place would be left for the existence of the idea.

The idea comes before my mind as in suspension and as loose from a certain subject, and so far it floats. But none the less as an adjective it qualifies another subject. It is not predicated of this other subject, but it comes as attached to it or as inhering there. This other subject may be more or less specialized or more or less vague and general, and the union again between this subject and the idea may be more or less implicit. It may amount to little more than the immediate inherence of one aspect in a felt whole. But in every case of a floating idea this other subject and its attachment can be found. The idea in short, held free from one subject, coalesces more or less immediately with another subject from which in varying degrees it is distinct.

Thus in negation the idea denied is not in the proper sense predicated of another subject. But this idea in every case qualifies an alternative more or less distinct, and hence nowhere floats absolutely. The idea repelled is, in other words, felt to fall somewhere else. It may qualify another alternative more or less specified before the mind, or it may coalesce with that vague whole which comes to us as the residue of the Universe. But to existence unsupported within a void it never attains.

This qualification apart from explicit judgement can by reflection everywhere be turned into formal predication. Whether before that we should speak of judgement I need not discuss. The point is that apart from predication ideas can qualify a subject. Hence you cannot conclude that, where predication fails, ideas, if present, must float, since the possibility of informal union between ideas and reality destroys this conclusion. The reader may now have realized the bearing and the importance of the [34] above distinction, and I will go on to explain and justify it in detail by considering various instances of floating ideas. We find obvious examples in negation and supposition, in the use of imperatives and questions, and in the world of imagination and of mere idea. I will deal first with the case of imaginary ideas.

The imaginary in general is defined by exclusion from the real. It is something which positively possesses the character of this or that real world and hence suggests its inclusion there, but on the other hand is shut out from the limits of the world in question. And the world which excludes is primarily the world of actual fact. This world, we saw above, is made by construction from my real body. It is the region, in short, which is taken as continuous with that basis.[8] Whatever, having more or less the character of this series, nevertheless falls outside it, is imaginary, or, taken more generally, the imaginary is whatever is excluded by actual fact. And in a secondary sense the imaginary is what in the same way falls outside of any kind of world which is taken as actual. Now if an idea is admitted to be imaginary (which we have seen means unreal), how, it will be objected, can such an idea be the adjective of reality? And this problem is solved, we have seen, by the plurality of real worlds. The idea is repelled from one sphere but qualifies another, and in this other sphere is real. Reality, we feel, is a whole which extends beyond any special world. It is something which comes to us as wider than the distinctions we make in it. Hence, wherever an idea is repelled by a subject, there remains another field which in some sense is real. In this field the idea falls positively, inheres in it and qualifies it, and, when we reflect, we can express this inherence in a judgement. The idea, before we so reflect, is not a predicate, but the idea of the other [35] hand is still not free. It is in the air, if you will, but you must add that it qualifies this air which is its support and reality.

Consider for example the world inhabited by the characters in some novel. Things not only here are so or otherwise in actual literary fact, but beyond this fact we recognize a world of reality. And this world does not consist in or depend on the mere event that Balzac or Thackeray chose to write down this or that detail.[9] It is the same elsewhere and in every world of the arts. The imaginary, we all say, has its laws, and, if so, we must go on to add, it has its own truth and own life, and its ideas, floating in reference to common fact, are hence attached to this its own world of reality. Thus again in abstract science, where we should refuse to say that truth is imaginary, we could hardly assert the existence of any and every truth as an actual fact. On the other hand, whatever we might protest, we feel and know that truth somewhere must be real. Nay, even in the practical relation of desire and will, ideas are felt somehow to be real. Indeed, their reality in collision with their non-existence makes the conflict in

---

[8] In the second part of this chapter I will further discuss the nature of the basis mentioned above.

[9] See on this point Prof. [Bernard] Bosanquet's *Knowledge and Reality* (London: Swan Sonnenschein, 1892)], pp. 144 ff., followed by Prof. James in his *Psychology*, ii. 292.

which we suffer. We suffer there most where most we feel that the idea has reality superior to the existence which excludes it. Our will is moved by, and it unawares insists on, the reality in another world of that idea which it brings here into fact. The star that I desire does not wander outcast and naked in the void. My heart is drawn to it because it inhabits that heaven which is felt at once to be its own and mine.

In the end and taken absolutely (to repeat this) there can be no mere idea. Reality is always before us, and every idea in some sense qualifies the real. So far as excluded it is excluded only from some limited region, and beyond that region has its world. To float in the absolute sense is impossible. Flotation means attachment to another soil, a realm other than that sphere which [36] for any purpose we take here as solid ground and as fact. Now the region which we oppose to fact may be a distinct world, or may be a residue more or less unspecified. It may be this or that province of the ideal, or it may be no more than the undefined space which falls beyond what we distinguish as fact. But the province, or the mere residual space or vague background, is still reality felt as positive, and to this reality the idea is bound.[10]

We may deal rapidly with the position of the idea in imperatives and questions. The nature of an imperative has been discussed by me elsewhere (in *Mind*[a] . . .), and we have no need to enter on that general topic. But with regard to reality it is with the idea here as in the practical relation generally. The idea, ordered to exist in our world, qualifies already the world of ideas and has reality there. The same thing holds again in interrogatives. In a question we have some known aspect of reality before us, which we regard, at least here, as actual fact. We have next the suggestion of an idea, more or less specified or again undefined, which we assume to be somehow connected with our known fact. We have finally a demand for further knowledge in this direction. The demand is addressed to another mind, or even secondarily to our own, or again to material nature. The further knowledge (of which we have the idea) is absent from our known

---

[10] The idea again may be excluded from the subject taken simply and in itself, or again from the subject taken merely as so far known. The negation in the latter sense may, if we please, be called privative.

---

[a] NS 13 (1904), 4–5; repr. in *CE*, ch. xxviii, 'The Definition of the Will', 552–4.

fact. But on the other hand this knowledge, the answer to our question, is not fetched from nowhere. We take it to be truth which already is there and which in some sense exists.[11] It already, that is, qualifies another realm of reality, and to this realm it is attached.

[37]   We may pass from this to consider the case of supposition and hypothetical judgement. In supposition we use an idea which in one connection is true and is real. This ideal truth we bring into relation with a 'fact' taken in another sphere, in order to discover what result comes in a certain direction. This result is truth which is considered now, as before, to qualify and to be rooted in the ideal world. Supposition in short presupposes that the actual or real fact is not the whole of reality. It implies that there are other spheres, or other provinces of the same sphere, all connected in a wider Universe. Hence ideas once more never float except relatively. Their suspension involves a positive attachment to a point of support taken elsewhere.

I may perhaps be allowed to dwell somewhat longer on the problem raised by hypothetical judgement. It is obviously impossible for me here to discuss this fully in regard either to its psychological origin or logical value, and I must content myself with calling attention to a point which is essential. In a hypothetical judgement we have an assertion, and it is really idle to dispute this. If you suppose something then something follows, and, unless you know that this is so, you cannot say it. There is an assertion, but this assertion (properly) is not of actual fact. On the other side you have before you a datum which in some sense you take to be fact and actually real. And there is some connection, you assume, between this fact and your ideal truth. But in spite of this connection the fact is not the subject of your judgement, or rather it never is so except improperly and through mere implication.

In order to understand the hypothetical judgement we must
[38] keep in mind the following essential aspects. (1) The subject of

---

[11] The reader possibly may object that, in the case of the future which I am to make, the above account will not hold. I reply that it holds here unquestionably as it holds elsewhere, and that otherwise the attempt at prevision would be meaningless. The difficulty is caused by the nature of a real fact which is future, a construction which is full of radical inconsistency. But in any case, if the idea of the future cannot qualify the world of fact and truth, it still does not float but is attached to the imaginary world.

this judgement is never the actual fact. (2) On the other hand the actual fact to some extent enters into the judgement. And (3) in many cases the judgement contains an unavowed implication. It more or less covertly implies, that is, a certain connection between its subject and the actual fact.

(1) In every hypothetical judgement there is actual fact to which the subject is opposed. This actual fact may be a perceived existence, or again it may belong to some ideal or imaginary world. But in every case the use of 'if' marks a distinction between what we think and what is otherwise real. If a square could be round then something follows, which does not follow from an actual square. And 'if you attacked that man he would defend himself' does not make its assertion about that man. The man is not attacked, the square is not round, and you do not even suggest that either is so. And in 'if he goes there he will succeed' you do not say that he will go there. From him, as you know him, that predicate is absent, and your 'if' means that you are *not* speaking of the known actual man. In every case you are speaking of that which you suppose, and whatever you suppose you *ipso facto* oppose to what you take to be real. Otherwise there would be no sense in supposing and no meaning in 'if'.

(2) On the other side your assertion clearly in some sense refers to the actual fact. For otherwise, and if there were no connection, who could think of supposing? If your assertion had positively or negatively nothing to do with your actual reality, it would be meaningless or at least must lose its hypothetical form. Thus on the one side you are dealing in some sense with actual fact. The subject of your judgement on the other hand is not an actual fact. But the actual fact is referred to and to some extent it enters into the subject of the judgement. We have first the actual man who is not attacked and who is not the subject, and we have next the supposed, the ideal, man of whom the judge- [39] ment is true. If these two men are the same, our 'if' at least implies that we do not know this, while on the other side our 'if' implies that these men are connected. There is in short enough known identity between the two men to warrant a supposition. We thus assert about the ideal man but also refer to the other man. Our reference assumes that certainly between the two there is a partial identity, while our supposition means that, for any-

thing we really know, there is a difference which on the whole is superior and prevails.[12]

(3) So much as the above belongs to the essence of hypothetical judgement. Many cases, however, present an additional aspect, which has given rise to difficulty and to error. We have often a further implication as to the amount of identity between the ideal subject and the fact, and, owing to this implication, the judgement, while hypothetical in form, may assert or deny of the actual. In *si vales bene est* there is an implied identity, between the supposed and the actual, sufficient to justify the use of *est*. On the other hand in *si tacuisses philosophus esses* we assume a known difference, between the two cases of yourself, sufficient to warrant a denial of the conclusion in fact. This implied identity or difference can exist in a variety of degrees, and the actual meaning conveyed by the judgement may depend upon this implication. But this implication, we must not forget, falls outside the hypothetical form. It is often absent from it, and when present it may even be said to contradict it, since it involves knowledge on a point where the use of 'if' assumes ignorance. Hence this accidental meaning conveyed by some hypothetical [40] judgements is foreign to the essence of the hypothetical form. And a want of clearness on this point must everywhere, I think, preclude an understanding of that essence.

With these brief but, I fear, too lengthy remarks, I must pass from the hypothetical judgement. Assuming everywhere, as that does, various realms of reality and truth, the consideration of it has tended to confirm our main conclusion. The ideas which float have in every case another world in which they are based and secured.

When we pass to the alleged existence of floating ideas in the case of negation, we find a subject too intricate and too difficult for discussion here. I must content myself with a summary state-

[12] A hypothetical judgement (to state this otherwise) is itself always universal, but it implies that there is a question of bringing a designated case under this universal judgement. It implies that this question is worth considering, and (taken strictly) it implies that the answer is unknown.

I should remind the reader that in the above discussion I assume throughout the correctness of the account of existential judgements which I have given elsewhere. See my *Principles of Logic* ['The Categorical and Hypothetical Forms of Judgement', repr. above, Part I, Ch. 2.].

ment of the conclusion which I adopt.[13] By negation I understand a denial of the intelligible and not a mere refusal to entertain the unmeaning. And the main point here is this, that all negation is relative. Negation, whatever else it is, is repulsion, repulsion not absolute but from a subject formed by distinction within reality. Reality therefore is always wider than the subject which negates, and beyond this subject we have always a region taken in some sense to be real. And the idea, which is repelled from the subject, falls within this other world and qualifies it.

I do not mean that in all negation the alternative is distinct. The alternative on the contrary may be unspecified in various degrees. Our other world may amount to no more than that vague residue which remains after the subject has been selected. But, however undefined this other may be, it is the region into which the banished idea is sent. The idea never floats, like Mahomet's coffin, between both worlds, or somehow hangs nowhere. And the idea once more belongs to and qualifies that world which it inhabits. I do not mean that the idea, when repelled from one subject, must be predicated of another subject. Predication, we have seen above, [41] is not asserted wherever floating ideas are denied (p. 33[b]). The union of the repelled idea with the other world may be no more than a coalescence in feeling, and in various degrees may be immediate. But this union, we have seen, is a qualification and amounts to a bond. And with this summary result I must pass from the claim of floating ideas to exist in negation.

I have now in various instances attempted to justify the denial [42] of floating ideas. If the principle has been made clear to the reader, I think that further detail would be superfluous. Ideas float, but they float relatively, and there is another ground always which supports them, and of which they are adjectives. They need not be predicated of this ground, and, if such a necessity is assumed, then the denial of floating ideas, I agree, is untenable. But this necessity rests, I urge, upon a false alternative. Without predication an ideal content can qualify more or less immediately a subject from which it is distinct. And such a qualification is all that our conclusion requires.

[13] On the subject of negation I would refer the reader to Prof. Bosanquet's admirable *Logic*.

[b] See above, pp. 234-5.

Every possible idea therefore may be said to be used existentially, for every possible idea qualifies and is true of a real world. And the number of real worlds, in a word, is indefinite. Every idea therefore in a sense is true, and is true of reality. The question with every idea is how far and in what sense is it true. The question is always whether, qualifying reality in one sense, the idea qualifies reality in another sense also. For, true in one world, an idea may be false in another world, and still more false if you seek to make it true of the Universe.

II. It may serve to throw light upon the whole subject if I go on to discuss briefly a well-known doctrine. We often hear that [43] between an object as imaginary and the same object as real there is no difference in content, or at least that such a difference, where it exists, is not essential. This doctrine is often stated as axiomatic or as at any rate incontestable, and certainly I do not doubt that it possesses truth. On the other hand the truth possessed by it seems partial and limited. And in the end and in principle the doctrine must even be called false.

About its plausibility there is no question. What is the difference, we are asked, between a real and an imaginary shilling, and, if they differ as shillings, how do they differ? Suppose that they differ, then take this point of difference, whatever it is, and in imagination remove it. There will now no longer be any diversity in content between the two shillings, which still remain two. This contention obviously is plausible, and, though there are difficulties—to my mind insoluble—which result from its acceptance, the prevalence it has acquired is not surprising.

On the other hand, when we reflect, the counter-doctrine seems no less plausible. The real shilling, it has been remarked, does things, where the imaginary shilling has no power. The former is an active and in some sense a permanent constituent of the real world. And this difference appears to be essential and to affect the internal content of the shilling. You may perhaps deny this, and may attempt to argue that any such difference falls outside the two shillings. They are to differ, that is, barely in and through their external relations and not at all in themselves; and of course continuance will be a mere matter of external context. But this is to assume that a thing's relations, which make all the difference to other things, or at least all the difference beyond itself, make no difference whatever to itself. And this assumption, if it is tenable, seems at least not free from difficulty. For in the end the doubt is suggested whether in the end, when you have removed the relations, there is any shilling at all left.

You may answer perhaps that this abstract difficulty leaves you [44] unmoved. At any rate, when the 'real' external relations are cut off, what in fact is left is no more or less than the imaginary shilling. But this answer, I will go on to show, apart from any objection based on general principle, is in practice unavailing. For we have not to deal merely with two shillings, the one real and the other fancied. There is not on one side a single 'real' world of fact and on the other side a single world that I call 'imaginary'. On the contrary a man has, as we saw, an indefinite plurality of worlds.[14]

Now this diversity of worlds, and the presence of the same object in various worlds, seems to bear on our problem. If on the one side you agree that these worlds are diverse, each through a different content, it seems natural to think that the object's quality may be affected in each case by this difference. But if on the other side all these worlds are to be diverse without differing in content, such a doctrine, if tenable, has surely at least ceased to be plausible. It seems to commit us to the view that there is an indefinite number of distinctions without any difference, or that there are differences between things which do not really differ. For myself such a conclusion tends to the dissolution of all things, whether real or imaginary, and at any rate there will be few, I think, to whom it commends itself at once as plausible.

If now leaving general considerations we test our doctrine by applying it to special cases, we discover that at least it has limits. The whole distinction in short between the imaginary and the real tends, as we apply it, to become invalid. The first instance I will take is the case of the Universe or Reality, for it is better, I think, here not to use the instance of God. Can we speak of the Universe as being merely real or as being merely imaginary? Is it not on the other hand plain that such a distinction falls within the Universe? If we oppose the real to the imaginary, then clearly [45] the Universe is neither or both. Taken as a whole it falls on neither side of this opposition, and is not comprised in either the real or the imaginary world. Both these worlds on the contrary

---

[14] In a work of fiction, for instance, we have the imaginary worlds of the characters over against their real world, and so on indefinitely.

are contained within the Universe. So far then as we maintain the hard distinction between imaginary and real, we can neither say that All is real nor that All is imaginary. This distinction, and with it the whole doctrine which we are considering, has proved inapplicable or mistaken.

Again, let me take the case of my real self. My real self, as I am now aware of it, appears to be unique, and in contrast with it I have a variety of imaginary selves. Now, if the doctrine in hand is correct, the difference between my imaginary selves and my real self does not rest on content. It must on the other hand somehow consist in mere external relations. But this conclusion, if in the end it is not senseless, seems contrary to what experience here suggests. The distinction between imaginary and real seems, at least here, to rest on a felt difference, and, where there is a felt difference, it is natural to assume a diversity in content. To suppose that my real and imaginary selves are in themselves interchangeable, and that there is no diversity here except in that which falls outside each, seems, in the presence of the actual fact, to be untenable if not unmeaning. Thus, as applied to the Universe, we found that the doctrine which we examine proved invalid, while now in the case of my real and my imaginary self it seems even vicious.

But the doctrine without doubt possesses truth, truth not unlimited but partial. So far as you can abstract from the diversity of your different worlds, whether real or imaginary, you can take their contents as merely the same. And to a certain extent and in many cases it is legitimate and useful so to abstract. But, while the doctrine taken in this sense is true, in any other sense it seems not [46] true. It is, first, not true that the content so abstracted is in the strict sense imaginary. This content on the contrary is so far neither real nor imaginary. And again it is not true that all the diversity from which you abstract must consist in something other than content. You cannot take this diversity as everywhere something external, which leaves objects unaffected in their character. For in the end the whole distinction of imaginary from real fundamentally rests, we shall find, on a difference in quality. If, to repeat, you abstract from the difference between the imaginary and the real, you obviously so far have no difference of any kind between them. But, if on the other hand the difference between them is to be maintained, it must rest in the end on a difference in felt content.

What is the imaginary? This is a question which up to a certain point we have answered already. The imaginary, we saw, is not something indifferent, to which reality could simply be added. The imaginary is qualified by exclusion from real existence, and apart from that exclusion it loses its character. And real existence, I have now to urge, depends on a positive quality.

My 'real world', we saw, is a construction from my felt self. It is an inconsistent construction, and it also in the last resort depends on my present feeling. You may protest that its basis is really my normal waking self, but in the end you have no way of distinguishing such a self from the self which is abnormal. In the end my foundation is and must be my present self, whatever that happens at the moment to be. In madness or drunkenness we have the distinction of imaginary from real, and the distinction seems here to be as good as elsewhere. Nay even in dream I may construct another world which is the environment of my dream-body, and may oppose to this reality a mere imaginary world. The basis of the opposition everywhere is, in a word, present feeling, and one present feeling, if you take reality so, stands as [47] high as another. And the conclusion suggested is that the above opposition of 'real existence' to 'mere imagination' is in the end invalid and breaks down.

But, however arbitrary my procedure, my real world is taken as that which is continuous with my normal waking felt self. And it is by exclusion from this real world that the imaginary is made. Thus if I and a hundred other men were to dream the same dream, and in somnambulism were to act from our dreamt world, this world would remain unreal because not continuous with the world of my self as normal and waking. By virtue of exclusion from this world the realm of the imaginary is defined. And it is only at a stage of mind which is comparatively late that such a division is made. Thus the gulf fixed between imaginary and real existence, however necessary and useful it may be, is at once arbitrary and novel.

And the points to which I would direct the reader's attention are these. (i) The existence of the imaginary depends upon my real world, and (ii) the existence of my real world depends on a felt quality.

(i) A content is not made imaginary by mere privation and through simple failure. If you abstract from all relation to what is called my real world, you have so far not got the imaginary. Abstract truths, for instance, do not express 'real' matters of fact, but they fall elsewhere than in the realm of mere imagination. This realm is made by positive exclusion from the special world which I call real. And in a word if you desire to turn 'imaginary' into 'real', you cannot effect this by mere addition. You require also to subtract the above exclusion, though, this subtraction being unimportant practically, has been generally ignored.

(ii) And my real world, difference from which and exclusion by which, we have seen, is the essence—on what does that rest? It rests on a quality, on a felt content, on that of which I am aware [48] when I say 'this myself which is now'. I experience this content when I feel the difference between the mere idea and the actuality of my present self. But it is impossible for me to bring this content wholly before me as an object. With every object I have still the difference felt between this object and my felt self. And, if this were not so, the difference and the relation between subject and object would vanish. And thus what I call my real world, the world which is made by a construction from my self, depends in the end on a content, a content not explicit but positive, not brought before me but felt. If you take away this content, and the exclusion by this content, then at one stroke you have removed the characters of both imaginary and real. And if such a mere felt quality seems but a precarious foundation for our edifice, that is precisely the conclusion which I desire to suggest. For what I call my real world is something other than Reality. It is a construction, required for certain ends and true within limits, but beyond those limits more or less precarious, negligible, and in the end invalid.[15]

---

[15] It is useless to insist that my real world is real because it is the world where we all meet really through the real connections of our real bodies. For, as was remarked above, in my dreams my own dream-body possesses its world of things and of other persons; and this order of things, while I dream, is real to myself. Nay an indefinite number of persons might, for all we know, dream a world of identical content, in which each with a difference occupied his proper place. And if you ask for the criterion by which to decide between my dreamt and my waking worlds, something more is required than a mere arbitrary choice. You are led in the end to find that the superiority of my waking world lies in its character, in the greater order and system which it possesses and effects. But, with this, the hard division has turned into a question of degree, and this question once raised will tend to carry us still further.

The imaginary then is made by exclusion from my real world. It rests in the last resort on a felt difference from a felt unique quality, and this, I apprehend, is a difference in content. Such a [49] result, I admit, entails difficulties which I do not here discuss. But, if we reject it, we seem forced to conclusions which to my mind are far less tolerable. For I cannot see how things or orders of things are to be distinct, if they are not different, or what in the end can be meant by a relation which is merely external.

The difference between the real and imaginary thus rests in the end upon content. So far as you abstract from the difference, the content of both worlds is obviously the same. For many purposes the abstraction is permissible and useful, but it is not everywhere valid. And so the doctrine of the identity in content between real and imaginary has but partial truth. When you take the instance of the Universe or again of my real self, the doctrine proves inapplicable or vicious.

We have hence been led once more to the main theme of this chapter. The difference between my world of fact and my other worlds is important and necessary, but the exaggerated value we often tend to attach to it is really illusory. Its pretensions are in practice refuted incessantly by experience of other kinds. And, when we examine its theoretical claim to possess ultimate truth, we find that this is founded on arbitrariness, is built up in inconsistency, and ends in obscurity. The difference for us between real and unreal is vital. This can hardly consist in a division founded on felt quality condemned for ever to be latent, and, while seeking for another foundation, we found none which is intelligible. Hence this difference, vital for us, must be sought and be discovered elsewhere. It must depend on the internal character of those various worlds which claim our allegiance. And our impassable gulf and our hard and fast division will have to give way to degree and to differences in value.

I may remark in passing that the real world is by some writers defined so exclusively, that whatever is perceptible but to one person becomes unreal. But obviously any man might under individual conditions have an experience which would not be shared by others, and which would yet belong to the order of events in the real world of fact.

On Truth and Practice

In the short extract we have included from this paper Bradley rejects a view which portrays the notion of truth as secondary to that of practice. However, he allows that at an early stage in the development of mind 'the intellect directly subserves practice' (*ETR* 75, below, p. 249).

We might characterize Bradley's position as follows:

In the psychological order of things 'in the beginning is the deed'. In other words within the time-order of any particular human life truth will first come to play a role in activities in which the individual's aim is the achievement of ends other than truth. Purely theoretical activities, or activities of the intellect *as such*, i.e. activities of that faculty which makes truth itself an end, must be seen as a late development of the human mind, not only in the individual but also in the race.

But in the logical order of things, on Bradley's view, the beginning lies not in the deed but in the word. The notion of truth cannot be satisfactorily defined in terms of the notion of working in practice. If we are to be able to distinguish (1) cases in which the agent's idea of the means really works, and its realization actually enables the achievement of the aim as intended, from (2) cases in which the idea, in a weak sense of the term, works but does so merely by chance, we must reintroduce the notion of the idea, in the former case, corresponding with the facts of the situation, i.e. being true. So Bradley says: 'If my idea is to work it must correspond to a determinate being which it cannot be said to make. And in this correspondence, I must hold, consists from the very first, the essence of truth' (*ETR* 76, below, p. 250).

The main point of the extract is the claim that the notion of truth is logically prior to that of working in practice. However, the latter quotation presents an exegetical difficulty. Does it commit Bradley to a correspondence theory of truth?

In 'On Truth and Copying' Bradley makes clear the sense of the term in which he rejects a correspondence theory of truth. However, he allows that there is a perfectly acceptable sense in which we can speak of our ideas as corresponding to facts. We can do so in contexts where we can make a relatively clear distinction between what he calls 'perceptional

'On Truth and Practice' is repr. from *ETR*, ch. iv.

and reflective thinking' (*ETR* 108, below, pp. 255–6; cf. also 118–20, below, pp. 263–4). In the context of self-consciously intentional actions of the kinds that Bradley exemplifies in 'On Truth and Practice' we can make just such a distinction.

For a system of beliefs which are from the very earliest stage all-important in our practical lives, namely those with respect to spatio-temporally locatable things in the immediate vicinities of our bodies (cf. *ETR* 34, above, pp. 235–6), the successively *given* contents of our waking sense-perceptions will play a fundamentally important role in the process whereby we bring *system*, or truth, into our thinking, i.e. bring our beliefs into correspondence with 'the facts' (cf. *ETR* 208–9, below, pp. 300–2; *PL* 63–6, above, Part I, Ch. 2; but cf. *PL* 487, not reprinted here).

It is in this sense, I take it, that, for Bradley, from the very first the essence of truth will consist in correspondence with a determinate being it cannot make. However, in such an account the notion of correspondence need not be (and, of course, in reading Bradley, must not be) construed in the sense which Bradley finds objectionable in 'On Truth and Copying' (cf. *ETR* 107 ff., below, p. 253 ff.).

G.S.

In maintaining that truth essentially does not consist in the mere [75] practical working of an idea, I would first of all remove a probable misunderstanding. For myself I have always held that at the beginning of its course the intellect directly subserves practice, and that between practice and theory there is as yet no possible division. . . . Again I hold that in the end theory and practice are one. I believe in short that each is a one-sided aspect of our nature. And for me the ultimate reality is not a mere aspect or aspects, but it is a unity in which every distinction is at once maintained and subordinated. On the other hand, wherever the word 'truth' has its meaning, that meaning to me cannot be reduced to bare practical effect. And at our human level, and throughout at least some tracts of our life, the words 'true' and 'false' have to me most certainly a specific meaning. The nature of this I cannot here attempt to point out, but I hold that it is other than the mere fact that an idea works or fails practically. It is on account of this denial, I presume, that I am to be termed an 'intellectualist', and this denial I will now proceed to justify.

The view that truth everywhere subserves practice directly seems to me contrary to fact; but, even where this is the case, truth itself is not merely practical. This distinction appears, as I have said, to be often ignored. At an early and unreflective stage of mind no idea will be retained unless it works practically, or unless at least [76] it practically satisfies me. We can have at this level no reflection on disappointment, failure and falsehood. And hence I agree that here there is no truth except where an idea works practically. But to go from this to the conclusion that truth's essence even here lies wholly in such working, is a further step which to me seems not permissible. The idea works, but it is able to work not simply because it is there and because I have chosen it. It is able to work because, in short, I have chosen the right idea.

Everywhere in conation and will there is an idea which is opposed to existence. And this existence nowhere is characterless, but it is a determinate being. And the character of this being again is not something inert. On the contrary it is an element in the whole situation, and it dictates to my idea as well as submits to dictation. If my idea is the right one, and if it works, this, we may say, is because the nature of the whole situation selected it. My idea, I agree, then reacts, and I agree that it then makes the situation to be different. But to speak as if the entire nature of the situation were first made by the idea seems really extravagant. If my idea is to work it must correspond to a determinate being which it cannot be said to make. And in this correspondence, I must hold, consists from the very first the essence of truth. I will proceed to show this first on the positive side, and then again where in failure and in falsehood we meet the opposite of truth. But I shall take our experience now at a level more removed from its lowest point, and shall consider it at a stage where reflection is possible.

(*a*) The fact which first offers itself is the case of finding means to a positive end. I desire, let us say, to cross a stream in order to gather fruit. The stream is swollen, and there is hence a gap between my idea and its reality. On this let us suppose that I retain my general idea of crossing, and that other ideas as to the particular manner of crossing are suggested. This is in the main [77] what we understand by finding means to an end. Now these ideas, I agree, may all be said to be practical ideas. My end will remain my crossing somehow, and the means will probably consist in my doing something so as to cross. But these means surely must correspond to the actual nature of the stream, and surely to suggest that my ideas manufacture that correspondence is absurd. The stream is wider lower down, so that there I may wade. The stream is full of rocks higher up, so that there I may leap. If I will only wait quietly the stream is falling of itself. If I will only sit still, my companion has promised that he will come with a float. My end is practical doubtless, and my means still are the idea of myself doing something—if at least you stretch that so as to include my waiting till something happens of itself or is done by another. But when you ask what it is which makes each idea right or wrong, you cannot exclude its agreement or its discord with fact other than my will. And to ignore this aspect of the case, or to treat this aspect as if it were something somehow immaterial, to my mind, I must repeat, is wholly unprofitable. In selecting my means I am forced to consider their relation to the facts, and, if my idea works, it is because of this relation which is not made by my idea. And it is in this relation that we have to seek the distinctive nature of truth. Or we may say that the whole situation, inward and outward, dictates to me the selection of such an idea as can work, and that hence to treat this *congé d'élire* merely as my act on the situation is a foolish pretence. Let us take again the case where I go hunting and where my end is the capture of some beast. I obviously here may have to reflect carefully on the nature of the means. Where the animal is, and what it is likely to do under certain conditions, all this I may have to infer from a general knowledge of its nature and from a variety of indications that I gather from facts now perceived. And, if others are to co-operate, I have to take account also of their natures and of their probable conduct. The whole of this is [78] fact to which my idea has got first to correspond. It has, that is, first to be true as a condition of its working. On the other side doubtless the idea of the means is dependent on the end, and doubtless, if you remove the end, you remove at one stroke the idea and its truth. But from this you cannot logically conclude that the entire truth was made by your end and your ideas. It would be as rational first to insist that without the given facts there are in fact no ideas and no truth, and then go on to infer that in the end truth and will consist barely in what comes to my mind.

(*b*) I shall be charged, I do not doubt, with idle insistence on the obvious. But where I understand little more than that there is a denial of what to me are plain facts, no course is possible to me except thus to insist on the obvious. And so I proceed to view the facts from their negative side. When, at a certain mental stage, I fail, I do not at this stage merely try again and again, but I retain my failures and use them to determine my conduct. My being carried away by the stream if I attempt to cross here, my falling amongst the rocks if I try to cross there, my being captured by my enemies if I remain where I am—these ideas remove possibilities and they qualify the situation by narrowing it. They are practical ideas, and in the end they may subserve another idea which actually works. But, taken in and by themselves, you can hardly say that they work directly. On the other hand, however indirectly, they do seem to make an assertion about things which are other than my will. And taken as ideas of my 'doing' they have to fall under the head of 'avoiding'. But that avoidance is based, I submit, on what things do to me. It depends on a character in things which hinders me or even actively makes me suffer. For we are not to say, I presume, that I avoid evils merely because of my desire to do something in the way of avoidance.

[79] We may see this more evidently where I am not engaged in any positive pursuit, but where a danger threatens me from which terrified I desire to escape. It is dusk and the man-eating tiger will be coming, and I do not know how to avoid him whether by this course or by that. And surely, in order to find some idea which will 'do', I must before all things consider his nature and what he on his side is likely to do. The same thing is evident again where my enemies are human. My end is practical, but surely my ideas about the means must be dictated to me by something which is clearly not myself. And this forced agreement of my ideas with a nature other than my volition is, I presume, that which in general we understand by truth. . . .

3

On Truth and Copying

Bradley's aim in this short, difficult essay is to defend his view of the nature of truth by showing how it avoids the mistakes of two other views (for an earlier statement of his view see 'Thought and Reality', Part II, Sect. 1, Ch. 6, above). Bradley calls the first mistaken view the correspondence or copy theory of truth. According to this theory, truth consists in corresponding to or 'copying' reality (pp. 254–7). The second mistaken view is the pragmatic theory; according to it truth is what 'holds' or 'works' (pp. 257–9). As the title suggests, Bradley is more concerned with the copy theory than with the pragmatic theory. But to use his criticisms of the copy theory as a springboard for a defence of his own view, Bradley needs to show that the pragmatic theory is not a viable alternative.

The essay has four parts. In the first part (pp. 254–9), Bradley briefly explains and criticizes the copy theory and the pragmatic theory. The main error of both, he claims is that they separate truth, knowledge, and reality. By this he seems to mean that they define truth by reference to something taken by each theory to be external to it. In the case of the copy theory, this is the reality that it copies; in the case of the pragmatic theory, it is the end it realizes. His argument against this is that we cannot meaningfully assert the existence of any external thing unless we know what it is. But to know what it is requires possessing the truth, at least to some degree, about it. Hence it cannot be separate from truth.

In the second part of the essay (pp. 259–63), Bradley shows how correcting this mistake lays the groundwork for his own view. Since the mistake consists in separating truth, knowledge, and reality, Bradley proposes to avoid separating them. He expresses this by saying that they should be identified. Like Joachim, whose discussion of the correspondence theory provided the occasion for this essay,[a] Bradley seems to assume that any view of the nature of truth will also provide a criterion for the evaluation of truth claims. Since truth is not defined by reference

'On Truth and Copying' was first pub. in *Mind*, NS 16 (1907). Repr. here from *ETR*, ch. v.

[a] H. H. Joachim, *The Nature of Truth* (Oxford: Clarendon Press, 1906), 7–30, esp. 22–4.

to anything external, it follows that truth claims are not evaluated by anything external. As Bradley puts it, '[W]e must attempt . . . to judge truth from its own standard' (p. 260). Since truth and knowledge cannot be separated, he concludes that we must evaluate truth claims by their coherence with our knowledge.

There is, however, a problem with this view which Bradley recognizes. Our knowledge is not now and, in his opinion, never will be complete. But if this is the case, then it can never provide an absolutely satisfactory criterion for the evaluation of truth claims. In other words, this view of the nature of truth includes a criterion for evaluating truth claims that will inevitably be imperfect. It will evaluate some claims incorrectly. Bradley puts this paradoxically by saying that truth is defective, even when judged by its own standard.

In the third part of the essay (pp. 261–3), Bradley argues that this alleged problem is not a problem but an essential feature of truth. It is part of the nature of truth, he claims, that it includes a criterion that is not absolute. In his view the truth is something that we will always seek and never find, something that we can approach progressively, but never reach. Bradley thinks this conclusion is supported by his account of the relation between thought and reality in *Appearance and Reality*. His position there is that truth is a property of thought as embodied in judgements. For thought to be true it must characterize reality consistently. But, as Bradley argues in 'Thought and Reality', no judgement can do this. To become consistent a judgement would have to overcome the relation it bears to reality and *become* reality. In so doing it would cease to be a judgement and hence cease to be the sort of entity that could be true. Truth by nature thus requires *per impossibile* identity with reality (without this a judgement would be different from reality and so relational, inconsistent, and untrue) *and* difference from reality (since judgements are by definition related to reality and hence different from it). Bradley concludes that truth must be identical with reality yet different from it where this difference is internal to the nature of truth.

In the fourth and final section of the essay (pp. 263–6), Bradley explains what is correct about the copy theory, how it is related to the pragmatic theory, and how both are superseded by his own theory.

J.A.

[107] The idea that truth consists in mere copying is suggested from many sides. A man through language and ideas has to convey fact to other men, and how can he do this unless his ideas copy

fact so far as the purpose requires? And, in dealing practically with the present or the future situation, unless I have mirrored in my mind the main features of that situation, how can I hope to succeed? And in recalling the past we are bound above all things not to alter it, and how can we avoid this unless in some way, however indirect, we produce a copy? Finally truth implies agreement amongst the ideas of separate individuals. And, since this agreement is not made by one or another individual, and so not by all of them, it therefore seems due to all of them following one original fact. But unless they mentally repeat this fact, how, it will be asked, can they follow it?

The above view is natural, but, even as it stands, seems hardly consistent with itself, for how the past or future can be copied is at least not evident. And it is soon in trouble, as is well known, [108] with regard to the sensible properties of things. But, not to dwell on this, the whole theory goes to wreck in principle and at once on a fatal objection. Truth has to copy facts, but on the other side the facts to be copied show already in their nature the work of truth-making. The merely given facts are, in other words, the imaginary creatures of false theory. They are manufactured by a mind which abstracts one aspect of the concrete known whole, and sets this abstracted aspect out by itself as a real thing. If, on the other hand, we exaggerate when we maintain that all facts are inferences, yet undeniably much of given fact is inferential. And if we cannot demonstrate that every possible piece of fact is modified by apperception, the outstanding residue may at least perhaps be called insignificant.[1] Or (to put it from the other side) if there really is any datum, outward or inward, which, if you remove the work of the mind, would in its nature remain the same, yet there seems no way of our getting certainly to know of this. And, if truth is to copy fact, then truth at least seems to be in fact unattainable.

If the above objection cannot be met (and I do not know how it can be met) the theory in principle is ruined. In the end truth is not copying; but it is possible, while admitting this, to attempt to save the theory in a modified form. We may draw a distinction

[1] I am not assuming here that we have no feelings so elementary as to be unmodified by apperception. But any assumption on the other side seems hazardous and could at any rate not extend far. Cf. ['On Truth and Coherence', repr. below], p. [295].

between perceptional and reflective thinking. As to what is perceived we may allow that we cannot argue that this is copied, but in any case, we may go on to urge, our ideas must copy our perceptions. And thus, after all, our secondary and reflective truth must seek to mirror reality. But the position taken here, though founded on a distinction, which in itself is important, for the purpose in hand seems wholly ineffectual. And, apart from such [109] difficulties as might once more be raised as to given facts which are past and future, we have only to apply this view in order to find it break down in our hands.

Disjunctive, negative, and hypothetical judgements cannot be taken as all false, and yet cannot fairly be made to conform to our one type of truth. And in general the moment we leave perceived facts and seek explanation—which after all is implied in the desire for truth—we find that we are moving away from the given. Universal and abstract truths are not given facts, nor do they merely reproduce the given, nor are they even confined to the limits of actual perception. And in the end, when we come to general truth about the Universe, it seems impossible to regard this as transcribed from the given Universe. Our truths in short can all of them in some sense be verified in fact, but, if you ask if they all are copied from fact, the answer must be different. And we are driven to admit that, at least when we pass from individual truths, our truth no longer represents fact but merely 'holds' or 'is valid'. And, asking what these phrases mean, we are forced to perceive that both truth and reality go beyond the perceived facts. The given facts in other words are not the whole of reality, while truth cannot be understood except in reference to this whole.[2]

We saw in the first place that given facts are even themselves not merely given, but already even in themselves contain truth. And secondly we have seen that, even if the perceived facts were given, truth cannot merely transcribe them. And, since truth goes beyond the given, it is impossible to understand how truth can copy reality. For, before the reality has been reached, there is no original to copy, and, when the reality has been attained, that

---

[2] This is the main conclusion which was urged in my *Principles of Logic*. It did not occur to me that I should be taken there or anywhere else to be advocating the copy-theory of truth.

attainment already is truth, and you cannot gain truth by transcribing it.

I will now break off the consideration of that view for which truth consists in copying fact, and will endeavour briefly to indicate a better way of resolving the problem. But I must begin by pointing out the main error which, if left unremoved, makes the problem insoluble. This error consists in the division of truth from knowledge and of knowledge from reality. The moment that truth, knowledge, and reality are taken as separate, there is no way in which consistently they can come or be forced together. And since on the other hand truth implies that they are somehow united, we have forthwith on our hands a contradiction in principle. And according to the side from which the subject is approached, this contradiction works itself out into a fatal dilemma. [110]

This defect in principle has been illustrated by the view we have been examining, and it may repay us to notice in a different case the result of the self-same error. An attempt is sometimes made to escape from difficulty by insisting that truth is merely what 'holds', or is what merely 'serves' or merely 'works'. But since these phrases are relative and, I presume, relative to something which is known, we have at once a division of truth from knowledge. On the one side is known reality, and on the other side is mere truth, and in short we have repeated the error of that view which took truth as a copy. And the fatal result of our proceeding soon becomes manifest. Truth is merely to be that which subserves something else, and I am to know that this is so, and that this is so is true. But such a truth about truth seems itself to go beyond truth, and our theory is dissolved in self-contradiction.

Let us consider this more in detail. We are, it seems, to take an end, such say as the abstraction of practical success or of felt pleasure, and we are to understand truth as a means, an external means, to this end. And what, we may hear, can be more plain and intelligible that this? It is, I agree, almost as clear as the former view for which truth merely copied things, and perhaps this suggestion may be an omen. But first let us ask as to our end, is this known or unknown? If it is unknown, how do we know that it is an end served by means? And, if it is known, then what are [111] we going to say of *this* knowledge? Is it true? Can we discuss it? Have we got a truth about our end, and, if so, does 'about' mean no more than merely subserving? I do not myself know how these particular questions should be answered, but in general I cannot see how to defend truth which is external to knowledge or knowledge which is external to reality, and with this I must pass to another difficulty which attaches to the present view. Truth has been taken as being *merely* the means to an end, and we naturally understand this to say that truth is *really* the means. But here at once arises a well-known puzzle. The end, we all agree, in a sense dictates the means, but on the other hand the end, we are accustomed to think, must choose those means which are really possible. We are hence, given the end, in the habit of discussing the means. We have to consider, in short, about suggested means whether they are means really and in truth. But, with this, we seem to have knowledge and truth and reality, certainly all in relation with the one real end, but on the other side all external to it and apparently more or less independent of it. We started in other words by saying 'Truth is nothing beyond that which subserves', and we have ended in explaining that 'Truth is that which in fact and in truth subserves'. And when in a given case a question is raised as to this fact and truth, it is answered apparently by appealing to something other than the end. Any such appeal obviously is inadmissible; but, when we reject it, we seem now to have excluded all truth about our means, just as before we seemed to have no knowledge nor any truth about our end.[3]

[112]   And a prescribed remedy, if I rightly understand, is to throw overboard all preconceived ideas as to truth and reality. Truth is merely the ideas which are felt in a certain way, and are felt to dominate in a mind or in a set of minds, and any further question as to their truth is senseless. You may indeed ask psychologically, if you please, how they have come to dominate, but, however they have come to dominate, their truth is the same. If you and I disagree we both so far have truth, and if you argue with me and persuade me, that is one way of agreement. But, if

---

[3] One is, I presume, naturally led to avoid this difficulty by maintaining that our knowledge in the end is intuitive. We have, that is to say, an experience in which reality, truth, and knowledge are one. But, with this, there is an end at once and in principle of the view that truth is an external means to something else. And on our new ground the problem of Error, the question how we can hold for true what is false, obviously threatens to become pressing.

you prefer to knock me on the head, that, so far as truth goes, is the same thing, except that now there is truth not in two heads but one. And as to there being any other truth *about* all this state of things, or in short any truth at all beyond mere prevalence, the whole notion is ridiculous. And, if you deny this, you do but confirm it, since your denial (though of course true) must also be false, since it is true only because in fact it has prevailed. And if you want further proof, you can perhaps demonstrate all this by a downward deduction. For either this or the copy-theory must be the truth about truth, and as the copy-theory will not work, this by inevitable consequence remains as true. But there is no one, I think, who is ready apart from some reserve to accept wholly the above result.

It would be easy, passing on, to point out how the same main error, appearing in other forms, works itself out from other sides into conflicting dilemmas. But the limits of this chapter compel me to proceed. The division of reality from knowledge and of knowledge from truth must in any form be abandoned. And the [113] only way of exit from the maze is to accept the remaining alternative. Our one hope lies in taking courage to embrace the result that reality is not outside truth. The identity of truth, knowledge and reality, whatever difficulty that may bring, must be taken as necessary and fundamental. Or at least we have been driven to choose between this and nothing.

Any such conclusion, I know, will on many sides be rejected as monstrous. The last thing to which truth pretends, I shall hear, is actually to be, or even bodily to possess, the real. But though this question, I know, might well be argued at length, the issue in my judgement can be raised and can be settled briefly. Truth, it is contended, is not to be the same as reality. Well, if so, I presume that there is a difference between them. And this difference, I understand, is not to be contained in the truth. But, if this is so, then clearly to my mind the truth must so far be defective. How, I ask, is the truth about reality to be less or more than reality without so far ceasing to be the truth? The only answer, so far as I see, is this, that reality has something which is not a possible content of truth. But here arises forthwith the dilemma which ruined us before. If such an outstanding element is known, then so far we have knowledge and truth, while, if it is not known, then I do not know of it, and to me it is nothing. On the one hand to divide truth from knowledge seems impossible, and on the other hand to go beyond knowledge seems meaningless.

And, if we are to advance, we must accept once for all the identification of truth with reality. I do not say that we are to conclude that there is to be in no sense any difference between them. But we must, without raising doubts and without looking backwards, follow the guidance of our new principle. We must, that is, accept the claim of truth not to be judged from the outside. We must unhesitatingly assert that truth, if it were satisfied itself, and if for itself it were perfect, would be itself in the fullest sense the entire and absolute Universe. And agreeing to the uttermost with this claim made by truth, we must attempt, truth and ourselves together, to judge truth from its own standard.

[114]

I will endeavour first to point out briefly in what this standard consists. The end of truth is to be and to possess reality in an ideal form. This means first that truth must include without residue the entirety of what is in any sense given, and it means next that truth is bound to include this intelligibly. Truth is not satisfied until we have all the facts, and until we understand perfectly what we have. And we do not understand perfectly the given material until we have it all together harmoniously, in such a way, that is, that we are not impelled to strive for another and a better way of holding it together. Truth is not satisfied, in other words, until it is all-containing and one. We are not obliged here, I think, to inquire further how these aspects of the idea of system are related, and whether, and in what sense, they have their root in a single principle. It is sufficient here to insist that both aspects are essential to truth, and that any theory which ends in dividing them is certainly false.

But, when we judge truth by its own standard, truth evidently fails. And it fails in two ways, the connection between which I will not here discuss.[4] (i) In the first place its contents cannot be made intelligible throughout and entirely. A doubt may indeed be raised whether even in any part they are able wholly to satisfy, but this again is a question on which here it is unnecessary to enter. For in any case obviously a large mass of the facts remains in the end inexplicable. You have perpetually to repeat that

[4] The reader is referred on this [to 'Coherence and Contradiction', repr. below, Part II, Sect. 2, Ch. 6].

things are so, though you do not fully understand how or why, and when on the other hand you cannot perceive that no how or [115] why is wanted. You are left in short with brute conjunctions where you seek for connections, and where this need for connections seems part of your nature.[5] (ii) And, failing thus, truth fails again to include all the given facts, and any such complete inclusion seems even to be in principle unattainable. (*a*) On the one hand the moment's felt immediacy remains for ever outstanding, and, if we feel this nowhere else, we realize at each moment the difference between the knower and his truth. (*b*) And on the other hand the facts before us in space and time remain always incomplete. How is it possible for truth to embrace the whole sensible past and future? Truth might understand them (do you say?) and so include them *ideally*. Well but, if truth could do as much as this, which I myself think not possible, truth after all would not include these facts *bodily*. The ideal fact after all and the sensible fact will still differ, and this difference left outside condemns truth even as ideal. And in short we are entangled once more in our old dilemma. We have an element given which in no way we can get inside the truth, while on the other side, if we leave it out, truth becomes defective. For there seems really no sense in endeavouring to maintain that what remains outside is irrelevant.

With this at first sight we have ended in bankruptcy, but perhaps we may find that the case is otherwise and that our failure has carried us to success. For we were looking for the connection between truth and reality, and we discovered first that no external connection is possible. We then resolved to take truth as being the same with reality, and we found that, taken so, truth came short of its end. But in this very point of failure, after all, lies the way to success. Truth came short because, and so far as, it could not become that which it desired to be and made sure [116] that it was. Truth claimed identity with an individual and all-inclusive whole. But such a whole, when we examine it, we find itself to be the Universe and all reality. And when we had to see how truth fails, as truth, in attaining its own end, we were being shown the very features of difference between truth and reality.

[5] You want in other words to answer the question 'What' by and from the object itself, and not by and from something *else*.

And in passing over into reality and in thus ceasing to be mere truth, truth does not pass beyond its own end nor does it fail to realize itself. Hence, being the same as reality, and at the same time different from reality, truth is thus able itself to apprehend its identity and difference. But, if this is so, we seem to have reached the solution of our problem.[6]

Truth is the whole Universe realizing itself in one aspect. This way of realization is one-sided, and it is a way not in the end satisfying even its own demands but felt itself to be incomplete. On the other hand the completion of truth itself is seen to lead to an all-inclusive reality, which reality is not outside truth. For it is the whole Universe which, immanent throughout, realizes and seeks itself in truth. This is the end to which truth leads and points and without which it is not satisfied. And those aspects in which truth for itself is defective, are precisely those which make [117] the difference between truth and reality. Here, I would urge, is the one road of exit from disastrous circles and from interminable dilemmas. For on the one side we have a difference between truth and reality, while on the other side this difference only carries out truth. It consists in no more than that which truth seeks itself internally to be and to possess.

Truth, we thus can say, at once is and is not reality, and we have found that the difference is not external to truth. For truth would be satisfied in its own self-sought completion, and that completion would be reality. And if you ask how truth after all stands to reality, and whether after all truth is not a copy, the answer is obvious. Apart from its aspect of truth the reality would not be the reality, and there surely is no meaning in a copy which makes its original. In truth and in other aspects of the Universe we find one-sidedness and defect, and we may go on to see that everywhere the remedy for defect lies in the inclusion of other aspects more or less left out. But as for comparing the Universe, as it is apart from one aspect, with the Universe as complete, such a comparison is out of our power. And it is even, when we reflect, ridiculous to seek to discover by thinking what the Universe would be like without thought. You cannot take reality to pieces and then see how once more it can be combined

---

[6] From this basis we can deal with the difficulty as to truth's being able consistently to pronounce itself imperfect. The dilemma that arises here was noticed by me and solved by a distinction [*AR* 482–5, repr. above, pp. 202–5].

to make reality. And thus, if we are asked for the relation of truth to reality, we must reply that in the end there is no relation, since in the end there are no separate terms. All that we can say is that, in order for truth to complete itself into reality, such and such defects in truth itself would have to be rectified.

That there are difficulties in the way of this solution I readily admit,[7] but difficulties and impossibilities, I urge, are not the [118] same thing. And any other exit from our maze is, I submit, closed impassably. On the one hand we must not use words that have no positive sense, and, with this, all reality that falls outside experience and knowledge is, to my mind, excluded. On the other hand we cannot rest in that which, when we try to think it, conflicts with itself internally, and is dissolved in dilemmas. But, in order to know that the Universe is a whole with such and such a general nature, it is not necessary to perceive and to understand how such a Universe is possible, and how its various aspects are held apart and together. We desire to know this, I agree, but I fail myself to see how we can, and I think that with less than this we can gain positive knowledge enough to save us from mere scepticism.[8]

If we now return to that view for which truth is a mere copy of things, we have seen that in the end no such doctrine is admissible. But from a lower point of view it may be convenient to speak of truth as corresponding with reality and as even reproducing facts. In the first place the individual in truth-seeking must subject himself. He must (I cannot attempt to explain this here) suppress ideas, wishes and fancies, and anything else in his nature which is irrelevant to and interferes with the process of

[7] One difficulty, on which stress has been rightly laid, is that we have no direct experience of any total experience which comprises in itself finite centres (cf. ['Thought and Reality', repr. above, Part II, Sect. 1, Ch. 6]. I do not however myself see that this is more than a difficulty.

[8] By scepticism I of course do not mean any positive view as to knowledge in general, and still less any kind of conclusion supported by proof. I mean by it denial or doubt with regard to the existence *de facto* for me of that which satisfies intellectually. This denial or doubt rests certainly on a positive basis, but, so long as the basis is not made explicit and the denial remains particular, the basis itself is not denied, and the position remains consistent. On the other hand the scepticism which itself poses as a doctrine, which deals in general truth, and in a word claims to be *de jure*, to my mind does not understand itself. No consistent scepticism can, in my opinion, offer a reasoned proof of itself, nor can a consistent scepticism maintain any general positive doctrine, or indeed any universal thesis of any kind whatever.

truth-seeking. And hence in a sense the individuals can have something in common, correspondence to which is essential for truth. Secondly, in truth-seeking the individual (once again I cannot try to explain this) must follow the object. Our understand-

[119] ing has to co-operate in the ideal development of reality, and it has not, like will, to turn ideas into existences. And thus following the object the ideas of the individual in a sense must conform to it. In the third place reflection, as we have seen, must take up sensible qualities as given matter, and it must accept also more or less brute conjunctions of fact. Intelligence of itself does not recreate the given past nor does it procreate entirely the given present or future. And it may be said to wait on and to follow a course of events which it is powerless to make. And, finally, to some extent language and truth must seek even to copy perceived facts, and, as we saw, to convey them faithfully, though of course

[120] in a partial manner. In the above senses truth may be spoken of as corresponding to facts, and it is right and proper as against one-sided theories to insist on this correspondence.[9] But, as we have seen, such a way of speaking is not permissible in the end.

I will ask, in conclusion, how what we may call the copy-theory of truth is affected by the connection between thought and volition. That in some sense thought depends on desire and will is even obvious, and it is doctrine in which most of us perhaps have, we may say, been brought up. But it is a doctrine on the other hand which can be interpreted in various ways. If in the first place truth is made wholly to depend in its essence on the individual's desire, then in this case, naturally, since truth itself goes, the copy-theory of truth goes also, together with every other sane theory of truth. But otherwise, if you simply take truth to be copying, the desire for truth will be a desire for copying, and by laying emphasis on the aspect of desire I do not see that you add anything.

Further, if you adopt a one-sided intellectual view, and maintain that reality is an original system of thought which you try to rethink, or a world of ideal essences whose presence you desire—it seems useless in such a case to speak about copying, since copying is excluded. There may be an original here, but, whatever else you are doing, you do not copy that original, since

---

[9] ['On Truth and Practice', repr. above, Part II, Sect. 2, Ch. 2.]

obviously you have no original before you to copy. The realization in detail of a general end is clearly in itself not repetition, and on the other side, as clearly, repetition and reproduction cannot all be called copying. Hence to ask here why we should desire to copy, is obviously irrelevant. The rational question to ask is about our desire for reproduction and repetition or for the [121] presence in or to our minds of a self-existent reality.

But, if we adopt a more concrete view, all such questions become idle. On such a view my desire and my will to have truth is the will and the desire of the world to become truth in me. Truth is a mode of the self-realization of myself and of the Universe in one. And if you ask why the full reality cares to spill itself into gratuitous vessels, or whence and why to me comes this mania for turning myself into a superfluous receptacle or instance—the answer is ready. Such inquiries are based on and betray a most stupendous misconception. The Universe is nowhere apart from the lives of the individuals, and, whether as truth or otherwise, the Universe realizes itself not at all except through their differences. On the other side the individuals, if they are to realize themselves personally, must specialize this common life of which truth is one aspect. And to suppose that the individuals can seek their end and their reality somehow apart (say in the abstraction of mere practice or of private pleasure) is in the end really meaningless. Thus truth, the same in all, is from the other side not wholly the same, since difference to it is vital and it gains difference in each. The personal diversity of the individuals is hence not superfluous but essential. For viewed from one side this diversity brings with it fresh quality, and from the other side, even so far as truth is common to the individuals, it must be taken none the less as modified in each case by its fresh context. But I must hasten here to add that no such general doctrine can be verified in detail.

The process of knowledge is, on any view like this, not something apart and by itself. It is one aspect of the life of the undivided Universe, outside of which life there is no truth or reality. And to speak here of copying as in a mirror, we may once more repeat, is absurd. If you like to add that the absurdity is heightened when we remember that life in general, and knowledge in particular, imply will and desire, to this naturally I make no objection. But for myself I have always been contented to know that the whole suggestion of copying is here ridiculously irrelevant. Still, as according to some critics my destiny is to illustrate what they call 'intellectualism', this chapter, if I could understand it, is doubtless a blind flutter against the limits of my cage.

4

On Our Knowledge of
Immediate Experience

In the Supplementary Note added to 'On Our Knowledge of Immediate Experience' Bradley says, '[I]n metaphysics we start, in some sense, from what is given, and . . . hence the question as to what is given at the start is fundamental and vital' (p. 292). For Bradley this fundamental starting-point is immediate experience or feeling. Its importance in Bradley's philosophy is apparent in a number of ways. For example, Bradley claims that we are able to predicate our ideas of reality through our contact with it in immediate experience ('The Categorical and Hypothetical Forms of Judgement', above, pp. 31–90) and that immediate experience is a main source of our idea of the absolute ('The General Nature of Reality (cont.)', above, pp. 139–52). Yet Bradley's conception of immediate experience is very unusual. Immediate experience, he claims, is a continuous and unified felt whole in which a distinction between subject and object is not yet present. Even though we are able to make distinctions within it and so abstract objects from it, immediate experience remains the ever-present non-objective background of our thought which is present in feeling. This conception sets the problem for the present essay. If this is the nature of immediate experience then it is difficult to see how Bradley or anyone else could know that it is. If there is no distinction between subject and object in immediate experience, then immediate experience is not the object of immediate knowledge. Since it provides the non-objective background for non-immediate or discursive knowledge, it would seem not to be an object of it either. How, then, can we know anything about immediate experience? In 'Our Knowledge of Immediate Experience' Bradley tries to answer this question by explaining how we might infer the existence of immediate experience and hence make it an object of consciousness.

Aside from a brief introduction in which Bradley states the problem and outlines his solution, and the conclusion and Supplementary Note where he stresses the metaphysical importance of immediate experience, the essay falls into three parts. In the first part (pp. 161–6) Bradley

'On Our Knowledge of Immediate Experience' was first pub. in *Mind*, NS 18 (1909). Repr. here from *ETR*, ch. vi.

discusses two psychological problems. He uses these problems to introduce the psychological principles on which he relies in inferring the existence of immediate experience. The first problem is whether paying
attention to some aspect of experience alters it. Bradley argues that it
does not. One of the two principles he invokes in his argument is that it
is possible to become aware of a change in what is given without paying
attention to what has changed and thus without, at the same time, making it an object of consciousness. The other principle is that we can
recall to consciousness (Bradley's word is 'reproduce') feelings that have
not been objects of attention. The second problem is a related one concerning introspection. When in introspection we notice and consequently
make an object of something that is felt, have we a reason for thinking
that we have done so correctly? Do we, in other words, have any reason
to believe that we can introspect our feelings without distorting them?
Bradley argues that we do. Immediate experience serves as a *criterion* for
judging the correctness of introspective claims. For just as we can be
aware of a change in immediate experience without making what has
changed an object, we can be aware of a change in immediate experience
when we introspect and hence abstract an object from it. But we need
not be aware of a change in this process. The original feelings remain
part of immediate experience even if they are objectified. If we are not
aware of any change in immediate experience during the process of
introspection, then we have a reason for thinking that we have intro-
spected correctly.

In the second part of the essay (pp. 278–82) Bradley explains his view
of immediate experience. He takes it to be the content of a unified state
of awareness 'which though non-relational, may comprise simply in itself
an indefinite amount of difference' (p. 279). This sounds more paradoxical than it is. Bradley thinks that relations hold only between objects
and that we can be aware of a relation only when we have abstracted its
terms from immediate experience by making them objects of attention.
By saying that immediate experience contains diversity without relations
Bradley means that it is a state in which we are aware of diversity, e.g.
change, without being aware of diverse or changing *objects*.

In the third part of the essay (pp. 282–90) Bradley attempts to answer
two questions: (1) How can immediate experience serve as a criterion?
and (2) How can it become an object? In his discussion of introspection
he has already anticipated his answer to (1). He thinks that we can feel a
concordance or a disharmony between what we think about an object
and the immediate experience which forms the background of our
awareness of it. By attending to this background we can abstract further
features of the object and so enlarge the content of the object by adding
these features to it. If this additional content is inconsistent with what

we have thought about the object, we will find the enlarged object to be contradictory and we will reject what we have thought about it. For example, I may be marginally aware of what I take to be a world map on the wall of a library room. By focusing my attention on the map I can notice features which I did not previously notice, like the colour of New Guinea. Since containing a coloured representation of New Guinea is consistent with being a world map, I now have an additional reason for thinking that it is a world map. However, if I focus my attention on what I take to be the world map and notice features inconsistent with it being a world map, like a representation of numerous craters, I will have reason to think that it is not a world map. Immediate experience, by being incorporated into objects, thus serves as a criterion for judging claims about them.

Bradley's answer to (2), How can immediate experience become an object?, draws heavily on the preceding discussions. In his answer to (1) he says that an object may be felt as discordant and enlarged from experience to become more satisfactory. This involves reproducing the felt features of the object. By extending this process ideally, in imagination, for example, he thinks we are able to form the idea of a complete, satisfying object. There are two obvious sources of the material by means of which we can form the idea of a complete object: (*a*) it may come from another object or (*b*) it may come from an undiscriminated area within the object. In both of these cases we feel the addition as new. We can be aware of this feeling without making it an object. But there is also a third case (*c*). Here the enlarged content does not come from either of these sources. In this case we feel an expansion of the object, so we know that it is being enlarged. But we lack any feeling of newness of the kind we have when the object is enlarged from within itself or from some other object. So the object must be enlarged by something that is non-objective and hence non-relational. Consequently, we infer the existence of a non-objective and non-relational experience as the source of the enlargement of the object. By so doing we make immediate experience an object of thought.

J. A.

In this chapter I am to treat of a difficulty which arises in con- [159] nection with immediate experience. The scope of the discussion must however be limited. Problems will be raised on all sides with which here I shall be unable to deal. And even on the main

point I must be satisfied, if I have shown how the question
presses for an answer.

I have had occasion often to urge the claims of immediate
experience, and to insist that what we experience is not merely
objects. The experienced will not all fall under the head of an
object for a subject. If there were any such law, pain and pleasure would be obvious exceptions; but the facts, when we look at
them, show us that such a law does not exist. In my general feeling at any moment there is more than the objects before me, and
no perception of objects will exhaust the sense of a living emotion. And the same result is evident when I consider my will. I
cannot reduce my experienced volition to a movement of objects,
and I cannot accept the suggestion that of this my volition I have
no direct knowledge at all. We in short have experience in which
there is no distinction between my awareness and that of which it
is aware. There is an immediate feeling, a knowing and being in
one, with which knowledge begins; and, though this in a manner
[160] is transcended, it nevertheless remains throughout as the present
foundation of my known world. And if you remove this direct
sense of my momentary contents and being, you bring down the
whole of consciousness in one common wreck. For it is in the
end ruin to divide experience into something on one side experienced as an object and on the other side something not experienced at all.

The recognition of the fact of immediate experience opens the
one road, I submit, to the solution of ultimate problems. But,
though opening the road, it does not of itself supply an answer
to our questions. And on the other side in itself it gives rise to
difficulties. With regard to these there are some points which I
have dealt with elsewhere, and other points which perhaps I have
failed wholly to see. There are again questions which have come
before my mind, but have been passed over, or at most have
been touched on by the way. It is one of the latter which in these
pages I shall attempt to discuss. The problem was noticed by me
years ago, and Prof. Stout in my opinion did well to insist on its
urgency.[1] This difficulty may be stated by asking, How immediate
experience itself can become an object. For, if it becomes an
object, it, so far, we may say, is transcended, and there is a

---

[1] In the *Proceedings of the Aristotelian Society*, 1902–3 [pp. 1–28].

doubt as to how such transcendence is possible. On the one hand as to the fact of immediate experience being transcended we seem really certain. For we speak about it, and, if so, it has become for us an object. But we are thus led to the dilemma that, so far as I know of immediate experience, it does not exist, and that hence, whether it exists or not, I could in neither case know of it. And with such a result the existence of immediate experience becomes difficult to maintain, and the problem which has been raised calls urgently for treatment and solution.

The solution, if I may anticipate, is in general supplied by con- [161] sidering this fact, that immediate experience, however much transcended, both remains and is active. It is not a stage which shows itself at the beginning and then disappears, but it remains at the bottom throughout as fundamental. And, further, remaining it contains within itself every development which in a sense transcends it. Nor does it merely contain all developments, but in its own way it acts to some extent as their judge. Its blind uneasiness, we may say, insists tacitly on visible satisfaction. We have on one hand a demand, explicit or otherwise, for an object which is complete. On the other hand the object which fails to include immediate experience in its content, is by the unrest of that experience condemned as defective. We are thus forced to the idea of an object containing the required element, and in this object we find at last theoretical satisfaction and rest.

This may be stated in general as the solution of our problem, and we might proceed forthwith to work out this solution in detail. I have however thought it better to begin by examining two difficulties well known to psychologists. My object in thus digressing is to show that our problem is not merely metaphysical, recondite and negligible, but that the principles applied in treating it cannot elsewhere be ignored. . . . Of the two difficulties just mentioned the first concerns Attention and the second Introspection.

I. With regard to the effects of attention there is a familiar puzzle. I am going here to take attention in the sense of noticing, without entering into any inquiry as to its nature. We all, when our attention is directed to our extremities or to some internal organ, may become aware of sensations which previously we did not notice. And with regard to these sensations there may be a [162] doubt whether they were actually there before, or have on the other hand been made by our attending. And, though this question may seem simple, it really is difficult. Can we directly compare attention's object with something to which we do not at all attend? To answer in the affirmative appears not easy. Can we then recall what we have not noticed, and, now attending to this, compare it with some other object? If reproduction necessarily depended on attention, any such process would seem impossible. But, since in any case this view of reproduction must be rejected as erroneous, we may reply confidently that the above comparison is a thing which actually happens. Still, asserting the possibility and the general principle, we have not removed all doubt as to the special fact. For how do I know in a given case that my present attending has not vitally transformed its result? Am I to postulate that in principle attention does not and cannot alter its object? Such an assumption, so far as I see, could hardly be justified. Certainly, apart from such an assumption, we may argue that any effect of attention requires time, and that hence, if the sensation appears as soon as we attend, the sensation must have preceded. And this inference is strengthened when we are able to pass thus repeatedly and with the same result from inattention to its opposite. Still at its strongest an argument of this kind seems far from conclusive. And in any case I cannot think that no more than this is the actual ground of our confidence when we refuse to believe that attention has made the thing that we feel. I agree that in some cases we recollect our state before attention supervened, though such a recollection in most cases, I should say, is absent. And again usually, and if you please always, we have the persisting after-sensation or after-feeling of our previous condition. But, all this being admitted, the question as to the actual ground of our confidence remains. In order to [163]   compare our previous state we *ex hyp.* are forced now to attend to it, and there is a doubt whether we can assume generally that attention does not alter. We have therefore to ask whether we are in a maze with no legitimate exit, and whether such a result, if accepted, does not throw doubt on the whole subject of this chapter.

I will state briefly what I take to be the real way of escape. (*a*) We must first assume that anything remains the same except so far as I have reason to take it as altered. The assumption is everywhere necessary, and may be called fundamental.[2] (*b*) Next we must hold that apart from any attention we may be aware of a change in our condition. Without anything which could in any ordinary sense be called attending, we can experience a difference when a change takes place in our general or special felt state. (*c*) There is again an experienced change when attention (say to a feeling B) supervenes, and this particular experience is felt otherwise than as a mere change, say from A to B. Hence from the absence of this special feeling, as well as from the presence of the ordinary feeling of change to B, we infer that our sensation B does not depend on attention, but was previously there. We have, that is, on one side a mode of feeling when one sensation, A, merely changes to another sensation, B, while on the other side, when I attend to B, though that attention brings a change of feeling, it does not bring the same mode as goes with such a mere transition as from A to B. I therefore assume that the change made by my attending is not a change to B itself. And we may perhaps add that when, while already attending to B, I go on to observe it more specially, I may still fail to gain any feeling of change either to or from B, though on the other hand I am of course aware of a change in myself. Now I am not suggesting that in the above we have a demonstrated conclusion, but it furnishes, I think, the ground for our view as to attention's limits. Further this view, once suggested, justifies itself in working. And it leaves us with this main result that we have feelings, such as those of change from A to B, and that, though these feelings have not been attended to, they are both real and reproducible. In any case apart from this assumption there seems to be no way of exit from disastrous puzzles. . . .

II. We may pass now to a kindred difficulty attaching to what [166] is called Introspection. Can I observe my own present state, and, if not that, what in the end can I observe? And, putting on one side all reference to attention, let us attempt to deal briefly with

---

[2] I do not mean by this that it is ultimate and self-evident, for, if a thing remains, there must *ex hyp.* be some change about it. We therefore have to abstract from this change. We find a certain connection of content in the thing, or between the thing and its context, and we take this connection as true, and as hence not to be made false by any mere circumstance. Such a truth, like all truth, is an abstraction, and a doubt may be raised as to its ultimate legitimacy. But this is the principle which underlies and justifies our practical assumption and procedure whenever we assume that something remains the same amid change.

this puzzle. To say that my present state is not observed and that I depend wholly on memory, leads us (as in part we have already seen) into a position which is not tenable. Let us agree, rightly in my opinion, that I can reproduce that which at the time of its occurrence was not an object, yet where is the warrant that my reproduction is accurate? I can hardly postulate that here there are no errors, and how are the errors to be corrected? And on the other side, if I can thus remember my past state, it seems strange that I am unable to make it an object while present. The appeal to memory seems therefore in any case inadmissible; and further for myself I am unable to verify in introspection this constant presence of memory. To myself, when I try to observe exhaustively, say, some internal sensations, the idea that I am struggling to remember them seems even ridiculous. To myself I appear to be observing something which *is*, and, apart from certain unsound views, I have found no reason to discredit this appearance. What I feel, that surely I may still feel, though I also and at the same time make it into an object before me. And any view for which this is impossible begins, I think, by conflict with fact, and ends, I am sure, in inability to explain facts. That I cannot make an object of the whole of my felt self all at once, so much is certain in fact, and the principle seems clear.[3] But that I can observe nothing of what I now feel, seems the false inference of a perverse theory.

[167]   But with this we are left face to face with a difficulty like the former one. Introspection is the attempt to observe my actual contents, and thus to take them as qualifying a construction called my self. To do this without residue, we agreed, was impossible, but that limitation need not trouble us. The difficulty and the problem arise in connection with the general mass that at any moment is felt but certainly is not throughout an object before me. Take an emotional whole such as despondency or anger or ennui. A part of this doubtless consists in that which, whether as sensation or idea, is before my mind. Any such object or objects we can observe, and, when we cannot keep them in view, we can postulate that they remain unaltered except so far as we have

---

[3] The principle involved is this, that, in order to have an object at all, you must have a felt self before which the object comes.

reason to suppose a change.[4] But in an emotional whole there are other felt elements which cannot be said to be before my mind. And now I desire both to bring these before me and to know that I have accomplished this task correctly.

With regard to the second of these points we must recall some results already reached. We have to assume that a change in feeling is felt, not in general merely, but as a change of this or that character. When my mood alters I feel, not a mere difference, but my mood to be different. And, on the other side, observation of my mood is felt as a difference but not as an alteration of my mood. We may take it in general to be the case that observation does not alter.[5] Thus, when for instance in despondency I observe my visceral sensations, these feelings are translated into objects, into perceptions and ideas, but none the less, though translated, the original feelings remain. Hence (and this is the point) the persisting feelings can be felt to jar or to accord with [168] the result of observation. For we have seen that generally in feeling we may experience the disagreement of elements. We have seen that a fresh fact, such as observation itself, must become an element contained in a new felt whole. And thus, when I pass psychically from despondency to despondency observed, I have not only a general sense of change to something new, but I feel more specially the presence or absence of novelty and an agreement or a jar with the object before me. When to my felt emotion, that is, its translation is added, I am aware of a harmony or discrepancy between that addition and what went before and still remains.[6] Apart from theory we should all agree that, when

[4] This is a mere application of the general postulate which we noticed before. It is unnecessary to discuss here our various special grounds for supposing the presence or absence of change.

[5] On the other side it is true that observation of my feelings may, according to the conditions, go on to increase or to suppress them. But I think that this point may be ignored here.

[6] I am in a certain felt state which I go on to observe. The description which results from the observation is an object added to my former felt state, and is now itself an element in a new felt state. This object gives me (*a*) a feeling of change, but (*b*) not a change of my special felt mood, say, anger. The description further, if correct, brings (*c*) a sense of harmonious addition without change, and if incorrect, (*d*) a feeling of incongruity. If the incongruity is positive (α), I feel a jarring new element. If it is negative (β), there is still a sense of discord, since defect has a positive quality. And there is, in this latter case especially, an instability in the object induced by ideal supplementation. This instability is largely the work of that which is merely felt.

despondent or angry, a man can feel that a description of such states is right or wrong, though he may be unable to compare this description with another object. Again we should agree that, when not despondent, a man may assent to a description of despondency, because he feels himself, as we say, into it, or may dissent because he cannot do so—and this though in neither case he could assign a special ground. And what happens here, I presume, is that the description excites feelings which tend to fill themselves out to the content of the usual felt state. And between this content and the description offered there is then experienced, as above, the sense of agreement or jar. I have not forgotten that, in order to test the truth of a description, a man may appeal to the usages of language, or again possibly may recall [169] some definite action or other symptom, or set of symptoms, from the past of himself or another. But, apart from an appeal to present feeling, nothing of this kind, however important it may be, is sufficient by itself, I would submit, to account for the facts.

I will now in passing touch briefly on the question of means. By what means and how am I able in, say, despondency to make an object of that which I feel? I am not inquiring how we come to have an object at all, nor am I even asking as yet how feeling in general can come to be an object. The question is limited at present to the above case of an emotion, but it has a more general bearing which will show itself later. And the point of importance is this. In any emotion one part of that emotion consists already of objects, of perceptions and ideas before my mind. And, the whole emotion being one, the special group of feeling is united with these objects before my mind, united with them integrally and directly though not objectively.[7] And this I think, supplies us with an answer to our question. For when the object-part of our emotion is enlarged by further perception or idea, the agreement or disagreement with what is felt is not merely general and suffused, but is located through the object in one special felt group. And this special connection and continuity with the object explains, I think, how we are able further to transform what is observed by the addition of elements from what is felt. There are features in feeling (this is the point) which already in a sense

---

[7] Again even on the object-side of the emotion there will of course be a greater or less extent of non-analysed content.

belong to and are one with their object, since the emotion contains and unites both its aspects.

Finally if we reject the idea that what is felt can serve to judge of what is before us, let us consider the position in which we are left. The attempt to fall back on memory, we have seen, resulted in failure, and what else remains to us? You may say, 'The object satisfies me or not, and that is the whole of it and the end of it.' [170] But assenting to this very largely, if not in the main, I cannot agree that no more is to be said as to the special satisfaction. The object, you may reply, in the end is found to be self-contradictory or harmonious; but once more here, while agreeing in principle, I cannot sit down content with such a mere generality. Why, when my mood is incompletely or wrong described, does the object go on to jar with itself and to be found self-inconsistent? There is more at work here, we saw, than the associations of language, and there is more even than any redintegration,[a] ideal or active, merely from the object by itself. For, with merely that, there is no accounting for the whole of the agreement or jar that I feel. You may appeal here to 'dispositions', and may argue that in one case my dispositions are satisfied and in the other case are restless. But if the disposition is not felt or in any way experienced, and to me is absolutely nothing but its effects, such an explanation once more seems insufficient. For in observing my mood I do not seem to be satisfied with the result, or to reject it, for no reason except that I find myself moved, I know not how, in this direction or the opposite. I seem on the contrary to myself to be engaged throughout and to be face to face with actual fact, and, wherever I dissent from or agree to an observed result, I seem to have a reason in this actual fact. And further I do not seem to have a mere general reason, but on the contrary something specific which I directly know and experience. The object before me is unstable and it moves so as to satisfy me; and in this point and so far we are perhaps all agreed. Where I go on to differ is that I insist that, in addition to other influences (whose working I admit), the object is moved also by that which is only felt. There are connections of content now actually present in

---

[a] Bradley defines 'redintegration' as follows: 'Any part of a single state of mind tends, if reproduced, to re-instate the remainder; or Any element tends to reproduce those elements with which it has formed one state of mind. This may be called the law of Redintegration' (*PL* 304).

feeling, and these are able to jar with the object before me. And they are able further to correct that object by supplementation [171] from themselves. And this, I submit, is the one account of the matter which on all sides is satisfactory.

We have now considered the problem offered both by Introspection and by Attention, and we have been led in each case to the same main result. These puzzles are insoluble unless that which I feel, and which is not an object before me, is present and active. This felt element is used, and it must be used, in the constitution of that object which satisfies me, and apart from this influence and criterion there is no accounting for the actual fact of our knowledge. We must go on now to deal more directly with the main question of this chapter. We must ask how immediate experience is able to make a special object of itself. The principles which we have laid down and have hitherto applied will furnish us, I trust, with a satisfactory answer.

I must however, before proceeding further, try to explain what I mean by immediate experience. . . . I use . . . immediate experi- [173] ence to stand for that which is comprised wholly within a single state of undivided awareness or feeling. As against anything 'unconscious', in the sense of falling outside, this is immediate as being my actual conscious experience. And further it is immediate as against those other special and mediated developments which throughout rest on it, and, while transcending, still remain within itself. I will now . . . attempt briefly to explain this difficult and most important sense of immediacy.

Questions at once arise on some of which we may first touch in passing.

(*a*) Was there and is there in the development of the race and the individual a stage at which experience is merely immediate? And, further, do we all perhaps at moments sink back to such a level? [174] We all (at least usually) have in what we experience the distinction of subject and object, or at any rate (it may not mean the same thing) the awareness of an object as a not-self. If we like to take 'consciousness' as the state in which we experience a not-self, we may thus ask if there ever was or ever is an experience which is in this sense wholly subconscious. In such a state there would be feeling, but there would not be an object present as an 'other'. And we should so far not be aware of any distinction between that which is felt and that which feels. For myself I think it probable that such a stage of mind not only, with all of us, comes first in fact, but that at times it recurs even in the life of the developed individual. But it is impossible for me to enter further on the matter here . . . What I would here insist on is the point that feeling, so understood, need not be devoid of internal diversity. Its content need not in this sense be simple, and possibly never is simple. By feeling, in short, I understand, and, I believe, always have understood, an awareness which, though non-relational, may comprise simply in itself an indefinite amount of difference. There are no distinctions in the proper sense, and yet there is a many felt in one. We may thus verify even here what we may call, if we please, an undeveloped ideality. And, not only this, but such a whole admits in itself a conflict and struggle of elements, not of course experienced as struggle but as discomfort, unrest and uneasiness. We may, I think, go on to add that the whole in feeling can feel itself present in one part of its content in a sense in which it does not so feel itself in another part. And of course change in its contents will be felt, though not experienced properly as change. Nor do I see reason to doubt that the laws of Redintegration and also of Fusion[b] (if we admit such a law) will hold in this field.

(*b*) I have thought it better to deal so far with the stage, real or supposed, where experience is merely immediate. But, in order to avoid controversy, I shall in this chapter consider this no further. And for our present purpose we need not assume that such a stage of mere feeling is even possible. I shall here take experience to exist always at the level where there is the distinction of object and subject, and a theoretical and practical relation holding between them.[8] I do not mean of course that this relation itself always exists for consciousness in the form of a relation proper uniting and dividing two terms. On the contrary we have no such object, I must insist, except so far as we have reached

[175]

---

[8] We may, as was noticed above, speak of this stage as 'consciousness' in contrast with mere feeling.

[b] Bradley states the law of fusion as 'Where different elements (or relations of elements) have any feature the same they may unite wholly or partially. The more wholly they unite the more their differences are destroyed, with a transfer of strength to the result' (*CE* 211).

self-consciousness; and to suppose that we are always self-conscious would to myself seem absurd. It is however impossible for me here to discuss these questions, on which I have entered elsewhere . . . and I must pass on to emphasize a further point which seems here all-important.

(c) Whether there is a stage where experience is *merely* immediate I have agreed to leave doubtful. Feeling is transcended always, if you please, in the sense that we have always contents which are more than merely felt. But on the other side at no moment can feeling ever be transcended, if this means that we are to have contents which are not felt. In a sense, therefore, we never can at any time pass beyond immediate experience. The object not-self, and again the object and subject related before my mind, all this is more than mere feeling. But again the whole of it would be nothing for me unless it came to me as felt; and that any actual experience should fall somewhere outside of feeling seems impossible. At every moment my state, whatever else it is, is a whole of which I am immediately aware. It is an experienced non-relational unity of many in one.[9] And object and subject and every possible relation and term, to be experienced at all, must fall within and depend vitally on such a felt unity.

At any moment my actual experience, however relational its contents, is in the end non-relational. No analysis into relations and terms can ever exhaust its nature or fail in the end to belie its essence. What analysis leaves for ever outstanding is no mere residue, but is a vital condition of the analysis itself. Everything which is got out into the form of an object implies still the felt background against which the object comes, and, further, the whole experience of both feeling and object is a non-relational immediate felt unity. The entire relational consciousness, in short, is experienced as falling within a direct awareness. This direct awareness is itself non-relational. It escapes from all attempts to exhibit it by analysis as one or more elements in a relational scheme, or as that scheme itself, or as a relation or relations, or as the sum or collection of any of these abstractions. And immediate experience not only escapes, but it serves as the basis on which the analysis is made. Itself is the vital element within

[176]

---

[9] I need not ask here if it is possible for my experience to consist of one single feeling.

which every analysis still moves, while, and so far as, and however much, that analysis transcends immediacy.

Everything therefore, no matter how objective and how relational, is experienced only in feeling, and, so far as it is experienced, still depends upon feeling. On the other side the objective and the relational transcend the state of mere feeling and in a sense are opposed to it. But we must beware here of an error. We cannot speak of a relation, between immediate experience and that which transcends it, except by a licence. It is a mode of expression found convenient in our reflective thinking, but it is in the end not defensible. A relation exists only between terms, and those terms, to be known as such, must be objects. And hence immediate experience, taken as the term of a relation, becomes so [177] far a partial object and ceases so far to keep its nature as a felt totality.

The relation (so to express ourselves) of immediate experience to its felt contents, and specially here to those contents which transcend it, must be taken simply as a fact. It can neither be explained nor even (to speak properly) described, since description necessarily means translation into objective terms and relations. We possess on the one side a fact directly felt and experienced. On the other side we attempt a description imperfect and half-negative. And our attempt is justified so far as the description seems true, so far, that is, as though inadequate, it does not positively jar, and again is felt positively to agree with our felt experience.

(*d*) There are several points which I cannot discuss here, but may notice in passing. The felt background, against which the object comes, remains always immediate. But, on the other hand, its content may to some extent show mediation. Parts of this content may have at some time been elements included in the object, and may have been internally distinguished into relations and terms. However, none the less now, this relational content forms part of the felt background. Again in the object not-self, on the other side, we may find tracts the contents of which have never been analysed. They are, so to speak, nebulae in which the non-relational form still persists internally, and in which the complexity does not go beyond simple sensuous co-inherence. And, as we saw in the case of an emotion, the matter contained in these nebulae, and in the not-self generally, is continuous as to its content with that matter which remains merely felt. It is impossible, however, here to enlarge on these questions. and I cannot ask here how far the not-self both in its origin and its essence is [178] distinctively practical. Nor can I point out how far and in what sense we have special not-selves depending on various relations, permanent and transitory, to special selves. I must hasten onwards to attempt to deal directly with the main problem of the present chapter.

I will, however, before proceeding, venture to repeat and to insist upon this main conclusion. Immediate experience is not a stage, which may or may not at some time have been there and has now ceased to exist. It is not in any case removed by the presence of a not-self and of a relational consciousness. All that is thus removed is at most, we may say, the *mereness* of immediacy. Every distinction and relation still rests on an immediate background of which we are aware, and every distinction and relation (so far as experienced) is also felt, and felt in a sense to belong to an immediate totality. Thus in all experience we still have feeling which is not an object, and at all our moments the entirety of what comes to us, however much distinguished and relational, is felt as comprised within a unity which itself is not relational.

We may now approach the two main questions of this chapter, (i) How can immediate experience ever serve as a criterion? and (ii) How can immediate experience itself become an object and a not-self, since *ex hyp.* it essentially is no object? The first of these questions, after what has gone before, may be dealt with briefly.

1. I am not discussing here the general problem of the ultimate criterion.[c] We may perhaps agree that the criterion consists in that which satisfies our wants, and is to be found where we have felt uneasiness and its positive opposite. That in which I feel myself affirmed, and which contents me, will be the general head under which falls reality, together with truth, goodness, and beauty. But I cannot enter further on this here, or inquire as to

---

[c] See 'The General Nature of Reality', repr. above, Part II, Sect. 1, Ch. 4.

the special characters of these diverse satisfactions.[10] What on the
other hand I wish here to emphasize is the point that I do not
take immediate experience as being in general the criterion. I do
not say that in agreement merely with the content of this we are
to find in all cases our answer to the question of truth and reality. The inquiry as to why an object contents or does not content
me, how it satisfies or does not satisfy a demand of my nature,
cannot in all cases be met by an appeal to the actual content of
my feeling. Hence the problem before us is limited to a special
issue. How, we must ask, in the cases where my immediate experience does serve as a criterion of truth and fact, is it able to perform such an office?

We have already in the main anticipated the answer. I can feel
uneasiness, we found, both general and special apart from any
object or at least without regard to any object in particular.
Again I can have a sense of uneasiness or its opposite in regard
to a particular object before me. I do not, so far, make an object
of my uneasiness and hold it before me in one with the object;
but so far, without actually doing anything of this kind, I feel the
jarring or unison specially together and in one with the object.
And we have now to ask how this disagreement can become a
contradiction before me in the object, so that I am not merely
dissatisfied with that but can go on to reject it as unreal.

What is required is that the object should itself become
qualified by the same content which was merely felt within me.
As soon as this qualification has appeared, I have actually before
me in the object that which previously was felt within me to be
harmonious or to jar in regard to the object. The feeling (to   [180]
speak roughly) remains what it was, but it no longer is merely
grouped round and centred in the object. The feeling itself is also
before me in the object-world, and the object now confronts me
as being itself satisfactory or discordant. My description, e.g., is
seen to come short, or to be otherwise conflicting, when compared with the corrected idea of my actual emotion.

I will now notice briefly the various ways in which the object
can gain its fresh qualification. The object naturally is unstable
and in constant change. Apart from what we may call external

---

[10] I assume here that goodness is not to be used for the general term which is
equivalent to satisfaction in general. But whether goodness is to be used in a
wider or a narrower sense, is to myself a question merely of nomenclature.

alteration, there are reactions from the subject. Even where these are non-acquired, they often tend to make the requisite change in the object. And then, as we have seen before, there is redintegration from the object both physical and psychical. This redintegration again is all-pervasive, and holds good beyond the object-world and within the region of mere feeling. Hence the object, having been continuous with what is felt in me, both generally and in special groups, becomes an ideal centre and bond. It has a tendency both to restore and to qualify itself by associated content whether foregone or present. And further, as soon as this qualification from whatever cause has taken place, the identity of the content before me and within me is felt. Thus I am no longer merely satisfied or in unrest with regard to the object, but the object contains for me and itself is that which I feel must be accepted or rejected.

We are attempting here to deal briefly with a difficult point which tends on all sides to lose itself in complications. I am endeavouring, therefore, so far as I can, to narrow and simplify the issue. We may feel satisfied or otherwise when we have contents felt to be harmonious or jarring, and further a perceived object may also in feeling be an element and an important element in a special felt group. Then, when the object (as may happen from various causes) itself acquires the content which before in feeling gave satisfaction or unrest, I become aware of the perceived object as that which in itself gives satisfaction or discord. And according to the nature of the dissatisfaction and of that which is done to remove it from the object, our general criterion acts in various specific ways. But all that concerns us here is the case where the particular content, which lies in my feeling, is used in order to judge of an object before me.

[181]

We may recur to our former instance of an emotional state. If I shrink from or am attracted by some person, and do not know how this happens, I may endeavour accurately to realize the detail of my feelings, and perhaps to discover the real nature of the conduct which the object suggests. We have here an object, perceived and thought of, and on the other side we have dim uneasy feelings in myself which are not objective and before me. Let, however, the object from any cause—an instinctive action, a chance sensation or an oscillation of emphasis—develop its content in a certain direction, and the situation may at once be changed. That which formerly was but felt in regard to the object has become now, also and as well, a quality of the object. And it may satisfy us because it is that qualification which answers to what we felt and still feel. I know now what my feelings actually were, and whether and how far they were that for which I took them. And I understand now how the person himself has perhaps a character which suggests this or that behaviour towards him. In either case an object has been judged of in accordance with and from the content of immediate experience, and that experience has acted as a criterion of the object.

2. From this hurried treatment of a difficult problem I pass on to deal at last directly with the special subject of this chapter. We must ask how immediate experience is able to know itself and to become for us an object. That such knowledge exists in fact seems to me incontestable. Immediate experience certainly cannot [182] make an object of itself throughout and in all its individual detail. And such a result not only fails in fact to be achieved but is impossible essentially. We can, however, set our immediate experience before us not only in partial detail but in its main general character. We can know about it as a positive experience, an awareness of many in one which yet is not relational; and I must attempt to point out the steps by which such a conclusion may be reached. But I am not here offering any genetic account of the matter. That inquiry, however important, may here fortunately be ignored. The idea of immediate experience, once suggested, is, like other ideas, verified by its working. And all that I am concerned with here is to show that the origin of the suggestion is itself not in principle inexplicable.

(i) We can in the first place have before us as an object the idea of a complete reality. Our actual object, as we saw, is unstable, and its advance (so far as it advances) in a certain main direction tends generally to remove uneasiness and to bring satisfaction.[11] Hence we can form (I need not ask how) the idea of an object with all uneasiness removed entirely, an object which utterly satisfies. But this means an object with nothing that is really outside it in the form of an 'elsewhere' or a 'not-yet'. The 'elsewhere' or the 'not-yet' that falls really outside the object,

---

[11] I am not saying that *every* satisfactory addition to the object is preceded by uneasiness and fulfils a felt need or want. That in my opinion would be going at least beyond the facts.

precludes (this seems obvious) entire satisfaction. We hence are led to think of an object without any external 'elsewhere' or 'not-yet', an object which in some sense contains within itself, and already is qualified by, every real possibility. We form in other words the idea of an all-inclusive Reality. And this idea, being set before us, may so far satisfy us as true and real. The Reality with anything outside of it will now not merely be felt as defective, [183] but will in addition be discrepant with its own idea. And anything now that is suggested or that can be suggested, if it fails to be there *in* our actual object, must be made somehow *of* the actual object, if at least that object is to be complete.[12]

(ii) I have thus the idea of an object which is complete and all-inclusive, while on the other hand the object actually before me is incomplete. But this perceived object is changed and, let us here say, is changed by addition. And, with this, the source of the added elements goes on to become for me a problem. (*a*) These elements, I proceed to judge, come to me in part from the unknown not-self. This is an inevitable inference, the nature and validity of which it is perhaps not necessary here to discuss. We have hence, in this unknown province, a reality which has the form of an object not-self, but which on the other side is not present actually before me in perception. And this reality must be set down as included within my complete object. (*b*) Again within that object which I actually perceive there are contained (as we saw) tracts more or less undistinguished internally. These tracts are nebulae the contents of which have on the one hand manifoldness, but on the other hand are more or less without the relational form. They have within them adjectives which sensuously inhere and cohere, though these adjectives have not yet been

---

[12] The reader will bear in mind that I am not asking here if the above idea is *true*. That is a question which here may be ignored. There are two points which I may notice in passing. (*a*) It may possibly be suggested that, instead of taking everything as *of* the object, I may take it as merely *together with* the object, and that this exception is fatal. But in this case I reply that the 'together' has now itself become the object—an object in my judgement most unsatisfactory but still answering the purpose of the text. (*b*) Again it may be said with regard to the 'not-yet' that, given a *recurrence* of a certain character, the 'not-yet' may be harmless. To this I answer that in such a case the 'not-yet' qualifies this character which recurs, and in some sense is included within this character, and that taken as really external it still means incompleteness. But, obviously, innumerable difficulties attaching to what is said in the text may occur to the reader, and must here be passed by.

ordered. But, as our knowledge increases, these sensuous wholes go on more or less to be broken up and discriminated. And the [184] object, which of course is continuous throughout, appropriates the result of this process. Hence the object now possesses to some extent actually all its contents in a discriminated form, and for the rest it can assume (rightly or wrongly) that the same result, though not actual, is possible. The object will now include for us both its distinguished and undistinguished contents, the latter taken as distinguished ideally though not in actual detail. How far and in what precise sense it is proper to attribute reality to these unmade distinctions, we are not concerned here to inquire. It is enough for us that the idea of the complete object now includes within itself an objective 'not-yet' external to its actual detail, and again an objective 'not-yet' lying undistinguished within the fact which is given. And, having concluded so much, the self so far is satisfied with the idea before it, and it feels that this idea is somehow true and real.

Now in the above two cases (we must go on to observe) there is a difference, a difference which is felt. When an addition is made to our object from the outside we feel this addition as new. I do not mean that in this respect it does not matter how the alteration of the object is made, and that, however the addition comes, we have precisely the same feeling. I admit the diversity, but I must insist that, in spite of this diversity, we have, when the object is added to from outside itself a specific feeling of newness, and that this feeling differs from that which comes when the object develops itself from within itself. In the latter case (the case of what we called nebulae) the content was actually there though it was not yet distinguished, and the content was already felt as being there; while in the former case (the case of addition from without) the content was not felt at all. The added features in both cases are felt as new, but in the one case these features arrive from a world which is unfelt, while in the other case the features already were somehow present in my actual awareness. [185] And the difference between the two arrivals shows itself in each case in a different feeling. The reader who finds a difficulty here should recall the results we have accepted as true. In the first place everything, the object included, is actually felt, and, in the second place, a change in feeling itself also is felt. All that we have added here is the conclusion, that in the two cases distinguished above there is in each case a specific felt difference.[13]

(*c*) But beyond these two cases we have also a third. An addition may be made to our object, but neither from the unknown not-self without it nor from the undistinguished tracts within itself. We saw that, when a felt emotion is described, a man may feel that the description agrees or does not agree with an actual fact of which he is aware. And yet we found that this experienced fact, by which the description is measured, has contents not objectively before the man even in an undistinguished form. The object in its wavering, and in its movement to complete itself through redintegration and otherwise, changes in directions which cause on one side satisfaction and on the other side uneasiness. And it is, largely or mainly, because these suggestions are felt to be in unison or discord with something already felt as present, that they are accepted or rejected. In something of the same way (we need not trouble ourselves here with the difference) the beautiful reality may seem to give you what you wanted, though what you wanted you did not know, or may seem to say for you what you always meant and could never express. This experience may doubtless in part be illusory. The want in part may not actually have been there before it was merged in satisfaction, and the meaning may in part never have gone before its expression. But upon the other side the experience certainly conveys to us things that are not perceived but were actually felt within us. Again earlier in this chapter we saw how in psychological introspection my self is put before me as an object, an object to be completed ideally. And its content, we went on to perceive, is filled up in part out of elements which I merely feel, and which in no sense are before me in the shape of an object. And we may once more remind ourselves in general how the object is continuous in substance with the content that merely is present in feeling, and hence tends persistently to complete itself by that content.

[186]

But, the fact being as above, how is the self ever to become aware of this fact or even to suspect its existence? How is the merely felt to become in that character an object? In the main, I

---

[13] I am of course not supposing that the consciousness which we are considering, knows at the present stage about these feelings all that we from the outside and at a later stage perceive.

think, this question has by now been answered. When my object is increased and the addition comes from that which was and is felt, there is, in such a case, first, a positive sense of expansion and of accord. And there is, next, an absence of the feeling of complete otherness and newness. We have not here quite the same experience as when the object is increased from the undistinguished not-self, but we have an experience more or less similar. This felt absence of disturbance, and this positive sense of something the same although new, prevent my attributing the change to that actual object-world which extends beyond my object. Can I then take the change as arising from the undistinguished tracts present within my actual object? Once more here, we find, the path is closed. For the feeling here, though similar, is not the same as that of which in the present case I am aware. Again, however much I develop the object in idea, I seem always to be left with a sense of defect. Further in some cases (through a persisting after-perception or otherwise) I can reproduce the special object as it was experienced before the addition. And here I find that the new feature does not in fact fall even within the undiscriminated parts of that object.

To repeat, my object, felt to be unsatisfactory, is changed and [187] now is qualified by an addition. This addition gives a positive sense of agreement and unison. It is without the sensation of disturbance, and it gives the feeling of identity with what went before. On the other side this feeling differs from that which I experience when the object is developed from its own undistinguished tracts. And in recalling the change of the object, where this is possible, there is, in passing between the earlier and the later object, a feeling of difference. And this difference remains even when I attend to those contents of the object which are not discriminated. For the above reason I cannot set down the change as due to the object even so far as that is undistinguished.

Generally then my object is added to, and the new matter cannot be taken as without a source. But in the first place the matter is not felt as wholly new but as something already there and mine. And, in the second place, what is new cannot come from the object-world. It goes beyond my actual object, and yet I cannot attribute it to the non-perceived object-world, or again to any non-relational nebula contained within my object. The origin of my experience therefore is non-objective and it is also non-relational; but, on the other side, positively, it comes to me as something which already was present to me. The idea, therefore, is suggested of an experience neither objective nor relational but, in a word, immediate. And this idea, being suggested (no matter how it is suggested), satisfies me so far, and is accepted as true and real. The process outlined above may, if you please, contain logical flaws. Whether that is or is not the case, I am not concerned to discuss. And the true history and the real genetic origin of the idea reached, you may contend, has escaped me. That would be an objection which once more I am not called on to answer. I claim to have shown how the idea of immediate experience can be brought before the mind, however otherwise normally it may be brought there. But the idea, once suggested, is verified by its working, and its acceptance does not logically depend upon the manner of its discovery.

The whole process which I have sketched may be briefly resumed thus. Our actual object fails to satisfy us, and we get the idea that it is incomplete and that a complete object would satisfy. We attempt to complete our object by relational addition from without and by relational distinction from within. And the result in each case is failure and a sense of defect. We feel that any result gained thus, no matter how all-inclusive so far, would yet be less than what we actually experience. Then we try the idea of a positive non-distinguished non-relational whole, which contains more than the object and in the end contains all that we experience. And that idea, as I have endeavoured in these pages to show, seems to meet our demand. It is not free from difficulty, but it appears to be the one ground on which satisfaction is possible. . . .

[189]   In some such manner it, however, seems possible to reach the idea of immediate experience. That experience we have seen is a positive non-relational non-objective whole of feeling. Within my immediate experience falls everything of which in any sense I am aware, so far at least as I am aware of it. But on the other side it contains distinctions which transcend its immediacy. This my world, of feeling and felt in one, is not to be called 'subjective', nor is it to be identified with my self. That would be a mistake at once fundamental and disastrous. Nor is immediate experience to be taken as simply one with any 'subliminal' world or any uni-

verse of the Unconscious. However continuous it may be with a larger world, my immediate experience falls, as such, strictly within the limits of my finite centre. But again to conclude from this that what falls within these limits is merely myself, would be an error entailing in the end theoretical ruin. The above idea of immediate experience is not intelligible, I would add, in the sense of being explicable; but it is necessary, I would insist, both for psychology and for metaphysics.

Its larger application would go far beyond the scope of these [190] pages. Nothing in the end is real but what is felt, and for me nothing in the end is real but that which I feel. To take reality as a relational scheme, no matter whether the relations are 'external' or 'internal', seems therefore impossible and perhaps even ridiculous. It would cease to be so only if the immediacy of feeling could be shown to be merely relational. On the other side relations in fact do exist and immediacy in fact is transcended.[14] And, just as we cannot explain the possibility of finite centres of feeling, so we cannot explain how this transcendence of feeling is possible. But the fact remains that feeling, while it remains as a constant basis, nevertheless contains a world which in a sense goes beyond itself. And when we seek for a unity which holds together these two aspects of our world, we seem to find given to us nothing but this unity of feeling which itself is transcended. Hence, as I have urged elsewhere, we are driven to postulate a higher form of unity, a form which combines the two aspects neither of which can be excluded. That such a form is given to us directly in any experience[15] I have never pretended. On the other hand against its possibility I have nowhere found a conclusive objection. And because this satisfies our demands, and because nothing but this satisfies them, I therefore conclude that such an idea, so far as it goes, is final and absolute truth. But, however

[14] We never in one sense do, or can, go beyond immediate experience. Apart from the immediacy of 'this' and 'now' we never have, or can have, reality. The real, to be real, must be felt. This is one side of the matter. But on the other side the felt content takes on a form which more and more goes beyond the essential character of feeling, i.e. direct and non-relational qualification. Distinction and separation into substantives and adjectives, terms and relations, alienate the content of immediate experience from the form of immediacy which still on its side persists. In other words the ideality, present from the first, is developed, and to follow this ideality is our way to the true Reality which is there in feeling.

[15] Given, that is, adequately and as required. I am not forgetting the claim of, e.g., our aesthetic experience.

[191] that may be, I trust that the humbler contentions of this chapter may in their way be useful. I have felt throughout that everything here which I have been able to say, could and should have been somehow put more simply. But if, while so far agreeing with me, the reader is nevertheless led to reflect further on this difficult theme, my main end will have been accomplished. The problem which has occupied us, however sterile and baffling it may appear, threatens, if left unresolved, to bring danger or even theoretical destruction.

SUPPLEMENTARY NOTE

[199] In republishing the foregoing article I would call attention to the metaphysical importance of [its] doctrine. Most of us, no doubt, agree that in metaphysics we start, in some sense, from what is given, and that hence the question as to what is given at the start is fundamental and vital. And the divergence of the answers, stated or implied, is a point which we are bound to recognize and deal with. There is, for instance, a well-known view that, whatever is given at first, it is not the One Reality; and that hence the One must be reached, if at all, by some supervening process. Our beginning, it is asserted, is with the mere Many. Or we may hear that we have to start with the correlation of subject and object, which correlation, we find later, we cannot transcend.

Disagreeing otherwise, I would emphatically endorse this last result. If what is given is a Many without a One, the One is never attainable. And, if what we had at first were the mere correlation of subject and object, then to rise beyond that would be impossible. From such premises there is in my opinion no road except to total scepticism. This is the ground, inherited of course from others, on which I may say that I have based myself always. If you take experience as above, then all the main conclusions which I advocate are assuredly wrecked. And nothing, I presume, is gained by simply urging against myself and others a result on which we ourselves have consistently stood.

But what is more important to discuss is, I should say, the truth of the premises. The doctrine that what is given at the start is a mere Many or a mere correlation, is, we contend, a fatal error. This, we maintain, is no genuine fact, but is a fundamental perversion of the fact. And while we are ready to inquire as to what would follow from any premisses alleged, we insist that the truth of the premisses is first in question, and we submit that, after all, it is perhaps better to begin by asking as to the [200] nature of what is actually experienced.

Any one who has read the foregoing paper (not to speak of what I have written elsewhere), will, I think, see that for me at no stage of mental development is the mere correlation of subject and object actually given. Wherever this or any other relation is experienced, what is experienced is more than the mere relation. It involves a felt totality, and on this inclusive unity the relation depends. The subject, the object, and their relation, are experienced as elements or aspects in a One which is there from the first. And thus to seek to extrude the One from what at first is experienced, is in every case to mistake for fact what really is sheer abstraction.

Everywhere, and not only here, a mere relation is in my view an abstraction, which never is given and could never be real. The experienced fact is not the mere terms and the relation. Over and above these it involves another aspect of given totality, and without this aspect the experienced fact is not given. And the same remark, of course, applies to the contention that what is first given is a bare Many.

I regret to repeat here once more what I have urged through so many years and so often. But, as long as what I hold to be fundamental fact is so much ignored, I have no choice but from time to time to repeat what to me seems indubitable.

As to what would follow if I am here in error, and if a mere Many or a bare correlation were actually given, I will add a few words. Relations (this, I presume, must follow) would be at least as real as their terms and would have ultimate reality. What, however, is to be said about the experienced 'togetherness' of terms and relations, I do not know. Not only does the 'together' seem to me, on this ground, to fall outside of knowledge and reality, but the whole fact of experience and knowledge has to my mind become non-existent and even impossible. Whether, if we start from the above basis, any subject could ever become aware of any other subject, I will not offer to discuss. But that the God of Theism could have his place in such a world, unless that world were radically changed, to myself seems inconceivable.

[201]   But is it not better, I would ask once more, to begin by a discussion as to what is actually given in experience? Is it not better to recognize that on this point there is no agreement, and little more than a variety of conflicting opinions? The opinion which I myself, with others, have adopted, may of course be erroneous. But obviously I cannot desert it because certain doctrines, on the rejection of which it long ago was based, are assumed to be true.

5

On Truth and Coherence

In this paper Bradley argues that the only test of truth that a person can apply, even in the case of the deliverances of his current sense-perceptions and memories, is *system*. System, he maintains, has two essential aspects: coherence and comprehensiveness.

A corollary of this view is that there are no infallible judgements of sense-perception. If we descend to the level of mere feeling in search of incorrigibility then, Bradley argues, we will arrive at something which cannot deliver either truth or falsity (*ETR* 205-6, below, pp. 298-9). So he rejects an epistemology according to which empirical knowledge is to be construed as a statically descriptive edifice (*ETR* 209, below, pp. 301-2) resting on a foundation of incorrigible and logically independent facts provided by the contents of sense-perception. On Bradley's view our systems of belief are to be seen not merely as descriptive, but also as explanatory and as confronting data conjecturally (cf. editorial introduction to Part II, Sect. 2, Ch. 6, below).

Any particular fact of sense-perception will be given, not independently of others, but within an interrelated manifold of facts. It will also be given, in the waking experience of a normal adult human being, in the context of more or less comprehensive systems of belief. Normally, particular facts, given at particular moments either in perception or by memory or as learned from other people, will feed consistently into a person's beliefs with respect to his 'real' world in space and time (*ETR* 208, below, p. 301; also cf. 215, below, p. 306). We will as a matter of principle accept as trustworthy (except when we have special reasons to do otherwise) our memories and the testimony of other people whom we take in general to view the world as we ourselves do. If we did not do this, and if we could then order our worlds at all, we could certainly not do it as systematically as we do by adopting those principles (*ETR* 212-3, below, pp. 303-4).

Nevertheless, on occasions, putative 'facts' of sense-perception and memory will conflict with contents in our systems of standing beliefs. If

---

'On Truth and Coherence' was first pub. in *Mind*, NS 18 (1909). Repr. here from *ETR*, ch. vii. It was partly a response to Russell's 'On the Nature of Truth', *Proceedings of the Aristotelian Society*, NS 7 (1906-7). It might also be seen as a total rejection of logical atomism.

such conflict does occur then whether the 'fact' is to be rejected or whether, by a suitable reassessment of truth-values in the contents of our standing beliefs, it is to be accepted will be decided by reference to the test of comprehensiveness. The question always is: Which of these courses of action would consistently account for the *most* data from all the data currently available from all sources, i.e. not merely from sense-perception, memory, and others, but also from the unlimited thought constructions we can, more or less fancifully, entertain (*ETR* 214–15, below, pp. 305–7)?

Bradley acknowledges that there will be certain facts of perception and memory concerning his real world (namely those essential to his personal identity) that a person will not be able to reject (*ETR* 216–17, below, pp. 307–9; cf. also 211, below, p. 303). However, Bradley argues, even such incorrigible facts would, relatively to the way in which they would be present in a wider experience (in particular in the limiting case of a totally comprehensive experience), properly be classed as errors (*ETR* 218, below, pp. 308–9).

G.S.

[202] [Whether] coherence will work as a test of truth in the case of facts due to sensible perception and memory is the issue to which here I confine myself, neglecting the question as to other truths whose warrant also is taken as immediate. What I maintain is that in the case of facts of perception and memory the test which we do apply, and which we must apply, is that of system. I contend that this test works satisfactorily, and that no other test will work. And I argue in consequence that there are no judgements of sense which are in principle infallible.

There is a misunderstanding against which the reader must be warned most emphatically. The test which I advocate is the idea of a whole of knowledge as wide and as consistent as may be. In speaking of system I mean always the union of these two aspects, and this is the sense and the only sense in which I am defending coherence. If we separate coherence from . . . comprehensiveness,

[203] then I agree that neither of these aspects of system will work by itself. How they are connected, and whether in the end we have one principle or two, is of course a difficult question. I hope to return to this,[1] but it is impossible for me to touch on it here. All

---

[1] See ['Coherence and Contradiction', repr. below, Part II, Sect. 2, Ch. 6].

that I can do here is to point out that both of the above aspects are for me inseparably included in the idea of system, and that coherence apart from comprehensiveness is not for me the test of truth or reality. . . .

For the sake of clearness let me begin by mentioning some things in which I do *not* believe. I do not believe in any know-ledge which is independent of feeling and sensation. On sensation and feeling I am sure that we depend for the material of our knowledge. And as to the facts of perception, I am convinced that (to speak broadly) we cannot anticipate them or ever become independent of that which they give to us. And these facts of perception, I further agree, are at least in part irrational, so far as in detail is visible. I do not believe that we can make ourselves independent of these non-rational data.

But, if I do not believe all this, does it follow that I have to accept independent facts? Does it follow that perception and memory give me truths which I must take up and keep as they are given me, truths which in principle cannot be erroneous? This surely would be to pass from one false extreme to another. Our intelligence cannot construct the world of perceptions and feel-ings, and it depends on what is given—to so much I assent. But that there are given facts of perception which are independent and ultimate and above criticism, is not to my mind a true con- [204] clusion. On the contrary, such facts to my mind are a vicious abstraction. We have, I should say, the aspect of datum, and we have the aspect of interpretation or construction. . . . And why, I ask, for the intelligence must there be datum without interpreta-tion any more than interpretation without datum? To me the opposite holds good, and I therefore conclude that no given fact is sacrosanct. With every fact of perception or memory a modified interpretation is in principle possible, and no such fact therefore is given free from all possibility of error.

The reason for maintaining independent facts and infallible judgements, as I understand it, is twofold. (1) Such data, it may be said, can be actually shown. And (2) in any case they must exist, since without them the intelligence cannot work. . . .

(1) I doubt my ability to do justice to the position of the man who claims to show ultimate given facts exempt from all possible error. In the case of any datum of sensation or feeling, to prove that we have this wholly unmodified by what is called

'apperception' seems a hopeless undertaking. And how far it is supposed that such a negative can be proved I do not know. What, however, is meant must be this, that we somehow and somewhere have verifiable facts of perception and memory, and also judgements, free from all chance of error.

I will begin here by recalling a truth familiar but often forgotten . . . In your search for independent facts and for infallible truths you may go so low that, when you have descended beyond the level of error, you find yourself below the level of any fact or of any truth which you can use. What you seek is particular facts [205] of perception or memory, but what you get may be something not answering to that character. I will go on to give instances of what I mean, and I think that in every case we shall do well to ask this question, 'What on the strength of our ultimate fact are we able to contradict?'

(*a*) If we take the instance of simple unrelated sensations or feelings, *a, b, c*—supposing that there are such things—what judgement would such a fact enable us to deny? We could on the strength of this fact deny the denial that *a, b and c* exist in any way, manner or sense. But surely this is not the kind of independent fact of which we are in search.

(*b*) From this let us pass to the case of a complex feeling containing, at once and together, both *a* and *b*. On the ground of this we can deny the statement that *a* and *b* cannot or do not ever anyhow co-exist in feeling. This is an advance, but it surely leaves us far short of our goal.

(*c*) What we want, I presume, is something that at once is infallible and that also can be called a particular fact of perception or memory. And we want, in the case of perception, something that would be called a fact for observation. We do not seem to reach this fact until we arrive somewhere about the level of 'I am here and now having a sensation or complex of sensations of such or such a kind'. The goal is reached; but at this point, unfortunately, the judgement has become fallible, so far at least as it really states particular truth.

(*α*) In such a judgement it is in the first place hard to say what is meant by the 'I'. If, however, we go beyond feeling far enough to mean a self with such or such a real existence in time, then memory is involved, and the judgement at once, I should urge, becomes fallible. . . . Thus the statement made in the judgement is liable to error, or else the statement does not convey particular truth.

(β) And this fatal dilemma holds good when applied to the [206] 'now' and 'here'. If these words mean a certain special place in a certain special series or order, they are liable to mistake. But, if they fall short of this meaning, then they fail to state individual fact. My feeling is, I agree, not subject to error in the proper sense of that term, but on the other side my feeling does not of itself deliver truth. And the process which gets from it a deliverance as to individual fact is fallible.

Everywhere such fact depends on construction. And we have here to face not only the possibility of what would commonly be called mistaken interpretation. We have in addition the chance of actual sense-hallucination. And, worse than this, we have the far-reaching influence of abnormal suggestion and morbid fixed idea. This influence may stop short of hallucination, and yet may vitiate the memory and the judgement to such an extent that there remains no practical difference between idea and perceived fact. And, in the face of these possibilities, it seems idle to speak of perceptions and memories secure from all chance of error. Or on the other side banish the chance of error, and with what are you left? You then have something which (as we have seen) goes no further than to warrant the assertion that such and such elements can and do co-exist—somehow and somewhere, or again that such or such a judgement happens—without any regard to its truth and without any specification of its psychical context. And no one surely will contend that with this we have particular fact.

The doctrine that perception gives us infallible truth rests on a foundation which in part is sound and in part fatally defective. That what is felt is felt, and cannot, so far as felt, be mistaken— so much as this must be accepted. But the view that, when I say 'this', 'now', 'here', or 'my', what I feel, when so speaking, is carried over intact into my judgement, and that my judgement in consequence is exempt from error, seems wholly indefensible. It [207] survives, I venture to think, only because it never has understood its complete refutation.[2] That which I designate, is not and

---

[2] I am of course referring here to Hegel. This is a matter to which I shall return (see ['Coherence and Contradiction'] repr. below,) I am naturally not attempting to deal here with the whole subject of Error [see 'Error', repr. above, Part II, Sect. 1, Ch. 7. Part II, Sect. 2, Ch. 6].

cannot be carried over into my judgement. The judgement may in a sense answer to that which I feel, but none the less it fails to contain and to convey my feeling. And on the other hand, so far as it succeeds in expressing my meaning, the judgement does this in a way which makes it liable to error. Or, to put it otherwise, the perceived truth, to be of any use, must be particularized. So far as it is stated in a general form, it contains not only that which you meant to say but also, and just as much, the opposite of that which you meant. And to contend for the infallibility of such a truth seems futile. On the other side so far as your truth really is individualized, so far as it is placed in a special construction and vitally related to its context, to the same extent the element of interpretation or implication is added. And, with this element, obviously comes the possibility of mistake. And we have seen above that, viewed psychologically, particular judgements of perception immune from all chance of error seem hardly tenable.

(2) I pass now to the second reason for accepting infallible data of perception. Even if we cannot show these (it is urged) we are bound to assume them. For in their absence our knowledge has nothing on which to stand, and this want of support results in total scepticism.

It is possible of course here to embrace both premisses and conclusion, and to argue that scepticism is to be preferred to an untrue assumption. And such a position I would press on the notice of those who uphold infallible judgements of sense and memory. But personally I am hardly concerned in this issue, for I [208] reject both the conclusion and the premisses together. Such infallible and incorrigible judgements are really not required for our knowledge, and, since they cannot be shown, we must not say that they exist.

In maintaining that all sense-judgements are liable to error it would be better no doubt first to discuss the nature of error. But, since this is impossible here, let me state how much I take to be admitted or agreed on. I understand it to be admitted that some judgements of perception are fallible, and that the question is simply whether this description applies to all such judgements without exception. But, if some at least of these judgements are to be called fallible, what are we to understand by that word? We each of us have a world which we call our 'real' world in space and time. This is an order, how made and based on what, it is impossible here to inquire.[3] But facts of sense are called imaginary or erroneous, when in their offered character they do not belong to this 'real' order in space or time. They all belong to it of course as facts in some one's mental history, but otherwise they do not qualify the 'real' order as they claim to qualify it. We therefore relegate them to the sphere of the erroneous or the imaginary, unless we are able to modify and correct their claim so that it becomes admissible. So much as this I must take here to be admitted on both sides, though it is more than possible, I fear, that I may have thus unknowingly perverted the issue. Still, unless the question by some means is cleared, I see no way of proceeding. And the issue, as I understand it, will now be as follows. Are there any judgements of perception or memory, purporting to qualify the 'real' world, which must necessarily qualify that world as they purport to qualify it? Or on the other hand are all such 'facts' capable in principle of being relegated to the world of error, unless and until they are corrected?

This I take to be the issue, but there is a distinction which, [209] before proceeding, the reader must notice, the distinction between *my* experience and *my* world and the world in general. It is one thing to say that there are truths which in and for my personal experience are fundamental and incorrigible, and it is another thing to assert that the same truths are infallible absolutely. This distinction will become clearer as we advance, for I will begin by confining the question to my personal experience. Is there any truth of perception which here is fundamental and infallible, and incapable of being banished to the world of fancy?

I agree that we depend vitally on the sense-world, that our material comes from it, and that apart from it knowledge could not begin. To this world, I agree, we have for ever to return, not only to gain new matter but to confirm and maintain the old. I agree that to impose order from without on sheer disorder would be wholly impracticable, and that, if my sense-world were disorderly beyond a certain point, my intelligence would not exist. And further I agree that we cannot suppose it possible that *all* the judgements of perception and memory which for me come first, could in fact for me be corrected. I cannot, that is, imagine

---

[3] See ['On Floating Ideas and the Imaginary', repr. above, Part II, Sect. 2, Ch. 1].

the world of my experience to be so modified that in the end none of these accepted facts should be left standing. But so far, I hasten to add, we have not yet come to the real issue. There is still a chasm between such admissions and the conclusion that there are judgements of sense which possess truth absolute and infallible.

We meet here a false doctrine largely due to a misleading metaphor. My known world is taken to be a construction built upon such and such foundations. It is argued, therefore, to be in principle a superstructure which rests upon these supports. You can go on adding to it no doubt, but only so long as the supports remain; and, unless they remain, the whole building comes down. But the doctrine, I have to contend, is untenable, and the [210] metaphor ruinously inapplicable. The foundation in truth is provisional merely. In order to begin my construction I take the foundation as absolute—so much certainly is true. But that my construction continues to rest on the beginnings of my knowledge is a conclusion which does not follow. It does not follow that, if these are allowed to be fallible, the whole building collapses. For it is in another sense that my world rests upon the data of perception.

My experience is solid, not so far as it is a superstructure but so far as in short it is a system. My object is to have a world as comprehensive and coherent as possible, and, in order to attain this object, I have not only to reflect but perpetually to have recourse to the materials of sense. I must go to this source both to verify the matter which is old and also to increase it by what is new. And in this way I must depend upon the judgements of perception. Now it is agreed that, if I am to have an orderly world, I cannot possibly accept all 'facts'. Some of these must be relegated, as they are, to the world of error, whether we succeed or fail in modifying and correcting them. And the view which I advocate takes them all as in principle fallible. On the other hand, that view denies that there is any necessity for absolute facts of sense. Facts for it are true, we may say, just so far as they work, just so far as they contribute to the order to experience. If by taking certain judgements of perception as true, I can get more system into my world, then these 'facts' are so far true, and if by taking certain 'facts' as errors I can order my experience better, then so far these 'facts' are errors. And there is no 'fact' which possesses an absolute right. Certainly there are truths with which I begin and which I personally never have to [211] discard, and which therefore remain in fact as members of my known world. And of some of these certainly it may be said that without them I should not know how to order my knowledge. But it is quite another thing to maintain that every single one of these judgements is in principle infallible. The absolute indispensable fact is in my view the mere creature of false theory. Facts are valid so far as, when taken otherwise than as 'real', they bring disorder into my world. And there are to-day for me facts such that, if I take them as mistakes, my known world is damaged and, it is possible, ruined. But how does it follow that I cannot to-morrow on the strength of new facts gain a wider order in which these old facts can take a place as errors? The supposition may be improbable, but what you have got to show is that it is in principle impossible.[4] A foundation used at the beginning does not in short mean something fundamental at the end, and there is no single 'fact' which in the end can be called fundamental absolutely. It is all a question of relative contribution to my known world-order.

'Then no judgement of perception will be more than probable?' Certainly that is my contention. 'Facts' are justified because and as far as, while taking them as real, I am better able to deal with the incoming new 'facts' and in general to make my world wider and more harmonious. The higher and wider my structure, and the more that any particular fact or set of facts is implied in that structure, the more certain are the structure and the facts. And, if we could reach an all-embracing ordered whole, then our certainty would be absolute. But, since we cannot do this, we have to remain content with relative probability. Why is this or that fact of observation taken as practically certain? It is so taken just so far as it is *not* taken in its own right. (i) Its validity is due to [212] such and such a person perceiving it under such and such conditions. This means that a certain intellectual order in the person is necessary as a basis, and again that nothing in the way of sensible or mental distortion intervenes between this order and what is given. And (ii) the observed fact must agree with our world as already arranged, or at least must not upset this. If the fact is too

---

[4] A possible attempt to do this will be discussed towards the close of the chapter, p. [307].

much contrary to our arranged world we provisionally reject it. We eventually accept the fact only when after confirmation the hypothesis of its error becomes still more ruinous. We are forced then more or less to rearrange our world, and more or less perhaps to reject some previous 'facts'. The question throughout is as to what is better or worse for our order as a whole.

Why again to me is a remembered fact certain, supposing that it is so? Assuredly not because it is infallibly delivered by the faculty of Memory, but because I do not see how to reconcile the fact of its error with my accepted world. Unless I go on the principle of trusting my memory, apart from any special reason to the contrary, I cannot order my world so well, if indeed I can order it at all. The principle here again is system. . . .

The same account holds with regard to the facts of history. For instance, the guillotining of Louis XVI is practically certain, because, to take this as error, would entail too much disturbance of my world. Error is possible here of course. Fresh facts conceivably might come before me such as would compel me to modify in part my knowledge as so far arranged. And in this modified arrangement the execution of Louis would find its place as an error. But the reason for such a modification would have to be considerable, while, as things are, no reason exists. And take again the case of an historical fact which is called more or less isolated. Mr. Russell[5] has instanced the honourable death of a late prelate, and has urged (as I understand) that on any view such as mine I have just as much reason to believe that this prelate was hanged. The fact is supposed to be isolated, and on mere internal evidence either alternative is taken, I presume, as equally probable. Now, of course I agree that we have innumerable cases where on mere internal evidence we are unable to distinguish between fact and fancy, but the difficulty that is supposed to arise I am unable to see. For the criterion with me is not mere absence, within the limits of this or that idea, of visible discrepancy. The question with me everywhere is as to what is the result to my real world. ['Error'[a].] Now, confining myself to a

[213]

---

[5] *On the Nature of Truth* [*Proceedings of the Aristotelian Society*, NS 7 (1906–7),] pp. 33, 35. [These passages are repr. in Bertrand Russell, *Philosophical Essays* London: Allen & Unwin, 1966, 134–8.]

[a] Repr. above, Part II, Sect. 1, Ch. 7.

certain case, the acceptance on the one side of the mere fancy or on the other side of the attested fact may, so far as I see, be in itself the same thing to my world. But imagine my world made on the principle of in such a case accepting mere fancy as fact. Would such a world be *more* comprehensive and coherent than the world as now arranged? Would it be coherent at all? Mr. Russell, I understand, answers in the affirmative[b] (p. 33), but it seems to me that he has misconceived the position. To take memory as in general trustworthy, where I have no special reason for doubt, and to take the testimony of those persons, whom I suppose to view the world as I view it, as being true, apart from special reason on the other side—these are principles by which I construct my ordered world, such as it is. And because by any other method the result is worse, therefore for me these principles are true. On the other hand to suppose that any 'fact' of perception or memory is so certain that no possible experience could justify me in taking it as error, seems to me injurious if not ruinous. On such a principle my world of knowledge would be ordered worse, if indeed it could be ordered at all. For to accept all the 'facts', as they offer themselves, seems obviously impossible; and, if it is we who have to decide as to which facts are infallible, then I ask how we are to decide. The ground of validity, I maintain, consists in successful contribution. That is a principle of order, while any other principle, so far as I see, leads to chaos.[6] [214]

'But', it may still be objected, 'my fancy is unlimited. I can therefore invent an imaginary world even more orderly than my known world. And further this fanciful arrangement might possibly be made so wide that the world of perception would become for me in comparison small and inconsiderable. Hence, my perceived world, so far as not supporting my fancied arrangement, might be included within it as error. Such a consequence would or might lead to confusion in theory and to disaster in practice.

---

[6] To the question if the above principle is merely 'practical', I reply, 'Certainly, if you take "practice" so widely as to remove the distinction between practice and theory.' But, since such a widening of sense seems to serve no useful purpose, I cannot regard that course as being itself very 'practical'. I answer therefore that the above principle is certainly not merely practical.

---

[b] *On the Nature of Truth.*

And yet the result follows from your view inevitably, unless after all you fall back upon the certainty of perception.'

To this possible objection, I should reply first, that it has probably failed to understand rightly the criterion which I defend. The aspect of comprehensiveness has not received here its due emphasis. The idea of system demands the inclusion of all possible material. Not only must you include everything to be gained from immediate experience and perception, but you must also be ready to act on the same principle with regard to fancy. But this means that you cannot confine yourself within the limits of this or that fancied world, as suits your pleasure or private convenience. You are bound also, so far as is possible, to recognize and to include the opposite fancy.

This consideration to my mind ruins the above hypothesis on [215] which the objection was based. The fancied arrangement not only has opposed to it the world of perception. It also has against it any opposite arrangement and any contrary fact which I can fancy. And, so far as I can judge, these contrary fancies will balance the first. Nothing, therefore, will be left to outweigh the world as perceived, and the imaginary hypothesis will be condemned by our criterion.

And, with regard to the world as perceived, we must remember that my power is very limited. I cannot add to this world at discretion and at my pleasure create new and opposite material. Hence, to speak broadly, the material here is given and compulsory, and the production of what is contrary is out of my power. After all due reservations have been made, the contrast in this respect between the worlds of 'fact' and of fancy will hold good. You cannot, as with fancies, make facts one to balance another at your pleasure. And (if we are to go still further) the riches of imagination even as regards quantity are deceptive. What we call our real world is so superior in wealth of detail that to include it, as outweighed in quantity, within some arrangement which we merely fancy, is to my mind not feasible. The whole hypothesis which we have considered seems to have been shown on more than one ground to be untenable.

But if I am asked, 'Were it otherwise, what becomes of your criterion?' though I think the question unfair, I will answer it conditionally. In that supposed case I would modify my criterion. I would say, 'The truth is that which enables us to order most coherently and comprehensively the data supplied by immediate experience and the intuitive judgements of perception'.[7] But this answer, I repeat, is merely conditional, and I do not believe that [216] the condition holds good. For I believe that our criterion, applied without modification, gives it proper place to mere fancy. And in any case (need I add?) it does not follow that particular judgements of perception and memory, all or any of them, are infallible.

But there is an objection which perhaps for some time has been troubling the reader. 'After all' (he may say) 'my experience has got to be mine. If you went beyond a certain point in modifying my known world, it might possibly be a superior world but it would be no world for me. And from this it follows that something, and something given, is in my world fundamental, and that, while my world remains mine, this something is indispensable and infallible. And the fact, if it is fact, that I cannot produce this element fails to show that it is not there.' Now it is one thing, I reply, to allow the existence of a fundamental element, and it is another thing to admit this in the form of an infallible judgement. I wish to emphasize this distinction and to insist that, if there is to be an infallible judgement, that judgement must be produced. On the other hand, I do not seek to deny in every sense the fact of the fundamental element. We are here in a region which so far is perhaps little understood, but for our purpose fortunately the whole question is irrelevant.

We must remind ourselves of the distinction which we laid down above. Conceivably a judgement might be fundamental and

---

[7] As I am not committed to this answer, I can hardly be called on to explain it further. But I may remind the reader that immediate experience and perceptional judgement is not all of one kind. Aesthetic perceptions, for instance, will not fall under the head of mere fancies. Where the 'fancy' represents some human interest, it ceases, in proportion to the importance of the interest, to be mere fancy or, properly, fancy at all.

Again, to pass from this to another point, I may be asked whether the instance of a man in collision with a new environment to which he cannot adapt himself presents no difficulty to our general criterion. In our case none, I reply, since we hold all such knowledge for relative. A difficulty arises only in the case of those who take judgements as absolute. We must, however, remember that, in the above instance of collision between inner and outer worlds, it would be wrong to assume that the man who prefers his inner world goes always against the weight of his immediate and intuitive experience.

[217] infallible for me, in the sense that to modify it or doubt it would entail the loss of my personal identity, while yet to another mind that modification or that doubt might be possible and necessary. Of course I do not mean that anything which is something for me, could by a wider experience be taken as something which in no sense exists. I mean that the character in which it offers itself to me in judgement might by a wider experience be seen to need correction, and might, apart from that correction, be classed as error. I am speaking here (the reader will remember) about particular 'facts' of feeling, perception or memory. And with regard to these I do not see the way by which I am to pass from relative to absolute infallibility, and I do not know how to argue here from an assumed necessary implication in my personal existence to a necessity which is more than relative. Am I to urge that a world in which my personal identity has been ended or suspended has ceased to be a world altogether? Apart from such an argument (which I cannot use) I seem condemned to the result that all sense-judgements are fallible.

The repugnance excited by this conclusion seems due to several grounds. Our immediate experience is not fallible, and this character (we have seen) is mistakenly transferred to those judgements which claim to deliver that experience. And further we had the false identification of knowledge with a mechanical superstructure supported by an external foundation. But behind this we have the demand for absolute reality in the shape of self-existent facts and of independent truths. Unless reality takes this form it seems to be nowhere, and so we go on to postulate absolute knowledge where no more than probability is attainable. Again, if the conclusion and the principle advocated here are accepted, the whole Universe seems too subject to the individual knower. What is given counts for so little and the arrangement
[218] counts for so much, while in fact the arranger, if we are to have real knowledge, seems so dependent on the world. But the individual who knows is here wrongly isolated, and then, because of that, is confronted with a mere alien Universe. And the individual, as so isolated, I agree, could do nothing, for indeed he is nothing. My real personal self which orders my world is in truth inseparably one with the Universe. Behind me the absolute reality works through and in union with myself, and the world which

confronts me is at bottom one thing in substance and in power with this reality. There *is* a world of appearance and there *is* a sensuous curtain, and to seek to deny the presence of this or to identify it with reality is mistaken. But for the truth I come back always to that doctrine of Hegel, that 'there is nothing behind the curtain other than that which is in front of it'.[8] For what is in front of it is the Absolute that is at once one with the knower and behind him.

The conclusion advocated in these pages is, however, but limited. With regard to the two aspects of coherence and comprehensiveness I have in these pages not asked if they are connected in principle. I have merely urged that it is necessary to use them in one, and that here and here alone we have the criterion of perceived and remembered truth. And I have argued that in principle any judgement of perception or memory is liable to error, and I have urged that, if this is not so, the right conclusion is to chaos. But to some of the points here left unsettled I shall return.

---

[8] I believe these to be Hegel's words, but I cannot give any reference for them. Almost the same words will, however, be found in *Phänomenologie* (second edition), p. 126. This is the last page of the division marked A. III.

6

Coherence and Contradiction

This essay is a continuation of Bradley's defence of coherence as a criterion of truth. In the previous essay, 'On Truth and Coherence', Bradley defended coherence against a series of objections. One of these objections was that it would be possible to invent a fantasy world which would be more coherent than the real world. By Bradley's criterion it would then seem that judgements describing the fantasy world would be true, while those describing the real world would not. Bradley replies to this objection by saying that it misconceives his position. Coherence as a criterion of truth also includes comprehensiveness and no fantasy world will be as coherent *and comprehensive* as the real world (cf. *ETR* 214–5, above, pp. 305–7). Bradley's primary aim in the present essay is to show that this is not simply an *ad hoc* defence, because coherence and comprehensiveness are essentially connected. They are aspects of a single principle which Bradley refers to as 'system'.

Bradley also has a secondary aim: to defend his position against pragmatist criticisms. Pragmatists like Dewey claimed that Bradley was inconsistent in using an intellectual criterion for truth and reality, namely, the absence of contradiction, while admitting that reality contains elements which are not intellectual and hence not the sorts of thing that could be contradictory or non-contradictory.[a] In this defence Bradley attempts to meet this objection by showing that the use of his intellectual criterion justifies the inclusion of non-intellectual elements in reality. This secondary aim explains why Bradley opens his essay as he does. In the introductory pages (pp. 312–13) Bradley reaffirms his view, taken from *Appearance and Reality*, that truth is what satisfies the intellect (Appendix, § II, above, p. 210). But the intellect, he claims, is connected with other aspects of our being, for example, our practical desires. Because of this connection our intellects cannot be satisfied unless other aspects of ourselves are also satisfied (see 'The General

'Coherence and Contradiction' was first pub. in *Mind*, NS 18 (1909). Repr. here from *ETR*, ch. viii.

[a] See e.g. John Dewey, 'The Intellectualist Criterion for Truth', in *John Dewey: The Middle Works 1899–1924*, iv (Carbondale, Ill.: Southern Illinois University Press, 1977), 50–75.

Nature of Reality (cont.)', above, pp. 143–50). Consequently, Bradley's intellectual criterion recognizes the importance of the satisfaction of practical aspirations, something strongly insisted upon by the pragmatists. At the same time it does not reduce truth, as Bradley thought pragmatism did, to the satisfaction of desires.

In accordance with this secondary aim Bradley next briefly rejects a purely intellectual view of reality from which the essential connection between coherence and comprehensiveness can be defended (pp. 314–15). This view depends solely on the nature of thought. It holds that any object other than the whole of reality *explicitly* or *visibly* contradicts itself. It alleges that the concepts used to describe any object, my pen, for example, can only do so consistently by describing it not in isolation but as part of the whole of reality. From this it follows that any description which is not all-inclusive (i.e. comprehensive) is explicitly contradictory. Comprehensiveness is thus an aspect of coherence and not something added to it in an *ad hoc* way.

The problem with this position, from Bradley's perspective, is twofold. First, it holds that an object will fail to satisfy the intellect only if its descriptions contain a contradiction. It will thus be the presence of a contradiction, something accessible only in thought, which fails to satisfy the intellect. This is a problem for Bradley because it leaves no role for non-intellectual satisfactions in defining truth and reality. The second problem from Bradley's perspective is that the alternative view holds that the description of an object may be both coherent and comprehensive. This is a problem because on Bradley's view no judgement could be both coherent and comprehensive except as a matter of degree.

It is against this background that Bradley defends the unity of coherence and comprehensiveness. He claims that his criterion for truth in *Appearance and Reality* requires their unity. He supports this by explaining, first, how an object, even if we do not find it to be contradictory, may still not satisfy the intellect, or, to use his expression, may be 'defective' (pp. 314–16). This is because, he claims, an object may fail to satisfy us because it is incomplete relative to immediate experience, a claim Bradley explains in more detail in 'On Our Knowledge of Immediate Experience' (see esp. pp. 282–5, above). The presence of immediate experience in this explanation is Bradley's attempt to do justice to the pragmatist insistence that reality transcends thought.

He then explains how, on his view of judgement, an object which is not comprehensive, i.e. which is 'felt' as defective without being explicitly contradictory, must still *be* contradictory (pp. 316–20). This explanation relies on his view of judgement and on his account of the relation between thought (which is embodied in judgements) and reality. On this basis Bradley claims that any two judgements with different contents which are not construed as conditionals must be taken as contradictory. He then argues that we can never specify all of the conditions included in any conditional. From this he concludes that any judgement about any object, including one merely 'felt' to be defective, becomes contradictory at the point where we are unable to supply further conditions. This allows him to conclude that according to the criterion of truth he gave in *Appearance and Reality* coherence and comprehensiveness are aspects of the same principle (pp. 320–2), while satisfying the pragmatist demand for a reality that is not purely intellectual.

J.A.

[219] In the preceding chapter I pointed out how coherence and comprehensiveness are the two aspects of system, and I attempted to justify the claim of system as an arbiter of fact. In the chapter which follows I am to endeavour to show how system stands to contradiction. The question is difficult and could in any case here be dealt with but imperfectly, and the reader again must excuse me if I approach it by a circuitous route.

What in the end is the criterion? The criterion of truth, I should say, as of everything else, is in the end the satisfaction of a want of our nature. To get away from this test, or to pass beyond it, in the end, I should say, is impossible. But, if so (the suggestion is a natural one), why should we not set forth, or try to set forth, the satisfaction of our nature from all sides, and then accept and affirm this statement as truth and reality? That in practical life we should do this, at least in some sense, I am fully agreed. But I cannot on the other hand endorse generally such an answer in philosophy, for I am unable to see how by such a plan we avoid theoretical shipwreck. . . .

I would take this opportunity to say that, with regard to the principle of non-contradiction as a test of truth, I agree in the main with what Prof. Bosanquet has urged in his *Individuality and Value*, pp. 49 foll. and 265 foll. [See Bernard Bosanquet, *The Principles of Individuality and Value* (London: Macmillan, 1927).] One contradicts oneself in principle in asserting that there is no beauty or virtue, as much as in asserting that there is no truth. Certainly, as Prof. Bosanquet points out, if a man chooses to deny the fact of beauty or virtue, you cannot, with that denial, formally convict him out of his own mouth, as you can if he asserts that there is no truth. And in this latter case there is a superiority in what may perhaps be called theoretical elegance. Still in philosophy our real object is not the dialectical confutation of an opponent. Our real object is the understanding of facts which cannot reasonably be denied.

Hence I have to remain so far in my old position.[1] If there is
to be philosophy its proper business is to satisfy the intellect, and
the other sides of our nature have, if so, no right to speak
directly. They must make their appeal not only to, but also
through, the intelligence. In life it is otherwise, but there is a
difference between philosophy and life. And in philosophy my
need for beauty and for practical goodness may have a voice,
but, for all that, they have not a vote. They cannot address the
intellect and insist, 'We are not satisfied, and therefore you also
shall not be satisfied.' They must be content to ask and to repeat,
'Are you in fact satisfied with yourself as long as we remain
unsatisfied? It is for you to decide, and we can only suggest.'
Hence, I conclude, I can philosophize with my whole nature, but
I cannot do this directly. On one hand the appeal is to the intellect, but on the other hand every aspect of my being can and
does express itself intellectually. And the question is how far, in
order to reach its special end which is truth, the intelligence has
to adopt as true the various suggestions which are offered. How
far, in order to satisfy itself, must its ideas satisfy all our needs?

In the above I am of course not assuming that the intellect is
something apart, working by itself, and, so to speak, shut up in a
separate room. On the contrary those who teach the implication
of all sides of our being with and in what we call thought, deny
no doctrine held by me. All that I maintain is that we have a
specific function, as such verifiable in fact, and claiming to possess special rights of its own. I insist that, unless we take that
claim seriously speculation is impossible. And, if any one differs
from me here, I would go on to urge that he is in conflict with
fact, and rests on inconsistency. And the result, I think, is confusion or total obscurity. . . .

It is obviously necessary therefore to inquire what does or
would satisfy the intellect. Such an inquiry I am not undertaking
in this chapter, but I may state the view which has commended
itself to my mind. Truth is an ideal expression of the Universe, at
once coherent and comprehensive. It must not conflict with itself,
and there must be no suggestion which fails to fall inside it.
Perfect truth in short must realize the idea of a systematic whole.

---

[1] [Cf. 'The General Nature of Reality', repr. above, Part II, Sect. 1, Ch. 1.]

And such a whole, we saw ['On Truth and Coherence'b], possessed essentially the two characters of coherence and comprehensiveness. I will therefore, without pausing here to raise and discuss difficulties, go on at once to ask as to the connection between these two characters. Have we in comprehensiveness and coherence two irreducible principles, or have we two aspects of one principle?

If we can adopt a well-known view the answer is plain. The whole reality is so immanent and so active in every partial element, that you have only to make an object of anything short of the whole, in order to see this object pass beyond itself. The object visibly contradicts itself and goes on to include its complementary opposite in a wider unity. And this process repeats itself as long as and wherever the whole fails to express itself entirely in the object. Hence the two principles of coherence and comprehensiveness are one. And not only are they one but they include also the principle of non-contradiction. The order to express yourself in such a way as to avoid visible contradiction, may be said in the end to contain the whole criterion.

No one who has not seen this view at work, and seen it applied to a wide area of fact, can realize its practical efficiency. But, for myself, if this solution of our puzzle ever satisfied me entirely, there came a time when it ceased to satisfy. And when [224] attempting to discuss first principles this was not the answer which I offered.[2] However immanent in each element the whole is really, I cannot persuade myself that everywhere in the above way it is immanent visibly. I cannot perceive that everywhere with each partial object we can verify the internal contradiction, and a passage made thus to a wider unity of complementary opposites. And, this being so, the question as to our two principles of coherence and comprehensiveness requires, so far as I am concerned, a modified answer.

To a large extent partial objects are seen (I at least cannot doubt this) to develop themselves beyond themselves indefinitely

---

[2] [*AR.*] I have perhaps fallen in places into inconsistency, but there was, I think, no doubt in my mind as to which of the two answers was the right one. There is, however, a natural tendency to pass from *really* to *visibly*, and this tendency may perhaps at times have asserted itself unconsciously.

---

b Repr. above, Part II, Sect. 2, Ch. 5.

by internal discrepancy. Everything, so far as it is temporal or spatial, does, I should say, thus visibly transcend itself, though, if there are many orders of time and space, the same self-transcendence will not hold between them. But I will not seek here to urge a principle as far as it will go, when I admit that, so far as I can see, it will not go to the end. The visible internal self-transcendence of every object is a thing which, as I have said, I cannot everywhere verify.

And the principle which in my book I used and stated was the following. Everything which appears must be predicated of Reality, but it must not be predicated in such a way as to make Reality contradict itself.[3] I adhere to this principle, and I will go on briefly to justify it with special reference to what we have called comprehensiveness and coherence. There are two main questions, I think, to which answers here are wanted. (1) If my object is really defective, and if it cannot develop itself for me beyond itself by internal contradiction, how otherwise can it do [225] this? (2) How and in what sense does an isolated object make Reality contradict itself?

(1) The object before me is not the whole of Reality, nor is it the whole of what I experience. The Universe (I must assume this here) is one with my mind, and not only is this so, but the Universe is actually now experienced by me as beyond the object. For, beside being an object, the world is actually felt, not merely in its general character but more or less also in special detail.[4] Hence, as against this fuller content present in feeling, the object before me can be experienced as defective. There is an unspecified sense of something beyond, or there may even arise the suggestion in idea of the special complement required. We may perhaps hesitate to say that the defective object itself suggests its own completion, and we may doubt whether the process should be called Dialectic. But at any rate a process such as the above seems to furnish the solution of our problem. Exactly how that idea comes by which the partial object is made good, is, on the view we have just sketched, a matter of secondary moment. The

---

[3] This is of course not the same thing as taking up a suggestion (whatever it may be), and then, if you fail to see that it is visibly inconsistent, forthwith calling it real [see 'On Truth and Coherence', repr. above, Part II, Sect. 2, Ch. 5].

[4] The reader is referred here specially to ['On Our Knowledge of Immediate Experience', repr. above, Part II, Sect. 2, Ch. 4].

important point is that with the object there is present something already beyond it, something that is capable both of demanding and of furnishing ideal suggestions, and of accepting or rejecting the suggestions made.

On a view such as this the essential union of comprehensiveness with coherence seems once more tenable. We have not only [226] connections in the object-world, temporal, spatial and other relations, which extend for us the content of a partial object. We have also another world at least to some extent actually experienced, a world the content of which is continuous with our object. And, where an element present in this world is wanting to our object, dissatisfaction may arise with an unending incompleteness and an endless effort at inclusion. The immanent Reality, both harmonious and all-comprehending, demands the union of both its characters in the object. The reader will notice that I assume here (*a*) that everything qualifies the one Reality, (*b*) that, when one element of the whole is made an object, this element may be supplemented even apart from visible inconsistency, and (*c*) that, to know Reality perfectly, you must know the whole of it, and that hence every partial object is imperfect. To this last point I shall return, but will proceed first to deal with the question asked as to Contradiction.

(2) For, the reader may object, 'Suppose for the sake of argument that I admit the above, I still do not see how Contradiction comes in. Why am I to add with you that the test of truth is its ability to qualify Reality without self-contradiction?' In replying to this I will first dispose of a point which possibly is obvious. If, in speaking of Reality, you say 'R is *mere a*', and if then, while you say that, another qualification, *b*, appears and is accepted, you contradict yourself plainly. To this your answer, I presume, will be, 'Yes, but I was careful *not* to say "mere *a*". I merely said "*a*", and between these two assertions there is a vital difference.' The question as to this vital difference may perhaps be called here the real issue. It is contended against me that I may first say 'R*a*' and then later 'R*b*' and then later 'R*c*' without any contradiction. For *a, b* and *c* may be separate, or, if related, they may be conjoined externally. Hence '*a* with *b*' (it is urged) is quite [227] consistent with '*a*', since '*a*' remains unaffected. It will hence be absurd to argue that by merely saying '*a*' the presence of '*b*' is denied.

My object here is to explain the sense of the doctrine which I advocate far more than to make this doctrine good against all possible competitors. And hence, if in what follows I seem to the reader to be assuming all that has to be proved, I must ask him to bear this warning in mind. Certainly I must assume here that the view of judgement which I hold is correct, and it is on this view that what follows is really founded. I have at least seen no other view of judgement which to myself seems tenable, but this is a point on which I cannot attempt to enter here. I assume then that in judgement ideas qualify Reality, and further that in judgement we have passed beyond the stage of mere perception or feeling. The form of qualification present in these cannot, as such, be utilized in judgement. And the question is whether in judgement we have any mode of qualification which is in the end consistent and tenable. I do not think that we have any.[5]

In all predication I assume that the ultimate subject is Reality, [228] and that in saying 'Ra' or 'Rb' you qualify R by a or b. My contention is that, in saying 'Ra', you qualify R unconditionally by

[5] What follows in the text may perhaps be summed up thus. In feeling (with which we start) we have an immediate union of one and many, where the whole immediately qualifies the parts, and the parts the whole and one another. In judgement this immediate unity is broken up, and there is a demand for qualification otherwise. This 'otherwise' involves distinction and a relational plurality; and that, because simple qualification is now impossible, entails mediation and conditions. And, because in judgement we cannot completely state the conditions, we are forced into an indefinite process of bringing in new material and new conditions. The end sought by judgement is a higher form of immediacy, which end however cannot be reached within judgement.

It may perhaps assist the reader if I put the whole matter as follows. Take any object, and you find that, as it is, that object does not satisfy your mind. You cannot think it as real while you leave it just as it comes. You are forced to go outside and beyond that first character, and to ask, What, Why, and How. You must hence take your first object as included with something else in some wider reality. There is thus a demand so far, we may say, for comprehension.

On the other hand you want to know the object itself and *not* something else. Therefore, while going beyond the object, you must not leave it but must still follow it. If you merely conjoin it with something outside that is different and not itself, this in principle is contradiction. Hence what you want is connection and implication, where the object is its own self as contributing to a reality beyond itself. That now is coherence and comprehensiveness in one.

Of course the critic who ignores what Prof. Bosanquet and myself have urged as to the real meaning of contradiction, must expect to miss the sense of the doctrine which we advocate, each in his own way. Take a diversity (here is the point), a diversity used simply to qualify the same subject, and with that you have contradiction, and that is what contradiction means. The 'And' (see p. [320]), if you take it *simply* as *mere* 'And', is itself contradiction.

a, and that this amounts to saying 'mere *a*'. For is there, I ask, any difference between R and *a*? Let us suppose first that there is no difference. If so, by saying first R*a* and then R*b* you contradict yourself flatly. For *a* and *b*, I presume, really are different, and hence, unless R is different from *a* and *b*, what you (however unwillingly) have done is to identify *a* and *b* simply. But the simple identification of the diverse is precisely that which one means by contradiction.[6] If on the other hand, when I say R*a*, I suppose a difference between R and *a*, then once more I am threatened with contradiction, for I seem now to have simply qualified R by *a*, the two being diverse. The reader will recall that we are concerned here with judgement and not with mere feeling or perception. And the question to be answered is how in judgement we are to qualify one thing by another thing, the two things being different.

A natural answer is to deny that the judgements, R*a* and R*b*, are unconditional. That, it will be urged, was never meant. But, if it is not meant, I ask, ought it to be said, except of course for convenience and by a licence? Let it then be understood that the [229] above judgements hold good because R is somehow different from *a* and from *b*, and that the assertion is made under this condition, known or, I suppose, here unknown. The assertion then will really be 'R(*x*)*a*' and 'R(*x*)*b*', the *x* being of course taken to qualify R. But, if so, apparently 'R*a*' is true only because of something other than *a* which also is included in R. R is *a* only because R is beyond *a*, and so on indefinitely. Merely to say *a* is therefore, if our view of judgement is sound, equivalent to denying the above and to saying mere *a*; and that, since R is beyond mere *a*, seems inconsistent with itself. Contradiction therefore so far has appeared as the alternative to comprehensiveness, and the criterion so far seems to rest on a single principle.

If, in other words, you admit that the assertion 'R*a*' is not true unless made under a condition, you admit that no knowledge in the form R*a* can be perfect. Perfect knowledge requires that the condition of the predicate be got within the subject; and, seeking to attain this end (which, I assume, can never be completely real-

---

[6] For a discussion of the nature of contradiction the reader is referred to ['Contradiction, and the Contrary' repr. above, Part II, Sect. 1, Appendix], reprinted (with omissions) in *AR* since 1897, and may now be directed especially to Prof. Bosanquet's *Individuality and Value*, pp. 223 foll.

ized), we are driven to fill in conditions indefinitely. The attempt to deny this, so far as we have seen, seems to force you to the conclusion that *a* makes no difference to R and that *b* makes no difference to either. And, if so, upon our view of judgement you have said nothing, or else have fallen into self-contradiction.[7]

The general position here taken must, so far as I see, be [230] attacked either by falling back on designation or by the acceptance of mere external relations. I will say something more on these alternatives lower down, but will for the present seek to explain further the view which I hold. Judgement on that view is the qualification of one and the same Reality by ideal content. And, if we keep to this, we must go on to deny independent pieces of knowledge and mere external relations. The whole question may, perhaps, be said to turn upon the meaning and value of the word 'and'. Upon the view which I advocate when you say 'R is *a*, and R is *b*, and R is *c*', the 'and' qualifies a higher reality which includes R*a* R*b* R*c* together with 'and'. It is only within this higher unity that 'and' holds good, and the unity is more than mere 'and'. In other words the Universe is not a mere 'together' or 'and', nor can 'and' in the end be taken absolutely. Relatively—that is, for limited purposes—we do and we must use mere 'and' and mere external relations,[8] but these ideas become

[7] I will remind the reader once more that the above argument assumes that in judgement what is asserted is taken to qualify Reality, and that there is no other way of asserting. To those who believe in another way the above argument is not addressed. The same thing may again be put thus. The assertion of any object *a* is R*a*. Here, if R is not different from *a*, you have really no assertion. But, if R is different, you either deny this difference and so have a false assertion, or else you qualify R (that is, a higher R) both by *a* and this difference. Hence you have now asserted a manifold. But, as soon as you assert of R a manifold (however you have got it), there arises at once a question as to the 'how'. You cannot fall back on mere sense, because in judgement you are already beyond that; and on the other hand again you cannot simply identify. Hence you have to seek ideal conditions, and this search has to go on indefinitely. The above statement of course does not claim to show how these special conditions which you want are supplied. The process, that is, so far does not point to the particular complement which is required. Again, the reader must not understand me to suggest that, given a single feeling or sensation, we could by any logical process pass beyond it. I am on the contrary assuming that at the stage of judgement we are beyond any single feeling or sensation, if ever we were confined to one. In the foregoing the word 'logical' has been used (perhaps improperly) in a narrow sense; to mean simply a visible process of intrinsic implication. See above, p. [317] note.

[8] How the 'and' is to stand to the external relations seems doubtful. If 'and' itself is an external relation, then obviously, to unite it to its terms, you seem to want a further 'and', and so on indefinitely.

untenable when you make them absolute. And it would seem useless to reply that the ideas are ultimate. For the ideas, I presume, have a meaning, and the question is as to what becomes of that meaning when you try to make it more than relative, and whether in the end an absolute 'and' is thinkable.

[231]   That on which my view rests is the immediate unity which comes in feeling,[9] and in a sense this unity is ultimate. You have here a whole which at the same time is each and all of its parts, and you have parts each of which makes a difference to all the rest and to the whole. This unity is not ultimate if that means that we are not forced to transcend it. But it is ultimate in the sense that no relational thinking can reconstitute it, and again in the sense that in no relational thinking we can ever get free from the use of it. And an immediate unity of one and many at a higher remove is the ultimate goal of our knowledge and of every endeavour. The aspects of coherence and comprehensiveness are each a way in which this one principle appears and in which we seek further to realize it. And the idea of a whole something of this kind underlies our entire doctrine of judgement. You may seek, and I agree that it is natural to seek, for another view as to judgement and truth. But, so far as I see, that effort has resulted and will result in failure.

Judgement, on our view, transcends and must transcend that immediate unity of feeling upon which it cannot cease to depend. Judgement has to qualify the Real ideally. And the word 'idea' means that the original unity has so far been broken. This is the fundamental inconsistency of judgement which remains to the end unremoved, and which in principle vitiates more or less all ideas and truth. For ideas cannot qualify reality as reality is qualified immediately in feeling, and yet judgement seeks in vain to escape from this foregone method. And thus, aiming to reconstitute with its ideas the concrete whole of one and many, it fails,

---

[9] Cf. [above, pp. 267–94]. and ['On Our Knowledge of Immediate Experience', repr. above, Part. II, Sect. 2, Ch. 4]. In my view (I am here of course in the main following Hegel) the 'and' is a developed and yet degraded form of the immediate unity, and throughout implies that. Make the contents of the felt totality both objective and relational, and then abstract from any special character of the relations and any special character of the totality—and you have got what you mean by 'and'. But the point to be emphasized here is that, if you abstract *altogether* from the totality, you have destroyed your 'and'. The 'and' depends essentially upon the felt totality, and of course cannot generate its own foundation.

and it sinks through default into the abstract identity of predicate [232] with subject. But this is a result at which it did not aim and which it cannot accept as true. Judgement in the form 'R*a*' never meant that between R and *a* there is no difference. What is meant was to predicate its idea of, and to reconstitute with its idea, the old immediate reality. But since that whole and its way of unity were not properly ideal, and since now we are in the world of truth and ideas, the judgement has failed to express itself. The reality as conditioned in feeling has been in principle abandoned, while other conditions have not been found; and hence the judgement has actually asserted unconditionally *a* of R and R of *a*. And such an assertion, it perceives, is false. The way to remedy its falsehood is to seek the conditions, the new ideal conditions, under which 'R*a*' is true. To gain truth the condition of the predicate must be stated ideally and must be included within the subject. This is the goal of ideal truth, a goal at which truth never arrives completely; and hence every truth, so long as this end is not attained, remains more or less untrue.

Every partial truth therefore is but partly true, and its opposite also has truth. This of course does not mean that any given truth is merely false, and, of course also, it does not mean that the opposite of any given truth is more true than itself. These are obvious, if natural, misunderstandings of our view. But surely it should be clear that you can both affirm and deny 'R(*x*)*a*' so long as *x* remains unspecified. And the truth on one of these two sides surely becomes greater in comparison, according as on that side, whether of affirmation or denial, you are able to make the conditions more complete. But, as long as and so far as the conditions remain incomplete, the truth is nowhere absolute. 'It is possible to produce sparks by striking flint' is, I understand offered as an instance of unconditional truth. But the opposite of [233] this truth surely is also true. The thing clearly I should have said, is possible or not possible according to the conditions, and the conditions are not sufficiently expressed in the judgement. You have therefore so far a truth which can at once be affirmed and denied, and how such a truth can be absolute I fail to perceive. The growth of knowledge consists . . . in getting the conditions of the predicate into the subject. The more conditions you are able to include, the greater is the truth. But so long as anything remains outside, the judgement is imperfect and its opposite also is true. Certainly the truth of the opposite becomes progressively less, and may even be negligible, but on the other hand it never disappears into sheer and utter falsehood. . . .

[241]   Coherence and comprehensiveness then we have found to be each an integral aspect of system. In practice they may diverge, but they remain united in principle. And system is connected essentially with contradiction and its absence. For what is inconsistent is so far unreal, and a diversity, judged unconditionally to be real, we found was inconsistent, and such internal discrepancy tends to involve an indefinite passage beyond self. Further, apart from this, an object which is short of the whole tends naturally, we may say, to suggest its complement. And, since that suggested complement is absent in fact, reality thus contradicts itself. How the suggestion is made we have inquired. The object itself may through its own internal content pass for us visibly beyond its own limits, or, on the other hand, the addition may come to us

[242]   from that whole which we feel. And this whole, as felt, may contain, we saw, actually a special detail, or again a general character which was wanting in the object; or the whole may be present to us even more vaguely as a something beyond, a something which is not satisfied with what is before us. But when the suggestion is made, however it is made, we have a fresh predicate of Reality. Our object has thus become more comprehensive, and we must endeavour now to include this fresh predicate within it consistently. . . .

7

What is the Real Julius Caesar?

This was a previously unpublished paper, written in 1911, prompted by Russell's famous article 'Knowledge by Acquaintance and Knowledge by Description'.[a] It is particularly useful because it contains the best account of Bradley's difficult notion of a finite centre.

According to the theory of judgement that Russell held at the time (1) a particular subject, or self, S, will be able to understand the content of a judgement only if it is acquainted with the constituents, particular and universal, of the judgement and (2) S will be a possible object of acquaintance for S alone. Hence it follows that Caesar *qua* particular self, could not be a constituent of any judgements intelligible to anybody other than Caesar. Any subject non-identical with Caesar could have knowledge of Caesar only by description and therefore any judgements we could make about Caesar would be in logical form existential, and therefore general as opposed to singular (cf. *ETR* 425–6, below, pp. 336–8). Thus according to Russell's theory Caesar, as a constituent of Caesar's own judgement, is portrayed as something which could not conceivably be a constituent of other people's judgements when they have what passes for historical knowledge of Caesar. Caesar, *qua* particular subject of cognitive states and acts, is radically private and unknowable by anybody but himself (*ETR* 409, below, p. 326; cf. also 422–3, below, pp. 334–5). Bradley takes this to be a *reductio ad absurdum* of Russell's theory.

Bradley's own epistemologically basic notion is that of a finite centre of immediate experience: *ex hypothesi* the Universe as a whole is to be construed as immediately, or non-relationally, present in the experiences of a multiplicity of finite centres (one might usefully think of these as analogous to Leibniz's monads in everything except substantiality[b])

'What is the Real Julius Caesar?' is repr. here from *ETR*, ch. xiv.

[a] First pub. in *Proceedings of the Aristotelian Society*, 11 (1910–11); repr. in B. Russell, *Mysticism and Logic* (London: Longmans & Green, 1921), ch. x; for Russell's theory of judgement see 'On the Nature of Acquaintance' and 'The Philosophy of Logical Atomism', in B. Russell, *Logic and Knowledge*, ed. R. C. Marsh (London: Allen & Unwin, 1956).

[b] T. S. Eliot, 'Leibniz's Monads and Bradley's Finite Centres', *Monist*, 26 (1916), 566–76.

(*ETR* 409, below, p. 326). Objects of consciousness of general sorts, inner and outer, mental, physical, mathematical, or whatever, are *ex hypothesi*, without exception, distinguished within finite centres of immediate experience. Bradley proceeds to elucidate the relationship between the notion of finite centre of experience (*ETR* 410–12, below, pp. 326–8), and those of soul (*ETR* 414–16, below, pp. 328–30) and self (*ETR* 416–19, below, pp. 330–2).

As a limiting case the experience of a finite centre might in principle be *merely* immediate. In other words, there might within the centre of experience be no consciousness of objects of any kinds whatsoever (cf. Leibniz's category of 'bare' or unconscious monads). Within such a centre there would be no experiences possessing what Brentano called intentionality, or, to use Bradley's own term, 'ideality' (*ETR* 416, below, p. 330). There would therefore be no experience of difference, or opposition, between self and not-self. In consequence, in Bradley's sense of the term, there would be no immediately *felt self*. Thus an immediately felt self can exist within a finite centre of experience only if there are within in it objects of consciousness: objects (inner and/or outer etc.) which will be distinguished against a background of immediate feeling, this background being the felt self. It follows that the existence of a felt self might be merely momentary and will be momentary if the consciousness of objects is momentary (ibid.).

The felt self cannot be construed as existing in any kind of representable relation to the objects of consciousness distinguished within a finite centre. To borrow Wittgenstein's simile, the situation must be construed as like that which holds between the eye and its visual field.[c] The felt self could be represented in consciousness as related to an object only by making it (by what Leibniz called an act of apperception) an object of consciousness and thereby making it opposed to an immediately felt self. But then the erstwhile immediately felt self would of necessity have ceased to be an immediately felt self. Hence an immediately felt self can no more be brought within the limits of the world of propositionally describable objects than could the eye be brought within the limits of its own visual field.

Thus the immediately felt self must be construed, as Bradley puts it, to be less than the felt totality constitutive of a finite centre of immediate experience, but 'it remains intimately one thing with that finite centre within which [the] Universe appears' (*ETR* 418, below, p. 331). Other selves will not be immediately felt by S but will (assuming S to be a human being possessing a language and thus capable of apperception) be known by him as objects of his thoughts and thought-impregnated expe-

---

[c] L. Wittgenstein, *Tractatus Logico-Philosophicus*, trans. D. F. Pears and B. F. McGuinness (London: Routledge & Kegan Paul, 1961), §§ 5.631–5.6331.

riences. Other selves will not, in other words, fall within the immediately felt self that is opposed to the objects of S's own consciousness, inner and outer etc. (*ETR* 418–19, below, pp. 331–2).

However, according to Bradley's conception of the Absolute, the Universe exists only in and through a totality of finite centres of experience which are construed as ultimately interconnected with one another in virtue of one and all being modes, or ways, through which the one all-inclusive substance is realized. Hence there will be no theoretical problem in understanding how the contents of other immediately felt selves can be present in (or be, as Bradley also puts it, 'one in substance with') S's ideas of them (*ETR* 424–7, below, pp. 336–8). There will be no more theoretical difficulty, within the context of such a metaphysical structure, in understanding how intersubjective knowledge of the contents of the immediate feelings of others is possible than there is in understanding, within the context of our everyday framework of thought, how *intra*subjective knowledge of the contents of feelings is possible. According to that framework the contents of S's past feelings can be present in his thoughts at later dates because the thoughts and feelings are one and all *his*, i.e. are one and all interconnected as modes, or ways, in and through which one and the same enduring *individual* sentient being acts and suffers. His feelings are thus construed as being *one in substance* with his ideas or thoughts.

Russell's atomism in portraying each particular subject (1) as being in the strict metaphysical sense of the term an individual and (2) as being a possible object of his own acquaintance only does not allow such a theoretical solution to the problem of intersubjective knowledge.

So we can ask: What is the real Julius Caesar?

On Bradley's view Caesar was a self-conscious sentient being who was born x years ago (the reader must substitute for x), who lived for a determinate time and played an influential historical role in our real world of fact. In having a temporally extended felt self he was, in Bradley's sense of the term, a soul (*ETR* 421, below, p. 333). But Bradley argues that if, in philosophy, we are to make sense of the possibility of intersubjective knowledge, neither Caesar, nor anyone else in human history, could have been a *genuine* individual (i.e. a substance) in the strict metaphysical sense of the term.

G.S.

It may throw some light on the general position defended by [409] myself, if I briefly state the answer which in my opinion should be given to this question. I will begin by emphasizing what to myself is the main and vital issue. Mr. Russell in a recent essay ventures on the following assertion: 'Returning now to Julius Caesar, I assume that it will be admitted that he himself is not a constituent of any judgement which I can make.' To my mind the opposite of this admission appears to be evident. It seems to me certain, if such an admission is right, that about Julius Caesar I can have literally no knowledge at all, and that for me to attempt to speak about him is senseless. If on the other hand I am to know anything whatever about Caesar, then the real Caesar beyond doubt must himself enter into my judgements and be a constituent of my knowledge. . . .

The problem of the ultimate reality of Julius Caesar is obviously one which in a limited space cannot be thoroughly discussed. I can here deal with it but partially, and only on the assumption that the general conclusion which I have advocated is sound. To me the Universe is one Reality which appears in finite centres, and it hence is natural to ask at once if Julius Caesar is to be identified with a finite centre. The reply is obviously in the negative. A finite centre is not a soul, or a self, or an individual person. Hence in the following pages we have throughout to bear these distinctions in mind. And these distinctions are so important, and they seem to be so difficult to apprehend, that I must begin by attempting, even at considerable length, to make them clear to the reader.

[410]

There is, however, one point to which I must first call attention. The Universe to me is one Experience which appears in finite centres. I take this to be true, but on the other hand it is not the whole truth. It is the truth to my mind so far as truth is attainable by me, but it nevertheless remains imperfect, and in the end it is not intelligible. Our ultimate conceptions, that is, are necessary, and in a sense they are really ultimate. But there are features in them which without any satisfactory insight we have to accept, since we are able to do no better. The complete experience which would supplement our ideas and make them perfect, is in detail beyond our understanding. And the reader, throughout what follows, will, I hope, not ignore this general warning.

To proceed then, a finite centre, when we speak strictly, is not itself in time. It is an immediate experience of itself and of the Universe in one. It comes to itself as all the world and not as one world among others. And it has properly no duration through which it lasts. It can contain a lapse and a before and after, but these are subordinate. They are partial aspects that fall within the whole, and that, taken otherwise, do not qualify the whole itself. A finite centre itself may indeed be called duration in the sense of presence. But such a present is not any time which is opposed to a past and future. It is temporal in the sense of being itself the positive and concrete negation of time.[1]

The distinctions of a past and future beyond the present time, [411] and of one centre of experience as separate from others, are essentially the products of ideal construction. And the same remark holds with regard to the duration in time of any finite centre. Hence these ideas properly are true only of the world of objects, and in the end a finite centre (if we are to express ourselves strictly) is not an object. It is a basis on and from which the world of objects is made. We may speak, as I have spoken myself . . . of a finite centre's duration. But we can do this only on sufferance, and so far as by reflection we have transformed into an object the nature of that which lies behind objects.[2]

And thus in the end a finite centre has no identity with any past or future of itself. It has, or it contains, a character, and on that character its past and future depend. And the special quality which makes my self one self as against others, remains (I will return to this point) in unbroken unity with that character. But the identity of a centre or a self with itself in time is essentially ideal. Its being depends on construction and holds good only through a breach in the immediate given unity of what and that. And so, to speak strictly, there is in my life neither continuance nor repetition of a finite centre. For a centre is timeless, and for

[1] I will allow myself to add two passages from an early work of my own. 'The present is the filling of that duration in which the reality appears to me directly; and there can be no part of the succession of events so small or so great, that conceivably it might not appear as present.' . . . 'Presence is really the negation of time, and never can properly be given in the series. It is not the time that can ever be present, but only the content.' [Cf. 'The Categorical and Hypothetical Forms of Judgement', §§ 12–13, repr. above, Part I, Ch. 2.] The reader will of course not understand me here to claim originality for a doctrine which I inherited.

[2] From such a position as mine it is obvious that the question whether change is in the end real, admits of but one answer. The Universe contains change, but the Universe itself cannot change. I would gladly deal here or elsewhere with any arguments in favour of an opposite conclusion. But, to speak frankly, those arguments, so far as I know them, have failed to understand the position which they seek to attack.

itself it is not even finite as being itself one thing among others. To speak of its continuance and its sameness is to apply to it [412] expressions which we are forced to use, but which in the end and in their proper sense cannot be justified.

The duration of a finite centre in time, and a plurality of centres which do not share their immediate experiences as immediate, are (I would repeat) necessary ideas. They are conceptions without which we could not express ourselves, and through which alone we can formulate that higher truth which at once contains and transcends them. Such ideal constructions, on the one hand, beyond question are real, and their reality is affirmed both in thought and volition. But they are neither immediately given nor in the end are they wholly intelligible. They are special appearances the full and ultimate reality of which cannot in detail be known.

It is interesting to inquire into the stages of that process by which we enter into possession of our everyday world, and it is important to trace in outline that development by which we come to distinguish outward things from our selves, and our own self from others. But in principle we are concerned here not with the origin but with the nature of our knowledge. We have seen that a finite centre, so far as it exists as an object, so far as it endures in time, and is one of a number, is made and subsists by ideal construction. There really is within the Absolute a diversity of finite centres. There really is within finite centres a world of objects. And the continuance and identity of a finite centre, together with the separation of itself from all others, can become an object to that centre. These things are realities, and yet, because imperfect, they are but appearances which differ in degree. That they are supplemented and without loss are all made good absolutely in the Whole, we are led to conclude. But how in detail this is accomplished, and exactly what the diversity of finite centres means in the end, is beyond our knowledge. . . .

[414]   I will proceed to ask as to the meaning of a soul and again of a self. Neither of these ideas must be confused with what we call a finite centre, and with each there is a demand for careful distinction.

What is a soul? A soul is a finite centre viewed as an object [415] existing in time with a before and after of itself. And further the soul is a thing distinct from the experiences which it has, which experiences we take not as itself but as its states. The finite centre was an experience which is in one with its own reality. It comes to itself (we saw) immediately as a content which is the Universe. And thus, when by a construction you prolong the finite centre in time, you have still not arrived at the idea of a soul. In order to reach this, you must go on to distinguish the content as experienced from that which experiences the content. The latter, you must say, has these experiences, and yet has them not as other things but as states of itself. And to whatever other reality these experiences may be due, to whatever other world they may belong, and to whatever things, other than the soul, they may stand in relation, all this in one sense is indifferent. If you confine your attention to the soul as a soul, then every possible experience is no more than that which happens in and to this soul. You have to do with psychical events which qualify the soul, and in the end these events, so far as you are true to your idea, are merely states of the soul. Such a conception is for certain purposes legitimate and necessary, and to condemn it, while used within proper limits, is to my mind mistaken. But, outside these limits, what we call the soul is, I agree, indefensible. It is vitiated by inconsistencies and by hopeless contradictions into which there is here no need to enter further.[3]

Whether the soul is essentially one among other souls need not be discussed. I cannot myself see that an affirmative answer is necessary, but the question here seems not relevant. We may say the same of the doubt whether without a body a soul is possible. [416] And with regard to a soul's identity I will merely state that, so far as I see, this point, if it is to be settled, must be settled more or less arbitrarily. But such inquiries have little or no bearing on our purpose. We are concerned here simply with the distinction between a soul and a finite centre, and I will pass from this to consider a similar point with reference to the 'self'. How does a self stand towards a finite centre and again towards a soul? We have to do here, I agree, with an intricate and difficult problem.

---

[3] See [*AR* and 'A Defence of Phenomenalism in Psychology', in *CE*, vol. ii, ch. xxii]. The reader will bear in mind that, though feeling is in itself not an object, on the other hand, when you go on to view it as an event, you have so far made it objective. For psychology everything psychical which happens is in one sense an object, though most certainly not everything is an object for the individual soul in question.

And I regret that in what follows I can do no more than set down that result which to myself seems tenable.

The self in the first place is not the same as the finite centre. We may even have a finite centre without any self, where that centre contains no opposition of self to not-self. On the other hand we have a self wherever within a finite centre there is an object. An object involves opposition, theoretical and practical, and this opposition is to a self, and it must so be felt. As to the duration of a self, that in principle need be no more than momentary. If we keep to ordinary usage a different reply would have perhaps to be given, but the usage, so far as I can judge, does not rest on any principle. And, again, for myself I cannot see that to be a self implies what is called memory. Wherever you take a finite centre as containing the opposition of not-self to self, and as having, of course, some duration through which this opposition remains or recurs, you have reached that which we term a self. It is usual, of course, for the object to consist at least partly of other selves, but to my mind this feature is certainly not essential.

[417] We have, then, first (i) an immediate felt whole without any self or object.[4] Next (ii), where we find an object against a self, this opposition is still a content within a totality of feeling. And the relation (so to speak of it) is not yet itself an object. There is not as yet in the proper sense any relation, because the self, so far, itself is no object. And, even when the correlation of self and not-self has been objectified, this complex object comes against the self still in that way which (to be strict) is no relation. The manner in which, in order to be an object, the object is felt, must be expressed by a preposition. The preposition implies the presence of two things before us. And thus, if we are not to be silent, we have no choice but to use a form of statement, while we deny an implication involved in that form. Further (iii) the self, although not yet an object, is experienced content, and it is itself a limited content and is so felt. Any view for which the self is not thus experienced as limited content, leaves us in my judgement without any self that is experienced at all. But from such a result it would follow that the self must either remain completely unknown, or at least must be known as something which is no

---

[4] On this and the following points cf. ['On Our Knowledge of Immediate Experience', repr. above, Part II, Sect. 2, Ch. 4].

self. And again I do not understand how in any felt whole there is to be an opposition, unless, as against the object, the all-containing whole also itself becomes something limited. While remaining, that is, still the unbroken whole, it is felt also specially in one with a restricted content. This limited self (I would once more add) may in self-consciousness itself become, more or less, an object; but, notwithstanding this, it always must continue to be felt, and otherwise, as a self, it would bodily disappear. (iv) On the nature of that limited content felt as self I can here say nothing in detail. Far from remaining always the same, it varies greatly. There is much of it which from time to time has come before us as objective, and on the other hand there are elements which remain throughout in the background. And all this will be true even of that central group on which our personality seems to rest. But on these aspects of our problem I can here do no more [418] than touch in passing. (v) I will go on to emphasize the point which it is essential for us to keep in view. All that is experienced comes, we saw, within a finite centre, and is contained within that whole which is felt immediately. Now on the one side the self must be less than this felt totality, but on the other side the self must remain implicit in the unbroken unity of feeling. The self (to repeat this) may become an object, and yet the self still must also be felt immediately, or it is nothing. As so felt it still belongs to that world where content and being remain, at least formally, unseparated. The self's unity with that finite centre within which and before which the whole Universe comes, remains a unity which is implicit and non-relational. For, though it may come before the background as an object, the self (to repeat this) is a self only so far as it remains felt as in one with that whole background. I am fully aware that this statement is in one sense not intelligible. On the other hand to myself it serves to convey, if not to express, an indubitable and fundamental fact, a basis without which the world is ruined. And with this I must leave the matter to the reader's judgement.

(vi) The question why one finite centre, rather than any other, should be mine, can now be readily answered. My self, we have seen, depends on that which cannot become merely an object, and hence it remains intimately one thing with that finite centre within which my Universe appears. Other selves on the contrary are for me ideal objects, the being of which is made by

[419] opposition and construction.⁵ They have, as such, no content which, except as within an ideal construction, can be felt in immediate union with the given foundation of my world.

It is true that other selves and God are far more than mere ideal objects. On the contrary, the wills of others can, as we say, be taken up into mine or mine resolved into theirs. And, however we phrase it, this real unity of emotion and action is most certain; and I know that God's will or that of others is carried out in my volition into actual fact. Nay, in comparison with the reality of this higher common will, anything that is merely my own can be experienced as unreal and worthless. And yet, so far as within my centre the overruling end is realized, the volition is mine in a sense in which it belongs to no other being. It realizes and it expresses that which is felt as itself in unbroken unity with what is given, while it is only with a different centre that another's will can be felt as thus intimately one. I can be aware of a common will which is realized in and by myself. I can be sure that, present also in another person, this same common will is also felt directly as his own. But, though each of us knows certainly of the other's feeling, neither of us can experience it as it comes in direct unity with immediate experience.

It is only because it is an object that the other, for me, is another at all. Our joint experience, which I feel, I can feel as yours only on the strength of an ideal construction, which does not cease to be such because it is also a familiar fact. Our common feeling may in you, as in me, be referred ideally to both me and yourself. But that which in your experience makes in the end your feeling to be yours is no construction, while in my experi-
[420] ence it depends on and consists in nothing else. Here is the solution of the puzzle well known to those who reflect on life, and who are driven for ever alternately to affirm and to deny that thoughts and emotions are shared.

It does not follow from the above that I myself am my world, or that I possess any superior importance or reality. As against

⁵ That any mind should have an immediate and direct experience of another mind seems, to me at least, out of the question. So far as I know, the only ground for such a doctrine is to be found in a false alternative. There is an apparent failure to perceive the extent to which my knowledge even of my own self is itself ideal and not immediate. My self and other selves are, each alike, constructions made in my experience. But my self is connected there with the basis of feeling, as other selves, in my experience, most certainly are not connected.

the Universe, against the community or God, I may find myself, as we saw, to be trifling and contemptible. The nothingness of the self, in fear and in the condemnation of the higher Will, is familiar to us all. I have indeed a special and a singular reality possessed by naught else. This reality of mine is even indispensable to the Universe. But the same thing holds again of the meanest rudiment of fact or least vestige of appearance. That which is indispensable has its place; but what kind of place and what amount of value belongs to it we have still to ask. The World and God without myself are in the end inconceivable—so much is certain. But this tells us nothing as to the degree and as to the manner in which I serve to conduce to their reality. In short I cannot suppose that those critics who charge me with Solipsism can have much of an idea as to the position in which I stand. My self is not my finite centre, and my finite centre is but one amongst many, and it is not the Universe. It *is* the whole Universe entire and undivided, but it is that Universe only so far as it appears in one with a single centre. Feeling is the beginning, and it is the source of all material, and it forms the enfolding element and abiding ground of our world. But feeling is not that world, and it is not the criterion of Reality. The criterion for each of us is that system of developed content which we call true and good and beautiful. . . .

(vii) The intimate connection of the finite centre and the self leads us continually into error. We identify the two, and then, failing perhaps to distinguish the finite centre from the Universe, [421] we are landed in Solipsism. Or in any case the self, once confused with the prolonged finite centre, drifts into the position of a soul. And, since everything experienced within a soul must be taken as its adjective and state, we fall at once into dilemmas from which no exit is possible.

The true relation of the self to the soul may be now stated briefly. The soul is a self so far as within that soul we have the felt opposition of not-self to self. Whether within a soul there can at any time be more than one self, is a question which here we need not answer. For myself any decision on this point would have to remain more or less arbitrary. The same reply must be given if we are asked whether personal identity and the identity of the soul are indistinguishable or at least must coincide. But it is not necessary for us here to embarrass ourselves with these problems.

Passing them by, we may observe how a want of clearness as to the relative positions of soul and self leads us fatally to confusion or ruin. On the one hand the self is a content which falls within the soul, and must, I suppose, in a sense be regarded as its 'state'. Hence, if we forget to distinguish the self from the finite centre, which finite centre, as prolonged, we have turned into the soul-thing, the result is certain disaster. Every psychical content will belong to, and will be an adjective of, the self, while again the self will be an adjective and a state, in the end, of itself. On the other hand, if the soul be taken as an aggregation or collective unity, the self tends to become a mere 'ingredient' which with others is found in this vessel. The self has here been turned into a mere object and its essence has vanished. For that essence, as we saw, lived in feeling and was inseparable from immediate experience as a whole.

[422] The foregoing discussion has, I fear, been wearisome, though the importance and the difficulty of its subject is obvious. I will now pass from it to deal with the question of the individual's reality. What is it that we are to call the real Caesar? Let us begin at once by asking as to the limits of his being, and, again, let us start by assuming the following conclusions. A soul exists, as such, only for a certain period of some history, and the states of no soul can be observed directly by others. These two theses, let us add, will hold good of a self. What a man feels as himself is not accessible directly to others, and any such feeling is an event which falls within a single part of the time-series. The reader who is unable to endorse these statements, will perhaps, for the sake of argument, accept them provisionally. And is the real Caesar, let us now ask, confined within the boundary of such a limited soul or self?

(*a*) Even these limits, it may be argued, are already far too wide. The real Caesar is the man who is actually perceived, and, further, the man is not a body but is mental, and no one, we have agreed, but the man himself can perceive his own mind. The reality of Caesar must be therefore confined to his own self-knowledge. But from the above it follows that no one else, not even Caesar's own mother, even knew the real Caesar, and that we ourselves now are even more ignorant, if greater ignorance can exist. And yet, even with this, the being of Caesar has not been narrowed to its strict reality. For how much of Caesar was ever given even to himself in direct knowledge? That knowledge, whenever actual, was certainly confined to one present time. The past of Caesar and his future never came within his own experience. It was the being of a fleeting moment of which alone he was aware, and aware even of that, we may add, but imperfectly; and it is in this fragment or succession of fragments that at last we have reached the actual hero. In other words the real man has, if not essentially, at least mainly become a thing unknowable even by himself. And, again, for us on our side, he has become [423] simply nothing at all, and what we are to mean when we speak of him I cannot imagine. But this whole restriction of the individual's reality was founded on prejudice, and it leads inevitably, as we have seen, to theoretical ruin.

(*b*) If, however, leaving this error, we go on to fix other limits, and now confine the reality of Caesar within the period of his own lifetime, is our position more secure? On the contrary we seem left at once without any principle at all—unless the identification of Caesar with his perishing body is perhaps to serve as a principle. And in short our narrowing of his true being to the mere period in which he lived, seems once more to rest on prejudice. Based on no principle, it is in collision both with common sense and consistent theory, and may be finally dismissed.

How far then, we ask, is the reality of the individual to extend? It extends, I reply, in a word just so far as it works. As far as any man has knowledge, so far, I insist, the man himself really is there in what is known. And it seems even obvious that his reality goes out as far as what we call his influence extends. The real individual is in short 'that sphere which his activity doth fill'. The question within what limits a man feels and is aware of himself, does not, we saw, when it is answered, give you the bounds of his reality. And, if it is objected that the limits have now become too indefinite to be fixed, I reply that I both recognize and accept this consequence. It is a consequence which conflicts, so far as I see, with nothing better than prejudice.

Why should I be forced to believe that the great minds of the past, where they influence me, are unreal, and are themselves simply dead? Surely I am right to ask here for a reason, and for

a reason that will bear scrutiny. 'Then you imagine also', I perhaps may hear, 'that a man's will really can survive his death.'
[424]   Long ago, I reply, I have urged that this imagination is the fact
and the literal truth.[6] A man's will is there where that will is carried out into existence. This of course does not imply that the
man now feels and is directly aware of his will. It really denies
that the man's will is confined within the sphere of his direct
awareness. And, if this denial is not right, I am still waiting to
learn upon what ground it is wrong. For I am acquainted with
no ground which I at least could call rational.

We must accept a like consequence with regard to dead
Caesar's knowledge. A man actually must be there, wherever his
knowledge extends, even if that knowledge is of the unseen present or of the past or future. So far as Caesar in his own day
foresaw ours, his proper reality was not limited to his own world
or time. He was and he is present there, wherever anything that
the Universe contains was present to his mind. Caesar of course
was not, and he is not, in our own time as we ourselves now are
there. The distinction is obvious and to ignore it would be even
absurd. On the other hand this separation only holds within limits, and it is perfectly compatible with the real presence of Caesar
in his known object. The further result that Caesar's knowledge
will affect the being of, and will make a difference to, his object,
must again be affirmed. But as to the amount of such a difference
of course nothing is implied. Differences may be there, and yet
may fairly be called inappreciable. For certain of our purposes,
that is, they may be taken as negligible.

It is then not evident, it is far from being evident, that the real
Caesar is unable to come within my knowledge. He enters into
my judgement on the contrary just as I, if he had foreseen me,
might have been an actual constituent of his known world. Such
[425]   a view, I fully admit, brings with it its difficulties, but the denial
of it, so far as I see, entails absolute disaster. There surely can be
no knowledge of anything except what is real, nor about anything which itself falls outside our knowledge.

We are here confronted by that error which consists in the sun-
dering of ideal from real experience. If we know only by ideas, we

---

[6] ['On Active Attention', *CE* ii. 419–20. Cf. 'Pleasure, Desire, and Volition',
CE i. 267–8,] for the question as to the object of desire.

never (it is an old argument) are able to reach reality, that reality, at least, which we find in direct awareness. But the whole division, when you take it thus as absolute separation, is false. We never anywhere know merely by ideas, and in the end a mere idea is but a ruinous abstraction, just as, on the other hand, wherever we have an object, our knowledge cannot fail to be ideal. That ideal construction in which for us the entire past consists, is based on and is inseparable from present feeling and perception. If these do not support and do not enter into that extension of themselves which is the past, that past has disappeared. You may insist that Caesar, at least as he knew himself, falls outside of our construction, but even this contention, understood as you understand it, is false. My idea of Caesar is not in the full sense an immediate experience of Caesar's mind, and as to this there is no question. But I have none the less an idea of Caesar's immediate experience, and my idea is true, and, so far as it goes, it is real, and actually, so far, it *is* Caesar's own direct awareness of himself. The difference here is not a wall which divides and isolates two worlds. The immediate experience and the idea of it, are, on the contrary, one in substance and in reality. Why they should not be so, I fail to perceive, and I am convinced, that if they are not so, our knowledge is illusion.[7] There is immediate experience assuredly which for itself is not an object, nor has any idea of its   [426]

---

[7] When (to use the instance given by Mr. Russell in his essay referred to already) we assert that Scott was the author of *Waverley*, what we presuppose as true and real is the idea of a unique individual man at such and such a determinate place in our unique 'real' order of space and time. This idea, Mr. Russell contends, is not a constituent of any judgement. It is on the contrary, something indeterminate which falls outside our proposition.

Any such doctrine to my mind is both false and utterly ruinous. I urge that in connection with present perception, and by an ideal extension of that, we get the idea of a unique series and order, with a unique man at a certain part of that series and order. Such an idea is incomplete, but it is positive and determinate, and most assuredly it does enter into our judgement. And, if this is not so, then what Mr. Russell has to show is how our judgement can possibly be anything but senseless, and again how in fact our judgement even is possible.

With regard to Mr. Russell's contention that there are propositions without any denotation ['Knowledge by Acquaintance', in *Mysticism and Logic*, 224–5], I of course reject this. The sense in which all propositions have denotation, and all are existential, has been long ago discussed by me (I admit imperfectly) in my *Principles of Logic*. Cf. ['On Floating Ideas and the Imaginary', repr. above, Part II, Sect. 2, Ch. 1]. The general view advocated by Prof. Bosanquet and myself seems (I would venture to add) to be ignored by Meinong and again by Mr. Russell.

own being. But in the Universe as a whole any such falling apart of its complementary aspects is made good. And *ex hyp.* we are concerned here with a case where the immediate experience of the individual is known even to others.

The past and future (once more to repeat this) are ideal constructions which extend the given present. And our present world itself is a construction based on feeling and perception, 'construction' here meaning for us (the reader will note) a living outgrowth of the continuous reality. The past and future vary, and they have to vary, with the changes of the present, and, to any man whose eyes are open, such variation is no mere theory but is plain fact. But, though ideal, the past and future are also real, and, if they were otherwise, they could be nothing for judgement or knowledge. They are actual, but they must remain incomplete essentially. Caesar's direct feeling and self-awareness are known by us really. Our knowledge does not go far, but, so far as it goes, our idea is the veritable reality. And, if it were anything else, then once more surely we could have no idea of Caesar. The immediate experience which Caesar had of himself, if you take that, not in its general character, but in its unbroken felt totality of particular detail, remains inaccessible. It is a feeling which comes within our knowledge, but which we do not ourselves actually feel. Caesar's experience however, as thus inaccessible, does not fall within history. It is at once below, and (as some would add) above the temporal order of events. Our knowledge of the past and future is, in short, an actual and yet an imperfect knowledge of reality. In this we have seen that it is like the knowledge we possess of those persons who are nearest. And the same conclusion holds even as to that which we can know of our own selves. Any self-knowledge which contains a past or future of our selves, is ideal. Any distinction of our own self from that of others, and even any appearance of our self as an object of our own selves, will bear the same character. And, when you have narrowed your awareness to that which both in substance and in form is direct, have you anything left which you can fairly take as being by itself the genuine knowledge of your own self? But into the discussion of this last point I will forbear to enter here.[8]

[427]

---

[8] Cf. ['On Truth and Coherence', repr. above, Part II, Sect. 2, Ch. 5]. The reader will, I hope, bear in mind the difference between the felt basis on which the knowledge of self depends, and, on the other side, that knowledge itself.

The real individual then (we find) does not fall merely within a moment, nor is he bounded by his birth and death, nor is he in principle confined to any limited period. He lives there wherever the past or future of our 'real' order is present to his mind, and where in any other way whatever he influences or acts on it. If you complain that these limits are too indefinite, I will not ask you to reflect also whether the individual's reality does not pass even beyond the temporal order. I will content myself here with urging that at least any limit in time can in the end be seen to be arbitrary. We must treat the individual as real so far as anywhere for any purpose his being is appreciable. If this is to be inconsistent, it is still perhaps our least inconsistent course, and it is our way, our only way, of satisfactory knowledge.

8

On Our Fear of Death and Desire for Immortality

[451] It may perhaps assist the reader if I add . . . some further remarks on what is called the fear of death and the desire for immortality. I do not doubt that there is here some difference in our individual natures and sentiments, but the great divergence of opinion among us cannot, it seems to me, be justified on this ground. It rests mainly on what I am forced to regard as confusion and mental impotence. And it may be well for me perhaps to begin by setting down my own feelings, so far as I know them.

Certainly in a sense I fear death and desire future life. I shrink, perhaps more than I ought, from the pain of bodily destruction, from the cruelty of severance, and the infinite sadness of being torn from what one loves. And, the older I grow, the more I recoil from any forced venture in the dark. But I recognize that religion, if it were effective in me, would master these feelings. And in any case I know nothing of what is called the horror of [452] ceasing to be. Any fear of annihilation which may rise in my mind, seems in me to come merely from a momentary lapse into thoughtless confusion.

Again, as to personal survival, I should wish to survive if my future life were to be desirable, and I on my side to remain much what I am now. But, if my future life is to be undesirable, I am of course averse from it. And, if I am not to continue to be much what I am, the future life, being the life of another man, does not personally concern me.

I have spoken already of the hope that after death we might still, or once more, be young, and be with those with whom we would be, the hope that decay and parting are after all hardly real. If this could be more than a hope, then death, I suppose,

Repr. from *ETR*, ch. xv, Supplementary Note B; the Editors felt that an introduction to this note would be superfluous.

would have lost its worst terror. Apart from this, I should welcome of course the chance to undo some evil that I have done—if, that is, I did not fear that perhaps I might go on to do more, and if the hope of individual perfection appeared to me to be anything but insane. If I believed that whatever I do now would make all the difference to me hereafter, that of course might make me more careful; though to be sanguine about a future where all, no matter what, is retrievable, might possibly produce a different effect. And the idea that by my misdeeds I may be prolonging indefinitely an evil series of lives, would conceivably trouble me more if I regarded life as an evil. Such are my own feelings, which I do not suppose to be wholly typical, and, passing from these, I will consider more in general what is called the personal interest in immortality.

The question whether what I do and fail to do now, is to make any difference, worth considering, to any one after my death, must first be dismissed. An answer in the negative (I fully assent to this) would be a very serious matter, but we are not here concerned with it. I am assuming here that we are agreed that death does not end all, but that on the other hand my actions have [453] results beyond my own life, results of which I am bound to take account. But consequences to others than myself are not directly here in question. What I am to consider here is my own future, and I am about to ask, supposing that I have a future after death, as to the nature of my present interest in that. What kind of interest is it that I really take in the idea of my future life? Far from being plain, this question is extremely obscure. In asking it we usually do not realize what we mean by our self. And in the second place we fall constantly into sheer self-deception. We suppose ourselves to imagine certain situations, when what we really imagine is not these but something different.

That in which I take a personal, an individual, interest is the self which I actually feel, and feel as mine now. So far as I take this self to be in the past or future, and so far as I feel myself now in that past or future self, it is to me a matter of personal concern. Memory or anticipation (so much seems clear) is not all that is wanted. To some of my past which I remember, I remain indifferent, since it is alienated too far from my present feeling. And again, if I contemplate a future which is alienated in the same way, that future fails to concern me personally. To be felt as mine the past or future must be included within the self which I feel now, or (it is the same thing) I must feel myself individually into them. Memory and anticipation are thus by themselves insufficient, and yet on the other side memory seems clearly wanted for personal interest.

You may be tempted to deny this. You may suppose, for instance, the case of a letter written by me long ago and now wholly forgotten. If I read this letter, I recognize that there is in it something which is mine, and my interest is individual though I do not remember. Yes, I reply, but what I feel here as my own, is placed by me, however indefinitely, in my past, and that [454] depends upon memory. Otherwise it is much as when I read of another's past, or even of another's present, which has features felt to be akin to my own, or again when I meet some person in union with whom my felt personality expands. We have personal interest here doubtless in a sense, but we have not the individual concern felt in the prolongation of myself into the past and future.

Suppose after my death a man to exist who is to be very like myself. Certainly I prefer to feel that I have now perhaps helped such a man rather than another man less like me. And suppose that I myself am to exist after death and am to be altered considerably, the more I am altered the less and less personal concern do I now feel, until a point is reached where my interest really ceases to be special. The only personal identity which seems to count here is the degree and the amount of likeness in the felt self. From the other side, though felt sameness in character is wanted in order to have continuity recognized between myself now and then, this by itself is not enough. If I am to have an individual personal interest, I must suppose also a memory in the 'then'. I must imagine, for instance, a man after my death reading what I myself write now, and saying to himself, 'Yes, I wrote it.' He must not only feel it to be the expression of his self, but he must make that self continuous in the past (even if there are intervals) with my own. Here is the identity in which I can now take interest as personal to me myself. In whatever falls short of this I can feel a concern which, though never individual, may be special, special until by lessening degrees we arrive at that which is merely general.

It may help us if we consider the case of a man who, under an anaesthetic, has endured an operation as to which his memory is a blank. Let us suppose that a question is raised now as to whether at the time pain was present or absent. Would the man, if he is sure that he is in any case no worse now, take a personal [455] concern in the inquiry? And if the same question were raised as to a future operation, would the man, apart from fear that things might turn out badly otherwise, concern himself any more?[1] And, if not, why, if there is to be no memory, should he trouble himself as to whether his future life is to be his or another man's? To answer that, if he is obtuse about one thing, he need not be obtuse about another, does not help us to see where there really is obtuseness. And if you reply that the man in fact assumes that his state, while anaesthetized, is in any case so alienated as not to be his, while with regard to a future life that assumption is not made, I am not shaken in my conclusion. Your alleged fact in the first place seems at best very doubtful. And in any case this supposed alienation and its opposite are connected inseparably, I would urge, with the absence and presence of memory. The man in the past or in the future who knows nothing about me, whatever else he is, after all will not be myself. The interest that I feel in him may (to repeat this) be more or less special, but it never can really be individual.

I can of course transcend my present felt state. I can make an object of what goes beyond it and is even far removed from my life. And with regard to such things I can of course entertain a variety of feelings. In such objects I can take an interest which is in varying degrees special, and which again, from being impersonal, may alter till it becomes in a sense personal. So far, I presume, we are agreed. The question is whether my felt self can take an interest in anything as being its own individual self, unless it regards its present feeling as prolonged into that object. And the further question is whether I can suppose this felt iden- [456] tity to be there in the future, unless I assume also that the future self is aware of the connection between itself and me, as I now am. These questions I have to answer in the negative, and I am forced also to conclude that, where they are answered otherwise,

---

[1] He would take a personal interest in his future self, as that is to be while anaesthetized, if (*a*) that self is to feel and remember, or if (*b*) it is to be included in the memory of a later self which remembers. I am of course not assuming that the second alternative without the first is really possible.

we have confusion and a failure to be clear as to what really is
before the mind. Promise me, if I may repeat this, a future self
much the same as mine now, and promise me that my present
self shall hereafter be present in and present to that future self—
and I am here concerned individually. But, with anything less
than this, I find an identity which I cannot regard as truly personal, though in a diversity of ways and degrees I can take in it
an interest which is special.

This conclusion is obscured by the weakness of our imagination,
and by this I mean our difficulty in realizing what elements are
and what are not actually present in our object. There is a constant tendency to import into the object feelings and ideas which
are incompatible with that object, and which may even have been
formally excluded from its being. And to this tendency we, many
of us, seem a helpless prey. Thus, to shrink from pain and from
partial annihilation is rational, while, if the annihilation really is
total, there is nothing either to shrink or to shrink from. Our
fear comes from imagining ourselves present where we are explicitly set down as absent. What we actually fear is the process
where that which clings to itself is rudely torn away and apart;
while, on the other hand, the pain of sheer negation is an inconsistent and illusory idea. At sunset where, sunk before our eyes,

> Le soleil s'est noyé dans son sang qui se fige,

we listen in our hearts to the complaining of

> Un cœur tendre qui hait le néant vaste et noir,
> Du passé lumineux recueille tout vestige.[a]

[457] But, once the heart has ceased to beat, it is but folly to dream
that it feels. And again to suppose that I seek *merely* 'to go on'
after death, while at the same time I refuse to 'go on' as another
man, seems (to use plain words) to be something like stupidity.
For obviously I am here desiring for myself a great deal more
than merely to 'go on'. Again there is no illusion when we are
pained by the thought of parting from what we hold dear. The

---

[a] From Charles Baudelaire, 'Harmonie du Soir', in *Baudelaire* (Baltimore:
Penguin, 1964), 193. Francis Scarfe translates these lines literally as 'the sun that
drowned in its congealing blood, | A tender heart that hates the huge, black void,
| is gathering to itself all traces of the luminous past.'

struggle against the destruction of our being, while it lasts, is terrible, and the prospect of those whom we love missing us and suffering is cruel. And to sorrow for our loss of those who are dead is at once rational and human, while to imagine them on their side seeking to rejoin us in vain would be torture. But at once to suppose our dead to have ceased, and yet to grieve not for ourselves but for them, comes from mental confusion. Whether the dead now remember me or not may concern me vitally, but whether, if they do not remember, they are now themselves or some other self, can hardly make a difference to me. What they now have become makes of course a difference to the Universe. But how, if they recall nothing, personal continuance, or its absence, should be anything to me or them, I cannot imagine. Again, if we meet hereafter, and if (as some think) we are drawn, without memory, to one another once more, the question of our individual identities (so far as I see) is not likely to concern us. That what we have done in this life may cause our future love might be true, and yet, if nothing is remembered, individual continuance might to us then mean nothing. Where love is the passion of which poets speak, the whole inquiry might lack interest. Something has been revealed which is beyond time and sports with the order of events. There never was a before, and God has made the whole world for this present. The sum of the matter is this, that I understand gratitude towards a past, though I do not remember it, if that past has brought good, whatever it is, into my personal life. But mere individual survival,   [458] as an incentive to present affection, is to myself not intelligible.

> Ah, Moon of my Delight who know'st no wane,
> The Moon of Heaven is rising once again:
> How oft hereafter rising shall she look
> Through this same Garden after me—in vain![b]

The desolation that invades us, as we recall these lines, is due not wholly to illusion. That what we have left should search for us hereafter with grief and pain, distresses us in prospect, and this is rational. But illusion begins if we imagine ourselves at once as nothing, and at the same moment as struggling helplessly in darkness towards light and love. It may aid us perhaps in testing

---

[b] Edward, Fitzgerald, *The Rubáiyát of Omar Kmayyám*, verse 74.

the real nature of our sadness and our desire, if we go on to imagine another man hereafter in the same garden, filled with the same spirit and offering the same unaltered devotion, a devotion recognized rapturously as the same without change or loss. If, with that thought, we still suffer, our defeat is human. But, if we justify our pain, and if we insist that we have something here really worth grieving for, then either we do not understand, or we do not love. And, though what I am about to say will perhaps with some right be turned against myself, I must add that, if there were more love, there would, at least on such points, be less misunderstanding. The striving for personal and individual existence and satisfaction is no doubt good in its own place, but, whatever else it is, I cannot take it as essential to love or religion.

The reader will understand that the scope of the above remarks is limited. I have tried to point out the illusion involved in some fears and in some hopes about the hereafter. But I have not attempted to argue that all such fear is irrational. To die and go we know not where, to survive as ourselves, and yet to [459] become we know not what—such thoughts must always bring disquiet. If we are left with that and with no more than that, we have obviously some cause for apprehension. It is here that religion, if we have a decent religion, should come to our aid. Any but an inferior religion must on one hand condemn all self-seeking after death. But on the other hand it will assure us that all evil is really overcome, and that the victory (even if we do not understand how) lies with the Good.

FURTHER READING

The most complete bibliography of works by and about Bradley is Richard Ingardia, *Bradley: A Research Bibliography* (Bowling Green, Ky.: Philosophy Documentation Center, 1991). The works listed below comprise only a few of the many things written on Bradley's logic and metaphysics. We have included them only as suggestions for further reading.

Bradley's Major Works

Ethical Studies, 2nd edn. rev. (first pub. 1876; Oxford: Clarendon Press, 1927).

The Principles of Logic, 2nd edn., 2 vols. (first pub. 1883; Oxford: Clarendon Press, 1922; corr. imp. 1928).

Appearance and Reality, 2nd edn. (first pub. 1893; Oxford: Clarendon Press, 1897; 9th imp. 1930).

Essays on Truth and Reality (first pub. 1914; Oxford: Clarendon Press, 1962).

Aphorisms (Oxford: Clarendon Press, 1930).

Collected Essays, 2 vols. (Oxford: Clarendon Press, 1935).

Presuppositions of Critical History and Aphorisms, intro. Guy Stock (Bristol: Thoemmes Press, 1993).

Works by Bradley's Contemporaries

BOSANQUET, BERNARD, *Knowledge and Reality: A Criticism of Mr. F. H. Bradley's 'The Principles of Logic'* (London: K. Paul French, 1885).

DEWEY, JOHN, *The Influence of Darwin on Philosophy and Other Essays in Contemporary Philosophy*, esp. 'The Intellectualist Criterion of Truth', in *John Dewey: The Middle Works*, 15 vols., (first pub. 1910; Carbondale Ill.: Southern Illinois University Press, 1977), iv.

ELIOT, T. S., 'Francis Herbert Bradley', in *Selected Essays*, 2nd edn. (first pub. 1932; New York: Harcourt, Brace, 1950). This essay was first collected in *For Lancelot Andrewes: Essays in Style and Order* (London: Faber & Gwyer, 1928).

ELIOT, T. S., *Knowledge and Experience in the Philosophy of F. H. Bradley* (New York: Farrar, Straus, 1964). This is Eliot's dissertation, which he completed in 1916.

JAMES, WILLIAM, *A Pluralist Universe* (first pub. 1910; Cambridge, Mass.: Harvard University Press, 1977), esp. Lecture 2, 'Monistic Idealism'.

—— 'Bradley or Bergson', in *Essays in Philosophy* (Cambridge, Mass.: Harvard University Press, 1978). First pub. in *Journal of Philosophy*, 7 (1910), 29–33.

—— *Essays in Radical Empiricism* (first pub. 1912; Cambridge, Mass.: Harvard University Press, 1976), esp. 'The Thing and its Relations'.

MOORE, G. E., 'The Nature of Judgement', *Mind*, 8 (1899), 176–93.

—— 'The Conception of Reality', in *Philosophical Studies* (London: Routledge & Kegan Paul, 1922).

—— 'External and Internal Relations', in *Philosophical Studies* (London: Routledge & Kegan Paul, 1922).

ROYCE, JOSIAH, *The World and the Individual*, 2 vols. (New York: Macmillan, 1899–1901), esp. i, 'Supplementary Essay: The One, the Many, and the Infinite'.

RUSSELL, BERTRAND, 'The Monistic Theory of Truth', in *Philosophical Essays*, (2nd edn. first pub. 1910; London: Allen & Unwin, 1966).

—— 'Some Explanations in Reply to Mr. Bradley', *Mind*, 19 (1910), 373–8.

STOUT, G. F., 'Mr. Bradley's Theory of Judgement', *Proceedings of the Aristotelian Society*, 3 (1902), 1–28.

Works by More Recent Writers

ALLARD, JAMES, W., 'Bradley's Principle of Sufficient Reason', in Manser and Stock (eds.), *The Philosophy of F. H. Bradley*.

—— 'Bradley on the Validity of Inference', *Journal of the History of Philosophy*, 27 (1989), 267–74.

BLANSHARD, BRAND, *The Nature of Thought*, 2 vols. (London: Allen & Unwin, 1939), esp. ii. 445–70.

BRADLEY, JAMES, 'F. H. Bradley's Metaphysics of Feeling and its Place in the History of Philosophy', in Manser and Stock (eds.), *The Philosophy of F. H. Bradley*.

CANDLISH, STEWART, 'The Status of Idealism in Bradley's Metaphysics', *Idealistic Studies*, 11 (1981), 242–53.

—— 'Scepticism, Ideal Experiment, and Priorities in Bradley's Metaphysics', in Manser and Stock (eds.), *The Philosophy of F. H. Bradley*.

—— 'Idealism and Bradley's Logic', *Idealistic Studies*, 12 (1982), 251–9.

CANDLISH, STEWART, 'The Truth about F. H. Bradley', *Mind*, 98 (1989), 331–48.

CRESSWELL, M. J., 'Reality as Experience in F. H. Bradley', *Australasian Journal of Philosophy*, 55 (1977), 169–88.

—— 'Bradley's Theory of Judgement', *Canadian Journal of Philosophy*, 9 (1979), 575–94.

Crossley, David, 'Holism, Individuation, and Internal Relations', *Journal of the History of Philosophy*, 15 (1977), 183–94.

CUNNINGHAM, G. WATTS, *The Idealistic Argument in Recent British and American Philosophy* (London: Century, 1933), esp. 78–113, 382–407.

EWING, A. C., *Idealism: A Critical Survey* (London: Methuen, 1933), esp. 208–28.

FINDLAY, J. N., 'Bradley's Contribution to Absolute Theory', in Manser and Stock (eds.), *The Philosophy of F. H. Bradley*.

GLOUBERMAN, MARK, 'Interpreting Bradley: The Critique of Fact Pluralism', *History and Philosophy of Logic*, 9 (1988), 205–23.

GRAM, M. S., 'Bradley's Argument against Relations', *New Scholasticism*, 44 (1970), 49–63.

GRIFFIN, NICHOLAS, 'What's Wrong with Bradley's Theory of Judgement?', *Idealistic Studies*, 13 (1983), 199–225.

HOLDCROFT, DAVID, 'Bradley and the Impossibility of Absolute Truth', *History and Philosophy of Logic*, 2 (1981), 25–39.

—— 'Holism and Truth', in Manser and Stock (eds.), *The Philosophy of F. H. Bradley*.

HYLTON, PETER, *Russell, Idealism, and the Emergence of Analytic Philosophy* (Oxford: Clarendon Press, 1990), esp. 44–71.

JUBIN, B., 'F. H. Bradley on Referring', *Southern Journal of Philosophy*, 14 (1976), 157–68.

MANSER, ANTHONY, 'Bradley and Internal Relations', in G. N. A. Vesey (ed.), *Idealism: Past and Present* (Cambridge: Cambridge University Press, 1982).

—— *Bradley's Logic* (Totowa, NJ: Barnes & Noble, 1983).

—— 'Bradley and Frege', in Manser and Stock (eds.), *The Philosophy of F. H. Bradley*.

—— and STOCK, GUY (eds.), *The Philosophy of F. H. Bradley* (Oxford: Clarendon Press, 1984).

METZ, RUDOLF, *A Hundred Years of British Philosophy* (London: Allen & Unwin, 1938), esp. 322–45.

MONTAGUE, R. D. L., 'Wollheim on Bradley on Idealism and Relations', *Philosophical Quarterly*, 14 (1964), 158–64.

MUIRHEAD, J. H., *The Platonic Tradition in Anglo-Saxon Philosophy* (London: Allen & Unwin, 1931), esp. 219–304.

MURE, G. R. G., 'F. H. Bradley: Towards a Portrait', *Encounter*, 88 (1961), 28–35.

PALMER, ANTHONY, 'Parasites Cut Loose', in G. N. A. Vesey (ed.), *Idealism: Past and Present* (Cambridge: Cambridge University Press, 1982).

PASSMORE, JOHN, *A Hundred Years of Philosophy*, 2nd edn. (first pub. 1957; New York: Basic Books, 1966), esp. chs. 3 and 7.

—— 'Russell and Bradley', in Robert Brown and C. D. Rollins (eds.), *Contemporary Philosophy in Australia* (London: Humanities Press, 1969).

RANDALL, JOHN HERMAN, Jr., *Philosophy after Darwin: Chapters from 'The Career of Philosophy' Vol. 3 and Other Essays* (New York: Columbia University Press, 1977), esp. 160–208.

ROSS, JOSHUA JACOB, *The Appeal to the Given* (London: Allen & Unwin, 1970), esp. 22–30, 81–95, 146–9.

SCARROW, D. S., 'Bradley's Influence upon Modern Logic', *Philosophy and Phenomenological Research*, 22 (1961), 380–2.

SPRIGGE, T. L. S., 'Russell and Bradley on Relations', in George W. Roberts (ed.), *Bertrand Russell Memorial Volume* (New York: Humanities Press, 1979).

—— 'The Self and its World in Bradley and Husserl', in Manser and Stock (eds.), *The Philosophy of F. H. Bradley*.

STOCK, GUY, 'Bradley's Theory of Judgement', in Manser and Stock (eds.), *The Philosophy of F. H. Bradley*.

—— 'Negation: Bradley and Wittgenstein', *Philosophy*, 60 (1985), 465–76.

TACELLI, RONALD K., 'Cook Wilson as Critic of Bradley', *History of Philosophy Quarterly*, 8/2 (1991), 199–205.

TAYLOR, A. E., 'F. H. Bradley', *Mind*, 34 (1925), 1–12.

VANDER VEER, GARRETT, *Bradley's Metaphysics and the Self* (New Haven, Conn.: Yale University Press, 1970).

WALSH, W. H., 'F. H. Bradley', in D. J. O'Connor (ed.), *A Critical History of Western Philosophy* (New York: Free Press of Glencoe, 1964).

WOLLHEIM, RICHARD, *F. H. Bradley*, 2nd edn. (first pub. 1959; Baltimore: Penguin, 1969).

INDEX